BASEBALL

A DOUBLEHEADER COLLECTION OF FACTS, FEATS & FIRSTS

by the editors of
THE SPORTING NEWS

Co-Editor-Writer
JOE HOPPEL

Co-Editor-Researcher
CRAIG CARTER

Publisher
THOMAS G. OSENTON

Director, Specialized Publications
GARY LEVY

Managing Editor
MIKE NAHRSTEDT

Published in 1992 by
Galahad Books
A division of LDAP, Inc.
386 Park Avenue South
New York, New York 10016

Galahad Books is a registered trademark of LDAP, Inc.
Published by arrangement with THE SPORTING NEWS Publishing Co.
Design and typography by Tony Meisel, AM Publishing Services.

Library of Congress Catalog Card Number: 91-78351

ISBN: 0-88365-785-6

Printed in the United States of America.

CONTENTS

GAME ONE

GAME TWO

INTRODUCTION

Baseball, perhaps more than any other sport, lends itself to a constant examination and re-examination of its past. Baseball fans, often contending that their game is the only team sport that has remained basically unchanged in the last 50 years (in terms of the athletes' physical strength and playing abilities), use statistics and reminiscences as yardsticks for measuring yesterday's hero against today's superstar. There seemingly is no end to the comparisons—or to the discussions about *that* play, or *that* player, or *that* game. Or *that* trivia.

Baseball: A Doubleheader Collection of Facts and Firsts presents a detailed look at major league baseball's glorious, unusual and heretofore little-known moments and the famous and not-so-famous persons who played roles in those events. The book is at once a reference source—the first two chapters contain item-by-item reviews of the game's great achievements—and a trivia "who's who." After recounting baseball's dramatic happenings, the book focuses on the game's characters, goats, lesser-known feats, oddities, coincidences, "firsts," "lasts" and numbers, with emphasis on those who—until now—have been little more than footnotes to baseball history. All entries reflect records and situations as they were through the 1991 season.

GAME ONE

Atlanta's Hank Aaron receives congratulations from teammate Tom House and is embraced by his mother after hitting career homer No. 715 on April 8, 1974, breaking Babe Ruth's all-time record. House, a relief pitcher, caught the home run in the Atlanta bullpen and returned the ball to Aaron.

FIRST INNING
Dramatic moments
in hitting and baserunning,
with supporting casts

AARON'S 715th HOME RUN
On April 8, 1974, Hank Aaron of the Atlanta Braves became the major leagues' all-time home run king, hitting his 715th in a game against the Los Angeles Dodgers at Atlanta Stadium and surpassing Babe Ruth's total of 714.

Supporting Cast:
• **Al Downing.** Dodgers' pitcher off whom Aaron homered in the fourth inning and the losing pitcher in the Braves' 7-4 victory.
• **Darrell Evans.** Braves' third baseman who was on base when Aaron connected, having reached first on shortstop Bill Russell's error.
• **Joe Ferguson.** Downing's catcher.
• **Tom House.** Atlanta relief pitcher who caught Aaron's homer in the Braves' bullpen.
• **Ron Reed.** The Braves' starting and winning pitcher.

BOTTOMLEY'S 12 RUNS BATTED IN
St. Louis first baseman Jim Bottomley drove in a major league-record 12 runs on September 16, 1924, leading the Cardinals to a 17-3 triumph over Brooklyn at Ebbets Field. Bottomley went 6-for-6.

Supporting Cast:
• **Art Decatur.** Brooklyn pitcher off whom Bottomley collected six of his runs batted in. Decatur yielded a bases-loaded homer to Bottomely in the fourth inning and a two-run homer in the sixth.
• **Rube Ehrhardt.** Gave up a two-run single in the first inning.
• **Bonnie Hollingsworth.** Gave up a run-scoring double in the second.
• **Jim Roberts.** Gave up a run-scoring single in the ninth..
• **Tex Wilson.** Gave up a two-run single in the seventh. Wilson pitched in only one other major league game.

BROCK SURPASSES WILLS
Lou Brock of the St. Louis Cardinals broke Maury Wills' modern stolen-base record in 1974, getting his record-breaking 105th steal on September 10 against

Philadelphia at Busch Memorial Stadium. Brock finished with 118 steals.

Supporting Cast:
• **Bob Boone.** Phils' catcher when Brock broke Wills' record of 104 (set in 1962).
• **Ron Hunt.** Cardinals' batter when Brock made his seventh-inning steal.
• **Dick Ruthven.** Phils' pitcher when Brock stole second base.

CHAMBLISS' HOMER WINS PENNANT

Chris Chambliss of the New York Yankees hit a ninth-inning home run in Game 5 of the 1976 American League Championship Series, giving the Yanks a 7-6 victory over Kansas City and their first pennant in 12 years.

Supporting Cast:
• **George Brett.** Royals' third baseman whose three-run homer in the eighth inning off Grant Jackson tied the score, 6-6.
• **Mark Littell.** Relief pitcher off whom Chambliss homered.
• **Buck Martinez.** Littell's catcher.
• **Dick Tidrow.** Yankees' reliever who pitched the ninth inning and got the victory in the October 14 game at Yankee Stadium.

COBB FLEXES MUSCLES

Although he never hit more than 12 home runs in a season, Detroit's Ty Cobb had a three-homer game—and went 6-for-6 with five runs batted in—on May 5, 1925, against the St. Louis Browns at Sportsman's Park. Cobb's mark of 16 total bases—the Tiger star also singled twice and doubled—has been matched only by Lou Gehrig, Jimmie Foxx, Pat Seerey, Rocky Colavito and Fred Lynn in American League history.

Supporting Cast:
• **Joe Bush.** Permitted Cobb's first-inning homer and was the losing pitcher in the 14-8 game.
• **Milt Gaston.** Victim of Cobb's third homer, in the eighth inning.
• **Elam Vangilder.** Gave up a homer to Cobb in the second inning.

COLBERT'S DOUBLEHEADER SPREE

San Diego's Nate Colbert set a runs-batted-in record for a doubleheader on August 1, 1972, knocking in 13 runs as the Padres swept the Braves, 9-0 and 11-7, at Atlanta Stadium. Colbert slugged five home runs in the two games, tying the twin bill mark established by Stan Musial in 1954. The homers accounted for 12 of Colbert's RBIs, with the 13th coming in on a single.

Supporting Cast:
• **Jim Hardin.** Gave up a two-run homer to Colbert in the seventh inning of the nightcap.
• **Pat Jarvis.** Gave up a grand slam in the second inning of the nightcap.

- **Mike McQueen.** Gave up a solo homer in the seventh inning of the opener.
- **Ron Schueler.** Gave up a three-run homer in the first inning of the opener.
- **Cecil Upshaw.** Gave up a two-run homer in the ninth inning of the second game, capping Colbert's three-homer, eight-RBI performance in the nightcap and giving the Padre slugger a doubleheader-record 22 total bases (five homers, two singles).

CRONIN'S PINCH-HOMER FEAT

Joe Cronin, player-manager for the Boston Red Sox, slugged pinch-hit homers in both games of a June 17, 1943, doubleheader against the Philadelphia Athletics at Fenway Park. Cronin's accomplishment has been equaled only once—by Hal Breeden of the Montreal Expos, on July 13, 1973, at Atlanta.

Supporting Cast:
- **Don Black.** A's pitcher off whom Cronin hit a three-run pinch-homer in the eighth inning of the nightcap. Philadelphia won, 8-7.
- **Russ Christopher.** A's pitcher off whom Cronin hit a three-run pinch homer in the seventh inning of the opener. Boston won the first game, 5-4.
- **Lou Lucier.** Boston pitcher for whom Cronin batted in the opener.
- **Mike Ryba.** Boston pitcher for whom Cronin batted in the nightcap.

DiMAGGIO'S 56-GAME STREAK

Joe DiMaggio, New York Yankees' center fielder, compiled a major league-record 56-game batting streak in 1941. During the streak, DiMaggio batted .408 (91-for-223) with 15 home runs and 55 runs batted in. Immediately after being stopped, DiMaggio had a 16-game hitting streak—giving him hits in 72 of 73 games.

Supporting Cast:
- **Jim Bagby Jr.** Facing DiMaggio (hitless in two previous official at-bats) in the eighth inning of a July 17, 1941, game at Cleveland's Municipal Stadium the Indians' Bagby induced the Yankee standout to hit into a double play—ending DiMaggio's streak.
- **Lou Boudreau.** Cleveland shortstop who started the streak-ending double play (Boudreau to Ray Mack to Oscar Grimes).
- **Ken Keltner.** Cleveland third baseman who made two fine fielding plays on DiMaggio earlier in the game.
- **Joe Krakauskas.** Cleveland pitcher who, on July 16, 1941, gave up the last hit to DiMaggio during the Yankee player's streak.
- **Al Smith.** Cleveland pitcher who started against the Yankees on July 17, 1941, and held DiMaggio hitless in two official at-bats (the ground balls to Keltner). He also walked DiMaggio. Smith was the losing pitcher as New York won, 4-3.
- **Edgar Smith.** Chicago White Sox's pitcher against whom DiMaggio started his streak on May 15, 1941, with a first-inning single.

11

FISK'S 1975 WORLD SERIES HOMER
Leading off the bottom of the 12th inning of Game 6 of the 1975 World Series against the Cincinnati Reds, Boston catcher Carlton Fisk homered high off the left-field foul pole to give the Red Sox a 7-6 victory and tie the Series at three games apiece.

Supporting Cast:
• **Bernie Carbo.** Boston pinch-hitter whose three-run homer in the eighth inning off Rawly Eastwick tied the score, 6-6. It was Carbo's second pinch homer of the Series, tying the record set by Los Angeles' Chuck Essegian in 1959.
• **Pat Darcy.** Cincinnati pitcher off whom Fisk homered in Game 6, played October 21 at Fenway Park.
• **Rick Wise.** Winning pitcher for Boston, having worked the top of the 12th.

HARTNETT'S HOMER IN GLOAMIN'
Manager Gabby Hartnett's two-out home run in the ninth inning—as darkness was descending over Wrigley Field on September 28, 1938—lifted the Chicago Cubs to a 6-5 victory over Pittsburgh and a half-game lead on the Pirates in the National League pennant race. Until Hartnett connected, the Pirates had led the N.L. since July 12. The Cubs kept the league lead winning the pennant by two games.

Supporting Cast:
• **Mace Brown.** Pirates' pitcher off whom Hartnett homered on a two-strike pitch.
• **Billy Herman.** Cubs' player whose eighth-inning single tied the score, 5-5.
• **Tony Lazzeri.** Cubs' pinch-hitter whose eighth-inning double cut the Pirates' lead to 5-4.
• **Charlie Root.** Cubs' winning pitcher, having worked the top of the ninth.

HENDERSON TOPS BROCK'S MARK
Rickey Henderson of the Oakland A's broke Lou Brock's modern stolen-base record in 1982, recording his record-breaking 119th steal on August 27 against the Milwaukee Brewers at County Stadium. Henderson finished with 130 steals.

Supporting Cast:
• **Wayne Gross.** A's batter when Henderson broke Brock's record of 118 (set in 1974) with a third-inning steal of second base.
• **Doc Medich.** Brewers' pitcher when Henderson stole second.
• **Ted Simmons.** Brewers' catcher when Henderson set the record.

JACKSON'S THREE-HOMER SERIES GAME
Reggie Jackson of the New York Yankees walloped three home runs in Game

Boston's Carlton Fisk applies a little body English to his 12th-inning drive to left field in Game 6 of the 1975 World Series against Cincinnati. The ball stayed fair, hitting high off the foul pole and giving the Red Sox a 7-6 victory.

Rickey Henderson of Oakland shows off the base he stole on August 27, 1982, in Milwaukee, giving him 119 steals for the season and a modern major league record. Looking on is Lou Brock, the man whose record Henderson shattered.

6 of the 1977 World Series, becoming only the second player in Series history to accomplish the feat (Babe Ruth did it twice, in 1926 and 1928). Jackson's homers on October 18 at Yankee Stadium led the Yankees to a Series-clinching 8-4 victory over the Los Angeles Dodgers. Each homer was a first-pitch smash.

Supporting Cast:
- **Burt Hooton.** Dodgers' pitcher off whom Jackson hit a two-run homer into the right-field stands in the fourth inning.
- **Charlie Hough.** Pitcher off whom Jackson hit a leadoff homer into the center-field bleachers in the eighth inning.
- **Elias Sosa.** Pitcher off whom Jackson hit a two-run homer into the right-field stands in the fifth inning.

LAZZERI'S TWO GRAND SLAMS IN GAME
Playing against the Philadelphia Athletics on May 24, 1936, at Shibe Park, Tony Lazzeri of the New York Yankees became the first major leaguer to hit two bases-loaded homers in one game. Hitting three homers overall, Lazzeri drove in an American League-record 11 runs in the Yankees' 25-2 victory. Lazzeri also tripled in five official at-bats.

Supporting Cast:
- **George Turbeville.** A's pitcher off whom Lazzeri hit a bases-loaded homer in the second inning.
- **Red Bullock.** A's pitcher off whom Lazzeri hit a bases-loaded homer in the fifth inning.

LYNN TEES OFF ON DETROIT
Fred Lynn of the Boston Red Sox enjoyed one of the best days in big-league history on June 18, 1975, hitting three home runs and driving in 10 runs as the Red Sox pounded Detroit, 15-1, at Tiger Stadium. Lynn, who knocked in eight runs with his homers, also had a two-run triple and infield single in going 5-for-6.

Supporting Cast:
- **Joe Coleman.** Detroit pitcher off whom Lynn hit a two-run homer in the first inning and a three-run homer in the second.
- **Tom Walker.** Detroit pitcher off whom Lynn hit a three-run homer in the ninth inning.

MARIS' 61st HOME RUN
Playing against the Boston Red Sox in the regular-season finale on October 1, 1961, at Yankee Stadium, Roger Maris of the New York Yankees hit his 61st homer of the year to surpass Babe Ruth's single-season record of 60 (set in 1927).

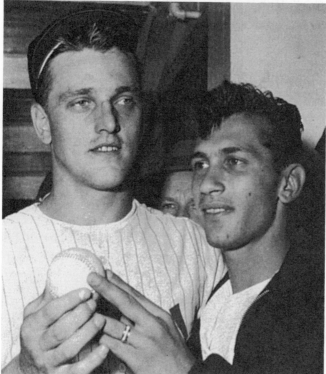

Roger Maris is greeted by Yogi Berra (8) after slugging his 61st home run of the 1961 season, then meets with Sal Durante, a 19-year-old fan from Brooklyn who retrieved his smash into the right-field stands.

Supporting Cast:
• **Sal Durante.** A 19-year-old fan from Brooklyn, he grabbed Maris' home-run ball 15 rows up in the right-field stands. In exchange for the ball, Durante received $5,000 and two trips to the West Coast.
• **Russ Nixon.** Boston's catcher when Maris homered.
• **Bill Stafford.** With relief help from Hal Reniff and Luis Arroyo, he was the winning pitcher in the Yankees' 1-0 victory.
• **Tracy Stallard.** Boston pitcher off whom Maris homered.
• **Carl Yastrzemski.** Boston's left fielder (he went 1-for-4) who was still an active major leaguer in 1982.

MAZEROSKI'S HOMER WINS WORLD SERIES
Leading off the bottom of the ninth inning of Game 7 of the 1960 World Series, Bill Mazeroski homered over the left-field wall at Pittsburgh's Forbes Field to give the Pirates a 10-9 triumph over the New York Yankees and their first Series championship in 35 years.

Supporting Cast:
• **Yogi Berra.** Yankees' longtime catcher who was in left field when Mazeroski hit his climactic homer in the October 13 game.
• **John Blanchard.** Yankees' catcher when Mazeroski homered.
• **Joe DeMaestri.** Yankees' utility infielder who replaced Tony Kubek in the eighth inning when the New York shortstop was struck in the throat by a bad-hop grounder.
• **Harvey Haddix.** Pirates' winning pitcher who replaced reliever Bob Friend with two on and no one out in the Yankees' ninth.
• **Tony Kubek.** Struck in the throat by Bill Virdon's sharply hit, bad-hop grounder in the Pirates' eighth, he was unable to make a play on Virdon. Virdon was credited with a hit in one of the key plays of the Pirates' five-run inning that overcame a 7-4 New York lead.
• **Mickey Mantle.** His ninth-inning single scored Bobby Richardson, cutting Pittsburgh's lead to 9-8.
• **Gil McDougald.** He scored New York's tying run (9-9) in the ninth on a play in which Berra grounded out to first baseman Rocky Nelson.
• **Hal Smith.** Having replaced Smoky Burgess as the Pirates' catcher in the top of the eighth, he hit a three-run homer in the bottom of the eighth off Jim Coates to give Pittsburgh a 9-7 lead.
• **Ralph Terry.** Yankees' pitcher off whom Mazeroski connected, making the Pittsburgh second baseman the only man to end a Series with a homer.

MONDAY'S HOMER
With the 1981 National League Championship Series tied at two games apiece and Game 5 deadlocked, 1-1, in the ninth inning, Rick Monday of Los Angeles hit a two-out, bases-empty home run at Olympic Stadium to give the Dodgers a 2-1 triumph over the Montreal Expos and the N.L. pennant.

Only once has a World Series ended with a home run, and the ecstasy of that moment is apparent as Pittsburgh's Bill Mazeroski heads for home after connecting against New York's Ralph Terry in the ninth inning of Game 7 of the 1960 Series.

Supporting Cast:
• **Ray Burris.** Expos' starting pitcher who left the October 19 game for a pinch-hitter in the eighth inning with the score tied, 1-1.
• **Steve Rogers.** Expos' pitcher who gave up the ninth-inning homer to Monday. Making only the third relief appearance of his big-league career, Rogers retired the first two batters he faced before Monday connected in the Monday afternoon game.
• **Fernando Valenzuela** Dodgers' starting and winning pitcher who needed last-out relief help from Bob Welch.

MUSIAL'S FIVE-HOMER DOUBLEHEADER
Stan Musial of the St. Louis Cardinals established a doubleheader home-run record on May 2, 1954, at old Busch Stadium, hitting five homers as the Cards split with the New York Giants (St. Louis won the opener, 10-6, but lost the nightcap, 9-7).

Supporting Cast:
• **Johnny Antonelli.** Giants' pitcher off whom Musial hit a bases-empty homer in the third inning of the opener and a two-run homer in the fifth inning of the first game.
• **Jim Hearn.** Gave up a three-run homer to Musial in the eighth inning of the opener.
• **Hoyt Wilhelm.** Gave up a two-run homer to Musial in the fifth inning of the nightcap and a bases-empty homer in the seventh inning of the second game.

ROSE'S 44-GAME STREAK
Pete Rose of the Cincinnati Reds equaled Wee Willie Keeler's all-time National League batting-streak mark in 1978, hitting safely in 44 straight games.

Supporting Cast:
• **Gene Garber.** Braves' pitcher whose ninth-inning strikeout of Rose on August 1 at Atlanta Stadium ended Rose's streak. Rose had lined into a double play against Garber in the seventh inning.
• **Larry McWilliams.** Braves' rookie pitcher who helped to stop Rose's streak August 1, retiring him on a liner in the third inning and a grounder in the fifth after walking him in the first.
• **Phil Niekro.** Braves' pitcher who allowed a sixth-inning single to Rose on July 31, enabling Rose to tie Keeler's mark (set in 1897).
• **Dave Roberts.** Chicago Cubs' pitcher off whom Rose started his streak June 14 with two hits.

RUTH'S THREE-HOMER SERIES GAMES
Babe Ruth put on a power display unprecedented in World Series history in 1926, then matched the feat in 1928. Ruth, New York Yankees' superstar,

Pete Rose acknowledges a standing ovation at Atlanta Stadium on July 31, 1978, after singling against the Braves and equaling the all-time National League batting-streak mark of 44 games. Ron Plaza, Cincinnati first-base coach, takes note of the "Pete" being flashed on a message board.

belted three home runs in Game 4 of each classic—and both performances came at Sportsman's Park against the St. Louis Cardinals.

Supporting Cast:
• **Grover Cleveland Alexander.** Cardinals' pitcher who gave up a bases-empty homer to Ruth in the eighth inning on October 9, 1928.
• **Hi Bell.** Cardinals' pitcher who gave up a two-run homer to Ruth in the sixth inning on October 6, 1926.
• **Flint Rhem.** Cardinals' pitcher off whom Ruth hit bases-empty homers in the first and third innings on October 6, 1926.
• **Willie Sherdel.** Cardinals' pitcher off whom Ruth hit a leadoff homer in the fourth inning on October 9, 1928, and a bases-empty homer in the seventh inning of the same game.

RUTH'S CALLED SHOT
Batting in the fifth inning of Game 3 of the 1932 World Series, New York's Babe Ruth—taunted by Cub fans at Wrigley Field—homered to deep center field after seemingly calling his shot. While many on hand at the October 1 game claimed Ruth pointed to the spot where he then hit the ball, others said the Yankee slugger made a gesture that really was never adequately explained.

After Babe Ruth hit three home runs in Game 4 of the 1926 World Series at St. Louis'
Sportsman's Park, the auto agency across the street on Grand Avenue took note of the
accomplishment. As the cracked glass in front of the Babe's image indicates, the dealer-
ship's showroom window was victimized by one of Ruth's drives.

Supporting Cast:
• **Lou Gehrig.** Yankees' first baseman who followed Ruth's fifth-inning shot with another homer, his second of the game.
• **George Pipgras.** The winning pitcher in the Yankees' 7-5 victory.
• **Charlie Root.** Cubs' pitcher who gave up the noted homer, a drive that broke a 4-4 tie. Root also yielded a three-run homer to Ruth in the first inning.
• **Joe Sewell.** Yankees' third baseman who preceded Ruth to the plate in the fifth. He grounded out to shortstop Billy Jurges.

RUTH'S 60th HOME RUN
Babe Ruth struck his 60th homer of the 1927 season on September 30, breaking the major league record of 59 he had achieved six years earlier.

Supporting Cast:
• **Walter Johnson.** Washington Senators' pitching great who—as a pinch-hitter in the ninth inning—made his last appearance as a big-league player in Ruth's 60th-homer game.
• **Mark Koenig.** New York Yankees' shortstop who was on third base with a triple when Ruth homered at Yankee Stadium.
• **Muddy Ruel.** Senators' catcher when Ruth connected.
• **Tom Zachary.** Senators' pitcher off whom Ruth homered in the eighth inning. The drive broke a 2-2 tie, sending the Yankees to a 4-2 triumph in the next-to-last game of the regular season.

SLAUGHTER'S MAD DASH
With Game 7 of the 1946 World Series tied with two out in the bottom of the eighth inning, St. Louis' Enos Slaughter raced home from first base on Harry Walker's hit to left-center field to give the Cardinals a 4-3 victory over the Boston Red Sox and the world championship.

Supporting Cast:
• **Harry Brecheen.** Cardinals' reliever who was the winning pitcher in the October 15 game at Sportsman's Park. He worked two innings.
• **Leon Culberson.** Boston center fielder who fielded Walker's hit and made the throw to the relay man. Culberson had entered the game in the top of the eighth as a pinch-runner.
• **Dom DiMaggio.** Boston center fielder whose two-run double in the eighth tied the score, 3-3. DiMaggio twisted his ankle rounding first and was replaced by Culberson.
• **Bob Klinger.** Boston reliever and losing pitcher off whom Walker got the game-winning hit.
• **Johnny Pesky.** Boston shortstop who hesitated in relaying Culberson's throw to the plate, helping Slaughter to score from first.
• **Harry Walker.** Cardinals' left fielder who made it to second base on his decisive hit and was credited with a double (not a single, as often reported).

Emerging from a cloud of dust in Game 7 of the 1946 World Series is St. Louis' Enos Slaughter, who raced home from first base with the Series-winning run on a hit by Harry Walker. Boston Catcher Roy Partee, up the third-base line, takes the late throw from shortstop Johnny Pesky as umpire Al Barlick focuses on Slaughter's slide.

THOMSON'S SHOT HEARD 'ROUND THE WORLD

Batting with one out in the bottom of the ninth inning of the third game of the 1951 National League playoffs, Bobby Thomson hit a three-run homer to give the New York Giants a 5-4 victory over the Brooklyn Dodgers and the N.L. pennant.

Supporting Cast:
• **Ralph Branca.** Dodgers' pitcher off whom Thomson homered in the October 3 game at the Polo Grounds, capping a four-run inning.
• **Al Dark.** Giants' shortstop who opened the bottom of the ninth with an infield single.
• **Clint Hartung.** Giants' reserve outfielder who ran for Don Mueller in the ninth when Mueller fractured his ankle sliding into third base.
• **Monte Irvin.** Only New York player to be retired in the ninth. He popped out.
• **Larry Jansen.** Giants' winning pitcher, having worked the ninth inning.
• **Whitey Lockman.** Giants' first baseman whose ninth-inning double scored Dark and sent Mueller to third.
• **Willie Mays.** A 20-year-old rookie, he was on deck when Thomson homered.
• **Don Mueller.** Giants' right fielder who followed Dark's hit with a single.
• **Don Newcombe.** Brooklyn's starting pitcher who took a 4-1 lead into the ninth but left after Lockman's double cut the lead to 4-2. With Hartung on third

Bobby Thomson was riding high after his pennant-winning home run for the New York Giants in 1951, while Giants Manager Leo Durocher and second baseman Eddie Stanky (wearing jacket) wrestled with their team's stunning success in the National League playoff against Brooklyn.

and Lockman at second, Brooklyn Manager Charlie Dressen brought in Branca to pitch to Thomson.
• **Al (Rube) Walker.** Branca's catcher when Thomson homered.

WILLIAMS' ALL-STAR SHOW
Ted Williams of the Boston Red Sox went 4-for-4 in the 1946 All-Star Game at Fenway Park, hitting two home runs and driving in five runs as the American League routed the National League, 12-0.

Supporting Cast:
• **Ewell Blackwell.** National League pitcher off whom Williams got a scratch single in the seventh inning of the July 9 game.
• **Kirby Higbe.** National League pitcher off whom Williams hit a leadoff homer in the fourth and a run-scoring single in the fifth.
• **Rip Sewell.** National League pitcher whose blooper pitch was hit for a three-run homer by Williams in the eighth inning.

WILLIAMS REACHES .400
"I don't care to be known as a .400 hitter with a lousy average of .39955," said Boston's Ted Williams, commenting on his playing status for a season-ending doubleheader against the Philadelphia Athletics on September 28, 1941. "If I'm going to be a .400 hitter," added the eager-to-play Williams, "I want to have more than my toenails on the line." Williams went 4-for-5 in the first game, boosting his average to .4039. Giving no thought to resting on his laurels, Williams went 2-for-3 in the second game to finish at .4057 (.406 in the record books).

Supporting Cast:
• **Fred Caligiuri.** A's pitcher off whom Williams singled and doubled in his first two at-bats in the nightcap. Caligiuri beat the Red Sox, 7-1, in a game called after eight innings because of darkness; it was one of only two victories he had in the majors. Caligiuri outpitched Boston's Lefty Grove, who took the loss while making his last major league appearance.
• **Dick Fowler.** A's pitcher off whom Williams singled and homered in his first two at-bats in the opener at Shibe Park.
• **Porter Vaughan.** A's pitcher off whom Williams singled in his third and fourth at-bats in the opener, which Boston won, 12-11.

WILLS BEATS COBB
Maury Wills of the Los Angeles Dodgers shattered Ty Cobb's modern stolen-base record in 1962, getting his record-breaking 97th steal on September 23 against the St. Louis Cardinals at old Busch Stadium. Wills finished with 104 steals.

Maury Wills of the Los Angeles Dodgers gave his shoes quite a workout in 1962 when he broke Ty Cobb's modern stolen-base record of 96. Wills finished the season with 104 steals, getting his last theft of the year against San Francisco in the N.L. playoffs.

Supporting Cast:
• **Jim Gilliam.** Dodgers' batter when Wills broke Cobb's record of 96 (set in 1915).
• **Larry Jackson.** Cardinals' pitcher when Wills stole second base in the seventh inning.
• **Carl Sawatski.** Cardinals' catcher when Wills stole.

SECOND INNING
Dramatic moments in pitching and fielding, with supporting casts

AGEE FOILS ORIOLES

Tommie Agee's defensive heroics in Game 3 of the 1969 World Series at Shea Stadium saved the Mets as many as five runs and led New York to a 5-0 triumph over the Baltimore Orioles, giving the Mets a two-games-to-one lead in the Series. Agee, New York's center fielder, also hit a leadoff homer in the first inning off Baltimore's Jim Palmer.

Supporting Cast:
• **Paul Blair.** Orioles' center fielder who came to bat with two out and the bases loaded in the seventh inning and Baltimore trailing, 4-0. Blair drove the ball to right-center field, where Agee, sliding on his stomach, made a one-handed catch.
• **Elrod Hendricks.** With Boog Powell (single) on first base and Frank Robinson (single) on third and New York ahead 3-0 in the fourth, Hendricks hit a smash to deep left-center, where Agee made a backhanded, fingertip catch at the base of the wall.
• **Gary Gentry.** Mets' pitcher off whom Baltimore's Elrod Hendricks hit his long drive with two out and two on in the fourth inning of the October 14 game.
• **Nolan Ryan.** Mets' pitcher off whom Blair hit his drive in the seventh. Ryan had just replaced Gentry, who had walked Mark Belanger, pinch-hitter Dave May and Don Buford after two Orioles had been retired.

ALEXANDER RESCUES CARDINALS

Having pitched a complete-game victory the day before, 39-year-old Grover Cleveland Alexander was summoned from the bullpen with two out and the bases loaded in the seventh inning and saved the St. Louis Cardinals' 3-2 victory over the New York Yankees in Game 7 of the 1926 World Series.

Supporting Cast:
• **Earle Combs.** Yankee center fielder whose leadoff single in the seventh started the Yanks' threat in the October 10 game at Yankee Stadium.
• **Lou Gehrig.** Yankee first baseman whose walk in the seventh filled the bases.
• **Jesse Haines.** Cardinals' starting and winning pitcher (6 2/3 innings) who gave way to Alexander (2 1/3 innings).

One of the Game 3 defensive gems turned in by Mets center fielder Tommie Agee in the 1969 World Series came with two out in the seventh inning and the bases loaded when Baltimore's Paul Blair drove a line drive to right-center field and Agee made a diving, one-handed catch.

• **Waite Hoyt.** New York's starting and losing pitcher.
• **Mark Koenig.** Yankee shortstop who sacrificed Combs to second in the seventh.
• **Tony Lazzeri.** Yankee rookie second baseman who struck out against Alexander with the bases loaded in the seventh.
• **Bob Meusel.** Yankee left fielder whose seventh-inning grounder forced Babe Ruth at second base and sent Combs to third.
• **Bob O'Farrell.** Cardinals' catcher.
• **Babe Ruth.** Yankee right fielder who drew an intentional walk in the seventh.

AMOROS' GAME-SAVING CATCH
With Brooklyn leading 2-0 in the sixth inning of Game 7 of the 1955 World Series and the Yankees having the potential tying runs on base, Dodgers' left fielder Sandy Amoros squelched New York's rally by making a sensational catch and then doubling up a Yankee baserunner. The Dodgers' lead stood up, giving Brooklyn its only Series championship.

Supporting Cast:
• **Yogi Berra.** Yankee catcher who, with runners on first and second and no one out in the sixth inning, lofted a drive down the left-field line. Amoros raced into the corner and made a glove-hand catch, turning the grab into a double play.
• **Jim Gilliam.** The man Amoros replaced in left field at the start of the Yankees'

28

Brooklyn's lone World Series championship came in 1955, thanks largely to the defensive heroics of left fielder Sandy Amoros. With two Yankees on base in the sixth inning of Game 7 and the Dodgers leading 2-0, Amoros raced to the left-field corner to snare Yogi Berra's fly ball and then doubled a runner off first.

sixth in the October 4 game at Yankee Stadium.

• **Billy Martin.** Yankee second baseman who started New York's sixth with a walk.

• **Gil McDougald.** Yankee third baseman who was doubled off first base after Amoros' catch. He had reached base on a bunt single.

• **Johnny Podres.** Brooklyn pitcher off whom Berra hit the drive to Amoros. Podres finished with an eight-hit shutout.

• **Pee Wee Reese.** Brooklyn shortstop whose relay throw to first baseman Gil Hodges after Amoros' catch doubled up McDougald.

• **Don Zimmer.** Brooklyn second baseman whose removal from the game in the top of the sixth for pinch-hitter George Shuba led to the move of Gilliam to second base and the insertion of Amoros into left field.

ARMBRISTER MAKES PRESENCE FELT

In his only official at-bat in World Series competition, coming October 14, 1975, at Riverfront Stadium against the Boston Red Sox, Cincinnati's Ed Armbrister was the focal point of a controversial no-interference ruling on his sacrifice-bunt attempt. The 10th-inning play in Game 3 helped the Reds to a 6-5 victory and a two-games-to-one lead in the Series, which they won in seven games.

Supporting Cast:

• **Larry Barnett.** Home-plate umpire who rejected the Red Sox's claim of interference on the play.

• **Rawly Eastwick.** Reds' reliever and winning pitcher for whom Armbrister batted in the 10th with the score tied, 5-5.

• **Carlton Fisk.** Boston catcher who collided with Armbrister while attempting to get to Armbrister's bunt in front of the plate, then threw wildly into center field (leaving Cincinnati with runners on second and third base). The play was ruled an error on Fisk.

• **Cesar Geronimo.** Reds' center fielder who led off the 10th with a single preceding Armbrister's attempted bunt.

• **Joe Morgan.** Reds' second baseman who, after an intentional walk to Pete Rose and a strikeout by pinch-hitter Merv Rettenmund in the 10th, drove in Geronimo with a fly over the head of Fred Lynn, Boston's drawn-in center fielder.

• **Jim Willoughby.** Red Sox's reliever and losing pitcher who gave way to Roger Moret after the Armbrister incident.

BEVENS LOSES SERIES NO-HIT BID

One out away from becoming the first man in history to pitch a World Series no-hitter, Floyd (Bill) Bevens of the New York Yankees lost his bid—and the game—on a two-run double in Game 4 of the 1947 World Series as the Brooklyn Dodgers beat the Yanks, 3-2.

Supporting Cast:
• **Hugh Casey.** Dodgers' reliever and winning pitcher. He pitched two-thirds of an inning.

• **Carl Furillo.** After catcher Bruce Edwards flied out to open the Dodgers' ninth in the October 3 game at Ebbets Field, center fielder Furillo drew a walk off Bevens (trying to protect a 2-1 lead).

• **Al Gionfriddo.** After third baseman Spider Jorgensen fouled out for the second out of the Dodgers' ninth, Gionfriddo went in to run for Furillo. With Pete Reiser at the plate, Gionfriddo stole second on a 2-1 pitch.

• **Cookie Lavagetto.** Dodgers' pinch-hitter whose ninth-inning double off the right-field wall scored Gionfriddo and Eddie Miksis, giving Brooklyn its only hit and a Series-squaring 3-2 victory.

• **Eddie Miksis.** He ran for Reiser in the Dodgers' ninth.

• **Pete Reiser.** A pinch-hitter for Casey in the Dodgers' ninth, he was walked intentionally after the count reached 3-1.

• **Eddie Stanky.** Dodgers' second baseman for whom Lavagetto pinch-hit in the ninth.

GIBSON STRIKES OUT 17 TIGERS

Bob Gibson of St. Louis struck out a World Series-record 17 batters in Game1 of the 1968 classic, in the Cardinals' 4-0 victory over the Detroit Tigers at Busch Memorial Stadium. Eleven Tigers struck out swinging in the October 2 game; five were called out on strikes and one bunted foul for a third strike.

PINELLI
STIRNWEISS
HENRICH
McQUINN
McGOWAN
PITLER
MIKSIS
GIONFRIDDO
BEVENS
BERRA
LAVAGETTO
GOETZ

The flight of Cookie Lavagetto's ninth-inning double, the positioning of the Yankees' defense and movement of Brooklyn baserunners is diagrammed during Game 4 of the 1947 World Series played at Ebbets Field. Lavagetto, whose hit gave Brooklyn a 3-2 victory and broke up Bill Bevens' no-hit bid, is escorted from the field by police and happy teammates.

Detroit first baseman Norm Cash comes up empty on a ninth-inning swing against Cardinals ace Bob Gibson during Game 1 action in the 1968 World Series. Cash was Gibson's record-breaking 16th strikeout victim en route to a game total of 17.

Supporting Cast:
• **Norm Cash.** With one out in the ninth inning, the Tigers' first baseman became Gibson's record-breaking 16th strikeout victim as the St. Louis pitcher surpassed Sandy Koufax's Series mark of 15 (set in 1963).
• **Willie Horton.** Tigers' left fielder, the game's final batter, was called out on strikes, giving Gibson 17 strikeouts.
• **Al Kaline.** After Tigers' shortstop Mickey Stanley singled to open the ninth, Kaline became Gibson's record-equaling 15th strikeout victim.
• **Tim McCarver.** Gibson's catcher.
• **Denny McLain.** Tigers' loser in the heralded pitching matchup. McLain was coming off a 31-victory season (he was the majors' first 30-game winner in 34 years), while Gibson posted a National League-record 1.12 earned-run average in 1968 and pitched 13 shutouts.

GIONFRIDDO'S CATCH
With two Yankees on base and the Dodgers ahead 8-5 in the sixth inning of Game 6 of the 1947 World Series, Brooklyn left fielder Al Gionfriddo denied New York a score-tying home run with an outstanding catch in front of the bullpen at Yankee Stadium. The Dodgers went on to win, 8-6, to even the Series at three games apiece, but the Yankees won the Series the next day.

Supporting Cast:
• **Yogi Berra.** Yankees' right fielder whose two-out single in the sixth inning put runners at first and second base.
• **Joe DiMaggio.** Yankees' center fielder whose two-out, sixth-inning drive with two runners on base was caught by Gionfriddo just as it appeared the ball might drop over the fence. Gionfriddo made a twisting, glove-hand catch near the 415-foot mark.
• **Joe Hatten.** Dodgers' pitcher off whom DiMaggio hit his sixth-inning drive in the October 5 game.
• **Eddie Miksis.** Dodgers' left fielder who was replaced defensively by Gionfriddo as the Yankees prepared to come to bat in the bottom of the sixth. Miksis had entered the game in the fifth inning as a pinch-hitter for left fielder Gene Hermanski, then went in to play left field.
• **George Stirnweiss.** Yankees' second baseman who walked in the sixth and advanced to second on Berra's single.

HADDIX PITCHES 12 PERFECT INNINGS
Harvey Haddix of the Pittsburgh Pirates pitched 12 perfect innings against Milwaukee on May 26, 1959, at County Stadium, only to end up a 1-0, one-hit loser to the Braves in 13 innings.

Supporting Cast:
• **Hank Aaron.** Braves' right fielder who drew an intentional walk from Haddix in the 13th inning of the 0-0 game.
• **Joe Adcock.** Braves' first baseman who, with one out and Felix Mantilla on second base and Aaron on first, hit a 13th-inning pitch from Haddix over the fence in right-center field. Aaron, figuring the ball had dropped at the fence and that Mantilla's run had ended the game, touched second base and headed for the dugout. Adcock circled the bases, but he was credited with a double— not a home run—because he was ruled out before reaching third base for having passed Aaron. Nevertheless, Adcock's hit made Milwaukee a 1-0 winner.
• **Lew Burdette.** Braves' winning pitcher who went the distance and permitted 12 hits (all singles).
• **Smoky Burgess.** Haddix's catcher.
• **Don Hoak.** Pittsburgh third baseman whose throwing error opening the Braves' 13th ended Haddix's perfection at 36 straight batters.
• **Felix Mantilla** Braves' second baseman was the first baserunner against Haddix, reaching first on Hoak's misplay. Mantilla had entered the game in the 11th inning, after Del Rice pinch-hit for second baseman Johnny O'Brien in the Braves' 10th.
• **Eddie Mathews.** Braves' third baseman who sacrificed Mantilla to second in the 13th.

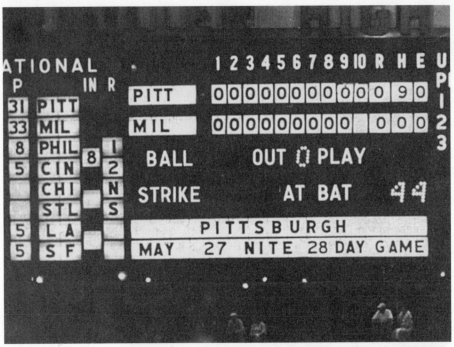

The scoreboard tells the story as Pittsburgh's Harvey Haddix enters the 10th inning of his 1959 gem against Milwaukee in perfect form, while Al Gionfriddo's catch of a long drive by Joe DiMaggio told the story in Game 6 of the 1947 World series. Gionfriddo's play kept the Yankees from tying the score and Brooklyn went on to win, 8-6.

HUBBELL'S ALL-STAR FEAT

Carl Hubbell of the New York Giants turned in one of the most memorable pitching performances in baseball history on July 10, 1934, at the Polo Grounds, striking out five straight American League All-Stars in the major leagues' second All-Star Game. Despite Hubbell's performance, the National League, ahead 4-0 after three innings, lost, 9-7.

Supporting Cast:
• **Babe Ruth.** After Charlie Gehringer (Detroit Tigers) and Heinie Manush (Washington Senators) singled and walked, respectively, to open the A.L.'s first, the Yankees' Ruth became Hubbell's first strikeout victim.
• **Lou Gehrig.** Yankees' first baseman who was Hubbell's second consecutive strikeout victim in the first inning.
• **Jimmie Foxx.** Philadelphia Athletics' slugger who was Hubbell's third straight strikeout victim in the first inning.
• **Al Simmons.** Chicago White Sox's outfielder who led off the second inning for the A.L. and became Hubbell's fourth straight strikeout victim.
• **Joe Cronin.** The second batter for the American League in the second inning, the Washington Senators' shortstop became Hubbell's fifth straight strikeout victim.
• **Bill Dickey.** New York Yankees' catcher who, after Cronin struck out in the second inning, ended Hubbell's strikeout streak with a single.
• **Lefty Gomez.** Yankees' pitcher who struck out after Dickey's hit, giving Hubbell six strikeouts in the first two innings (Hubbell did not record a strikeout in the third, his last inning of work).
• **Mel Harder.** Cleveland Indians' pitcher who hurled one-hit, shutout ball over the last five innings for the A.L. and was credited with the victory.
• **Van Lingle Mungo.** Brooklyn Dodgers' pitcher who was the National League's loser. He gave up four runs and four hits in the fifth inning.

Fernando Valenzuela, pitching for the National League and representing the Los Angeles Dodgers, struck out five consecutive American League batters in the 1986 All-Star Game.

JOSS PERFECT

Addie Joss of Cleveland was at his best on October 2, 1908—and it was out of necessity. Ed Walsh of the Chicago White Sox, Joss' pitching opponent that day in Cleveland, hurled one of the best games of his career. But Joss was even better, pitching a perfect game and winning, 1-0.

Supporting Cast:
• **John Anderson.** White Sox's pinch-hitter whose groundout completed Joss' perfect game. The at-bat was Anderson's last in a 14-year major league career.
• **Nig Clarke.** Joss' catcher.
• **Ossee Schreckengost.** White Sox's catcher who broke a finger in this game—

a game that proved Schreckengost's last in an 11-year big-league career.
• **Ed Walsh.** White Sox's losing pitcher who struck out 15 batters, allowed only four hits and walked one. Joss had three strikeouts.

LARSEN'S PERFECT GAME
On October 8, 1956, at Yankee Stadium, Don Larsen accomplished the unprecedented feat of hurling a no-hit game in the World Series. Larsen pitched a perfect game as the Yankees defeated the Brooklyn Dodgers, 2-0 in Game 5.

Supporting Cast:
• **Hank Bauer.** Yankee right fielder whose sixth-inning single scored Andy Carey with New York's second run. Carey had singled and advanced to second on Larsen's sacrifice.
• **Yogi Berra.** Larsen's catcher.
• **Roy Campanella.** Brooklyn catcher who, as the second batter in the ninth, grounded out to second baseman Billy Martin.
• **Carl Furillo.** Leading off the ninth, Brooklyn right fielder flied out to Bauer.
• **Sal Maglie.** Dodgers' losing pitcher who allowed only five hits, walked two batters and struck out five.
• **Mickey Mantle.** Yankee center fielder whose fourth-inning home run staked Larsen to a 1-0 lead.
• **Dale Mitchell.** Pinch-hitting for Maglie, he was the last out in Larsen's perfect game. The sequence of pitches: Ball one, outside; strike one, called; strike two,

Yankee pitcher Don Larsen receives a big hug from catcher Yogi Berra after striking out Brooklyn's Dale Mitchell to complete his perfect game in the 1956 World Series.

36

swinging; foul ball to the left, into the crowd; strike three called. The strikeout was the seventh of the game for Larsen.

• **Pee Wee Reese.** Brooklyn shortstop who was the only Dodger to reach ball three against Larsen. The second batter of the game, Reese was called out on strikes on a 3-2 pitch.

MALONEY, WILSON NO-HITTERS

Jim Maloney of Cincinnati and Don Wilson of Houston pitched back-to-back no-hitters in a 1969 Reds-Astros series, marking only the second time such a performance had occurred in major league history. Maloney beat the Astros, 10-0, on April 30 at Crosley Field, striking out 13 and walking five. Wilson foiled the Reds, 4-0, on May 1, walking six and striking out 13.

Supporting Cast:

• **Wade Blasingame.** Astros' starting and losing pitcher in Maloney's no-hitter.
• **Darrel Chaney.** Reds' shortstop who helped to preserve Maloney's no-hitter with a somersaulting catch of Johnny Edwards' sixth-inning looper into short left field.
• **Bobby Tolan.** Reds' right fielder whose three hits and four RBIs backed Maloney.
• **Denis Menke.** Astros' shortstop who had two hits and two runs batted in May 1 in support of Wilson. Third baseman Doug Rader hit a bases-empty home run, and Wilson contributed a sacrifice fly.
• **Jim Merritt.** Reds' starting and losing pitcher in Wilson's no-hitter.

MARTIN TO THE RESCUE

Trailing 4-2 with two out and the bases loaded in their half of the seventh inning, the Brooklyn Dodgers saw their hopes rise in Game 7 of the 1952 World Series when a popup near the mound seemed on the brink of going unattended. With two Dodgers having crossed the plate and another runner rounding third base, Yankee second baseman Billy Martin dashed in and grabbed the ball about knee-high. The score stood up, and the Yankees had their fourth straight World Series championship.

Supporting Cast:

• **Joe Collins.** Yankee first baseman who apparently would make the play on the seventh-inning popup, but he lost sight of the ball.
• **Billy Cox.** Brooklyn third baseman whose single helped the Dodgers fill the bases in the seventh.
• **Carl Furillo.** Dodgers' right fielder who led off the seventh with a walk.
• **Bob Kuzava.** Yankee relief pitcher who stood transfixed when the seventh inning popup was hit.
• **Pee Wee Reese.** Brooklyn shortstop whose seventh-inning walk loaded the bases.
• **Jackie Robinson.** Brooklyn second baseman who, on a 3-2 pitch, hit the

Second baseman Billy Martin saved the day for the Yankees when he made a running, knee-high catch of a bases-loaded, infield pop with two out in the seventh inning of Game 7 of the 1952 World Series.

popup that Martin snared in the October 7 game at Ebbets Field.

MAYS' REMARKABLE CATCH
With the opening game of the 1954 World Series between the Cleveland Indians and New York Giants tied, 2-2, in the eighth inning and two Indians on base, Giants' center fielder Willie Mays made an over-the-shoulder catch of a 460-foot smash while running with his back to the plate. Saved by Mays' remarkable play, the Giants went on to beat the Indians, 5-2, in 10 innings on the way to a Series sweep.

Supporting Cast:
• **Larry Doby.** Cleveland center fielder who led off the Indians' eighth with a walk. He moved to second on a single and tagged up and went to third after Mays' catch (but was left on base).
• **Marv Grissom.** Giants' reliever and winning pitcher who worked 2 2/3 innings.
• **Don Liddle.** Giants' relief pitcher who faced only one batter in the September 29 game at the Polo Grounds—Vic Wertz, who came to the plate with two runners on and no one out in the Indians' eighth.
• **Dusty Rhodes.** Giants' pinch-hitter who batted for left fielder Monte Irvin in the 10th inning and hit a game-winning three-run homer off Cleveland starter and loser Bob Lemon.
• **Al Rosen.** Cleveland third baseman whose eighth-inning single, following Doby's walk, brought on Liddle in relief of Giants' starter Sal Maglie.
• **Vic Wertz.** Cleveland first baseman who singled twice, doubled and tripled in the game . . . and hit the eighth-inning drive that Mays hauled in.

McLAIN NOTCHES 30th
Denny McLain of Detroit became the major leagues' first 30-game winner in 34 years on September 14, 1968, when the Tigers scored two runs in the bottom of the ninth inning and edged the Oakland A's, 5-4. McLain struck out 10 batters and walked one, allowing six hits. Not since Dizzy Dean won 30 games for the St. Louis Cardinals in 1934 had a big-league pitcher reached the select figure.

Supporting Cast:
• **Bill Freehan.** McLain's catcher in the game at Tiger Stadium.
• **Willie Horton.** Detroit left fielder whose one-out hit over left fielder Jim Gosger's head scored Mickey Stanley with the winning run in the ninth inning, boosting McLain's record to 30-5 (he finished at 31-6).
• **Reggie Jackson.** A's right fielder who hit a two-run home run and a bases-empty homer off McLain.
• **Al Kaline.** Pinch-hitting for McLain in the ninth with the Tigers trailing 4-3, he drew a leadoff walk.
• **Jim Northrup.** With one out in the Tigers' ninth and runners on first and

One of the more remarkable catches in baseball history occurred during the opening game of the 1954 World Series when New York Giants center fielder Willie Mays, his back to the plate, made an over-the-shoulder grab of a 460-foot drive off the bat of Cleveland's Vic Wertz.

Willie Horton's one-out, game-winning hit prompted this burst of excitement from Tiger teammates Al Kaline (left) and Denny McLain, who received credit for his 30th victory of the 1968 season.

• **Jim Northrup.** With one out in the Tigers' ninth and runners on first and third, the Detroit right fielder grounded to A's first baseman Danny Cater. Cater made a poor throw to the plate, allowing Kaline to score from third and Stanley to move from first to third.

• **Diego Segui.** A's losing pitcher who worked the final 4 1/3 innings.

• **Mickey Stanley.** Detroit center fielder whose one-out single in the ninth sent Kaline to third.

OAKLAND'S FOUR-PITCHER NO-HITTER

Trying to tune up his pitching staff for the 1975 American League Championship Series, Oakland Manager Alvin Dark used four pitchers in the A's regular-season finale on September 28—and the foursome responded with a no-hitter. Vida Blue, the A's starter and winner in a 5-0 victory over California at the Oakland Coliseum, held the Angels hitless for five innings. Blue walked two and struck out two.

Supporting Cast:

• **Glenn Abbott.** A's second pitcher who retired the Angels in order in the sixth inning.

• **Paul Lindblad.** A's third pitcher who retired the Angels in order in the seventh inning.

• **Rollie Fingers.** A's fourth pitcher who retired the Angels in order in the eighth and ninth innings, completing the four-man no hitter.

• **Reggie Jackson.** A's right fielder who hit two homers in the game and drove in three runs.

• **Dal Maxvill.** A's shortstop who, playing his last major league game, threw out the game's final batter.

• **Joe Pactwa.** Angels' pitcher who was appearing in his fourth and last major league game. Working in relief, he pitched the eighth inning (giving up a hit and a walk, but no runs).

• **Mickey Rivers.** Pinch-hitting for Angels' third baseman Dave Chalk, he grounded to Maxvill for the game's final out.

• **Gary Ross.** Angels' starting and losing pitcher who was making his only big-league appearance of the season.

On July 13, 1991, four Baltimore pitchers—Bob Milacki (six innings), Mike Flanagan (one), Mark Williamson (one), and Gregg Olson (one)—combined on a 2-0 against Oakland.

PERRY, WASHBURN NO-HITTERS

Gaylord Perry of San Francisco and Ray Washburn of St. Louis pitched consecutive no-hitters in a 1968 Giants-Cardinals series at Candlestick Park, the first such occurrence in big-league history. Perry stopped the Cardinals, 1-0, on the night of September 17, striking out nine and walking two. Washburn defeated the Giants, 2-0, the next afternoon, walking five and

1-0, on the night of September 17, striking out nine and walking two. Washburn defeated the Giants, 2-0, the next afternoon, walking five and striking out eight.

Supporting Cast:
• **Bob Gibson.** Cardinals' losing pitcher in Perry's no-hitter. He yielded only four hits and struck out 10 batters in going the distance.
• **Ron Hunt.** Giants' second baseman whose first-inning home run accounted for the only run in Perry's no-hitter and enabled San Francisco to beat St. Louis in the Cardinals' first game since clinching the National League pennant two days earlier.
• **Bob Bolin.** Giants' starting and losing pitcher in Washburn's no-hitter.
• **Mike Shannon.** Cardinals' third baseman who broke up a 0-0 game on September 18 with a run-scoring double off Bolin in the seventh inning.

RUDI'S CATCH
With the A's leading the Reds, 2-0, with one Cincinnati runner on base and no one out in the ninth inning of Game 2 of the 1972 World Series, Oakland left fielder Joe Rudi raced to the fence for a long drive and made a leaping, backhanded catch against the wall. The A's, who got a bases-empty homer from Rudi in the third inning, went on to win, 2-1, for a two-games-to-none lead in the Series, which they won in seven games.

Supporting Cast:
• **Rollie Fingers.** A's relief pitcher who ended the Reds' ninth-inning threat, getting the only batter he faced, pinch-hitter Julian Javier (batting for reliever Tom Hall), to foul out to first baseman Mike Hegan.
• **Jim (Catfish) Hunter.** A's starting and winning pitcher who lost his shutout with two out in the ninth in the October 15 game at Riverfront Stadium.
• **Hal McRae.** Cincinnati pinch-hitter who batted for shortstop Darrel Chaney in the ninth and singled across the Reds' only run.
• **Denis Menke.** Cincinnati third baseman who hit the long smash on which Rudi made an outstanding catch in the ninth.
• **Tony Perez.** Cincinnati first baseman who led off the Reds' ninth with a single preceding Menke's at-bat. Perez later went to second on right fielder Cesar Geronimo's low liner to first (Hegan knocked down the ball and retired Geronimo at the bag) and scored on McRae's hit.

SEAVER STRIKES OUT 10 STRAIGHT
Tom Seaver of the New York Mets set a major league record for consecutive strikeouts in one game on April 22, 1970, fanning 10 straight San Diego batters

Oakland left fielder Joe Rudi makes a leaping, backhanded catch against the wall to rob Cincinnati's Denis Menke and short-circuit a ninth-inning Reds' rally in Game 2 of the 1972 World Series.

A young Tom Seaver holds the Cy Young Award he was presented before an April 22, 1970, game against San Diego. Seaver celebrated the occasion by striking out a record 10 straight Padres en route to a record-tying game total of 19.

in the Mets' 2-1 triumph over the Padres. Seaver, presented with his 1969 Cy Young Award before the game at Shea Stadium, finished with a two-hitter and 19 strikeouts, with the strikeout total equaling the modern big-league mark for a nine-inning game set a year earlier by St. Louis' Steve Carlton against the Mets.

Supporting Cast:
• **Mike Corkins.** San Diego's starting and losing pitcher.
• **Clarence (Cito) Gaston.** San Diego center fielder who, as the Padres' second batter in the ninth inning, became Seaver's record-breaking ninth consecutive strikeout victim (the previous modern record of eight had been reached seven times through 1982).
• **Jerry Grote.** Seaver's catcher.
• **Al Ferrara.** San Diego left fielder who followed Gaston to the plate in the ninth and became Seaver's 10th straight strikeout victim, ending the game. Ferrara had accounted for the Padres' run with a second-inning homer.
• **Van Kelly.** San Diego third baseman who struck out leading off the ninth, enabling Seaver to tie the modern record of eight consecutive strikeouts.

SHORE 'PERFECT'
Coming on in relief when Boston's starting pitcher was ejected after issuing a walk to the game's first batter, Ernie Shore was on the mound for the Red Sox as 27 consecutive Washington players were retired in the first game of a June 23, 1917, doubleheader at Fenway Park. While Shore's feat is listed as a perfect game in most record books (with an asterisk alongside the entry), some baseball "purists" debate the point because of the leadoff walk. Shore won, 4-0, striking out two batters.

Supporting Cast:
• **Sam Agnew.** Boston catcher who entered the game with Shore when the Red Sox's starting battery departed after the game-opening walk. Agnew had a 3-for-3 day at the plate.
• **Doc Ayers.** Washington's losing pitcher.
• **Mike Menosky.** Washington pinch-hitter who made the final out against Shore.
• **Ray Morgan.** Washington second baseman who led off the game with a walk, then was thrown out trying to steal by Agnew (with reliever Shore pitching).
• **Brick Owens.** Home-plate umpire whose ejection of Boston's starting pitcher set the stage for Shore's masterpiece.
• **Babe Ruth.** Boston's starting pitcher who was thrown out of the game for disputing Owens' ball-and-strike calls on Morgan.
• **Pinch Thomas.** Boston's starting catcher who left the game with the banished Ruth after the walk to Morgan.

SWOBODA'S SERIES CATCH

With Baltimore runners on first and third base and the New York Mets leading, 1-0, in the ninth inning of Game 4 of the 1969 World Series, Mets right fielder Ron Swoboda made a diving, one-handed catch of a one-out liner. While a run scored on the play, Swoboda's catch prevented further damage and the Mets went on to win, 2-1, in 10 innings.

Supporting Cast:
• **Rod Gaspar.** Pinch-running for Mets' catcher Jerry Grote (who had doubled) in the 10th inning, he scored the winning run on Baltimore reliever Pete Richert's throwing error.
• **Brooks Robinson.** Baltimore third baseman who hit the ninth-inning liner on which Swoboda turned a "sure" rally-extending hit into a sacrifice fly.
• **Frank Robinson.** Baltimore right fielder who scored on Brooks Robinson's sacrifice fly after singling with one out in the ninth and advancing to third on first baseman Boog Powell's single.
• **Tom Seaver.** Mets' pitcher who went the distance in the October 15 game at Shea Stadium. Allowing only six hits he positioned the Mets for the Series clincher the next day.

TONEY, VAUGHN: NO HITS THROUGH NINE

When Fred Toney of the Cincinnati Reds and Jim Vaughn of the Chicago Cubs hooked up in a May 2, 1917, game in Chicago, the words "pitching duel" didn't begin to tell the story. After nine innings, it was a 0-0 game— and neither team had a hit. Cincinnati managed two hits and an unearned run in the 10th inning, though, and won, 1-0, as Toney finished with his no-hitter intact.

Supporting Cast:
• **Emil Huhn.** Toney's catcher.
• **Larry Kopf.** Cincinnati shortstop who got the first hit off Vaughn, a one-out single in the 10th inning.
• **Al Orth.** Home-plate umpire in the Toney-Vaughn double no-hitter.
• **Jim Thorpe.** Cincinnati right fielder and football great whose infield single in the 10th inning scored Kopf with the winning run.
• **Cy Williams.** Cubs' center fielder whose error on Cincinnati first baseman Hal Chase's 10th-inning fly ball enabled Kopf to move from first base to third.
• **Art Wilson.** Vaughn's catcher.

VANDER MEER'S CONSECUTIVE NO-HITTERS

Johnny Vander Meer is the only major leaguer in history to have pitched two straight no-hitters, accomplishing the feat in 1938 as he led the Cincinnati Reds to a 3-0 triumph over the Boston Bees on June 11 and a 6-0 victory over the Brooklyn Dodgers on June 15.

Facing Brooklyn in the first night game in Ebbets Field history, Johnny Vander Meer of the Cincinnati Reds delivers a pitch en route to his second straight no-hitter of the 1938 season.

Supporting Cast:

• **Max Butcher.** Brooklyn's losing pitcher in Vander Meer's second no-hitter.

• **Leo Durocher.** Brooklyn shortstop who was the last out in the June 15 game, which was the first night game in Ebbets Field history. Durocher flied to Cincinnati center fielder Harry Craft.

• **Debs Garms.** Boston third baseman who got the first hit off Vander Meer following his two no-hitters. Garms' one-out single in the fourth inning of a June 19 game ended Vander Meer's hitless streak at 21 2/3 innings.

• **Hank Leiber.** New York Giants' center fielder who got the last hit off Vander Meer before his two no-hitters. Leiber had a two-out single in the ninth inning of a June 5 game.

• **Ernie Lombardi.** Vander Meer's catcher in both no-hit games.

• **Danny MacFayden.** Boston's losing pitcher in Vander Meer's first no-hitter.

• **Ray Mueller.** Pinch-hitting for Boston first baseman Elbie Fletcher, he made the last out in the June 11 game at Crosley Field by grounding to Cincinnati third baseman Lew Riggs.

Cleveland second baseman Bill Wambsganss (top, left) wheels around and tags out Brooklyn's Otto Miller, completing an unassisted triple play in Game 5 of the 1920 World Series. Pete Kilduff, doubled off second base, is shown reaching third base as Indians third baseman Larry Gardner watches Wambsganss.

WAMBSGANSS' TRIPLE PLAY

The only triple play in World Series history was made in Game 5 of the 1920 classic—and it was an unassisted play by Cleveland second baseman Bill Wambsganss.

Supporting Cast:
• **Jim Bagby Sr.** Cleveland hurler who was the winning pitcher in the 8-1 game, going the distance and allowing 13 hits. In the fourth inning, Bagby became the first pitcher in Series history to hit a home run.
• **Burleigh Grimes.** Brooklyn starting and losing pitcher who gave up the first bases-loaded homer in Series history (to Cleveland right fielder Elmer Smith in the first inning) and the first Series homer by a pitcher (Bagby's drive).
• **Pete Kilduff.** Brooklyn second baseman who led off the fifth with a single.
• **Otto Miller.** Brooklyn catcher who followed Kilduff's fifth-inning single in the October 10 game with another single.
• **Clarence Mitchell.** Batting third in Brooklyn's fifth, the relief pitcher lined to Wambsganss at second for one out. Wambsganss then stepped on second base, doubling off Kilduff, and wheeled around to tag Miller (who had broken for second) to complete the triple play.

49

THIRD INNING
Goats, victims and
futile performances

JACK BILLINGHAM
The Cincinnati pitcher who gave up Hank Aaron's 714th career home run on April 4, 1974, in Cincinnati. The Atlanta Brave slugger's homer tied Babe Ruth's lifetime mark.

Supporting Cast:
• **Ralph Garr.** Braves' baserunner on second when Aaron homered.
• **Mike Lum.** Braves' baserunner on first when Aaron homered.

RALPH BRANCA
The losing pitcher in the first playoff game in major league history. Pitching for the Brooklyn Dodgers against the St. Louis Cardinals on October 1, 1946, Branca was the Dodgers' starter and loser in a 4-2 defeat.

Branca was the losing pitcher in three of the first five N.L. playoff games. Besides losing Game 1 in 1946 when the Dodgers dropped two straight games in the best-of-three playoff, Branca was charged with defeats in Games 1 and 3 of the 1951 playoff against the New York Giants.

Branca, whose 0-1 pitch to Bobby Thomson in the ninth inning of Game 3 of the '51 playoff ended in a pennant-winning home run (New York won, 5-4), had given up a two-run homer to Thomson in Game 1 (which the Dodgers lost, 3-1).

BOB BUHL
The Milwaukee Braves-Chicago Cubs pitcher who went 0-for-the-season as a batter in 1962. Going hitless in 70 at-bats, Buhl, who was traded to Chicago during the season, established the big-league mark for most at-bats in a season without getting a hit.

WILLIE DAVIS
The Los Angeles Dodgers' center fielder who made three errors in the fifth inning of Game 2 of the 1966 World Series, helping Baltimore to a 6-0 triumph (and the Orioles went on to sweep the Series). Davis lost two fly balls in the sun, with errors being charged on both plays, and threw wildly to third base after the second misplay.

Supporting Cast:
• **Paul Blair.** His fly ball to deep center field dropped at Davis' feet.
• **Andy Etchebarren.** His lazy fly to center glanced off Davis' glove for error No. 2. Davis grabbed the ball and made a bad throw to third for error No. 3, with Boog Powell and Blair scoring on the play. Etchebarren was doubled home by Luis Aparicio, capping the three-run inning.
• **Boog Powell.** He led off the Orioles' fifth with a single against Sandy Koufax (who was in a 0-0 duel with Baltimore's Jim Palmer at the time).

AL DOWNING
The Los Angeles Dodgers' lefthander who gave up Hank Aaron's 715th career homer on April 8, 1974, during a game in Atlanta. With the Braves' slugger needing one more homer to break his tie with Babe Ruth for the all-time record, Downing, the Dodgers' starting pitcher, avoided notoriety in the first inning by walking Aaron on four pitches. In the fourth, however, Downing became a footnote to baseball history when Aaron hit a 1-0 pitch over the fence in left-center. The two-run drive tied the score, 3-3, and the Braves went on to win, 7-4.

DON DRYSDALE
The Brooklyn and Los Angeles Dodgers' pitcher from 1956 through 1969 who gave up more home runs (17) to Hank Aaron, the career leader with 755, than any other hurler.

JACK FISHER
The Baltimore Orioles' pitcher who gave up a bases-empty home run to Boston's Ted Williams in the Red Sox slugger's final at-bat in the major leagues on September 28, 1960, at Fenway Park. Williams hit a 1-1 pitch into the seats in right-center field in the eighth inning.

Roger Maris hit his 60th homer of the 1961 season against Fisher, connecting in the Yankees-Orioles game of September 26.

CURT FLOOD
The Cardinals' center fielder who misjudged a seventh-inning drive during Game 7 of the 1968 World Series, helping to send the Detroit Tigers to the Series title. With St. Louis' Bob Gibson and Detroit's Mickey Lolich locked in a 0-0 duel and two Tigers on base, Flood broke in on the ball, realized he had misjudged it and ran back. The ball sailed past Flood, and both runners scored. Detroit went on to win the game, 4-1, and the Series, four games to three.

Supporting Cast:
• **Norm Cash.** He singled with two out in the Tigers' seventh.
• **Bill Freehan.** His run-scoring double capped the Tigers' three-run seventh.
• **Willie Horton.** He followed Cash's seventh-inning single with another single.

Game 2 of the 1966 World Series was just one of those days for center fielder Willie Davis (3) and the rest of the Los Angeles Dodgers. Davis, who had committed three errors an inning earlier, couldn't get together with right fielder Ron Fairly on this sixth-inning smash off the bat of Baltimore's Frank Robinson and the ball dropped in for a triple. The Dodgers made six errors in the game and lost, 6-0.

• **Jim Northrup.** Hitting the drive that Flood misplayed, Northrup was credited with a triple and two runs batted in.

RAY FOSSE
The catcher and representative of the Cleveland Indians in the 1970 All-Star Game who was bowled over at the plate in the 70 classic on a 12th-inning play that enabled the National League to defeat the American League, 5-4.

Supporting Cast:
• **Jim Hickman.** Chicago Cubs' player who delivered the game-winning single in the 12th.
• **Amos Otis.** The Kansas City Royals' center fielder who fielded Hickman's single and made the throw to the plate.
• **Pete Rose.** Racing for home on Hickman's hit, the Cincinnati Reds' star barreled into Fosse just as the ball arrived and scored the winning run.

FRED GLADDING
A relief pitcher who appeared in 450 big-league games from 1961 through 1973 and managed only one hit in the majors. Playing for the Houston Astros in 1969, Gladding singled off Ron Taylor of the New York Mets in the first game of a July 30 doubleheader. Gladding's lone hit in 63 major league at-bats came in an 11-run inning in which Houston's Denis Menke and Jim Wynn hit bases-loaded home runs.

TOMMY GLAVIANO
The St. Louis Cardinals' third baseman who made errors on three consecutive plays in the ninth inning of a May 18, 1950 game, giving Brooklyn four runs and a 9-8 victory. The Dodgers, who had trailed, 8-0, scored four runs in the bottom of the eighth, then closed within 8-5 with a run in the ninth and had the bases loaded with one out when Glaviano experienced his nightmare.

Supporting Cast:
• **Roy Campanella.** He hit a bases-loaded grounder to Glaviano, who made a wide throw to second on a force-play attempt. The error allowed a run to score, cut the Cardinals' lead to 8-6 and kept the bases loaded.
• **Eddie Miksis.** He grounded to Glaviano, whose wide throw to the plate allowed another run to score (making it 8-7 with the bases still loaded).
• **Pee Wee Reese.** His grounder went through Glaviano's legs, enabling the tying and winning runs to score.

BABE HERMAN
An extra-base hit with the bases loaded means two or three runs batted in. Usually. But Herman of the Brooklyn Dodgers hit a bases-full double against the Boston Braves on August 15, 1926, and came away with one RBI . . . and was victimized as part of a double play. With Hank DeBerry on third base,

After crashing into catcher Ray Fosse and scoring the winning run in the 12th inning of the 1970 All-Star Game, Pete Rose (left) surveys the damage he has done. National League teammate Dick Dietz hugs Rose, and Leo Durocher, an N.L. coach, applauds the play.

Dazzy Vance on second and Chick Fewster on first, Herman hit a George Mogridge pitch off the right-field wall. DeBerry scored, but Vance—seemingly in no hurry—got caught between third and the plate. Vance retreated to third, and Fewster slowed up between second and third so Vance wouldn't be forced to run home. Herman, meanwhile, was running with his head down—and he passed Fewster. With Herman joining Vance on third, Fewster sped up and soon there were three Dodgers at the bag. Herman was out for passing Fewster on the bases, and Fewster was out because Vance, as the lead runner who wasn't forced to advance home, had rights to third base.

KEN JOHNSON
Pitching for the Houston Colts against the Cincinnati Reds on April 23, 1964, he became the only man in major league history to lose a nine-inning, complete-game no-hitter.

Supporting Cast:
• **Joe Nuxhall.** He pitched a five-hitter in the Reds' 1-0 victory.
• **Pete Rose.** He reached second in the Reds' ninth when Johnson fielded his bunt attempt and threw wildly to first. Rose moved to third on a groundout and scored on second baseman Nellie Fox's error.

On July 1, 1990, at Chicago, Andy Hawkins of the New York Yankees pitched all eight innings of a complete-game no-hitter—but wound up a 4-0 loser to the White Sox.

FRED LINDSTROM
The New York Giants' third baseman who watched a bad-hop grounder bounce over his head for the game-winning hit in the 12th inning of Game 7 of the 1924 World Series against the Washington Senators.
Supporting Cast:
• **Earl McNeely.** His ground ball bounded over Lindstrom, giving the Senators a 4-3 victory and the Series title.
• **Muddy Ruel.** Given life when Giants' catcher Hank Gowdy misplayed his pop foul in the 12th, Ruel then doubled and later scored on McNeely's single.

MARK LITTELL
The Kansas City Royals' relief pitcher who gave up Chris Chambliss' pennant-winning homer in 1976. In 60 regular-season games during the season, Littell had allowed only one home run—to Detroit's Pedro Garcia—in 104 innings. But in the ninth inning of Game 5 of the '76 American League Championship Series, Chambliss hit Littell's first pitch to give the New York Yankees a 7-6 victory and the A.L. pennant.

MARK LITTELL
Pitching for the St. Louis Cardinals against the Philadelphia Phillies on August

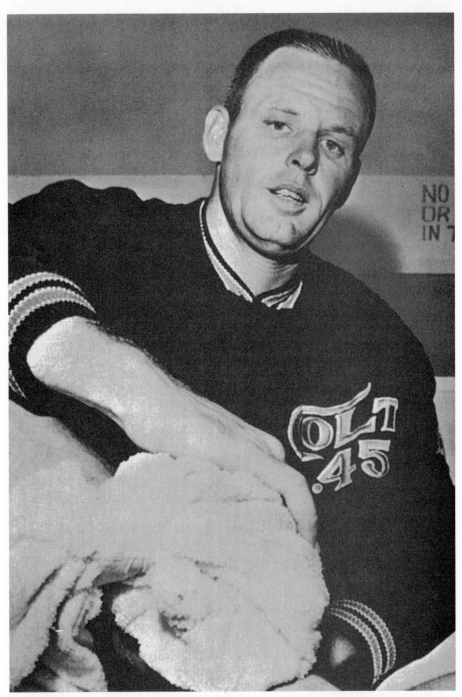

Not only did Houston's Ken Johnson lose a nine-inning, complete-game no-hitter on April 23, 1964, but the Colts' pitcher had to nurse a sore shin after being struck by a line drive the game against the Cincinnati Reds.

10, 1981, Littell surrendered Pete Rose's 3,631st career hit, a single, making Rose the National League's all-time hit leader.

ERNIE LOMBARDI
The Cincinnati Reds' catcher famous for his 1939 World Series "snooze." Amid the New York Yankees' Series-clinching three-run outburst in the 10th inning of Game 4, Lombardi failed to hold right fielder Ival Goodman's throw to the plate when Yankee baserunner Charlie Keller crashed into the Reds' catcher. Lombardi fell down and the ball rolled away, enabling Joe DiMaggio (whose single had been misplayed by Goodman) to circle the bases as Lombardi lay stunned. New York won, 7-4, to sweep the Series.

JIM MALONE
The Cincinnati Reds' pitcher who had a no-hitter through 10 innings against the New York Mets on June 14, 1965, but ended up with a two-hitter—and a 1-0 loss in 11 innings.

Supporting Cast:
• **Larry Bearnarth.** Mets' reliever and winning pitcher who worked the last three innings after replacing starter Frank Lary.
• **Johnny Lewis.** He led off the Mets' 11th with a home run. Roy McMillan singled later in the inning.

TIM McCARVER
The Philadelphia Phillies' catcher who, playing against Pittsburgh in the first game of a July 4, 1976, doubleheader, hit a bases-loaded drive over the right-

Knocked out of the play seconds earlier by baserunner Charlie Keller, Cincinnati catcher Ernie Lombardi is sprawled on the ground as Joe DiMaggio of the Yankees scores in the 10th inning of Game 4 of the 1939 World Series.

Johnny Lewis (left) of the Mets rounds third base on June 14, 1965, after leading off the 11th inning with a home run against Cincinnati's Jim Maloney, who had pitched no-hit ball through 10 innings but ended up a 1-0 loser. Coach Don Heffner is about to congratulate Lewis, while Reds third baseman Deron Johnson looks the other way.

field wall—but was denied a grand slam on the United States' Bicentennial. After hitting his second-inning smash, McCarver passed teammate Garry Maddox on the basepaths and was declared out. Maddox had held up at first base, thinking the ball might be caught.

MICKEY McDERMOTT
The Boston Red Sox pitcher who gave up home runs to Bob Nieman of the St. Louis Browns in his first two big-league at-bats on September 14, 1951. Nieman is the only player ever to accomplish the feat.

FRED MERKLE
The New York Giants' first baseman whose 1908 baserunning boner might have cost his team a pennant. With the pennant-contending Chicago Cubs and Giants tied, 1-1, with two out in the bottom of the ninth inning of a September 23 game, Merkle failed to touch second base when a Giant teammate delivered an apparent game-winning hit. The Cubs retrieved the ball and touched second base, forcing Merkle and negating the run. New York fans, thinking their team had scored on the play, swarmed the field, which led to a halting of the tie game. The game was made up October 8—when other National League clubs had finished their seasons and the Cubs and Giants were tied for first place with 98-55 records—and Chicago prevailed, 4-2, to win the N.L. pennant.

Supporting Cast:
• **Al Bridwell.** With two out in the ninth and Moose McCormick on third base and Merkle on first for the Giants, Bridwell hit safely into center field. Merkle, after seeing McCormick cross the plate, headed for the clubhouse instead of touching second base. The alert Cubs then made the run-nullifying force play on Merkle (a play that also deprived Bridwell of a hit).
• **Johnny Evers.** Cubs' second baseman who tagged second, forcing out Merkle.
• **Hank O'Day.** The home-plate umpire who made the ruling on Merkle and, because of the fans' rush onto the field, called the game a 1-1 tie.
• **Jack Pfiester.** Cubs' pitcher when the Merkle incident occurred.

JOHN MILJUS
The only pitcher in World Series history to end a classic with a wild pitch. With the score tied, 3-3, in the ninth inning of Game 4 of the 1927 Series, Pittsburgh's Miljus threw a wild pitch while facing Tony Lazzeri of the New York Yankees with the bases loaded. Miljus' errant pitch scored Earle Combs, enabling the Yanks to beat the Pirates, 4-3, and win the Series in four straight games.

STAN MUSIAL
The focal point—and victim—of a June 30, 1959, play in which two baseballs were in use at the same time. In the fourth inning, a 3-1 pitch from Bob Anderson of the Chicago Cubs got past catcher Sammy Taylor and St. Louis' Musial—hearing umpire Vic Delmore's ball-four call—headed for first base. Certain that the ball had struck Musial's bat, Taylor and Anderson ignored the loose ball and began arguing with Delmore. Musial, seeing the ball at the screen, took off for second base. Cubs' third baseman Al Dark ran in to retrieve the ball, grabbing it from a batboy. Dark then made a low throw to second base, where shortstop Ernie Banks scooped up the ball. Meanwhile, Delmore "automatically" reached into his pocket and gave Taylor a new ball. Anderson, seeing Musial en route to second, grabbed the ball and threw wildly toward second (with the ball going into center field). Musial, aware of only the ball thrown into center, ran toward third but was tagged out by Banks, who had the first ball. After considerable confusion and debate, the umpires ruled Musial out because he was tagged with the original ball in play.

MICKEY OWEN
The Brooklyn Dodgers' catcher whose passed ball cost his team a victory in the 1941 World Series. With two out and no Yankees on base and the Dodgers leading, 4-3, in the ninth inning of Game 4, a third strike on New York's Tommy Henrich got past Owen. The Dodgers, instead of wrapping up a victory that would have tied the Series at two games apiece, saw the Yankees break loose for four runs in the inning and win, 7-4. New York clinched the Series the next day.

A third strike on Tommy Henrich of the Yankees eludes Dodger catcher Mickey Owen with two out in the ninth inning of Game 4 of the 1941 World Series, setting the stage for a four-run inning and a 7-4 New York triumph.

Supporting Cast:
• **Hugh Casey.** Brooklyn relief pitcher whose strikeout of Henrich in the ninth inning was in vain.
• **Joe DiMaggio.** After Henrich reached base in the ninth, DiMaggio singled. Charlie Keller then doubled home Henrich and DiMaggio.
• **Joe Gordon.** With Keller on second base and Bill Dickey on first (with a walk) in the ninth. Gordon doubled home both runners to cap the four-run rally.
• **Johnny Murphy.** Yankees' reliever and winning pitcher who worked the final two innings.

BABE RUTH
The New York Yankee slugger whose ninth-inning basestealing attempt ended the 1926 World Series. With the Classic tied at three games apiece and the St. Louis Cardinals leading New York, 3-2, in Game 7 with two out in the Yankees' ninth, Ruth was thrown out attempting to steal second base after drawing his 11th walk of the Series.

Supporting Cast:
• **Bob Meusel.** Yankees' cleanup hitter who was at bat when Ruth was thrown out to end the Series.

• **Bob O'Farrell.** Cardinals' catcher whose throw to second baseman Rogers Hornsby caught Ruth in the ninth. Ruth, who stole second in Game 6, twice had 17 steals in a season during his career.

AL SMITH
Some misplays and misadventures are enough to leave a player crying in his beer. A fifth-inning home run by Charlie Neal of the Los Angeles Dodgers in Game 2 of the 1959 World Series is a good example. Al Smith, Chicago White Sox's left fielder watched as Neal's drive sailed over the wall. A fan, also following the flight of the ball, accidentally knocked a cup of beer off the ledge of the wall, sending the brew splashing onto Smith's head. The Dodgers went on to win the game, 4-3—the first of three consecutive Los Angeles triumphs on the way to a four-games-to-two Series victory.

FRED SNODGRASS
The New York Giants' center fielder who made an error in the 10th inning of the eighth and final game of the 1912 World Series, helping the Boston Red Sox to victory. But Snodgrass wasn't alone when it came to misdeeds as the Red Sox overcame a New York run in the top of the 10th with two runs of their own in the bottom of the inning (Boston won the game, 3-2, and the Series, four games to three, with one tie).

Supporting Cast:
• **Clyde Engle.** After the Giants had broken a 1-1 tie on Fred Merkle's run-scoring single, Engle led off Boston's 10th by hitting a fly ball to center that Snodgrass dropped for a two-base error.
• **Tris Speaker.** After Snodgrass' misplay on the routine fly, an out (Snodgrass made a great catch on Harry Hooper's drive) and then a walk, Speaker lofted a pop foul between first baseman Merkle and catcher Chief Meyers. The foul dropped between the players and Speaker, given another life, singled home Engle with the tying run.
• **Steve Yerkes.** After walking and advancing to third on Speaker's hit, Yerkes scored the winning run for Boston on Larry Gardner's long fly.

TRACY STALLARD
The Boston Red Sox' pitcher who yielded Roger Maris' 61st home run of the 1961 season. Stallard allowed the Yankees only one run and five hits in seven innings, giving up one walk and striking out five batters in the October 1 game in New York. Stallard got Maris to fly to left fielder Carl Yastrzemski in the first inning, was touched for the homer on a 2-0 pitch in the fourth and struck out Maris on a 3-2 pitch in the sixth. (In the eighth against reliever Chet Nichols, Maris popped to second baseman Chuck Schilling.) Maris' homer accounted for the only run of the game.

White Sox left fielder Al Smith received an unexpected shower during Game 2 of the 1959 World Series when a fan, intent on following the flight of a home run by the Dodgers' Charlie Neal, tipped a cup of beer onto his head.

CHUCK STOBBS
The Washington Senators' pitcher who surrendered a home run in 1953 to New York's Mickey Mantle that traveled an estimated 565 feet (as figured by Yankees' publicist Red Patterson). Mantle's homer, hit April 17 at Griffith Stadium, came when the Yankees' switch-hitter was batting righthanded against lefthander Stobbs. The ball caromed off the side of the football scoreboard in left field (the scoreboard was 460 feet from the plate) and landed in the backyard across the street at 434 Oakdale St. Later in the game, Mantle reached base on a bunt single.

RALPH TERRY
The New York Yankees' pitcher who surrendered Bill Mazeroski's ninth-inning, World Series-deciding home run in 1960. Called on in relief in the eighth inning of Game 7 after Hal Smith hit a three-run homer that gave Pittsburgh a 9-7 lead, Terry ended the Pirates' five-run inning by getting Don Hoak to fly to left field. Terry wasn't as fortunate in the next inning, though. After the Yankees tied the score with two runs in the ninth, Terry gave up Mazeroski's leadoff smash on a 1-0 pitch, ending one of the strangest Series in history. The Pirates became world champions despite being outscored, 55-27, and outhit, 91-60. The Yankees scored 16-3, 10-0 and 12-0 victories, while Pittsburgh won 6-4, 3-2, 5-2 and 10-9.

LEON WAGNER
As a rookie outfielder for the San Francisco Giants, he was the victim of a ruse on July 1, 1958, at Chicago's Wrigley Field. Tony Taylor of the Chicago Cubs hit a smash to left field that bounced into the Cubs' bullpen, and Chicago players jumped up and peered intently under the bench. Wagner scrambled around, looking for the ball; actually, it lay 45 feet down the line in a rain gutter. By the time Wagner realized he had been duped, Taylor had circled the bases for an inside-the-park home run.

RUBE WALBERG
The New York Giants, Philadelphia Athletics and Boston Red Sox pitcher (1923 through 1937) who gave up more home runs (17) to Babe Ruth than any other hurler.

DAVE WICKERSHAM
Entering an October 1, 1964, game (his final start of the year), the Detroit pitcher had compiled a 19-12 record in what proved his only real shot at a 20-victory year. But Wickersham was victimized in his bid for No. 20 . . . by himself. With the Tigers and New York Yankees locked in a 1-1 game in the seventh inning, the Yanks' Phil Linz was called safe on a close play at first base as the tie-breaking run scored. Wickersham, trying to get umpire Bill Valentine's attention, put his hand on the umpire, which meant an automatic ejection. Detroit went on to win, 4-2, with Mickey Lolich getting the victory. Wickersham

Mickey Mantle displays the home-run ball he hit an estimated 565 feet on April 17, 1953. The battered ball had caromed off the side of the football scoreboard at Washington's Griffith Stadium and landed in the backyard across the street.

As Giants catcher Bill Rariden (left) checks the action elsewhere on the field in the fourth inning of Game 6 of the 1917 World Serles, third baseman Heinie Zimmerman chases Eddie Collins of the White Sox across the plate during a rundown play.

never won more than 12 games in any other season, finishing his big-league career with a 68-57 record.

HACK WILSON

The Cubs' center fielder who lost a seventh-inning drive in the sun in Game 4 of the 1929 World Series between Chicago and the Philadelphia Athletics. The misplay turned into a key three-run, inside-the-park home run as the A's, down 8-0 entering the inning, erupted for 10 runs and seized a three-games-to-one lead in the Series when it seemed certain the Cubs had deadlocked the classic. Philadelphia wrapped up the Series in five games.

Supporting Cast:
• **Sheriff Blake.** Cubs' losing pitcher who faced two batters in the seventh

inning, giving up singles to Al Simmons and Jimmie Foxx.

• **Jimmie Dykes.** His two-run double off Pat Malone broke an 8-8 tie and capped the A's 10-run seventh.

• **Jimmie Foxx.** Foxx's single in the seventh scored Mickey Cochrane, tying the score, 8-8.

• **Mule Haas.** A's player whose smash was mishandled by Wilson and brought Philadelphia within 8-7.

• **Art Nehf.** Cubs' pitcher who was the victim of Haas' inside-the-park homer.

• **Eddie Rommel.** A's reliever and winning pitcher who worked the top of the seventh and allowed two hits, a walk and one run in his lone appearance of the Series.

• **Charlie Root.** Cubs' pitcher who took an 8-0 lead into the seventh. He retired only one batter in the inning and was charged with six runs.

• **Al Simmons.** He led off the A's seventh with a homer and singled later in the inning (eventually scoring the winning run).

TOM ZACHARY

While noted for having permitted Babe Ruth's 60th home run of the 1927 season, the pitcher has another link to Ruth. Only Zachary gave up home runs to Ruth in 1927 while pitching for two clubs, yielding No. 22 to the Yankees' Ruth on June 16 while a member of the St. Louis Browns and giving up No. 36 on August 10 and No. 60 on September 30 while with the Washington Senators.

HEINIE ZIMMERMAN

The New York Giants' third baseman who chased Eddie Collins of the Chicago White Sox across the plate on a rundown play in the fourth inning of Game 6 of the 1917 World Series. The play accounted for the first run in a three-run inning that sparked the White Sox to a 4-2 triumph and the Series title (four games to two).

Supporting Cast:

• **Happy Felsch.** With Collins and Joe Jackson on third and first base (after errors by Zimmerman and right fielder Dave Robertson) in a 0-0 game in the fourth inning, Chicago's Felsch grounded to pitcher Rube Benton. Seeing Collins break from third, Benton threw to Zimmerman. Zimmerman ran Collins toward the plate, but Collins darted past catcher Bill Rariden to make it a Zimmerman-Collins race to home. Collins won, helped on the play because Rariden, Benton and first baseman Walter Holke left the plate unattended.

• **Chick Gandil.** His two-run single followed the rundown play, giving White Sox pitcher Red Faber all the runs he needed.

FOURTH INNING
Other offensive and defensive feats; "only" achievements

HANK AARON
His two-run, 11th-inning home run off Billy Muffett of the second-place St. Louis Cardinals on September 23, 1957, clinched the National League pennant for the Milwaukee Braves. The Braves' 4-2 triumph gave Milwaukee a six-game lead over the Cards with five games left for both clubs.

BABE ADAMS
The only rookie pitcher to win three games in a World Series. Adams hurled three complete-game victories for Pittsburgh in the 1909 Series, defeating the Detroit Tigers 4-1, 8-4 and 8-0 as the Pirates won the classic in seven games. Adams had compiled a 12-3 record in 1909, his first full season in the majors, after appearing in one game for the St. Louis Cardinals in 1906 and four games for the Pirates in 1907.

JOE ADCOCK
The first of three men (excluding exhibition-game players) to reach the distant center-field bleachers at New York's Polo Grounds with a home-run drive after the bleachers were remodeled (and the distance to the fence lengthened) in 1923. Adcock, playing for the Milwaukee Braves, hit a homer off the New York Giants' Jim Hearn on April 29, 1953, that carried an estimated 475 feet.

Lou Brock of the Chicago Cubs and Hank Aaron of the Braves became the second and third players to reach the bleachers—and they did it on consecutive days. Brock connected against Al Jackson of the New York Mets on June 17, 1962, and Aaron hit his shot off Jay Hook of the Mets on June 18, 1962.

HAROLD BAINES
His home run, a solo drive off Milwaukee's Chuck Porter in the 25th inning, enabled the Chicago White Sox to score a 7-6 victory over the Brewers on May 9, 1984. Baines' clout marked the latest inning in which a homer had been struck in the big leagues.

The Brewers-White sox game had started the previous night and was suspended after 17 innings.

A young Hank Aaron gets a lift from his teammates after hitting an 11th-inning home run that defeated the second-place Cardinals and clinched the 1957 pennant for the Milwaukee Braves.

The flight of Milwaukee first baseman Joe Adcock's long Polo Grounds homer, an estimated 475-foot shot into the center-field bleachers in 1953, is diagrammed above.

JESSE BARNES
Winning pitcher in the fastest nine-inning game in big-league history. Pitching for the New York Giants against the Philadelphia Phillies in the first game of a September 28, 1919, doubleheader, Barnes beat the Phils, 6-1, in a 51-minute game.

JULIO BECQUER
Washington's leading base stealer in 1957 when the Senators established a major league club record for fewest steals, 13, in a season. Becquer had three steals.

JOHNNY BENCH
The only player in major league history with at least three career home runs in the All-Star Game, League Championship Series and World Series. During his 17-year big-league career, Bench, who came up with the Cincinnati Reds in 1967, had three homers in All-Star competition, five in Championship Series play and five in the World Series.

YOGI BERRA, JOSE CANSECO
The only players in World Series history to hit bases-loaded home runs in losing causes. Berra's second-inning grand slam in Game 2 of the 1956 Series staked the New York Yankees to a 6-0 lead over Brooklyn, but the Dodgers rebounded for a 13-8 triumph. Oakland's Canseco smashed his bases-full shot in the second inning of Game 1 of the 1988 Series, giving the A's a 4-2 lead over Los Angeles, but the Dodgers rallied for a 5-4 victory.

VIDA BLUE
Only pitcher in modern major league history to strike out 300 or more batters in a season without leading the league. Pitching for the Oakland A's, Blue struck out 301 American League hitters in 1971—but Detroit's Mickey Lolich fanned 308.

VIDA BLUE
The only American League pitcher to win an All-Star Game in the 20-year span from 1963 through 1982. Blue, representing the Oakland A's, was the starting and winning pitcher in the 1971 classic at Tiger Stadium in Detroit as the A.L. won, 6-4. Blue got the victory despite yielding three runs—all earned—in three innings of work.

Blue also is the only major league pitcher to win an All-Star Game for each league. Blue, representing San Francisco, pitched a scoreless seventh inning in the 1981 classic in Cleveland's Municipal Stadium and received credit for the win when the Nationals rallied for two eighth-inning runs and a 5-4 victory.No other pitcher has ever earned a decision for both the A.L. and N.L.

DAVE BOSWELL, DEAN CHANCE, JIM KAAT
Pitching for the Minnesota Twins in 1967, each recorded 200 or more strikeouts—the first time a major league team had three pitchers attain that figure in the same season. Chance struck out 220 batters, Kaat fanned 211 and Boswell was at 204.

Only one other big league threesome has reached the 200 strikeouts-per-man milestone. Pitching for the Houston Astros in 1969, Don Wilson had 235 strikeouts, Larry Dierker 232 and Tom Griffin 200.

LOU BOUDREAU
The only modern major leaguer to manage a team the entire year during which he won a batting championship. Boudreau, who managed the Cleveland Indians to a fifth-place tie with the Philadelphia Athletics in 1944, posted an American League-leading .327 batting average that season.

Rogers Hornsby led the National League in hitting with .403 and .387 averages in 1925 and 1928, years in which he replaced Branch Rickey and Jack Slattery as manager of the St. Louis Cardinals and Boston Braves, respectively. Hornsby managed the Cardinals for 115 games in 1925 and guided the Braves for 122 games in 1928.

CLETE, KEN BOYER
The only brothers to hit home runs in the same World Series—and they did it in the same game. Ken, St. Louis Cardinals' third baseman, homered against the New York Yankees in the seventh inning of Game 7 of the 1964 Series; Clete, New York third baseman, homered in the ninth inning. Ken also hit a grand slam in Game 4.

LOU BROCK
One of only three players to collect 3,000 or more hits and not attain a lifetime batting average of .300. Brock, who came up to the majors at the end of the 1961 season and played through 1979, had 3,023 hits for the Chicago Cubs and St. Louis Cardinals and a career average of .293.

Al Kaline (Detroit, 1953-74) had 3,007 hits and a .297 average, while Carl Yastrzemski (Boston Red Sox, 1961-83) had 3,419 hits and a .285 mark for his career.

LLOYD BROWN
The only pitcher to surrender two of Lou Gehrig's major league-record 23 career grand slams. Brown gave up bases-loaded home runs to the New York Yankees' slugger while pitching for the Washington Senators on August 31, 1931, and for the Cleveland Indians on May 13, 1934.

When St. Louis' Lou Brock got his 3,000th hit on August 13, 1979, Hall of Famer Stan Musial, a former Cardinal and also a member of the elite club, was there to present the ball.

JOHN BUZHARDT

The Philadelphia pitcher who beat the Milwaukee Braves, 74, in the second game of an August 20, 1961, doubleheader, ending the Phillies' 23-game losing streak (a modern major league record). Buzhardt also was the last Philadelphia pitcher to win before the streak, defeating the San Francisco Giants, 4-3, in the second game of a July 28, 1961, doubleheader.

LEON CADORE, JOE OESCHGER

Pitchers who went the distance on May 1, 1920, when Brooklyn and Boston played to a 26-inning, 1-1 tie in a game called because of darkness. En route to sharing the major league record for most innings pitched in one game, Brooklyn's Cadore and Boston's Oeschger matched zeroes over the last 20 innings. Cadore gave up 15 hits overall, walking five and striking out eight; Oeschger yielded only nine hits, walking three and fanning four.

JOHNNY CALLISON

Philadelphia Phillies' right fielder whose three-run homer off Dick Radatz of the Boston Red Sox in the ninth inning of the 1964 All-Star Game enabled the National League to defeat the American League, 7-4, at New York's Shea Stadium.

A big reception of National Leaguers was there to greet Philadelphia's Johnny Callison after his three-run, ninth-inning home run broke up the 1964 All-Star Game at New York's Shea Stadium.

HAL CHASE
The only lefthanded-throwing, righthanded-hitting player to win a major league batting title. Playing for the Cincinnati Reds in 1916, Chase hit a National League-leading .339.

TOM CHENEY
Washington Senators' pitcher who on September 12, 1962, established a big-league strikeout record for one game by fanning 21—although it took him 16 innings to accomplish the feat. Cheney, who beat the Baltimore Orioles, 2-1, on a homer by Bud Zipfel (the last of 10 that Zipfel hit in the majors), had 12 strikeouts after nine innings. Only one Baltimore starter, left fielder Boog Powell, did not strike out in the game.

CHUCK CHURN
Working in relief of Sandy Koufax, Churn was the winning pitcher on September 11, 1959, when Los Angeles handed Pittsburgh reliever Roy Face his only loss in an 18-1 season. The Dodgers beat the Pirates, 5-4.

TONY CLONINGER
The only player in N. L. history to hit two bases-loaded home runs in one game—and he was a pitcher. In a July 3, 1966, game in San Francisco, Atlanta's Cloninger hit first- and fourth-inning grand slams off the Giants' Bob Priddy and Ray Sadecki and added a run-scoring single in the eighth. Cloninger's nine runs batted in and seven-hit pitching led the Braves to a 17-3 triumph.

MICKEY COCHRANE, FRANKIE FRISCH
The managers in the last World Series in which both clubs had their field leaders in the lineup. Frisch, St. Louis Cardinals' manager and second baseman in the 1934 Series, batted .194 against Detroit in the classic (which the Cards won in seven games). Cochrane, Tigers' manager and catcher, hit.

DICK COFFMAN
Pitching for the St. Louis Browns on August 23, 1931, he ended Lefty Grove's winning streak at 16 games (which had tied the American League record for one season) by shutting out the Philadelphia Athletics, 1-0. Coffman pitched a three-hitter as Grove's record went to 25-3 (the A's pitcher finished at 31-4).

EDDIE COLLINS
Despite getting 3,309 hits in a major league career that started in 1906 and ended in 1930, Collins (who played for the Philadelphia Athletics and Chicago White Sox) failed to win a batting championship in the majors. Collins' lifetime average was .333.

Lou Brock is the only other big leaguer to amass 3,000 hits and not capture a hitting title. Brock, a .293 career hitter with the Chicago Cubs and St. Louis

Cardinals, totaled 3,023 hits from 1961 through 1979.

MORT COOPER
The only pitcher in major league history to lose two straight All-Star Games. Representing the St. Louis Cardinals, Cooper started the 1942 and 1943 games for the National League and was the loser in 3-1 and 5-3 decisions.

GAVVY CRAVATH
The major leagues' modern career home run king until displaced by Babe Ruth. Cravath, whose 11-season big-league career took him to Boston, Chicago and Washington in the American League and Philadelphia in the National and ended in 1920, had 119 lifetime homers (with a high of 24 in 1915). While playing for the Phillies, Cravath won five N.L. homer championships outright and shared another title.

Ruth, playing for the New York Yankees, hit his 120th career homer on June 10, 1921, connecting off Cleveland's Jim Bagby Sr.

BABE DAHLGREN
The player who moved into the New York Yankees' lineup at first base on May 2, 1939, in Detroit, ending Lou Gehrig's consecutive-game streak at 2,130. Gehrig played the last game of his streak—and of his career—on April 30, 1939. (The Yankees were not scheduled on May 1, 1939.)

ALVIN DARK
The first man to manage both the American League and the National League in the All-Star Game. Dark guided the A.L. team in 1963 and the N.L. All-Stars in 1975.

Dick Williams (A.L., 1968, 1973 and 1974; N.L. 1985) and Sparky Anderson (N.L., 1971, 1973, 1976 and 1977; A.L., 1985) are the only others to manage both leagues in All-Star competition.

DIZZY DEAN
With the National League pennant race having gone down to the final day of the 1934 season, Dean proceeded to win his 30th game of the year for the St. Louis Cardinals by defeating the Cincinnati Reds, 9-0, at Sportsman's Park. The Cardinals entered the last day one game ahead of the second-place New York Giants, who played Brooklyn in their season finale. While having little trouble overall with the Reds, Dean nevertheless got into a no-out, bases-loaded jam in the ninth inning. Word came that the Dodgers had beaten the Giants, 8-5, in 10 innings, ensuring the pennant for St. Louis. Dean then finished with a flourish, striking out Clyde Manion and Ted Petoskey and getting Sparky Adams to foul out.

The brothers Dean, Paul (left) and Dizzy, are pictured in a 1934 photo as members of the St. Louis Cardinals.

DIZZY, PAUL DEAN

The pitching brothers who established the major league record for fewest total hits, three, allowed by one team in a doubleheader. Pitching for the St. Louis Cardinals in the opening game of a September 21, 1934, twin bill, Dizzy Dean hurled a three-hitter as the Cards walloped Brooklyn, 13-0. In the nightcap, Paul Dean tossed a no-hitter as St. Louis beat the Dodgers, 3-0.

The Deans' record was tied on May 27, 1945, when Dave (Boo) Ferriss and Emmett O'Neill pitched one-hit and two-hit games, respectively, for the Boston Red Sox in a doubleheader against the Chicago White Sox.

In the two other doubleheaders in which one team allowed only three hits, the record-tying performances involved more than two pitchers. On June 21, 1964, Jim Bunning of the Philadelphia Phillies threw a perfect game against the New York Mets, then Rick Wise (notching his first big-league victory) and Johnny Klippstein combined on a three-hitter. On June 8, 1969, Cleveland's Sam McDowell pitched a two-hitter against California before four Indian pitchers (Mike Paul, Gary Kroll, Jack Hamilton and Stan Williams) combined for a one-hitter—in a 3-2 loss to the Angels.

BUCKY DENT

New York shortstop whose three-run, seventh-inning homer off Boston's Mike

Torrez overcame a 2-0 deficit and sparked the Yankees to a 5-4 triumph over the Red Sox in the one-game playoff for the 1978 American League East Division championship.

DOM, JOE DiMAGGIO
The only brothers with major league batting streaks of 30 or more games. Joe, playing for the New York Yankees, had his record 56-game streak in 1941. Dom, as a member of the Boston Red Sox, hit in 34 straight games in 1949.

JOE, VINCE DiMAGGIO
The only brothers in big-league history to hit homers in the All-Star Game. Joe, of the New York Yankees, hit one for the American League in 1939, while Vince, of Pirates, hit his for the National League in 1943.

JIGGS DONAHUE
Chicago White Sox's first baseman who singled in the seventh inning for the only hit off Ed Reulbach of the Chicago Cubs in Game 2 of the 1906 World Series. Reulbach and the Cubs prevailed, 7-1.

WILD BILL DONOVAN
First of only two pitchers who have lost final World Series games in consecutive years. Pitching for the Detroit Tigers, Donovan lost the 1908 finale to the Chicago Cubs and the last game in 1909 to the Pittsburgh Pirates.

Christy Mathewson of the New York Giants was the losing pitcher in the decisive games of the 1912 and 1913 Series against the Boston Red Sox and Philadelphia Athletics.

DON DRYSDALE
The only pitcher to start two All-Star Games in one season (from 1959 through 1962, the major leagues had two All-Star Games per year). Drysdale, Los Angeles Dodgers' hurler, had no decision in the National League's 5-4 first-game victory in 1959 at Forbes Field in Pittsburgh but was the loser in the American League's 5-3 second-game triumph in '59 at the Los Angeles Memorial Coliseum.

HOWARD EHMKE
Having pitched only 55 innings during the regular season, the 35-year-old Ehmke was a surprise starter in Game 1 of the 1929 World Series for the Philadelphia Athletics. Connie Mack had six pitchers on his staff with 11 or more victories—including 24-game winner George Earnshaw and 20-game winner Lefty Grove—but the A's manager opted for Ehmke, who had posted a 7-2 record, in the opener. Ehmke struck out a then-Series record of 13 Chicago Cubs as the A's won, 3-1, allowing eight hits, yielding the Cubs' lone run in the ninth inning.

KID ELBERFELD

The New York Highlanders' player who on August 1, 1903, collected all of his team's hits when Rube Waddell of the Philadelphia Athletics pitched a four-hitter. Sparked by Elberfeld's four singles, the Highlanders beat the A's, 3-2.

Billy Williams is the only other player in major league history to get all of his club's hits when the opposing pitcher allowed as many as four hits. Steve Blass of the Pittsburgh Pirates pitched a four-hit, 9-2 triumph over Chicago on September 5, 1969, and the Cubs' Williams hit two home runs and two doubles. Blass had four hits himself, including a homer.

DOCK ELLIS

The only National League pitcher to lose an All-Star Game in the 20-year period from 1963 through 1982. Ellis, representing the Pittsburgh Pirates, was the N.L.'s starter and loser at Detroit's Tiger Stadium in 1971 as the American League won, 6-4. Ellis, who gave up four runs in three innings, permitted two-run homers to Reggie Jackson and Frank Robinson in the third inning.

CHUCK ESSEGIAN

One of two players to slug two pinch-hit homers in a World Series. Batting for Los Angeles pitcher Johnny Podres in the seventh inning of Game 2 of the 1959 World Series, Essegian homered with the bases empty against Bob Shaw of the Chicago White Sox. In the ninth inning of Game 6, Essegian batted for Dodgers' right fielder Duke Snider and hit a bases-empty homer off Ray Moore.

Bernie Carbo of the Boston Red Sox, batting for pitcher Reggie Cleveland, hit a solo homer off Cincinnati's Clay Carroll in the seventh inning of Game 3 of the 1975 World Series. Pinch-hitting for pitcher Roger Moret in the eighth inning of Game 6, Carbo slammed a three-run homer off the Reds' Rawly Eastwick that tied the score, 6-6 (Boston went on to win, 7-6, in 12 innings).

BOB, KEN FORSCH

The only brothers to pitch nine-inning no-hitters in the major leagues. Pitching for the St. Louis Cardinals, Bob no-hit the Philadelphia Phillies in a 5-0 triumph on April 16, 1978, and then held the Montreal Expos hitless, 3-0, on September 26, 1983. Ken fired a no-hitter for the Houston Astros in 1979, stopping the Atlanta Braves, 6-0.

Ken's gem, which came April 7 in the Astros' second game of the '79 season, established the big-league record for the earliest calendar-date no-hitter. In 1984, Detroit's Jack Morris also pitched a no-hitter on April 7. Morris baffled the Chicago White Sox, 4-0.

DICK FOWLER

The only pitcher in modern big-league history to record a no-hitter for his only

Philadelphia A's pitcher Dick Fowler's only win of the 1945 season was a memorable one while Hal Griggs a journeyman pitcher for Washington had his memorable moment in 1957.

victory of the season. Fowler, who went 1-2 in 1945, held the St. Louis Browns hitless on September 9 as the Philadelphia Athletics notched a 1-0 triumph.

JIMMIE FOXX
Lone major leaguer to have hit 50 or more home runs in a season for two teams. Foxx slugged 58 homers for the Philadelphia Athletics in 1932 and 50 for the Boston Red Sox in 1938.

Willie Mays hit 51 homers for New York in 1955 and 52 for San Francisco in 1965, but it was for the same franchise, the Giants.

FRED FRANKHOUSE
Brooklyn Dodgers' pitcher who defeated Carl Hubbell and the New York Giants, 10-3, in the first game of a May 31, 1937, doubleheader, ending Hubbell's major league-record 24-game winning streak (over two seasons) by a pitcher.

Bill Lee of the Chicago Cubs had dealt Hubbell his last previous loss, stopping the Giants, 1-0, on July 13, 1936.

MILT GASTON
One of two American League pitchers who gave up as many as four home runs to Babe Ruth of the New York Yankees during Ruth's 60-homer season of 1927. Pitching for the St. Louis Browns, Gaston yielded Ruth's seventh 32nd, 33rd and 50th homers of the year.

Rube Walberg, Philadelphia A's pitcher, surrendered Ruth's second, sixth 14th and 44th homers of 1927.

FLOYD GIEBELL

He won only three games in the major leagues, but one of them clinched the American League pennant for the Detroit Tigers in 1940. Leading second-place Cleveland by two games entering a season-ending, three-game series against the Indians, Detroit decided to use Giebell—up from Buffalo—opposite Bob Feller in the first-game pitching matchup. Tigers' Manager Del Baker, figuring Feller (a 27-game winner) would be tough, thought it would be wise to hold out his aces—headed by Schoolboy Rowe—for use later in the series. Giebell, a 30-year-old who had beaten the Philadelphia A's eight days earlier after going 15-17 in the International League, outdueled Feller by pitching a six-hitter in a 2-0 triumph at Municipal Stadium on September 27. Feller permitted only three hits, but one was a two-run homer to Rudy York. Giebell's victory not only wrapped up the A.L. flag for Detroit—it was his last triumph in the majors.

LEFTY GOMEZ

The American League's starting pitcher in five of the first six All-Star Games. Gomez, of the New York Yankees, compiled a 3-1 All-Star record from 1933 through 1938 (failing to get a decision in 1934 and not appearing in 1936).

Another Lefty—Boston's Grove—started (and lost) for the A.L. in '36.

HANK GREENBERG

Detroit left fielder whose ninth-inning, bases-loaded home run in the opening game of a scheduled season-ending doubleheader at St. Louis clinched the 1945 American League pennant for the Tigers. Greenberg's homer off Nelson Potter overcame a 3-2 deficit, giving Detroit a 6-3 triumph over the Browns. The Tigers started the day with an 87-65 record and a one-game lead over Washington (87-67 and finished with its schedule). The second game was rained out after Detroit batted in the first inning.

HAL GRIGGS

Washington Senators' pitcher who had a cumulative 6-26 record in the big leagues, but who stopped Ted Williams' reaching-base streak in 1957. Boston's Williams, having reached first base in his previous 16 trips to the plate (a major league record), grounded out against Griggs on September 24.

RON HANSEN

Only man to play in the last games of both the original and second Washington franchises in the American League. Hansen played shortstop for the Baltimore Orioles on October 2, 1960, at Washington in the original Senators' last game before their relocation in Minnesota, and he was at third base for the visiting

Sandy Koufax mugs for the camera after pitching a perfect game against the Chicago Cubs on September 9, 1965. The four balls with zeroes signify the four career no-hitters Koufax compiled. Lou Johnson was Dodger hero No. 2, collecting the only hit of the 1965 game and scoring the only run after drawing a walk.

New York Yankees on September 30, 1971, when the second Senators played their last game before moving to Texas.

CARROLL HARDY
A .225 hitter in 433 big-league games, Hardy pinch-hit for Roger Maris and Ted Williams during his career. As a rookie in 1958, Hardy pinch-hit for Maris (then a second-year player) and hit a three-run homer off Billy Pierce in the 11th inning, giving the Cleveland Indians a 7-4 victory over the Chicago White Sox on May 18. On September 20, 1960, Hardy pinch-hit for Williams, who was unable to complete a first-inning at-bat after fouling a ball off his ankle, and lined into a double play against Baltimore's Hector (Skinny) Brown.

BOB HENDLEY
The losing pitcher in the only nine-inning complete game in major league history in which there was only one hit. Pitching for the Chicago Cubs at Los Angeles on September 9, 1965, Hendley allowed only a looping, opposite-field double by Lou Johnson in the seventh inning ... but the Dodgers' Sandy Koufax pitched a perfect game as Los Angeles won, 1-0. The Dodgers scored in the fifth inning, getting an unearned run when Johnson walked, moved to second on a sacrifice, stole third and continued home on catcher Chris Krug's high throw.

ROGERS HORNSBY
The lone player to bat .400 and slug 40 home runs in the same season. Hornsby hit .401 with 42 homers for the 1922 St. Louis Cardinals.

ROGERS HORNSBY, TED WILLIAMS
The only two-time winners of major league baseball's Triple Crown. Hornsby won the Triple Crown for the St. Louis Cardinals in 1922 (.401 average, 42 home runs and 152 runs batted in) and again in 1925 (.403, 39 homers and 143 RBIs). Williams captured the honor for the Boston Red Sox in 1942 (.356, 36 homers and 137 RBIs) and again in 1947 (.343, 32 homers and 114 RBIs).

RALPH HOUK
The only man to have World Series champions in his first two seasons as a major league manager. Houk led the 1961 and 1962 New York Yankees to Series triumphs over the Cincinnati Reds and San Francisco Giants.

REX HUDSON
The only man who pitched in just one major league game and surrendered a home run to Hank Aaron. Pitching against the Atlanta Braves on July 27, 1974, the Los Angeles Dodgers' Hudson gave up Aaron's 726th lifetime homer.

HANK HULVEY
The only man who pitched in just one big-league game and gave up a home

Larry Jaster, an 11-5 pitcher for the Cardinals in 1966, gets a handshake from Dick Hughes after shutting out the Los Angeles Dodgers for the fifth time in the '66 season.

run to Babe Ruth. Pitching against the New York Yankees on September 5, 1923, the Philadelphia Athletics' Hulvey permitted Ruth's 230th career homer.

JOE JACKSON
One of two players to hit .400 in a modern major league season without winning a batting championship that year. Cleveland's Jackson batted .408 in 1911, but Detroit's Ty Cobb had an American League-leading mark of .420.

Cobb compiled a .401 average for the Tigers in 1922, but George Sisler of the St. Louis Browns led the A.L. with .420.

LARRY JASTER
St. Louis Cardinals' pitcher who faced the National League champion Los Angeles Dodgers five times in 1966—and shut them out all five times, allowing only 24 hits (all singles) in 45 innings. Between the first and second shutouts,

Jaster was optioned to Tulsa for six weeks. He finished the '66 season with an 11-5 record and 3.26 earned-run average for the Cardinals.

JULIAN JAVIER

St. Louis Cardinals' second baseman whose two-out double in the eighth inning of Game 2 of the 1967 World Series was the only hit off Boston's Jim Lonborg. The Red Sox won, 5-0.

AL KALINE

The only major leaguer to hit 300 career home runs and not have 30 or more in one year. Kaline, who played for the Tigers from 1953 through 1974 and hit 399 homers, had a season high of 29 homers (achieved in both 1962 and 1966).

WILLIE KEELER

The only player to collect 200 or more singles in one season. Keeler singled 202 times for Baltimore of the National League in 1898.

DICKIE KERR

Chicago White Sox's pitcher who stood out in the 1919 World Series despite the fact eight of his teammates were later implicated in the Series-fixing "Black Sox" scandal. Kerr pitched a three-hit, 3-0 triumph over Cincinnati in Game 3 and went the distance in a 10-inning, 5-4 victory over the Reds in Game 6. Along with a 2-0 Series record, Kerr had a 1.42 earned-run average for his 19 innings of work.

HARMON KILLEBREW

One of only three players to hit 40 or more home runs while batting less than .250 in the same season—and he did it twice. Killebrew, playing for the Washington Senators, had 42 homers and a .242 average in 1959. Three years later, he hit 48 homers and batted .243 for the Minnesota Twins.

Gorman Thomas of the Milwaukee Brewers walloped 45 homers while batting only .244 in 1979, and the Detroit Tigers' Darrell Evans connected for 40 homers and a .248 batting mark in 1985.

RALPH KINER

The only player to hit All-Star Game home runs in three consecutive years. Representing the Pittsburgh Pirates, Kiner hit homers for the National League in 1949, 1950 and 1951.

RALPH KINER, JOHNNY MIZE

Major league baseball's only instance where the same two players shared a home-run championship twice. The Pirates' Kiner and the New York Giants' Mize tied for the National League homer titles in 1947 and 1948 with totals of 51 and 40.

DENNIS KINNEY

The lone pitcher in major league history to give up two pinch-hit, bases-loaded home runs in one season. Pitching for the American League's Cleveland Indians on May 6, 1978, Kinney yielded a pinch grand slam to Merv Rettenmund of the California Angels; on June 27, 1978, while a member of the National League's San Diego Padres, Kinney permitted a pinch grand slam to Jack Clark of the San Francisco Giants.

Hank Borowy is the only other pitcher to yield pinch grand slams in both leagues—but his misfortunes were more than three years apart. Pitching for the New York Yankees on July 15, 1945, Borowy gave up a pinch grand slam to Zeb Eaton of the A.L.'s Detroit Tigers; on September 11, 1948, while a member of the N.L.'s Chicago Cubs, Borowy surrendered a pinch grand slam to Ralph Kiner of the Pittsburgh Pirates.

CHUCK KLEIN

Playing for the Philadelphia Phillies in 1932, Klein shared the National League homer lead and topped the N.L. in stolen bases. Klein hit 38 homers, tying Mel Ott of the New York Giants, and had 20 steals.

Ty Cobb of the Detroit Tigers is the only other major leaguer to lead his league in homers and stolen bases in the same season. Cobb had American League-leading figures of nine home runs and 76 steals in 1909.

CHUCK KLEIN

His 1930 hit total of 250 ranks as the highest non-leading figure in major league history. Klein, of the Philadelphia Phillies, was second in the National League in 1930 to the New York Giants' Bill Terry, who had an N.L. record-tying 254 hits.

DAROLD KNOWLES

The only man to pitch in every game of a seven-game World Series. Knowles, Oakland A's relief ace, accomplished the feat in 1973.

Relievers Dan Quisenberry of Kansas City and Mike Marshall of Los Angeles are the only other pitchers to appear in every game of a World Series, with the Royals' Quisenberry pitching in all six games in 1980 and the Dodgers' Marshall pitching in all five games in 1974.

RON LeFLORE

The only player in major league history to lead the National and American leagues in stolen bases. LeFlore topped the American League with 68 steals while playing for the Detroit Tigers in 1978, and headed the National League with 97 steals while playing for the Montreal Expos in 1980.

A's pitcher Darold Knowles, shown receiving congratulations for Manager Dick Williams after finishing the opener of the 1973 World Series, was just getting started. Knowles pitched in all seven games of the '73 classic.

HECTOR MAESTRI
One of only three players to play for the American League's original Washington Senators franchise in its last season, 1960, and the expansion Senators franchise in its first season, 1961. Maestri, a pitcher, appeared in only two major league games in his career—one with each Washington franchise.

Rudy Hernandez and Hal Woodeshick, both pitchers, also played for both the '60 and '61 Senators.

MICKEY MANTLE
One of two major leaguers to hit 50 or more home runs in a season and fail to lead the league in that category. Mantle slammed 54 homers for the New York Yankees in 1961, but teammate Roger Maris captured American League honors with his record-setting 61.

Jimmie Foxx of the Boston Red Sox hit 50 in 1938, but finished second in the A.L. to Detroit's Hank Greenberg, who hit 58.

ROGER MARIS, CECIL FIELDER
The only major leaguers to bat less than .300 and hit 50 or more homers in the

same season. Maris batted .269 in 1961 when he hit 61 homers for the Yankees; Fielder wound up at .277 in 1990,when he hit 51 homers for the Tigers.

JIM MASON
The only player to hit a home run in his only World Series at-bat. Playing shortstop for the New York Yankees in Game 3 of the 1976 World Series, Mason homered off Pat Zachry of the Cincinnati Reds in the seventh inning.

CHRISTY MATHEWSON
Pitching for the New York Giants, he shut out Philadelphia three times in a six-day span during the 1905 World Series. Mathewson gave up four, four and six hits, struck out 18 batters and walked only one in winning 3-0, 9-0 and 2-0.

The Giants' other victory in their four-games-to-one triumph also was a shutout, with Iron Man Joe McGinnity winning Game 4, 1-0. The A's lone victory was a shutout, too, as Chief Bender won Game 2, 3-0.

Waite Hoyt of the New York Yankees is the only other man to pitch three complete games in a World Series without allowing an earned run, giving up two unearned runs in the 1921 classic. Hoyt beat the Giants, 3-0, in Game 2 and was a 3-1 victor in Game 5 before losing, 1-0, in Game 8.

WILLIE MAYS
The only player to collect three hits in each of two All-Star Games played in the same year. San Francisco's Mays went 3-for-4 for the National League in both the July 11, 1960, All-Star Game at Municipal Stadium in Kansas City, and the July 13, 1960, classic at Yankee Stadium.

Nellie Fox is the only other player to get two or more hits in each of two All-Star Games played in the same season. Fox, of the Chicago White Sox, singled twice in both of the 1959 classics.

JOE McGINNITY
Pitcher who in 1903 proved "Iron Man" was an apt nickname, setting a modern national League record of 434 innings pitched in one season and hurling three complete doubleheaders. McGinnity was 6-0 in the twin bills as the New York Giants defeated Boston, 4-1 and 5-2 (on August 1); Brooklyn, 6-1 and 4-3 (on August 8), and Philadelphia, 4-1 and 9-2 (on August 31).

Pitching for Baltimore of the American League in 1901, McGinnity completed doubleheaders against Milwaukee on September 3 (winning, 10-0, and losing, 6-1) and Philadelphia on September 12 (winning, 4-3, and losing, 5-4).

McGinnity's feat of pitching two complete games in one day five times is unequaled.

Baltimore pitcher Dave McNally gets a big greeting after connecting for his grand slam in Game 3 of the 1970 World Series against Cincinnati.

BILL McKECHNIE

The only man to manage three different franchises in the World Series. McKechnie managed the Pittsburgh Pirates in the 1925 Series, the St. Louis Cardinals in the 1928 classic and the Cincinnati Reds in 1939 and 1940. The '25 Pirates and '40 Reds were world champions.

DAVE McNALLY

The only pitcher to hit a bases-loaded home run in the World Series. Baltimore's McNally walloped his grand slam against Cincinnati's Wayne Granger in the sixth inning of Game 3 of the 1970 Series, helping the Orioles to a 9-3 victory on the way to a four-games-to-one Series triumph.

MINNIE MINOSO

Nine months past his 53rd birthday, Minoso became the oldest batter to get a hit in a major league game. Minoso, the Chicago White Sox's starting designated hitter in the first game of a September 12, 1976, doubleheader against the California Angels, singled in his first at-bat off Sid Monge. It was Minoso's only hit in eight at-bats that year.

Nick Altrock had just turned 53 when he collected a hit for the Washington Senators in 1929.

JOHNNY MIZE
The lone player in major league history to hit 50 home runs while striking out fewer than 50 times in the same season. Playing for the New York Giants in 1947, Mize walloped 51 homers and struck out only 42 times.

STAN MUSIAL
St. Louis Cardinals' left fielder whose first-pitch home run in the 12th inning off Frank Sullivan of the Boston Red Sox lifted the National League to a 6-5 triumph over the American League in the 1955 All-Star Game at Milwaukee's County Stadium.

STAN MUSIAL, DAVE WINFIELD
The only players to hit 400 or more home runs in the major leagues without slugging 40 or more in one season. Musial, who hit 475 homers for the St. Louis Cardinals in a big-league career that started in 1941 and ended in 1963, had a season high of 39 in 1948. Winfield has hit 406 homers through 1991. His single-season high was 37 with the Yankees in 1982.

ERNIE NEVERS
Pro Football Hall of Famer who gave up two of Babe Ruth's 60 home runs in 1927. Pitching for the St. Louis Browns, Nevers surrendered Ruth's eighth homer of the year on May 11 and the Yankee slugger's 41st of the season on August 27.

BOBO NEWSOM
One of two pitchers in major league history with more than 200 victories and a sub-.500 winning percentage. Newsom, whose big-league career started in 1929 and ended in 1953, won 211 games and lost 222 (.487).

Jack Powell, who pitched in the majors from 1897 to 1912, compiled a 247-254 record (.493).

SATCHEL PAIGE
A big-league rookie at age 42, Cleveland's Paige pitched his first complete game in the majors—a 5-0 shutout of the White Sox—before a sellout crowd of 51,013 at Chicago's Comiskey Park on August 13, 1948. Paige, who permitted five hits, was making his 12th appearance and second start since being signed by the Indians five weeks earlier.

Paige helped attract a record crowd for a major league night game, 78,382 fans, to Cleveland's Municipal Stadium on August 20, 1948—and pitched his second straight shutout, a three-hit, 1-0 triumph over Chicago.

Ernie Nevers earned his greatest fame as a pro football Hall of Famer, but he also pitched in the major leagues and allowed two of Babe Ruth's 60 homers during the 1927 season.

Satchel Paige, a 42-year-old rookie with Cleveland in 1948, watches on-field action while seated next to coach Muddy Ruel in late July.

TONY PEREZ
Cincinnati Reds' third baseman whose 15th-inning home run off Jim (Catfish) Hunter of the Kansas City A's gave the National League a 2-1 victory over the American League in the 1967 All-Star Game at Anaheim Stadium.

Third basemen accounted for all of the scoring in the '67 classic (the longest All-Star Game in history), with Dick Allen of the Phillies also homering for the N.L. and Brooks Robinson of the Baltimore Orioles homering for the A.L.

JOHNNY PESKY
The only player to lead his league in hits in the first three seasons in which he appeared in the majors. Playing for the Boston Red Sox as a rookie in 1942, Pesky led the American League with 205 hits. After spending the next three years in military service, Pesky topped the A.L. in hits in 1946 with 208 and in 1947 with 207.

Tony Oliva of Minnesota led the A.L. in hits in his first three full seasons, 1964 through 1966, after getting a total of seven hits in brief appearances with the Twins in 1962 and 1963.

FRITZ PETERSON, JOHN SMILEY
The only man in All-Star Game history to have pitched in the classic and not recorded an out. Pitching for the American League and representing the New York Yankees, Peterson faced one batter, Willie McCovey (who singled), in the ninth inning of the 1970 game at Riverfront Stadium in Cincinnati and then was replaced by Mel Stottlemyre. Pitching for the N.L. and representing the Pittsburg Pirates, Smiley faced two men in the seventh of the 1991 game at Toronto's SkyDome. He gave up a single to Joe Carter leading off the inning. Paul Miltor, the next batter, reached base safely when catcher Craig Biggio was called for interference. SMiley was then relieved by Rob Dibble.

TOM PHOEBUS
The most recent of nine pitchers who have tossed shutouts in their first two major league games. Making his big-league debut on September 15, 1966, Phoebus stopped the California Angels, 2-0, on four hits. On September 20, Phoebus defeated the Kansas City Athletics, 4-0, on a five-hitter.

Others breaking in with two shutouts: Al Spalding (Chicago, N.L., 1876), Monte Ward (Providence, N.L., 1878), Jim Hughes (Baltimore, N.L., 1898), Joe Doyle (New York, A.L., 1906), Johnny Marcum (Philadelphia, A.L., 1933), Dave (Boo) Ferriss (Boston, A.L., 1945), Al Worthington (New York, N.L., 1953) and Karl Spooner (Brooklyn, N.L. 1954).

WALLY PIPP
New York Yankees' first baseman who reportedly was not feeling well on June

The irony of Game 1 of the 1954 World Series was that Cleveland's Vic Wertz (right) hit a 460-foot drive that was caught by Willie Mays and New York's Dusty Rhodes (left) hit a ball approximately 260 feet that resulted in a game-winning home run.

2, 1925, and was scratched from the lineup. Pipp never got his job back as Lou Gehrig, who had pinch-hit the day before, started at first base June 2 against the Washington Senators in what became game No. 2 in Gehrig's record string of 2,130 consecutive games.

JACK QUINN
The oldest player in big-league history to hit a home run. Eight days shy of his 46th birthday, Quinn, a pitcher, homered for the Philadelphia Athletics against Chad Kimsey of the St. Louis Browns on June 27, 1930.

ED REULBACH
The only pitcher in big-league history to hurl shutouts in both games of a doubleheader. Pitching for the Chicago Cubs against Brooklyn on September 26, 1908, Reulbach scored a five-hit, 5-0 triumph in the opener and a three-hit, 3-0 victory in the second game. Johnny Kling was Reulbach's catcher for both games.

PAUL, RICK REUSCHEL
The only brothers to combine for a big-league shutout. Pitching for the Chicago Cubs against the Los Angeles Dodgers on August 21, 1975, Rick went the first 6 1/3 innings and Paul hurled the final 2 2/3 innings in a 7-0 triumph.

ALLIE REYNOLDS
The most recent of three pitchers who have won final World Series games in

consecutive years. Pitching for the New York Yankees in 1952 and 1953 Reynolds was the winning pitcher in the two clinchers against the Brooklyn Dodgers.

Art Nehf of the New York Giants won the final games of the 1921 and 1922 World Series against the Yankees, and the Yanks' Lefty Gomez beat the Giants in the 1936 and 1937 Series finales.

DUSTY RHODES
New York Giants' pinch-hitter whose three-run, 10th-inning home run off Cleveland's Bob Lemon gave the Giants a 5-2 victory in Game 1 of the 1954 World Series. Rhodes, batting for New York left fielder Monte Irvin, connected two innings after Giants' center fielder Willie Mays made a miraculous catch of a drive hit by Indians' first baseman Vic Wertz.

Again pinch-hitting for Irvin, Rhodes delivered a run-scoring single in the fifth inning of Game 2 that netted the Giants a 1-1 tie and later hit a bases-empty homer (after taking over for Irvin in left) as New York won, 3-1. In Game 3, Rhodes again batted for Irvin—and came through with a bases loaded single in the third inning, making him 4-for-4 in the Series (3-for-3 as a pinch-hitter) with seven runs batted in. Staying in the game, Rhodes struck out in his final two at-bats. Rhodes' services weren't required in Game 4 as the Giants completed a Series sweep.

PETE RICHERT
The only pitcher to strike out four batters in one inning in his first major league game. Pitching for the Los Angeles Dodgers on April 12, 1962, Richert struck out Cincinnati's Frank Robinson, Gordy Coleman, Wally Post and Johnny Edwards in the third inning. Coleman reached first base when catcher John Roseboro dropped a third strike.

FRANK ROBINSON
The only player in history to hit 200 or more home runs in both the National and American leagues. Robinson, who played in the majors from 1956 through 1976, hit 343 homers in the N.L. while playing for Cincinnati and Los Angeles, and 243 in the A.L. while playing for Baltimore, California and Cleveland.

Robinson is also the only player to hit home runs for both the National League and American League in All-Star Game competition. Representing Cincinnati, Robinson homered for the N.L. in the second All-Star Game of 1959; representing Baltimore, he homered for the A.L. in 1971.

FRANK ROBINSON, RUSTY STAUB
The players who hold the major league mark for homering in the most parks, 32, during regular-season play. Both hit home runs at these parks: Atlanta,

Atlanta Stadium; Baltimore, Memorial Stadium; Boston, Fenway Park; California, Anaheim Stadium; Chicago, Comiskey Park and Wrigley Field; Cincinnati, Crosley Field and Riverfront Stadium; Cleveland, Municipal Stadium; Detroit, Tiger Stadium; Houston, Colt Stadium; Kansas City, Royals Stadium; Los Angeles, Dodger Stadium; Milwaukee, County Stadium; Minnesota, Metropolitan Stadium; New York, Polo Grounds, Shea Stadium and Yankee Stadium; Oakland, Oakland Coliseum; Philadelphia, Connie Mack Stadium and Veterans Stadium; Pittsburgh, Forbes Field; San Diego, San Diego Stadium; San Francisco, Candlestick Park; Texas, Arlington Stadium.

Additionally, Robinson homered at these parks: Brooklyn, Ebbets Field; Jersey City (where Brooklyn played a total of 15 home games in 1956 and 1957), Roosevelt Stadium; Kansas City, Municipal Stadium; Los Angeles, Memorial Coliseum; St. Louis, Old Busch Stadium; San Francisco, Seals Stadium; Washington, Robert F. Kennedy Memorial Stadium.

Additionally, Staub homered at these parks: Houston, Astrodome; Montreal, Jarry Park and Olympic Stadium; Pittsburgh, Three Rivers Stadium; St. Louis, Busch Memorial Stadium; Seattle, Kingdome; Toronto, Exhibition Stadium.

Hank Aaron slugged home runs in 31 parks during his regular-season career in the big leagues.

BABE RUTH
The only starting pitcher in World Series history to bat anywhere but ninth in the order. In his last Series appearance as a pitcher, Ruth batted sixth in the lineup for the Boston Red Sox in Game 4 of the 1918 Series and grounded out, hit a two-run triple and sacrificed against the Chicago Cubs. After allowing a single and a walk to open the ninth inning, Ruth moved to left field and reliever Joe Bush nailed down the Red Sox's 3-2 victory. Boston went on to win the Series, four games to two.

Catcher Sam Agnew was Boston's ninth-place batter on the day pitcher Ruth hit in the sixth position. Agnew went 0-for-2 before being replaced by Wally Schang.

BABE RUTH
Owns the record for the longest complete-game pitching victory in a World Series. Pitching for the Boston Red Sox against Brooklyn in Game 2 of the 1916 Series, Ruth allowed only six hits in 14 innings and posted a 2-1 triumph in the lengthiest game in Series history.

NOLAN RYAN
Pitching for the California Angels in 1973, he established the modern major league record for most strikeouts in a season with 383. Ryan set the mark in his

Dodgers Manager Burt Shotton points out the heroes of the National League's 1950 All-Star Game victory at Comiskey Park in Chicago. Pittsburgh's Ralph Kiner hit a ninth-inning home run to tie the score and St. Louis' Red Schoendlenst won the game with a 14th-inning blast.

last start of the season, a September 27 game against the Minnesota Twins in which he struck out 16 batters in 11 innings and won, 5-4.

Rich Reese was Ryan's 383rd victim, enabling the California hurler to surpass the total of 382 strikeouts recorded by Sandy Koufax of the Los Angeles Dodgers in 1965. Five years earlier, Reese also was part of history when he struck out for the final out in Oakland pitcher Jim (Catfish) Hunter's perfect game against the Twins.

RED SCHOENDIENST
St. Louis Cardinals' second baseman whose 14th-inning home run off Ted Gray of the Detroit Tigers boosted the National League past the American League, 4-3, in the 1950 All-Star Game at Chicago's Comiskey Park.

PAT SEEREY
One of only 11 players in big-league history to hit four home runs in one game—accomplishing the feat for the Chicago White Sox on July 18, 1948—but he slugged only eight more homers (all in '48) in the majors, finishing with a career total of 86. Seerey's big game was the opener of an American League doubleheader against the Philadelphia A's, and his fourth homer of the contest—coming in the 11th inning gave the White Sox a 12-11 victory. Seerey, obtained from Cleveland earlier in the '48 season, saw his big-league career end the next year with a four-game stint with the White Sox; he was only 26 years old when he left the majors.

Joe Adcock of the Milwaukee Braves established a major league record for total bases, 18, in his four-homer game against Brooklyn in 1954. In addition to his homers, Adcock hit a double in the National League game.

The others to hit four homers in one game: Bobby Lowe, Boston, N.L., 1894; Ed Delahanty, Philadelphia, N.L., 1896; Lou Gehrig, New York, A.L., 1932; Chuck Klein, Philadelphia, N.L., 10 innings, 1936; Gil Hodges, Brooklyn, N.L., 1950; Rocky Colavito, Cleveland, A.L., 1959; Willie Mays, San Francisco, N.L., 1961; Mike Schmidt, Philadelphia, N.L., 10 innings, 1976, and Bob Horner, Atlanta, N.L., July 6, 1986.

DICK SISLER
Philadelphia left fielder whose three-run, 10th-inning home run off Brooklyn's Don Newcombe on the final day of the 1950 season wrapped up the National League pennant for the Phillies. Robin Roberts, collecting his 20th victory of the season, pitched the 4-1 triumph for the Phils, who entered the day with a one-game lead over the Dodgers. Besides foiling the Dodgers' pennant hopes, Sisler's smash also ruined Newcombe's bid to become a 20-game winner (he finished 19-11).

BILL SKOWRON
The only player to hit a bases-loaded home run in the final game of a World Series. Skowron's grand slam came in the seventh inning of Game 7 of the 1956 Series, capping the New York Yankees' scoring in a 9-0 victory over the Brooklyn Dodgers.

TRIS SPEAKER
The only American Leaguer other than Ty Cobb to lead the league in batting from 1907 through 1919. In that span, Detroit's Cobb won the A.L. hitting championship 12 times and captured the crown nine straight years before Cleveland's Speaker broke the string in 1916 with a .386 average (Cobb was runner-up at .371).

The Yankees' Moose Skowron (left) hams it up in the clubhouse with Johnny Kucks (center) and Yogi Berra after hitting a grand slam in the seventh game of the 1956 World Series, while Philadelphia's Dick sisler gets a hero's welcome after hitting his pennant-winning home run on the final day of the 1950 season.

RENNIE STENNETT

The only major leaguer since the turn of the century to collect seven hits in a nine-inning game. Stennett had four singles, two doubles and a triple in seven at-bats on September 16, 1975, leading the Pittsburgh Pirates to a 22-0 victory over the Chicago Cubs in the most lopsided shutout in modern big-league history. Stennett twice had two hits in one inning, tying the major league mark.

The next night, Stennett went 3-for-5 against the Philadelphia Phillies to set a modern record for most hits, 10, in two consecutive nine-inning games.

GENE STEPHENS

The only player in modern major league history to collect three hits in one inning. Playing for Boston against the Detroit Tigers on June 18, 1953, Stephens singled twice and doubled in the Red Sox's 17-run seventh inning (Boston won, 23-3).

BRUCE SUTTER

One of only two pitchers to win two straight major league All-Star Games. Representing the Chicago Cubs in 1978 and 1979, Sutter was the victor as the National League beat the American League, 7-3 and 7-6. In the 1978 game at San Diego Stadium, Sutter retired five straight batters in relief; in the 1979 game at Seattle's Kingdome, he pitched two scoreless innings as the last of seven N.L. pitchers.

Don Drysdale of the Los Angeles Dodgers was the winner for the N.L. in the 1967 and 1968 All-Star Games, pitching two scoreless innings of relief in a 15-inning, 2-1 triumph at Anaheim Stadium in '67 and hurling three scoreless innings as a starter in a 1-0 victory at Houston's Astrodome in '68.

GENE TENACE

The only player to hit home runs in his first two World Series at-bats. Playing for the Oakland A's against the Cincinnati Reds in the first game of the 1972 Series, Tenace walloped a two-run homer off Gary Nolan in the second inning and a bases-empty shot off Nolan in the fifth as the A's won, 3-2.

LEFTY TYLER

Boston Braves' pitcher who stopped New York, 8-3, in the second game of a September 30, 1916, doubleheader, ending the Giants' league-record 26-game streak. The Giants had won the opener, 4-0, behind pitcher Rube Benton.

The Giants started their streak September 7 when Ferdie Schupp pitched New York past Brooklyn, 4-1.

DIXIE, HARRY WALKER

The only brothers to win major league batting championships. Dixie, playing for the Brooklyn Dodgers in 1944, won the National League title with a .357

Pittsburgh's Rennie Stennett emphasizes his lucky number after collecting seven hits against the Cubs, then receives a plaque from National League President Chub Feeney in recognition of the feat.

figure. Harry, playing most of the 1947 season with the Philadelphia Phillies after starting the year with the St. Louis Cardinals, led the N.L. with a .363 mark.

JOHN MONTGOMERY WARD
The youngest pitcher in major league history to record a perfect game. At age 20, Ward pitched his gem on June 17, 1880, as Providence beat Buffalo, 5-0, in a National League game.

MAX WEST
One of only two players to hit a home run in his lone official All-Star Game at-bat. West, Boston Braves' outfielder, hit a three-run homer for the National League in the first inning of the 1940 classic at St. Louis' Sportsman's Park, then left the game in the second inning after crashing into the right-field wall.

Lee Mazzilli is the other player with a homer in his only official All-Star at-bat (through 1982), connecting for a score-tying pinch homer in the eighth inning of the 1979 game at Seattle's Kingdome. Mazzilli, representing the Mets, drew a game-winning, bases-loaded walk in the ninth for the National League.

HOYT WILHELM
Working in relief for the Chicago White Sox in the first game of a July 24, 1968, doubleheader, he set a major league record by making his 907th career appearance as a pitcher. Two days shy of his 45th birthday, Wilhelm took over for Tommy John in the ninth inning and retired the Oakland A's in order (on six pitches).

Wilhelm, whose big-league career began in 1952 and ended in 1972, finished with 1,070 lifetime appearances. Kent Tekulve ranks second on the all-time list with 1,050 and Lindy McDaniel is third at 987.

TED WILLIAMS
Boston Red Sox's left fielder whose two-out, three-run homer off Claude Passeau of the Chicago Cubs in the ninth inning of the 1941 All-Star Game gave the American League a 7-5 victory over the National League at Detroit's Briggs Stadium.

HOOKS WILTSE
One of three pitchers in major league history to hurl a complete-game no-hit victory that went extra innings. Pitching for the New York Giants against the Philadelphia Phillies on July 4, 1908, Wiltse held the Phils hitless in a 1-0, 10-inning triumph. Fred Toney and Jim Maloney, both of the Cincinnati Reds, pitched 1-0 no-hit victories against the Chicago Cubs in games that went 10 innings— and were 48 years apart. Toney's came on May 2, 1917, and Maloney's was on August 19, 1965.

Max West, who had homered for the National League in the first inning of the 1940 All-Star Game at St. Louis' Sportsman's Park, had to be removed from the game an inning later after crashing into the right-field wall.

RICK WISE
The only man in major league history to pitch a no-hitter and hit two home runs in the same game. Wise, pitching for the Philadelphia Phillies, held the Cincinnati Reds hitless on June 23, 1971, and slugged a two-run homer off Ross Grimsley and a bases-empty shot off Clay Carroll as the Phils won, 4-0.

EARLY WYNN
The only major leaguer to slug a pinch-hit, bases-loaded homer and also surrender one. Batting for Washington Senators' pitcher Roger Wolff on September 15, 1946, Wynn hit a grand slam off Johnny Gorsica of the Detroit Tigers. Pitching for the Chicago White Sox on May 28, 1961, Wynn gave up a pinch grand slam to Bob Cerv of the New York Yankees.

CARL YASTRZEMSKI
The only player in major league history whose record-book totals show more than 3,000 career hits but no 200-hit seasons. Boston's Yastrzemski had 3,419 hits in his career, with a season high of 191 for the 1962 Red Sox.

Cap Anson, who played for Chicago's National League club from 1876 through 1897, is credited with 3,081 hits and one 200-hit season. However, Anson's 200-hit season, 1887, was a year in which bases on balls were credited as hits (and Anson drew 60 walks). By modern standards, Anson would have had 164 hits—not 224—in 1887. And the same standards would leave Anson with 3,021 career hits . . . and no 200-hit seasons (with a high of 187 in 1886).

CARL YASTRZEMSKI
The player with the lowest league-leading batting average in major league history. Yastrzemski hit .301 for the Boston Red Sox in 1968, topping the American League.

RUDY YORK
Detroit Tigers' first baseman who singled in the second inning for the only hit off Claude Passeau of the Chicago Cubs in Game 3 of the 1945 World Series. The Cubs won, 3-0.

CY YOUNG
The only man to pitch major league no-hitters before and after 1900. Young pitched a no-hitter for Cleveland of the National League on September 18, 1897, then threw a perfect game for the Boston Red Sox on May 5, 1904. He pitched another no-hitter for the Red Sox on June 30, 1908.

JOEL YOUNGBLOOD
The only player in major league history to collect hits for two teams in one day. Youngblood started in center field for the New York Mets on August 4, 1982, at Chicago and hit a two-run single in the third inning off the Cubs' Ferguson

The scoreboard tells the story as Hoyt Wilhelm, nearly 45 years old, works during a 1968 game for the Chicago White Sox.

Expos, Youngblood left immediately to join his new team in Philadelphia. Arriving in time to be used as a defensive replacement for right fielder Jerry White in the sixth inning, Youngblood later singled off Steve Carlton to gain the additional distinction of being the only player in history to face two pitchers (Carlton, Jenkins) already in the 3,000-strikeout club in one day.

On May 30, 1922, Max Flack of Chicago and Cliff Heathcote of St. Louis went hitless in the first game of a Cubs-Cardinals doubleheader at Chicago. After the morning game, the outfielders were traded for each other and both played in the afternoon game, with Flack getting one hit in four at-bats and Heathcote going 2 for 4.

Youngblood, Flack and Heathcote are the only major leaguers to perform for two teams in one day (but only Youngblood played for two teams in two cities).

ROBIN YOUNT
The only man to have two four-hit games in World Series competition—and he did it within one Series. Playing for the Milwaukee Brewers against the St. Louis Cardinals in the 1982 Series, Yount had four hits in Game 1 and again in Game 5.

FIFTH INNING
Coincidences, oddities and ironies

HANK AARON
Atlanta right fielder who in 1969 homered in each of his team's League Championship Series games. Aaron, who hit home runs in all three games for the Braves in a sweep by the New York Mets, never played in another Championship Series (which became part of the major leagues' postseason play in '69).

HANK, TOMMIE AARON
Hank, the major leagues' career home-run king, and brother Tommie hit homers in the same game three times in their careers—all in 1962. They connected for the Milwaukee Braves on June 12 against the Los Angeles Dodgers, on July 12 against the St. Louis Cardinals and on August 14 against the Cincinnati Reds. No pitcher ever gave up homers to both brothers in the same game. The Aarons' lifetime homer total of 768 is the best of any brother combination (regardless of number). Hank hit 755, Tommie 13.

ALL-STAR, LCS, WORLD SERIES
No major leaguer has hit a home run in the All-Star Game, the League Championship Series and the World Series in the same season.

JOEY AMALFITANO, HARVEY KUENN
The only men to play on the opposing teams in two of Sandy Koufax's no-hitters. Amalfitano was San Francisco's second baseman and Kuenn was the Giants' left fielder in Koufax's 1963 no-hitter for the Los Angeles Dodgers, and both players were ninth-inning pinch-hitters for the Chicago Cubs in Koufax's 1965 perfect game for the Dodgers.

AMERICAN LEAGUE PLAYOFFS
There have been only two playoffs in American League history to decide a division or pennant winner—and both were one-game playoffs at Boston's Fenway Park. The Cleveland Indians defeated the Red Sox, 8-3, in a 1948 playoff for the A.L. pennant, and the New York Yankees beat Boston, 5-4, in a 1978 playoff for the A.L. East Division title.

NEAL BALL
Cleveland shortstop who was the first player in major league history to make an unassisted triple play—and the only man to turn such a play and hit a home

run in the same game. After making an unassisted triple play against the Boston Red Sox in the top of the second inning in the first game of a July 19, 1909 doubleheader, Ball homered off Charlie Chech in the bottom of the second.

Other players to make unassisted triple plays in the majors:
• **Bill Wambsganss,** second baseman, Cleveland Indians, October 10, 1920 (Game 5 of the World Series), fifth inning.
• **George Burns,** first baseman, Boston Red Sox, September 14, 1923, second inning.
• **Ernie Padgett,** shortstop, Boston Braves, October 6, 1923 (second game of doubleheader), fourth inning.
• **Glenn Wright,** shortstop, Pittsburgh Pirates, May 7, 1925, ninth inning.
• **Jimmy Cooney,** shortstop, Chicago Cubs, May 30, 1927, fourth inning.
• **Johnny Neun,** first baseman, Detroit Tigers, May 31, 1927, ninth inning.
• **Ron Hansen,** shortstop, Washington Senators, July 30, 1968, first inning.

All eight unassisted triple plays have occurred with runners on first and second base.

CLYDE BARNHART
The only player in modern major league history to get hits in three games in one day. Barnhart, the Pittsburgh Pirates' third baseman in all three games of an October 2, 1920, tripleheader against the Cincinnati Reds, managed two hits in the opener and one hit in each of the other two games.

Also playing in each game of the lone tripleheader in modern big-league history—and thus joining Barnhart in modern baseball's exclusive three-games-in-one-day club—were Pat Duncan and Morrie Rath of Cincinnati and Fred Nicholson and Cotton Tierney of Pittsburgh.

DICK BATES
Pitcher who appeared in only one big-league game—and that was with the 1969 Seattle Pilots (a club that spent only one season in Seattle before moving to Milwaukee and becoming the Brewers).

Three other players spent their entire major league careers with the Pilots. Miguel Fuentes pitched in eight games, Gary Timberlake pitched in two and Bill Williams appeared in four as a pinch-runner and outfielder.

BUDDY BELL, BILL BUCKNER
The only players in American League history to attain 200 or more hits in a season without batting .300. Playing for the Texas Rangers in 1979, Bell had 200 hits in 670 at-bats for a .299 average; toiling for the Boston Red Sox in 1985, Buckner collected 201 hits in 673 at-bats and also finished at .299.

Five National Leaguers have collected 200 or more hits in one year and not reached .300, with Joe Moore of New York being the first big leaguer to have such statistics. Moore went 201-for-681 (.29515) for the 1935 Giants. Maury Wills was 208-for-695 (.29928) for the 1962 Los Angeles Dodgers; Lou Brock went 206-for-689 (.29898, or .299 rounded off) for the 1967 St. Louis Cardinals, and Matty Alou was 201-for-677 (.29690, or .297) for the 1970 Pittsburgh Pirates. The fewest at-bats a 200-hit man can have and fail to record a .300 average is 668—and those were the exact at-bat and hit figures that Ralph Garr of the Atlanta Braves achieved in 1973 (668-200, .29940).

AL BENTON
The only pitcher to face both Babe Ruth and Mickey Mantle in a major league game. Benton, working for the Philadelphia Athletics, pitched to the Yankees' Ruth in 1934; as a member of the Boston Red Sox, he pitched against the Yanks' Mantle in 1952.

Bobo Newsom, who pitched against Ruth in 1934 while a member of the St. Louis Browns, appeared in a total of 41 games for the Washington Senators and Philadelphia A's in 1952 and 1953—but never faced Mantle (who was playing his second and third American League seasons). Newsom pitched only one inning of relief against the Yankees in those two years, and Mantle was out of the lineup because of an injury.

AL BENTON
The only player in major league history to have two sacrifice hits in one inning. Benton, Detroit Tigers' pitcher, laid down two sacrifice bunts during his club's 11-run third inning against the Cleveland Indians on August 6, 1941.

BEVENS, GIONFRIDDO, LAVAGETTO
Probably the most memorable players in the 1947 World Series (Bill Bevens for his near no-hit game, Al Gionfriddo for his catch of a long drive by Joe DiMaggio and Cookie Lavagetto for ruining Bevens' bid for the first no-hitter in Series history) neither Bevens, Gionfriddo nor Lavagetto played a major league game after the '47 Series.

DAVE BOSWELL
Minnesota Twins' pitcher who on October 5, 1969, lost to the Baltimore Orioles, 1-0, in 10 innings and struck out in all four of his at-bats in his only Championship Series game.

ROGER BRESNAHAN
Hall of Fame catcher whose first appearance in the major leagues was as a pitcher—and he threw a shutout in his debut. Pitching for Washington of the National League on August 27, 1897, Bresnahan stopped St. Louis, 3-0, on six hits.

GEORGE BRUNET
Kansas City Athletics' pitcher who issued five bases-loaded walks and hit another batter with the bases loaded during the Chicago White Sox's one-hit, 11-run inning on April 22, 1959. The White Sox drew 10 walks in the seventh inning off A's pitchers Tom Gorman, Mark Freeman and Brunet—and eight came with the bases loaded.

Preceding the run-scoring walks and hit-batsman RBIs, the White Sox scored their first two runs of the inning on Johnny Callison's single and on an error by A's right fielder Roger Maris. Chicago, a 20-6 winner, left three men on base in the seventh, an inning in which Kansas City also contributed three errors.

GEORGE BURNS
Philadelphia Athletics' player who batted twice as a pinch-hitter in the A's 10-run seventh inning in Game 4 of the 1929 World Series against the Chicago Cubs—and made two of his club's outs. Batting for pitcher Eddie Rommel, Burns made the first out of the inning by popping to shortstop Woody English. He later made the last out of the inning by striking out.

JOE BUSH
The only pitcher in modern major league history to win 25 or more games in a season without pitching a shutout. Compiling a 26-7 record for the 1922 New York Yankees, Bush pitched a pair of two-hitters and two four-hitters —but failed to throw a shutout.

NORM CASH
First baseman who reached a .300 batting average only once in a big-league career that started in 1958 and ended in 1974—but he won an American League batting championship by hitting .361 in 1961 while playing for Detroit. Cash's next highest average was .286, achieved in 1960 for the Tigers.

PETE CASTIGLIONE
Pittsburgh utilityman who in 1950 made one error all season at first base, two errors at second base, three errors, at third base and four while playing shortstop for the Pirates.

PHIL CAVARRETTA
Chicago Cubs' player (and manager) whose National League career ended in 1953 after he had appeared in 1,953 N.L. games. Cavarretta played for the Chicago White Sox in 1954 and 1955.

CESAR CEDENO
Houston Astros' center fielder who in 1980 grounded into double plays against the Philadelphia Phillies in all three of his career Championship Series games

Houston's Cesar Cedeno (right) couldn't avoid double plays—or injury—in the 1980 National League Championship Series.

(an ankle injury kept Cedeno out of Games 4 and 5 of the N.L. series).

CHICAGO CUBS
The only National League team not to have a winning record against the 1962 Mets, who established a modern big-league mark with 120 losses (while notching only 40 victories). The Cubs finished 9-9 against New York.

CHICAGO CUBS, CHICAGO WHITE SOX
Opponents the last time the World Series involved two first-time entrants in the classic—and this was in 1906. The Series, which began in 1903, had all-new teams in 1905 and '06 (there was no Series in '04), but in every year since at least one of the teams has played in the classic previously.

JOE CHRISTOPHER
One of nine players in major league history to appear in two perfect games. Christopher played for Pittsburgh in the 1959 game in which the Pirates' harvey Haddix pitched 12 perfect innings against the Milwaukee Braves, and he played for the New York Mets in the 1964 game in which Philadelphia's Jim Bunning pitched a perfect game.

Patsy Dougherty, Fred Parent, Ossee Schreckengost, Harry Hooper, Wes Covington, Jim Gilliam, Reggie Jackson and Alfredo Griffin also played in two perfect games. Dougherty and Parent played behind Cy Young in 1904 when the Boston pitcher hurled a perfect game against the Philadelphia A's, and they played for Chicago in 1908 when Cleveland's Addie Joss threw a perfect game against the White Sox. Schreckengost played against Young in '04 and against Joss in '08, while Hooper played behind Ernie Shore in the Boston pitcher's 1917 perfect game against Washington and behind Charley Robertson in the Chicago hurler's 1922 perfect game against Detroit. Covington played against Haddix in '59 and behind Bunning in '64. Gilliam played for the Brooklyn Dodgers in the 1956 World Series game in which Don Larsen of the New York Yankees pitched a perfect game, and he played for the Los Angeles Dodgers in 1965 when Sandy Koufax was perfect against the Chicago Cubs. Jackson played for Oakland in 1968 when the Athletics' Jim (Catfish) Hunter retired every batter in a game against Minnesota and was in California's lineup 16 years later when the Angels' Mike Witt didn't permit a baserunner in a game against Texas. Griffin played shortstop for the Dodgers when Los Angeles was victimized by Tom Browning in 1988 and by Dennis Martinez of the Montreal Expos in 1991.

ROCKY COLAVITO
An outfielder who slugged a total of 374 home runs for five big-league teams, he pitched in two games in the majors—and came up a winner on August 25, 1968, when he worked 2 2/3 innings of one-hit relief for the New York Yankees against the Detroit Tigers. Playing for the Cleveland Indians in 1958, Colavito did not allow a hit in a three-inning stint against the tigers on August 30.

Daryl Patterson of Detroit was the losing pitcher in Colavito's lone big-league pitching victory.

NATE COLBERT, STAN MUSIAL
As an 8-year-old in St. Louis, Colbert went out to old Busch Stadium (formerly Sportsman's Park) on May 2, 1954, to see the Cardinals play a doubleheader against the New York Giants. It proved quite a day—the Cardinals Musial set a major league record by hitting five home runs in the twin bill.

At age 26, Colbert, playing for San Diego, tied Musial's mark by slugging five homers in an August 1, 1972, doubleheader against Atlanta.

JIMMY COONEY
The lone player in major league history to be involved in two unassisted triple plays. Cooney was playing for the St. Louis Cardinals in 1925 when he was caught off second base in the unaided triple play turned by Glenn Wright of the Pittsburgh Pirates. In 1927, Cooney, playing shortstop for the Chicago Cubs, made an unassisted triple play against the Pirates. Both plays occurred at Forbes Field.

Ten years after he took the mound for the Cleveland Indians, Rocky Colavito delivered a pitch for the New York Yankees in 1968.

WES COVINGTON, HARRY HOOPER
The only men to play for the winning teams in two perfect games. Amazingly, one of the perfect games involving Covington was pitched. by the opposing hurler. Covington played for Milwaukee in 1959 when the Braves overcame Harvey Haddix's 12 perfect innings and beat Haddix and the Pittsburgh Pirates, 1-0, on one hit in the 13th inning (Haddix nevertheless was credited with a perfect game). Covington also played for the Philadelphia Phillies in 1964 when Jim Bunning pitched a 6-0 perfect game against the New York Mets. Hooper played for Boston in 1917 when Ernie Shore tossed a 4-0 perfect game against Washington and he was in the Chicago lineup in 1922 when Charley Robertson pitched a 2-0 perfect game against Detroit.

ALVIN DARK
The only person to manage three brothers in World Series competition. Matty and Felipe Alou played for Dark's San Francisco Giants in the 1962 Series, and Jesus Alou played for Dark's Oakland A's in the 1974 classic.

WILLIE DAVIS, RON FAIRLY, JIM GILLIAM
The only three teammates of Sandy Koufax to play in all four of the Los Angeles Dodger pitcher's no-hitters.

DIZZY DEAN, DENNY McLAIN
McLain was the last major league pitcher to win 30 games in a season, going 31-6 in 1968 for the American League's Detroit Tigers. Dean was the National League's last 30-game winner, posting a 30-7 record in 1934 for the St. Louis Cardinals. Both were righthanders who wore No. 17. In '34, Dean's Cardinals beat the Tigers in seven games in the World Series; in '68, McLain's Tigers defeated the Cardinals in seven games in the World Series.

JOE DiMAGGIO
The only player in big-league history to collect at least one All-Star Game hit at Yankee Stadium, the Polo Grounds and Ebbets Field. DiMaggio, New York Yankees' center fielder, homered in Yankee Stadium in the 1939 game, singled twice at the Polo Grounds in 1942 and singled and doubled at Ebbets Field in 1949.

VINCE DiMAGGIO
A National League outfielder for five teams (Boston, Cincinnati, Pittsburgh, Philadelphia and the New York Giants), he batted .249 in 1,110 major league games—compared with the .298 mark achieved by brother Dominic DiMaggio in 1,399 games with the Boston Red Sox and the .325 career figure attained by brother Joe DiMaggio in 1,736 games with the New York Yankees. As All-Star Game participants, Joe hit .255 in 11 games, Dom hit .353 in six games and Vince hit . . . 1.000 in two games (going 3-for-3).

Dizzy Dean (left) and Denny McLain had more in common than just pitching skill.

CHUCK ESTRADA
Baltimore's starting and winning pitcher in the five games in which teammate Jim Gentile hit all six of his bases-loaded home runs in the major leagues. (Gentile hit two grand slams for the Orioles in a May 9, 1961, game against the Minnesota Twins.)

RON FAIRLY
The only player to represent both Canadian major league teams in the All-Star Game, playing for the National League in 1973 as a member of the Montreal Expos and for the American League in 1977 as a member of the Toronto Blue Jays.

BILL FAUL
Cubs' pitcher who was on the mound when Chicago turned all three of its triple plays during the 1965 season.

In major league history, only one other pitcher—Will White of Cincinnati's 1882 American Association club—has been on the mound for three triple plays in one season. White took part in his team's second and third triple plays.

RICK, WES FERRELL
When Wes Ferrell of the Cleveland Indians pitched a no-hitter against St. Louis in 1931, one of the players in the Browns' lineup was catcher Rick Ferrell—Wes' brother.

The only other instance of a no-hit pitcher facing his brother occurred in 1904 when Jesse Tannehill of the Boston Red Sox hurled a no-hitter against Chicago. Jesse's brother, Lee, was the White Sox's third baseman that day.

AL FITZMORRIS, BOBBY SHANTZ
The only two-time selections in major league baseball's expansion drafts. Shantz was chosen by the new Washington Senators off the New York Yankees' roster in the 1960 American League expansion draft, and by the Houston Colt .45s off the Pittsburgh Pirates' roster in the 1961 National League expansion draft. Fitzmorris was picked by the Kansas City Royals off the Chicago White Sox's roster in the 1968 A.L. expansion draft, and by the Toronto Blue Jays off the Royals' roster in the 1976 A.L. expansion draft.

GEORGE FOSTER
The San Francisco batter for whom the Giants' Willie Mays pinch-hit on September 22, 1969, when Mays hit his 600th big-league home run.

JIMMIE FOXX, CHUCK KLEIN
The players who gave major league baseball its only Triple Crown "double" (two such winners in the same season)—and they were even from the same

city. Playing for the Philadelphia Phillies in 1933, Klein led the National League with a .368 batting average, 28 home runs and 120 runs batted in. Playing for the Philadelphia Athletics in '33, Foxx topped the American League with a .356 average, 48 homers and 163 RBIs.

FRANKIE FRISCH
He played the most games (50) in World Series history without hitting a home run. Frisch played in eight Series with the New York Giants (1921, 1922, 1923 and 1924) and St. Louis Cardinals (1928, 1930, 1931 and 1934) and had 197 at-bats.

JIM GILLIAM
The only player in major league history to appear in both a regular-season perfect game and a World Series perfect game. Gilliam played third base for Los Angeles when the Dodgers' Sandy Koufax pitched a perfect game against the Chicago Cubs in 1965, and he was at second base for Brooklyn when Don Larsen of the New York Yankees hurled a perfect game against the Dodgers in the 1956 World Series.

JOE GORDON
New York Yankees' second baseman who at the end of the 1946 season had played exactly 1,000 major league games and collected exactly 1,000 hits. Traded to Cleveland that fall, Gordon was unable to maintain his hit-a-game pace with the Indians. He finished his big-league career in 1950 with 1,530 hits in 1,566 games.

GOOSE GOSLIN
The only man to play in each of the Washington Senators' 19 World Series games. Goslin played in all seven games of both the 1924 and 1925 Series against the New York Giants and Pittsburgh Pirates, and in all five games of the 1933 Series against the Giants.

TED GRAY
Pitcher who appeared in only 14 games in the major leagues in 1955—but pitched for four teams that season. Gray had no record in two games with the Chicago White Sox, two games with the Cleveland Indians and one game with the New York Yankees, and he was 1-2 in nine games with the Baltimore Orioles.

LEFTY GROVE
One of two pitchers who gave up both a home run to Babe Ruth during the Yankee slugger's 60-homer season of 1927 and a hit to Joe DiMaggio during DiMaggio's 56-game batting streak in 1941. Pitching for the Philadelphia Athletics, Grove yielded a bases-loaded homer to Ruth on September 27, 1927 (Ruth's 57th homer of the year); pitching for the Boston Red Sox on May 25,

1941, he permitted a single to the Yankees' DiMaggio (the 11th straight game in which he batted safely).

Ted Lyons of Chicago gave up Ruth's 54th homer of the 1927 season on September 18, and the White Sox's pitcher surrendered two singles to DiMaggio in the first game of a doubleheader on July 13, 1941, as DiMaggio extended his string to 52 straight games.

BILLY HAMILTON
Philadelphia outfielder who captured the National League batting championship in 1891 with a figure that proved lower than his final career average. Hamilton, who won the '91 hitting title with a .338 mark, finished his career at .344.

Others winning big-league batting crowns with averages lower than their final lifetime marks:

Player, Club, League	Year	Title Avg.	Career Avg.
Dan Brouthers, Brooklyn, N.L.	1892	.335	.349
Elmer Flick, Cleveland, A.L.	1905	.308	.315
Ty Cobb, Detroit, A.L.	1907	.350	.367
Ty Cobb, Detroit, A.L.	1908	.324	.367
Edd Roush, Cincinnati, N.L.	1919	.321	.325
Ted Williams, Boston, A.L.	1947	.343	.344
Ted Williams, Boston, A.L.	1958	.328	.344
Rod Carew, Minnesota, A.L.	1972	.318	.328
Tony Gwynn, San Diego, N.L.	1988	.313	.328*

*Through 1991.

JACK HAMILTON
The only pitcher to surrender a big-league home run to Tommie Aaron but not to Tommie's brother, career home-run king Hank Aaron. Hamilton, pitching for the Philadelphia Phillies on April 26, 1962, gave up the first of Tommie's 13 career homers in the majors.

RON HANSEN
The most recent of eight big-league players to make an unassisted triple play—and the feat started a flurry of memorable activity for Hansen. Playing shortstop for the Washington Senators on July 30, 1968, Hansen turned an unassisted triple play in the first inning against the Cleveland Indians— but struck out four straight times against Sam McDowell. On July 31, Hansen fanned in his only two at-bats against Denny McLain of the Detroit Tigers. After walking in his first at-bat on August 1, Hansen snapped his string of six

Ron Hansen of the Washington Senators earned star billing on July 30, 1968, when he pulled an unassisted triple play against the Cleveland Indians.

consecutive strikeouts by belting a fourth-inning, bases-loaded homer off Detroit's Pat Dobson. The following day, Hansen was traded to the Chicago White Sox and that night he played third base against his old club, the Senators.

TOMMY HARPER
The only member of the Seattle Pilots to lead the American League in a major statistical category, topping the A.L. with 73 stolen bases in 1969.

HARRY HEILMANN
Detroit Tigers' outfielder who won American League batting championships in odd-numbered years from 1921 through 1927. Heilmann batted an A.L.-high .394 in 1921, .403 in 1923, .393 in 1925 and .398 in 1927.

WHITEY HERZOG
Kansas City A's right fielder who lined into an all-Cuban triple play on July 23, 1960. After Kansas City's Bill Tuttle and Jerry Lumpe led off the third inning of a game against Washington with singles, Herzog lined a 3-2 pitch to pitcher Pedro Ramos. Ramos caught the drive for out No. 1, then threw to first baseman Julio Becquer to double off Lumpe. Becquer fired the ball to shortstop Jose Valdivielso, who caught Tuttle off second base to complete the triple play.

CHUCK HILLER

Although finishing his eight-year major league career with only 20 home runs he hit the first bases-loaded homer for a National League team in World Series history. Hiller, San Francisco's second baseman in the 1962 Series, slugged his grand slam in the seventh inning of Game 4 off reliever Marshall Bridges of the New York Yankees. The homer snapped a 2-2 tie and led the Giants to a 7-3 triumph.

Ken Boyer of the St. Louis Cardinals hit the N.L.'s second—and only other— grand slam in the World Series. Boyer connected against Al Downing of the Yankees in the sixth inning of Game 4 of the 1964 classic, boosting the Cards from a 3-0 deficit to a 4-3 victory.

KEN HOLTZMAN

Oakland A's player whose World Series homer production (one) in 1974 surpassed his regular-season output (zero)—one of 14 times the feat has occurred in major league history. Holtzman, a pitcher who didn't have a plate appearance during the 1974 American League season (primarily because of the designated-hitter rule), became the most recent player to top his season homer total in the Series when he connected in Game 4 of the '74 classic against the Los Angeles Dodgers.

Pitcher Bob Gibson of the St. Louis Cardinals is the only player who twice has surpassed his regular-season homer mark in the Series, homering in Game 7 against the Boston Red Sox in 1967 and in Game 4 against the Detroit Tigers in 1968 after failing to connect during either season.

BILL HUNNEFIELD

Shortstop who played for the winning team in two no-hitters in his major league career and made a total of four errors in those games. Playing for the Chicago White Sox on August 21, 1926, Hunnefield committed the White Sox's only error as teammate Ted Lyons tossed a no-hitter against the Boston Red Sox. When Wes Ferrell of the Cleveland Indians pitched the American League's next no-hitter, on April 29, 1931, against the St. Louis Browns, Hunnefield made three errors at shortstop for the Tribe.

IKE, NIXON

It was Ike (Delock) pitching to (Russ) Nixon in the early 1960s for the Boston Red Sox. In 1960 (the last full year of the Dwight Eisenhower-Richard Nixon administration), Ike and Nixon led the Red Sox to a 13-4 victory over the Kansas City A's on June 23. Delock pitched a complete-game nine-hitter, and catcher Nixon went 3-for-5—a single, double and home run—and drove in four runs.

Chuck Hiller (right) of the San Francisco Giants became the first National League player to hit a bases-loaded homer in a World Series game, accomplishing the feat in Game 4 of the 1962 classic. Matty Alou (41) was among those offering congratulations.

Oakland pitcher Ken Holtzman, connecting for a home run against the Los Angeles Dodgers in 1974, is the last player to exceed his season homer total in the World Series.

RAY JANSEN

Playing third base for the St. Louis Browns on September 30, 1910, he got four singles in five at-bats in his only major league game.

NIPPY JONES

With the New York Yankees leading Milwaukee, 5-4, after 9 1/2 innings of Game 4 of the 1957 World Series, Jones led off the Braves' 10th as a pinch, hitter for pitcher Warren Spahn. Umpire Augie Donatelli called Tommy Byrne's first pitch to Jones a ball, but Jones insisted he had been struck on the foot—and the Milwaukee player set out to prove his point. Retrieving the baseball, Jones showed Donatelli a smudge of shoe polish on the ball. The umpire awarded him first base, and the Braves went on to score three runs for a 7-5 victory that tied the Series at two games apiece.

Twelve years later, in the fifth and final game of the 1969 World Series, another Jones—Cleon of the New York Mets—was awarded first base on a similar play. Leading off the sixth inning, Jones tried to avoid a pitch in the dirt from Baltimore Orioles hurler Dave McNally. Plate umpire Lou DiMuro called the pitch a ball. Mets Manager Gil Hodges retrieved the baseball and showed DiMuro that the ball contained smudges of shoe polish. The umpire then awarded Jones first base and the next batter, Donn Clendenon, belted a home run, cutting the Orioles' lead to 3-2. The Mets went on to win the game, 5-3, giving them their fourth straight win and the world championship.

With Donn Clendenon (left) looking on, Mets Manager Gil Hodges shows umpire Lou DiMuro a smudge of shoe polish on the ball during Game 5 of the 1969 World Series. The smudge proved that New York's Cleon Jones had been hit by a pitch from Baltimore's Dave McNally, and Clendenon followed with a home run.

ADDIE JOSS, JOHN LEE RICHMOND

Richmond, pitching for Worcester of the National League in 1880, hurled the big leagues' first perfect game (14 had been thrown through 1990), and Addie Joss pitched the majors' fourth perfect game in 1908 for Cleveland of the American League. Richmond later taught mathematics in a Toledo, Ohio, high school and one of his students was Norman Joss—Addie's son.

AL KALINE

Detroit player who was the only batter to face Rocky Colavito in both major league games in which Colavito, normally an outfielder, pitched. Colavito made one mound appearance for the Cleveland Indians in 1958 and one for the New York Yankees in 1968—and both games were against the Tigers.

JOHN KENNEDY

An infielder with Washington during years (1962, 1963) in which John Kennedy was President of the United States, the baseball-playing Kennedy was born on May 29—and so was the President. Baseball's Kennedy, born in 1941 (as opposed to 1917 for the President), also played for the Senators in 1964, then with the Los Angeles Dodgers, New York Yankees, Seattle Pilots, Milwaukee Brewers and Boston Red Sox in a career that ended in 1974.

DON KESSINGER

The most recent of three players in big-league history to receive either a putout or assist in three triple plays in one season. Kessinger, Chicago Cubs' shortstop, accomplished the feat in 1965.

Tom O'Brien had either an assist or putout in three triple plays for Rochester of the American Association in 1890 (he took part in the first two as a first baseman and the third one as a second baseman), and shortstop Donie Bush of the Detroit Tigers was credited with a putout or assist in three triple plays in 1911.

CHUCK KLEIN

The only player to win a Triple Crown in the major leagues and then be traded the following off-season. Playing for the Philadelphia Phillies in 1933, Klein led the National League with a .368 batting average, 28 home runs and 120 runs batted in. However, the financially strapped Phils traded Klein on November 21, 1933, to the Chicago Cubs for pitcher Ted Kleinhans, infielder Mark Koenig, outfielder Harvey Hendrick and an estimated $65,000.

JOE KUHEL

The only Washington player to hit a home run in the Senators' home park, Griffith Stadium, in 1945. Kuhel slugged a third-inning, inside-the-park homer off Bob Muncrief of the St. Louis Browns on September 7, 1945. Washington hit only 27 homers in the entire season, with Harlond Clift leading the club with eight.

Visiting players slugged only six homers at Griffith Stadium in '45, with Detroit's Rudy York hitting two. Milt Byrnes and Lou Finney, both of the Browns, Eddie Lake of the Boston Red Sox and Jeff Heath of the Cleveland Indians also homered at the Senators' park.

BILL KUNKEL
The home-plate umpire on August 10, 1971, when Harmon Killebrew of the Minnesota Twins hit his 500th career home run in a game against the Baltimore Orioles. While pitching for the Kansas City A's in 1961, Kunkel allowed three homers to the Twins' Killebrew.

WAYNE LaMASTER
The Philadelphia Phillies' starting pitcher on May 5, 1938, who was the loser against the Chicago Cubs although he didn't finish pitching to the Cubs' first batter. After the Phils failed to score in the top of the first inning, LaMaster worked the count to 2-1 on Chicago leadoff man Stan Hack before leaving the game because of a sore arm. Reliever Tommy Reis completed a base on balls to Hack (the walk was charged to LaMaster), and Hack eventually scored in the Cubs' four-run inning. Since the Phils never caught up—they ended up losing,

The Los Angeles Dodgers of 1965 and 1966 were able to field an all-switch-hitting infield of (left to right) Maury Wills, Jim Lefebvre, Jim Gilliam and Wes Parker.

21-2—LaMaster was charged with the defeat.

DON LARSEN
His first World Series victory was on October 8, 1956, at Yankee Stadium when he pitched a perfect game for the New York Yankees against the Brooklyn Dodgers, and his last Series triumph came exactly six years later —October 8, 1962—at Yankee Stadium when he beat the Yankees in relief while pitching for the San Francisco Giants. Larsen, who compiled a 4-2 career mark in Series play, pitched only one-third of an inning in Game 4 of the '62 classic but came out a winner when Chuck Hiller hit a bases-loaded homer for the Giants in a 7-3 triumph.

DON, THORNTON LEE
The only father-son combination to surrender home runs to Ted Williams of the Boston Red Sox. Williams, in fact, homered off the Lees as he was coming and going in the major leagues. As a Boston rookie, Williams homered off Thornton Lee of the Chicago White Sox in the first game of a September 17, 1939, doubleheader; playing his final season with the Red Sox, Williams connected off Thornton's son, Don, who was pitching for the Washington Senators in the opener of a September 2, 1960, twin bill.

JIM LEFEBVRE
One-fourth of the all-switch-hitting infield that the Los Angeles Dodgers used during the 1965 and 1966 seasons. Besides second baseman Lefebvre, the Dodgers' other switch-hit infielders were first baseman Wes Parker, shortstop Maury Wills and third baseman Jim Gilliam.

BOB LEMON
When Hall of Fame-bound Bob Feller pitched a no-hitter against the New York Yankees on April 30, 1946, the Cleveland pitcher had a future Hall of Famer playing behind him in center field—Lemon. Lemon, in the process of being converted into a pitcher, singled in four at-bats for the Indians.

DON LEPPERT, JOSE SANTIAGO
Don Eugene Leppert was a lefthanded-hitting second baseman who played in 40 games for the Baltimore Orioles in 1955 and batted .114, while Donald George Leppert was a righthanded-hitting catcher who played in 190 games from 1961 through 1964 with the Pittsburgh Pirates and Washington Senators (for whom he hit three of his 15 career homers in one game in 1963) and had a lifetime average of .229.

Jose Guillermo Santiago was a righthanded pitcher for the Cleveland Indians and Kansas City Athletics from 1954 through 1956, compiling a 3-2 record. Righthanded Jose Rafael Santiago, 34-29 in the majors, also pitched for the Kansas City A's (1963 through 1965) before spending the last five years (1966-

70) of his big-league career with the Boston Red Sox.

JOHN LUCADELLO
The first player in major league history to homer from both sides of the plate in one game for his only two homers of the season. Lucadello performed the feat on September 16, 1940, for the St. Louis Browns.

Only Ellis Burton, Larry Milbourne and U.L. Washington have matched Lucadello's accomplishment. Burton, playing for the Chicago Cubs, did it in the first game of a September 7, 1964, doubleheader; Milbourne, of the Seattle Mariners, followed on July 15, 1978, and Washington, as a member of the Kansas City Royals, became No. 4 on September 21, 1979.

For Lucadello and Washington, the homers were the first two of each player's big-league career; for Burton, the two homers were his last in the majors.

CONNIE MACK
The man who managed the Philadelphia Athletics for 50 of the club's 54 seasons in the American League. Mack piloted the A's from their inception in 1901 through 1950, with Jimmie Dykes taking over in 1951 and managing the club through 1953. Eddie Joost managed the A's in 1954, their last season in Philadelphia before relocating in Kansas City.

KEN MacKENZIE
The only pitcher to achieve a winning record for the 1962 New York Mets. MacKenzie, who worked in relief in 41 of the 42 games in which he appeared, posted a 5-4 record.

PAT MALONE, MILT WILCOX
The only men to play in the World Series for teams from both leagues under the same manager. Malone pitched with the National League's Chicago Cubs for Joe McCarthy in the 1929 Series and for the American League's New York Yankees under McCarthy in the 1936 Series. Wilcox pitched for the N.L.'s Cincinnati Reds for Sparky Anderson in the 1970 Series and for the A.L.'s Detroit Tigers under Anderson in the 1984 Series.

BILLY MARTIN
The only man to play in Don Larsen's World Series perfect game in 1956, Rocky Colavito's four-homer game in 1959 and Willie Mays' four-homer game in 1961. Martin was a teammate of Larsen and Colavito (with the New York Yankees and Cleveland Indians, respectively), and played against the San Francisco Giants' Mays while with the Milwaukee Braves.

EDDIE MATHEWS
The only man to play for the Boston Braves, Milwaukee Braves and Atlanta

Connie Mack's 50th year as Philadelphia A's manager is noted by his players and by American League President Will Harridge and Dodgers Manager Burt Shotton during spring training.

Braves. Mathews played for Boston in 1952, for Milwaukee from 1953 through 1965 and for Atlanta in 1966.

CHARLEY MAXWELL
Boston Red Sox's player who hit three home runs in 1951—the first three of his major league career—and each was a pinch-hit homer off a future Hall of Fame pitcher (Bob Feller of Cleveland, Bob Lemon of the Indians and Satchel Paige of the St. Louis Browns). Maxwell's smash against Paige was a grand slam.

CHARLEY MAXWELL
Outfielder who hit 40 of his 148 career home runs in the majors on Sunday, including four in a 1959 doubleheader against the New York Yankees and three in a 1962 twin bill against the Yanks. In '59, 12 of his 31 homers came on Sunday. Maxwell, who played for the Boston Red Sox, Detroit Tigers and Chicago White Sox from 1950 to 1964, had seven lifetime homers on Monday 21 on Tuesday, 19 on Wednesday, 13 on Thursday, 22 on Friday and 26 on Saturday. Of Maxwell's 40 Sunday shots, 12 were against New York.

WILLIE MAYS, DUKE SNIDER
The only two players to appear in both the 1951 and 1962 National League playoffs. Mays played for the New York Giants in '51 and for the San Francisco Giants in '62, and Snider played for the Brooklyn Dodgers in '51 and the Los Angeles Dodgers in '62.

JOE McCARTHY
New York Yankees' manager who didn't use any of the six Yankee players on hand for the 1943 All-Star Game at Philadelphia's Shibe Park. Apparently resenting accusations that he favored New York players in earlier All-Star Games and seemingly out to prove his American League team could win without the Yankees, McCarthy kept the six on the bench. And he proved his point—the A.L. defeated the National League, 5-3.

CLIFF MELTON
New York Giants' pitcher who on September 15, 1938, became the only man in major league history to give up back-to-back homers to brothers. In the fifth inning of a game with the Pittsburgh Pirates, Melton yielded consecutive homers to Lloyd and Paul Waner (Lloyd's shot was the 27th and last of his big-league career).

RUDI MEOLI
One of only two teammates of Nolan Ryan to play in as many as three of Ryan's seven no-hitters in the major leagues. Meoli was California's shortstop when Ryan pitched his first three no-hitters for the Angels—against the Kansas City Royals and the Detroit Tigers, both in 1973, and against the Twins in 1974.

Duke Snider (left) and Willie Mays met in the 1951 National League playoff between the Brooklyn Dodgers and New York Giants and again in the 1962 N.L. playoff between the Los Angeles Dodgers and San Francisco Giants.

Outfielder Leroy Stanton played for the Angels in Ryan's second, third and fourth no-hitters with California (No. 4 was against the Baltimore Orioles in 1975).

SAM MERTES
A 10-year major leaguer who broke up no-hitters in the 10th inning of both American League and National League games. Mertes singled in the 10th inning off Cleveland's Earl Moore after Moore had pitched no-hit ball for nine innings in an A.L. game against the Chicago White Sox on May 9, 1901. Moore lost, 4-2, in 10 innings, yielding two hits. On June 11, 1904, Mertes singled in the 10th inning off the Chicago Cubs' Robert Wicker after Wicker had pitched no-hit ball for 9 1/3 innings in an N.L. game against the New York Giants. Wicker won, 1-0, on a 12-inning one-hitter.

MIKE
The first name of the only three pitchers to defeat Ron Guidry of the New York Yankees in 1978. Guidry, winner of the American League's Cy Young Award in '78 when he compiled a 25-3 record, lost to Mike Caldwell of the Milwaukee Brewers, Mike Flanagan of the Baltimore Orioles and Mike Willis of the Toronto Blue Jays.

Guidry got revenge against the Mikes that year, beating Boston's Mike Torrez, 5-4, in the one-game playoff for the A.L. East Division championship.

BING MILLER
One of six players in World Series history to end the classic with a game-winning hit. Miller, playing for the Philadelphia Athletics in Game 5 of the 1929 Series, doubled off Pat Malone of the Chicago Cubs with two out in the ninth inning, scoring Al Simmons from second, giving the A's a 3-2 victory.

Other players with Series-ending hits:
• **Earl McNeely,** Washington Senators, 1924, Game 7. McNeely singled off Jack Bentley of the New York Giants with one out in the 12th inning, scoring Muddy Ruel from second base and giving the Senators a 4-3 triumph.
• **Goose Goslin,** Detroit Tigers, 1935, Game 6. Goslin singled off the Cubs' Larry French with two out in the ninth inning, scoring Mickey Cochrane from second base and boosting the Tigers to a 4-3 win.
• **Billy Martin,** New York Yankees, 1953, Game 6. Martin singled off Clem Labine of the Brooklyn Dodgers with one out in the ninth inning, scoring Hank Bauer from second base in a 4-3 victory.
• **Bill Mazeroski,** Pittsburgh Pirates, 1960, Game 7. Mazeroski homered against the Yankees' Ralph Terry to lead off the Pirates' ninth inning, giving Pittsburgh a 10-9 triumph.
• **Gene Larkin,** Minnesota Twins, 1991, Game 7. Larkin singled off the Braves Alejandro Pena with one out in the 10th inning, scoring Dan Gladden and giving the Twins a 1-0 victory.

Seeking good luck before the start of the 1935 World Series, Detroit outfielder Goose Goslin used a live rabbit—not just a rabbit's foot—as a charm. Goslin was rewarded, becoming one of only five players in history to end a Series with a game-winning hit.

BOB MILLER, BOB MILLER
Pitchers and teammates on the 1962 New York Mets. Robert Lane Miller, primarily a starter, was a righthander who compiled a 1-12 record for the '62 Mets. Robert Gerald Miller, a lefthanded reliever, posted a 2-2 mark for New York.

STU MILLER
San Francisco Giants' pitcher whose wind-caused balk helped the American League tie the National League in the ninth inning of the first All-Star Game of 1961, played in Candlestick Park. With the N.L. ahead, 3-2, in the ninth and Al Kaline on second base and Roger Maris on first for the A.L., Miller relieved Sandy Koufax. With Rocky Colavito at bat, gale-like winds blew Miller off the mound and the reliever was charged with a balk. With runners now on third and second, Colavito grounded to third baseman Ken Boyer. Boyer fumbled the ball, enabling Kaline to score the tying run. The N.L. went on to win, 5-4, in 10 innings—and Miller got the victory.

DALE MITCHELL
The only man to have played in the last World Series game of both the Brooklyn Dodgers and New York Giants. Mitchell pinch-hit for Cleveland against the Giants on October 2, 1954 (the day New York completed a sweep of the Indians), and pinch-hit for Brooklyn on October 10, 1956 (the day the New York Yankees won Game 7 of that Series).

JOHNNY MIZE
St. Louis Cardinals' first baseman whose ejection from the final game of the 1936 season enabled Walter Alston, future managerial standout with the Brooklyn and Los Angeles Dodgers, to appear in his only major league game. Mize was thrown out in the seventh inning, and Alston was his replacement at first base against the Chicago Cubs. In his lone big-league at-bat, Alston struck out against Lon Warneke.

GEORGE MULLIN
The only pitcher to appear in a World Series after losing 20 games during that year's regular season. Mullin, who compiled a 20-20 record for the Detroit Tigers in 1907, was 0-2 against the Chicago Cubs in the '07 Series.

JOHNNY NEUN
While unassisted triple plays are rare in the big leagues (only eight have been performed), Neun's unassisted triple play for the Detroit Tigers against Cleveland on May 31, 1927, was the second in two days in the majors. On May 30, 1927, shortstop Jimmy Cooney of the Chicago Cubs turned an unassisted triple play in the fourth inning of a game against the Pittsburgh Pirates.

Neun's unaided triple play is the only one to end a game, with the first baseman's ninth-inning heroics wrapping up a 1-0 victory over the Indians for Detroit pitcher Rip Collins. It was Collins' only shutout of the '27 season.

NEW YORK YANKEES, SAN FRANCISCO GIANTS
Teams that traded victories in every other game of the 1962 World Series (one club won all odd-numbered games and the other won all even-numbered games). The Yankees became world champions by winning Games 1, 3, 5, 7; the Giants took Games 2, 4 and 6.

The only other time the sequence occurred in the Series was in 1909 when the Pittsburgh Pirates beat the Detroit Tigers in every other game to win the classic, four games to three.

JOE NIEKRO
He hit only one home run in his 22-year major league career—and that was off his brother, Phil. Houston's Joe outpitched Atlanta's Phil in a May 29, 1976, game, and Joe's seventh-inning homer against his older brother helped the Astros beat the Braves, 4-3.

JIM O'ROURKE
The only man to play in major league baseball's first game and also compete in the majors after the turn of the century. Playing for Boston against Philadelphia in the National League's first game on April 22, 1876, O'Rourke singled off Alonzo Knight for the first hit in big-league history. A minor league manager in 1904 at age 52, O'Rourke longed to play one more time for the New York Giants (a team he helped to N.L. pennants in 1888 and 1889)—and Giants' Manager John McGraw acceded. O'Rourke caught the first game of a September 22 doubleheader against Cincinnati and collected one hit in his career-ending game as the Giants clinched the pennant, winning, 7-5, behind pitcher Joe McGinnity.

ERNIE PADGETT
Boston Braves' shortstop who turned an unassisted triple play on October 6, 1923, in only his fourth big-league game—and is the only major leaguer to make an unaided triple play in his club's final game of the season.

JIM PALMER
The only man to appear in all six World Series in which the Baltimore Orioles have played. Palmer pitched for the Orioles against the Los Angeles Dodgers in 1966, against the New York Mets in 1969, against the Cincinnati Reds in 1970, against the Pittsburgh Pirates in 1971 and 1979 and against the Philadelphia Phillies in 1983.

JIM PERRY
The losing pitcher in three of the four no-hitters hurled in the American League between the 1970 and 1973 All-Star Games. Pitching for Minnesota, Perry was

victimized in September of 1970 when Vida Blue of the Oakland A's threw a no-hitter against the Twins. Pitching for Detroit, Perry was victimized in April of 1973 when Steve Busby of the Kansas City Royals hurled a no-hitter against the Tigers, and in July of 1973 when Nolan Ryan of the California Angels also tossed a no-hitter against Detroit.

Kansas City's Bruce Dal Canton was the losing pitcher in the other A.L. no-hit game during that span, falling victim when California's Ryan threw a no-hitter against the Royals in May of 1973.

JIMMY PIERSALL
After hitting his 100th career home run on June 23, 1963, while playing for the New York Mets, he ran around the bases backward—but in sequence—against the Philadelphia Phillies. Piersall's drive, which came off Dallas Green, was his only National league homer (Piersall hit 103 homers in a 1,694-game American League career that was sandwiched around his 40 games with the Mets).

BABE PINELLI
The umpire whose last game behind the plate in the major leagues was on

While Babe Pinelli (center) ended his umpiring career on the bases in Games 6 and 7 of the 1956 World Series, it was Game 5 for which he will be remembered. Pinelli worked behind the plate for the final time that day when Don Larsen (left) and Yogi Berra formed a perfect-game battery.

134

October 8, 1956—the day Don Larsen of the New York Yankees pitched a perfect game against the Brooklyn Dodgers in Game 5 of the World Series. Pinelli, who began umpiring in the National League in 1935, retired after the 1956 season.

PIRATES, YANKEES, TIGERS, ROYALS

The only four teams in World Series history to come from three-games-to-one deficits and win the title in a seven-game Series—and the Pirates have done it twice. Pittsburgh rebounded against the Washington Senators in 1925 and against the Baltimore Orioles in 1979, the Yankees rallied against the Milwaukee Braves in 1958, the Tigers captured Games 5, 6 and 7 against St. Louis in 1968 and Kansas City roared back to bounce the Cardinals in 1985.

HUBERT (SHUCKS) PRUETT

A 29-48 career pitcher who in his first 11 head-to-head meetings with Babe Ruth struck out the Yankee slugger eight times, walked him twice and induced him to hit back to the mound. Pruett, who pitched three years (1922-24) with the St. Louis Browns before finishing his career in the National League, went against Ruth 33 times in 14 games (all in the American League) and struck him out 14 times in 25 official at-bats. Ruth wasn't exactly helpless when facing the lefthander, though, batting .280 against him overall (with two homers among his seven hits). And Ruth went 3-for-5 off Pruett during the pitcher's final season in the A.L.

PEE WEE REESE

Dodgers' shortstop who was the only man to play in all 44 World Series games—spanning seven Series (1941, 1947, 1949, 1952, 1953, 1955 and 1956)— between Brooklyn and the New York Yankees.

WILBERT ROBINSON

Holder for 32 years of the major league record for most RBIs for one game, 11, Robinson was the opposing manager on September 16, 1924, when Jim Bottomley of the St. Louis Cardinals broke his record. Playing against Robinson's Brooklyn Dodgers, Bottomley drove in 12 runs as the Cards won, 17-3.

Playing for Baltimore of the National League on June 10, 1892, Robinson went 7-for-7 (six singles and a double) against St. Louis and knocked in 11 runs in a 25-4 victory.

COOKIE ROJAS

One of two men to play on teams that were beaten in no-hitters pitched by both Sandy Koufax and Nolan Ryan. Rojas was Philadelphia's center fielder in the 1964 game in which Los Angeles' Koufax hurled a no-hitter against the Phillies, and he was Kansas City's second baseman in the 1973 game in which California's Ryan threw a no-hitter against the Royals.

Robert Lane (Bob) Miller was the New York Mets' starting and losing pitcher in the 1962 no-hitter thrown by the Dodgers' Koufax, and he relieved (but had no decision) for Detroit when the Angels' Ryan fired a no-hitter against the Tigers in '73.

JOHN ROSEBORO
Los Angeles Dodgers' player who caught two of Sandy Koufax's four no-hitters. Roseboro caught Koufax's no-hit game against the New York Mets in 1962 and the lefthander's gem against the San Francisco Giants in 1963.

Doug Camilli was the Dodgers' catcher when Koufax threw a no-hitter against the Philadelphia Phillies in 1964, and Jeff Torborg caught for Los Angeles in Koufax's perfect game against the Chicago Cubs in 1965.

JOSE SANTIAGO
The only pitcher in World Series history to lose a game in which he hit a home run. Santiago, the Boston Red Sox's starting pitcher in Game 1 of the 1967 Series, homered off St. Louis' Bob Gibson in his first Series at-bat but ended up a 2-1 loser to the Cardinals. Pitchers have homered 13 other times (never more than once in a game) in Series play; they have 11 victories in those games and two no-decision outcomes.

MIKE SCHMIDT
Philadelphia Phillies' third baseman who on June 10, 1974, hit one of the longest singles in major league history. With Dave Cash and Larry Bowa on base in the first inning, Schmidt hit a pitch from Houston's Claude Osteen that seemed to be a tape-measure drive. However, the ball deflected off a speaker hanging in fair territory in center field at the Astrodome. It was the first ball to hit a speaker in fair territory, and the ground rules stated the ball was in play. Neither baserunner scored as the ball caromed back onto the field, leaving Schmidt with a single. (The speaker hangs 117 feet off the ground, 329 feet from home plate.)

OSSEE SCHRECKENGOST
The first of only two men to play in two major league games in which their teams were victimized by perfect games. Schreckengost, a catcher, played for the Philadelphia Athletics in 1904 when Cy Young of Boston pitched a 3-0 perfect game against the A's, and he played for the Chicago White Sox in 1908 when Cleveland's Addie Joss hurled a 1-0 perfect game.

Alfredo Griffin played shortstop for the Dodgers when Los Angeles was victimized by Cincinnati's Tom Browning, 1-0 in 1988. Three years later, Griffin played shortstop when Montreal's Dennis Martinez pitched a 2-0 perfect game against the Dodgers.

DIEGO SEGUI
The only man to play for both the Seattle Pilots and the Seattle Mariners. Segui compiled a 12-6 pitching record for the Pilots in 1969 (their lone American League season before moving to Milwaukee and becoming the Brewers), but was 0-7 for the first-year Mariners in 1977.

MIKE SHANNON
St. Louis Cardinals' player who collected two hits in four at-bats in the opening game of each of his three World Series appearances (1964, 1967 and 1968).

BOBBY SHANTZ
A major league pitcher for 16 seasons, he hurled only one inning in All-Star Game competition—and struck out all three batters he faced. Relieving for the American League in the fifth inning of the 1952 game at Philadelphia's Shibe Park, Shantz struck out Whitey Lockman, Jackie Robinson and Stan Musial. The Philadelphia A's pitcher was denied a chance of matching Carl Hubbell's 1934 All-Star Game feat of five consecutive strikeouts, though, as rain ended the game after five innings. The National League won, 3-2.

BILL SHARMAN
Although he never played in a major league game, Sharman was ejected from one. An outfielder who had batted .286 for Class AA Fort Worth of the Texas League during the 1951 season, Sharman was called up to Brooklyn in September. Riding the bench in a September 27 game at Braves Field in Boston, Sharman suddenly found himself banished when umpire Frank Dascoli ejected Dodger catcher Roy Campanella and pitcher Preacher Roe after a disputed play at the plate and cleared the Brooklyn bench as well. With the Dodgers in a tight pennant race, Sharman never got into a game . . . and he soon turned his attention fully to basketball (a sport in which he made the Hall of Fame after a standout career with the Boston Celtics).

ENOS SLAUGHTER
The only player to appear in both the 1946 and 1959 National League playoffs. He played for the St. Louis Cardinals in the '46 playoff against the Brooklyn Dodgers, and for the Milwaukee Braves in the '59 playoff against the Los Angeles Dodgers.

REGGIE SMITH
Outfielder-first baseman who hit homers from both sides of the plate in one game four times in the American League and twice in the National League. Smith accomplished the feat for the A.L.'s Boston Red Sox in 1967, 1968, 1972 and 1973 and for the N.L.'s St. Louis Cardinals in 1975 and 1976.

Bill Sharman was highly visible as a basketball player after his disappearing act on the Brooklyn Dodgers' bench.

Ted Simmons, Chili Davis and Eddie Murray are the only others in history to homer both right-and-lefthanded in one game in both leagues.

WARREN SPAHN
As a rookie pitcher for the Boston Braves in 1942, Spahn was credited with one complete game—but he had a 0-0 record in four appearances. Pitching against the New York Giants in the second game of a September 26 doubleheader at the Polo Grounds, Spahn was trailing, 5-2, in the bottom of the eighth inning when hundreds of youngsters ran onto the field. The youths refused to return to their seats, so umpire Ziggy Sears forfeited the game to the Braves, 9-0— leaving Spahn with a no-decision outcome, but with his first complete game in the majors.

TIM STODDARD

Baltimore Orioles' pitcher whose World Series single in 1979 came in the only plate appearance of his major league career and made him one of only eight players to collect more hits in a World Series than in that year's regular season. Through the 1982 season, Stoddard had never gone to the plate except for his eighth-inning at-bat in Game 4 of the '79 Series when he grounded a single off Kent Tekulve of the Pittsburgh Pirates.

Other players with one World Series hit and none in the regular season are Joe Hoerner of the St. Louis Cardinals (1968), Bill Lee of the Boston Red Sox (1975), Will McEnaney of the Cincinnati Reds (1975), Jesse Orosco of the New York Mets (1986) and Mike Moore of the Oakland Athletics (1989). Ken Holtzman of the Oakland A's (1974) and Luis Tiant of the Red Sox (1975) had two Series hits and no regular-season hits.

Washington pitcher Dean Stone won the 1954 American League All-Star Game the easy way—he never retired a batter.

Cincinnati's Billy Bates had one hit in the 1990 Series but none during brief regular-season duty with the Reds. Earlier in the '90 season, Bated has collected three hits for the Milwaukee Brewers.

DEAN STONE
The winning pitcher in the 1954 All-Star Game at Cleveland's Municipal Stadium although he didn't retire a batter. Stone, Washington Senators' pitcher, entered the game with two out in the top of the eighth inning and his American League squad trailing, 9-8. With Duke Snider at bat for the National League, Red Schoendienst broke from third base in an attempt to steal home. Stone hurried his motion and threw to catcher Yogi Berra in time to retire Schoendienst. While he left the game in the bottom of the eighth for a pinch-hitter (Larry Doby, who homered), Stone notched the victory as the A.L. broke loose for three runs in that inning and an 11-9 triumph. Virgil Trucks worked the ninth inning for the A.L.

FRANK THOMAS
The only man to play in the New York Giants' last game in history and the New York Mets' first game. Thomas played first base for the Pittsburgh Pirates on September 29, 1957, against the Giants, who were playing their last game before moving to San Francisco in 1958; he was in left field for the Mets on April 11, 1962, when they made their debut against the St. Louis Cardinals.

BOBBY TOLAN
The only man to play in both games of the back-to-back no-hitters of San Francisco's Gaylord Perry and St. Louis' Ray Washburn in 1968 and both games of the consecutive no-hitters by Cincinnati's Jim Maloney and Houston's Don Wilson in 1969. Tolan played left field for St. Louis in the game, against Perry and right field behind Washburn, and he was in right field for Cincinnati in the Maloney and Wilson no-hitters.

JEFF TORBORG
The only player to catch no-hitters thrown by both Sandy Koufax and Nolan Ryan. Torborg caught Koufax's last no-hitter, a perfect game for the Los Angeles Dodgers against the Chicago Cubs in September of 1965, and he caught Ryan's first no-hitter—for the California Angels against the Kansas City Royals in May of 1973.

DICK TRACEWSKI
Infielder who played in both Sandy Koufax's 15-strikeout game in the 1963 World Series and Bob Gibson's 17-strikeout game in the 1968 Series (Koufax's total had broken Carl Erskine's Series mark of 14, set in 1953, and Gibson then surpassed Koufax). Tracewski played second base behind the Dodgers' Koufax against the Yankees in '63, and was a late-inning defensive replacement at third base for the Tigers against Gibson and the Cardinals in '68.

Virgil Trucks (left) and Hank Greenberg celebrate after leading Detroit to a 4-1 victory over the Chicago Cubs in Game 2 of the 1945 World Series. Trucks pitched a seven-hitter for his only triumph of the year (he spent most of the season in the military service), and Greenberg hit a three-run homer.

Roger Maris was the only other player to appear in both games, playing right field for the Yankees in '63 and the same position for the Cardinals in '68. Maris struck out once against Koufax (Tracewski did not bat against Gibson).

VIRGIL TRUCKS
The first of only two pitchers to win more games in the World Series than in the regular season preceding the classic. In the military service for most of the 1945 season, Trucks didn't pitch for the Detroit Tigers until the final game of the year—and he received no decision in a 5 1/3-inning stint. However, Trucks started twice against the Chicago Cubs in the '45 Series and pitched the Tigers to a 4-1 victory in Game 2 (in Game 6, he had no decision).

Steve Crawford, 0-2 for the Boston Red Sox in the 1986 regular season, won Game 2 or the '86 Series while working in relief against the New York Mets.

RUSS VAN ATTA
New York Yankees' pitcher who threw a five-hit shutout and had four singles in four at-bats against the Washinton Senators in his big-league debut on April 25, 1933. Van Atta, who later pitched for the St. Louis Browns, never managed another shutout in the majors (although his career lasted into the 1939 season).

BILL VIRDON
The only manager of the New York Yankees since the opening of Yankee Stadium in 1923 never to have managed the Yanks in that ballpark. Virdon was the Yankees' manager in 1974 and part of 1975—years in which the Yanks used New York's Shea Stadium as their home because of the extensive remodeling of Yankee Stadium.

BOBBY WALLACE
The man who spent the most years, 25, in the major leagues as an active player without being on a pennant-winning team. Wallace played from 1894 through 1918 with Cleveland and St. Louis of the National League and for St. Louis of the American League.

LLOYD, PAUL WANER
The only brother combination in big-league history to be involved in an unassisted triple play. In a May 30, 1927, game, Pittsburgh's Paul Waner hit a drive to shortstop Jimmy Cooney of the Chicago Cubs for out No. 1. Cooney caught Lloyd Waner off second base and stepped on the bag, then tagged the Pirates' Clyde Barnhart (who was running from first base).

PAUL (PEE WEE) WANNINGER
New York Yankees' shortstop who had a role in the beginning of Lou Gehrig's consecutive-game streak and who (less than a month earlier) had helped to snap the record string that Gehrig eventually surpassed. Wanninger gave way

Yankee shortstop Pee Wee Wanninger left a June 1, 1925, game for pinch-hitter Lou Gehrig—and that at-bat started Gehrig's record streak of playing in 2,130 consecutive games.

Hoyt Wilhelm homered in his first big-league at-bat, but the pitcher never connected again in a 21-season career.

to pinch-hitter Gehrig in the eighth inning of a June 1, 1925, game against the Washington Senators, thereby starting Gehrig's major league-record streak of playing in 2,130 consecutive games. On May 6, 1925, Wanninger replaced Everett Scott at shortstop for the Yankees, ending Scott's consecutive-game streak at 1,307 (the big-league mark until shattered by Gehrig).

HERB WASHINGTON

A non-pitcher who played in 105 regular-season games in the big leagues—but never batted. A track star at Michigan State, Washington was signed by Oakland A's Owner Charlie Finley for use as a pinch-running specialist. Washington, who played in 92 games for the A-s in 1974 and 13 in 1975, had

31 career steals (in 48 attempts) and scored 33 runs. He pinch-ran in three games of the 1974 World Series against the Los Angeles Dodgers, but stole no bases.

HOYT WILHELM
Pitcher who hit a home run in his first major league at-bat but failed to hit another one in a career that spanned 21 seasons. Batting for the New York Giants in the fourth inning of an April 23, 1952, game against the Boston Braves, Wilhelm connected against rookie Dick Hoover. Wilhelm finished his career with 432 official at-bats.

The April 23, 1952, game was Hoover's second and last in the majors, and Wilhelm's drive was the only homer he allowed in the big leagues.

HACK WILSON
Chicago Cubs' slugger who in 1930 set a major league record with 190 runs batted in and a National League mark with 56 home runs—but didn't hit a grand slam that season.

WILLIE WILSON
Kansas City Royals' outfielder who hit six home runs in 1979—five of them inside the park. Wilson's only over-the-fence homer in '79 was a June 15 shot at Milwaukee off the Brewers' Mike Caldwell.

SIXTH INNING
Notable firsts

FELIPE, JESUS, MATTY ALOU
Brothers who were the first batters in the first regular-season major league games at Busch Memorial Stadium in St. Louis, San Diego Stadium and Atlanta Stadium. Felipe, of the Atlanta Braves, was the first hitter at Busch Memorial Stadium on May 12, 1966; Jesus, of the Houston Astros, was the first to bat at San Diego Stadium on April 8, 1969, and Matty, a member of the Pittsburgh Pirates, was the leadoff hitter at Atlanta Stadium on April 12, 1966.

EMMETT ASHFORD
The major leagues' first black umpire, he umpired in the American League from 1966 through 1970.

EARL AVERILL
Cleveland Indians' player who collected the first pinch hit in All-Star Game history, singling in the sixth inning on July 6, 1933.

BOB BAILOR
The first player picked by the Toronto Blue Jays in the American League expansion draft of 1976. Bailor, a shortstop, was selected off the Baltimore Orioles' roster.

DAN BANKHEAD
The first black pitcher in major league history. Relieving Brooklyn starter Hal Gregg in the second inning of an August 26, 1947, game against Pittsburgh, Bankhead worked 3 1/3 innings and allowed 10 hits and six earned runs. He did not figure in the decision.

Batting in the bottom of the second inning, the Dodgers' Bankhead homered in his first big-league at-bat. He connected off the Pirates' Fritz Ostermueller.

ROSS BARNES
A second baseman for Chicago's National League team, he slugged the first home run in major league history on May 2, 1876. Barnes connected against Cincinnati's Cherokee Fisher.

GINGER BEAUMONT
Pittsburgh center fielder who was the first batter in World Series history on October 1, 1903. Beaumont flied out for the Pirates against Cy Young of the Boston Red Sox.

Jackie Robinson (right), the first black to play in modern big-league baseball, was joined in Brooklyn later in th 1947 season by Dan Bankhead, the first black pitcher in the majors.

ERWIN BECK
Cleveland second baseman who hit the first home run in American League history, connecting off John Skopec of Chicago on April 25, 1901.

YOGI BERRA
New York Yankee who belted the first pinch-hit home run in World Series history, connecting off Ralph Branca of the Brooklyn Dodgers in the seventh inning of Game 3 of the 1947 Series.

JOE BLACK
First black pitcher to win a World Series game. After starting only two of the 56 regular-season games in which he pitched for the Brooklyn Dodgers in 1952, Black started Game 1 of the '52 Series and beat the New York Yankees, 4-2, on a six-hitter.

PAUL BLAIR
Baltimore center fielder who was the first man to bat in a night World Series game. As the leadoff hitter in Game 4 of the 1971 Series, Blair singled for the Orioles against the Pittsburgh Pirates.

RON BLOMBERG
The first designated hitter in major league history. Playing in the April 6, 1973, American League game between New York and Boston, the Yankees' Blomberg drew a bases-loaded walk off Luis Tiant in the first inning and finished the day with one hit in three official at-bats. The Red Sox won, 15-5.

JOE BOWMAN
Philadelphia Phillies' pitcher who lost the first night game in major league history, May 24, 1935, at Cincinnati.

EDDIE BRESSOUD
The Houston Colt .45s' first pick in the National League expansion draft of 1961. Bressoud, an infielder, was selected from the San Francisco Giants' roster.

KEN BRETT
Pitching for the Chicago White Sox against the Toronto Blue Jays on April 7, 1977, Brett was the loser in the first American League game played in Canada.

LOU BROCK
St. Louis Cardinals' outfielder who was the first player to bat in a major league game in Canada, April 14, 1969, against the Montreal Expos.

OLLIE BROWN
Outfielder who was the first choice of the San Diego Padres in the National

League's 1968 expansion draft. Brown was taken from the San Francisco Giants' roster.

WILLARD BROWN
The first black player in American League history to hit a home run. Pinch-hitting for Joe Schultz of the St. Louis Browns on August 13, 1947, Brown drilled an inside-the-park homer off Hal Newhouser of the Detroit Tigers in the second game of a doubleheader.

WILLARD BROWN, HANK THOMPSON
The first two black players to appear together in a modern major league game. Brown played right field and Thompson second base for the St. Louis Browns in a July 20, 1947, game against the Boston Red Sox.

BYRON BROWNE, DON YOUNG
Chicago Cubs' outfielders who in their first major league game faced Sandy Koufax of the Los Angeles Dodgers on September 9, 1965—the night Koufax pitched a perfect game and won, 1-0. Browne batted sixth and played left field; Young led off and played center field.

BILLY BRUTON
Braves' player who hit the first major league home run at Milwaukee's County Stadium. Playing in his second big-league game on April 14, 1953, Bruton slugged a 10th-inning homer off Gerry Staley of the St. Louis Cardinals to give Milwaukee a 3-2 triumph. Bruton's drive, which bounced off the glove of St. Louis right fielder Enos Slaughter and over the fence, was the only homer for the Braves' outfielder in 151 games that season.

JIM BUNNING
The first man to pitch for both leagues in All-Star Games. After appearing for the American League in 1957, 1959, 1961 (twice), 1962 and 1963, Bunning pitched for the National League in the 1964 classic (and again in 1966).

BEN CHAPMAN
New York Yankees' outfielder who was the first man to bat for the American League in an All-Star Game. Chapman grounded out to third baseman Pepper Martin of the St. Louis Cardinals on July 6, 1933.

CHICAGO CUBS
The first National League team to draw one million fans in one year, attracting 1,159,168 in 1927.

LOU CHIOZZA
Philadelphia Phillies' second baseman who was the first player to bat in a major league night game. Chiozza grounded out to shortstop Billy Myers of the

Hank Thompson (left) and Willard Brown, the first black players to appear together in a modern major league game, sit with St. Louis Browns' Manager Muddy Ruel after signing to play with the Browns in July of 1947. Rob Blomberg became the first designated hitter in major league history on April 6, 1973.

Cincinnati Reds in the May 24, 1935, game at Cincinnati's Crosley Field.

COMISKEY PARK
Chicago stadium where the National League first won an All-Star Game at an American League site. After losing eight consecutive games in A.L. parks, the N.L. won, 4-3, in 14 innings in 1950 at Comiskey Park, home of the A.L.'s Chicago White Sox.

MORT COOPER
Pitcher for the St. Louis Cardinals who lost the first night All-Star Game in history, July 13, 1943, at Philadelphia's Shibe Park.

RAY CULP
Philadelphia Phillies' pitcher who gave up Hank Aaron's first home run as a member of the Atlanta Braves on April 20, 1966. The homer was the 399th of Aaron's major league career.

BILL DAHLEN
The first player in World Series history to steal home. Playing for the New York Giants against the Philadelphia Athletics in 1905, Dahlen stole home in the fifth inning of Game 3.

CLAY DALRYMPLE
Philadelphia player whose two-out, pinch single in the eighth inning was the only hit off San Francisco's Juan Marichal in the pitcher's first major league game, played July 19, 1960. Marichal and the Giants beat the Phillies, 2-0.

DIZZY DEAN
St. Louis Cardinals' standout who in 1936 became the first National League pitcher to win an All-Star Game.

PAUL DERRINGER
Reds' pitcher who started and won the first night game in major league history on May 24, 1935, at Cincinnati against the Philadelphia Phillies.

VINCE DiMAGGIO
Pittsburgh Pirates' center fielder who hit the National League's first home run in a night All-Star Game, connecting off Tex Hughson in the ninth inning of the 1943 contest.

BILL DINNEEN
Pitcher for the Boston Red Sox who tossed the first shutout in World Series competition, blanking the Pittsburgh Pirates in Game 2 of the 1903 classic. He was also the first former World Series player to umpire in a Series. He umpired in 1911 when the Philadelphia A's played the New York Giants.

LARRY DOBY, HANK THOMPSON
The first black players to oppose each other in a major league game. In the first game of an August 9, 1947, doubleheader between the Indians and Browns, Doby appeared as a pinch-hitter for Cleveland and Thompson played second base for St. Louis.

BOBBY DOERR
Boston Red Sox's second baseman who hit the first home run in a night All-Star Game, connecting against Mort Cooper in the second inning of the 1943 classic.

PATSY DOUGHERTY
Boston right fielder who was the first player to hit two home runs in one World Series game, accomplishing the feat against Pittsburgh in Game 2 of the 1903 Series.

DAN DRIESSEN
The National League's first designated hitter. With the N.L. using a designated hitter only in even-numbered World Series (a format that began in 1976), Driessen got his chance with Cincinnati in the '76 Series against the New York Yankees. Driessen, who flied out in his first at-bat in the second inning of Game 1, batted .357 in the Series as the Reds' DH.

DON DRYSDALE
Los Angeles Dodgers' pitcher who threw the first All-Star Game and World Series pitches on the West Coast, both in 1959 (when the second All-Star Game of the year was played August 3 at the Los Angeles Memorial Coliseum and Game 3 of the '59 Series was played at the Coliseum on October 4).

DON DRYSDALE
The man who threw the first pitch in the first indoor All-Star Game, 1968, at Houston's Astrodome.

HOWARD EHMKE
Philadelphia Athletics' pitcher who on April 15, 1927, yielded the first of Babe Ruth's 60 home runs that season.

GLENN ELLIOTT
Boston Braves' pitcher who gave up Jackie Robinson's first major league hit. Robinson, playing for the Brooklyn Dodgers on April 17, 1947, collected a bunt single.

GEORGE FALLON
St. Louis Cardinals' shortstop who was the first batter to face Cincinnati's Joe Nuxhall when the Reds' pitcher made his debut in the majors at age 15 on

June 10, 1944. Fallon grounded out against the youngest player in big-league history.

HOBE FERRIS
Boston second baseman who committed the first error in World Series history, fumbling a ball hit by Pittsburgh's Kitty Bransfield in the first inning of Game 1 of the 1903 classic.

FIRST TEAMS
Many players have not achieved their greatest fame in the majors with their original big-league teams. Included among such players are:

Player	First Club	Debut Year
Joe Adcock	Cincinnati Reds	1950
Gus Bell	Pittsburgh Pirates	1950
Roger Bresnahan	Washington Senators	1897
Lou Brock	Chicago Cubs	1961
Mordecai Brown	St. Louis Cardinals	1903
Lew Burdette	New York Yankees	1950
Jesse Burkett	New York Giants	1890
Johnny Callison	Chicago White Sox	1958
Dolph Camilli	Chicago Cubs	1933
Norm Cash	Chicago White Sox	1957
Stan Coveleski	Philadelphia A's	1912
Sam Crawford	Cincinnati Red	1899
Joe Cronin	Pittsburgh Pirates	1926
Mike Cuellar	Cincinnati Reds	1959
Al Dark	Boston Braves	1946
Paul Derringer	St. Louis Cardinals	1931
Elmer Flick	Philadelphia Phillies	1898
Curt Flood	Cincinnati Reds	1956
George Foster	San Francisco Giants	1969
Nellie Fox	Philadelphia A's	1947
Woodie Fryman	Pittsburgh Pirates	1966
Al Gionfriddo	Pittsburgh Pirates	1944
Burleigh Grimes	Pittsburgh Pirates	1916
Jesse Haines	Cincinnati Reds	1918
Bob Hazle	Cincinnati Reds	1955
Waite Hoyt	New York Giants	1918
Randy Hundley	San Francisco Giants	1964
Joe Jackson	Philadelphia A's	1908
Ferguson Jenkins	Philadelphia Phillies	1965
Tommy John	Cleveland Indians	1963
Deron Johnson	New York Yankees	1960
Don Larsen	St. Louis Browns	1953

Ernie Lombardi	Brooklyn Dodgers	1931
Al Lopez	Brooklyn Dodgers	1928
Dolf Luque	Boston Braves	1914
Bill Madlock	Texas Rangers	1973
Roger Maris	Cleveland Indians	1957
Bing Miller	Washington Senators	1921
Manny Mota	San Francisco Giants	1962
Art Nehf	Boston Braves	1915
Bobo Newsom	Brooklyn Dodgers	1929
Bill Nicholson	Philadelphia A's	1936
Lefty O'Doul	New York Yankees	1919
Claude Osteen	Cincinnati Reds	1957
Amos Otis	New York Mets	1967
Roger Peckinpaugh	Cleveland Indians	1910
Herb Pennock	Philadelphia A's	1912
Billy Pierce	Detroit Tigers	1945
Lou Piniella	Baltimore Orioles	1964
Babe Ruth	Boston Red Sox	1914
Bob Turley	St. Louis Browns	1951
Dazzy Vance	Pittsburgh Pirates	1915
Dixie Walker	New York Yankees	1931
Bucky Walters	Philadelphia Phillies	1934
Bill White	New York Giants	1956
Ken Williams	Cincinnati Reds	1915
Hack Wilson	New York Giants	1923

FRANKIE FRISCH
St. Louis Cardinals' second baseman who hit the first National League home run in an All-Star Game, belting a sixth-inning homer off Alvin Crowder of the Washington Senators on July 6, 1933.

RALPH GARR
Outfielder for the Chicago White Sox who in an April 7, 1977, game against the Toronto Blue Jays became the first American League player to bat in Canada.

LOU GEHRIG
New York Yankees' first baseman who committed the first error in All-Star Game history when he dropped a foul fly ball in the fifth inning on July 6, 1933.

LEFTY GOMEZ
New York Yankee and American League hurler who threw the first pitch in All-Star Game competition on July 6, 1933, was the winning pitcher in the first classic and had the first run batted in.

Longtime Milwaukee Braves slugger Joe Adcock made his major league debut in a Cincinnati Reds uniform in 1950. Adcock played three seasons with the Reds before being traded to the Braves as part of a four-club deal in 1953.

JACK GRANEY
Cleveland Indians' left fielder who was the first player to bat against Babe Ruth (then a pitcher with the Boston Red Sox) in a major league game, July 11, 1914.

ELI GRBA
The Los Angeles Angels' first choice in the American League expansion draft in 1960. Grba, a pitcher, was picked from the New York Yankees' roster.

STAN HACK
Chicago Cubs' third baseman who was the first batter in a night All-Star Game, leading off the 1943 classic with a single.

The 1947 Philadelphia A's had a young-looking second baseman named Nellie Fox.

CHICK HAFEY
Cincinnati Reds' left fielder who singled in the second inning for the first hit in All-Star Game history, July 6, 1933.

BILL HALLAHAN
St. Louis Cardinal who was the first man to pitch for the National League in the All-Star Game and also the losing pitcher in the first classic, July 6, 1933.

LUKE HAMLIN
Brooklyn Dodgers' pitcher who lost to the Cincinnati Reds in the majors' first televised game, August 26, 1939.

TOMMY HARPER
The first batter in Seattle Pilots' history. Harper, a second baseman, led off the Pilots' first game on April 8, 1969, at Anaheim by doubling off Jim McGlothlin of the California Angels.

JOE HARRIS
Washington right fielder who became the first player to hit a home run in his first World Series at-bat. Harris homered for the Senators against the Pittsburgh Pirates in the second inning of Game 1 of the 1925 Series.

EARL HARRIST
The first pitcher to face Larry Doby of Cleveland when Doby became the first black player to appear in an American League game on July 5, 1947. Pitching for the Chicago White Sox, Harrist struck out the Indians' Doby (who was pinch-hitting for pitcher Bryan Stephens in the seventh inning).

FRANK HAYES
Athletics' catcher who hit the first home run in an American League night game, connecting against Cleveland at Philadelphia on May 16, 1939.

MIKE HEGAN
The first player to hit a home run for the Seattle Pilots, connecting off Jim McGlothlin of the California Angels on April 8, 1969.

BABE HERMAN
Cincinnati Reds' player whose home run against the Brooklyn Dodgers on July 10, 1935, was the first in a major league night game.

BILL HOFFER
Cleveland pitcher who lost the first game in American League history, against Chicago on April 24, 1901.

BOBO HOLLOMAN
The first pitcher in modern major league history to toss a nine-inning no-hitter in his first starting assignment. After four relief appearances earlier in the 1953 season, Holloman started for the St. Louis Browns against the Philadelphia Athletics on May 6. The rookie held the A's hitless in a 6-0 triumph, walking five batters and striking out three. Holloman also had two hits and three runs batted in (the only hits and RBIs of his big-league career). Holloman won only two more games, and on July 23 he owned a 3-7 record. At that juncture, he was sold to Toronto of the International League—never to return to the majors.

Wilson Alvarez of the Chicago White Sox held the Baltimore Orioles hitless in his first big-league start, August 10, 1991. Alvarez walked five and struck out seven in his 7-0 victory at Baltimore. The game was AAlvarez's first with the White Sox and only his second in the major leagues. Two years earlier, Alvarez relieved in a game for the Texas Rangers but failed to retire a bater. He allowed three runs on three hits and two walks in losing to Toronto.

Leon Ames of the New York Giants began his big-league career by pitching a five-inning no-hitter against St. Louis in the second game of a September 14, 1903, doubleheader. The game was called because of darkness.

CARL HUBBELL
Pitching for the New York Giants against the Boston Braves on April 16, 1935, Hubbell gave up Babe Ruth's first National League home run. The homer was Ruth's 709th career shot in the major leagues.

JOHNNY HUMPHRIES
Cleveland Indians' pitcher who beat the Athletics in the American League's first night game, May 16, 1939, at Philadelphia.

LARRY JASTER
Montreal Expos' hurler who threw the first major league pitch in Canada on April 14, 1969, against the St. Louis Cardinals.

JERRY JOHNSON
Toronto Blue Jays' pitcher who won the first American League game played in Canada, defeating the Chicago White Sox on April 7, 1977.

MACK JONES
Playing for the Montreal Expos against the St. Louis Cardinals on April 14, 1969, he hit the first major league home run in Canada.

RUPPERT JONES
The first selection of the Seattle Mariners in the American League's 1976 expansion draft. Jones, an outfielder, was chosen off the Kansas City Royals'

St. Louis Browns pitcher Bobo Holloman holds the game ball he received for his 1953 no-hitter against the Philadelphia A's and expresses his hope for the future with crossed fingers. The old crossed-finger trick did not work.

roster.

SAM JONES
The first black pitcher in major league history to toss a no-hitter, throwing a 4-0 gem for the Chicago Cubs against the Pittsburgh Pirates on May 12, 1955.

Jones also was the first black hurler to lose a game in which an opponent pitched a no-hitter. Warren Spahn of the Milwaukee Braves tossed a 1-0 no-hitter against Jones and the San Francisco Giants on April 28, 1961.

BRUCE KISON
Pittsburgh Pirates' reliever who was the winning pitcher against the Baltimore Orioles on October 13, 1971, in the first night game in World Series history. Kison worked 6 1/3 innings of one-hit, scoreless relief.

BILL KLEM
The home-plate umpire at Cincinnati on May 24, 1935, when the Reds and Philadelphia Phillies played the first night game in big-league history.

DAVE KOSLO
New York Giants' pitcher who gave up the first home run by a black player in major league history. Facing the Brooklyn Dodgers on April 18, 1947, Koslo surrendered a homer to Jackie Robinson.

HOBIE LANDRITH
Catcher who was the first player selected by the New York Mets in the National League expansion draft of 1961. Landrith was drafted off the San Francisco Giants' roster.

DON LARSEN
The starting and losing pitcher for Baltimore in its return to the American League in 1954 (the city's 1901-02 franchise became the New York Yankees). Larsen and the Orioles lost, 3-0, to the Detroit Tigers on April 13.

TOMMY LEACH
Pittsburgh Pirates' third baseman who collected the first hit in World Series play, tripling in the first inning off Cy Young of the Boston Red Sox on October 1, 1903.

BOB LEMON
Cleveland Indians' pitcher who hurled the American League's first night no-hitter, beating the Detroit Tigers, 2-0, on June 30, 1948, at Briggs Stadium.

Johnny Vander Meer's second of two straight no-hitters in 1938 was the National League's first night no-hit game.

EMIL (DUTCH) LEONARD
Washington Senators' hurler who was the winning pitcher in the first night All-Star Game, played July 13, 1943, at Shibe Park in Philadelphia.

LOS ANGELES DODGERS
The first major league club to attain three million in attendance in one year, attracting 3,347,845 fans in 1978.

CONNIE MACK
The first manager of an American League squad in All-Star Game history, piloting the A.L. in 1933.

FRED MARBERRY
Washington Senators' pitcher who on July 23, 1925, surrendered the first of Lou Gehrig's record 23 bases-loaded home runs in the major leagues.

PEPPER MARTIN
St. Louis Cardinals' third baseman who was the first batter in All-Star Game history on July 6, 1933. Martin grounded out to American League shortstop Joe Cronin of the Washington Senators.

DAL MAXVILL
Playing for the St. Louis Cardinals against the Montreal Expos, Maxvill slugged the major leagues' first bases-loaded homer in Canada on April 14, 1969.

VON McDANIEL
After two relief appearances, this St. Louis Cardinal pitcher (just out of high school) shut out the Brooklyn Dodgers, 2-0, on two hits in his first major league start on June 21, 1957. In his seventh start, he beat the Pittsburgh Pirates, 4-0, on a one-hitter and allowed one baserunner. The 18-year-old McDaniel, brother of longtime relief specialist Lindy, finished the season with a 7-5 record and a 3.21 earned-run average. But, losing his pitching rhythm, Von pitched in only two more big-league games (both in 1958) and was through as a major leaguer at age 19.

DAN McGINN
Montreal Expos' relief pitcher who won the first big-league game played in Canada, beating the St. Louis Cardinals on April 14, 1969.

JIM McGLOTHLIN
The first man to pitch against the Seattle Pilots—and he lasted only one-third of an inning for the California Angels, taking the loss in a 4-3 game played on April 8, 1969.

JOHN McGRAW
The first manager of a National League team in All-Star Game history, piloting the N.L. in 1933.

MILWAUKEE BRAVES
The first National League club to hit two million in attendance in one season, drawing 2, 131,388 fans in 1954.

DON MINCHER
First baseman who was the first pick of the Seattle Pilots in the 1968 American League expansion draft. Mincher was selected off the California Angels' roster.

DON MINCHER
The first—and only—member of the Seattle Pilots to appear in the All-Star Game. Mincher, pinch-hitting for Denny McLain in the fourth inning of the 1969 game, struck out against Bob Gibson.

WILLIE MITCHELL
Cleveland Indians' hurler who lost to Babe Ruth of the Boston Red Sox on July 11, 1914, when Ruth pitched and won his first big-league game.

RICK MONDAY
The first player selected in major league baseball's first amateur free-agent draft, chosen by the Kansas City Athletics in June of 1965.

MANNY MOTA
Infielder-outfielder who was the first player taken by the Montreal Expos in the National League's expansion draft in 1968. Mota was selected off the Pittsburgh Pirates' roster.

LES MUELLER
Detroit Tigers' pitcher who on April 17, 1945, surrendered the first hit, a single, in the major league career of Pete Gray, the St. Louis Browns' one-armed outfielder.

BILLY MYERS
Cincinnati shortstop who made the first hit in a major league night game. Leading off the first inning for the Reds against the Philadelphia Phillies in a May 24, 1935, game, Myers doubled.

ROGER NELSON
The first selection of the Kansas City Royals in the American League's expansion draft of 1968. Nelson, a pitcher, was picked off the Baltimore Orioles' roster.

NEW YORK YANKEES
The first big-league club to draw one million (1,289,422 in 1920) and two million (2,265,512 in 1946) in attendance in one season.

MICKEY OWEN
Brooklyn Dodgers' catcher who slugged the first pinch-hit home run in All-Star Game history, connecting in the 1942 classic. Owen did not homer in 133 regular-season games that year.

SATCHEL PAIGE

The first black pitcher to take the mound in the World Series. Paige worked two-thirds of an inning for the Cleveland Indians in Game 5 of the 1948 World Series against the Boston Braves, allowing no hits or walks.

Dan Bankhead of the Brooklyn Dodgers was the first black pitcher to appear in a World Series, but he was used only as a pinch-runner in Game 6 of the 1947 classic.

CLARENCE (ACE) PARKER

Future Pro Football Hall of Famer who in the first at-bat of a two-year career in big-league baseball slammed a pinch-hit home run for the Philadelphia Athletics. Parker connected against Wes Ferrell of the Boston Red Sox on April 30, 1937.

ROY PARMELEE

Philadelphia Athletics' pitcher who lost to the Cleveland Indians in the first night game in American League history, May 16, 1939, at Philadelphia.

ROY PATTERSON

Chicago hurler who made the first pitch in American League history on April 24, 1901, against Cleveland and was the winning pitcher in the A.L.'s first game.

MARTY PATTIN

The first pitcher in the history of the Seattle Pilots. Pattin was the starter and winner—he worked five innings—in the Pilots' 4-3 triumph over the California Angels on April 8, 1969.

HERB PENNOCK

Pitcher for the Boston Red Sox who gave up Babe Ruth's first home run as a New York Yankee on May 1, 1920. It was Ruth's 50th lifetime homer.

GAYLORD PERRY

Cleveland Indians' pitcher who gave up Hank Aaron's first American League home run (the 734th homer of Aaron's big-league career). Aaron connected on April 18, 1975, as a member of the Milwaukee Brewers.

EDDIE PHELPS

Pittsburgh Pirates' catcher who in Game 1 of the 1903 World Series became the first man to strike out in Series play. Phelps fanned in the first inning against Cy Young of the Boston Red Sox, but reached first base when the ball got away from catcher Lou Criger.

DEACON PHILLIPPE
the winning pitcher in the first World Series game in history. Pitching for the Pittsburgh Pirates on October 1, 1903, Phillippe hurled a six-hit, 7-3 victory against the Boston Red Sox.

OLLIE PICKERING
Cleveland right fielder who was the first batter in American League history, going to the plate against Chicago on April 24, 1901.

LOU PINIELLA
The first designated hitter in World Series history. Playing for the New York Yankees against the Cincinnati Reds in Game 1 of the '76 Series, Piniella led off the second inning with a double.

JAMIE QUIRK, DAN QUISENBERRY
The majors' first "Q" battery. With Quirk catching for the Kansas City Royals in an April 13, 1980, game against the Detroit Tigers, Quisenberry came on as a relief pitcher in the seventh inning.

VIC RASCHI
Pitching for the St. Louis Cardinals against the Milwaukee Braves on April 23, 1954, he gave up the first home run of Hank Aaron's major league career.

ROBIN ROBERTS
The first man to pitch under artificial-turf conditions in the major leagues, hurling for the Houston Astros in an April 18, 1966, game against the Los Angeles Dodgers at the Astrodome. The Astrodome, which opened in 1965 and had natural grass during its first season, began the 1966 season with only an AstroTurf infield, but its outfield was covered with synthetic grass later in the year.

FRANK ROBINSON
The first black manager in major league history, making his debut as Cleveland's pilot on April 8, 1975, when the Indians played their American League season opener against the New York Yankees. In the Tribe's lineup as a designated hitter, Robinson homered against Doc Medich in the first inning.

Robinson also was the first black manager in National League history, making his debut for the San Francisco Giants on April 9, 1981.

BILL ROHR
Boston pitcher who in his first big-league game in 1967 went 8 2/3 innings without allowing a hit before Elston Howard of the Yankees—on a 3-2 pitch—singled. Rohr, whose batterymate (Russ Gibson) also was making his debut in the majors, finished with a one-hit, 3-0 triumph in New York's home opener—

Frank Robinson gets a cold greeting from John Lowenstein after hitting a first-inning home run in his debut as Cleveland's player-manager.

but he pitched in only nine more games for the Red Sox and 17 for the Cleveland Indians before bowing out of the big leagues in 1968 at age 23.

SCHOOLBOY ROWE
The first player to appear for both leagues in All-Star Game competition. Rowe, representing the Detroit Tigers, pitched for the American League in 1936; as a member of the Philadelphia Phillies, he pinch-hit for the National League's Warren Spahn in 1947.

JOE RUDI
Left fielder who played his first game for Oakland on May 8, 1968—the night that Jim (Catfish) Hunter of the A's pitched a perfect game against the Minnesota Twins. Rudi had played 19 games for the Kansas City A's in 1967.

BABE RUTH
New York Yankees' right fielder who hit the first home run in All-Star Game competition, connecting in the third inning off Bill Hallahan of the St. Louis Cardinals on July 6, 1933.

JOHNNY SAIN
The first pitcher to face Jackie Robinson in the majors. Sain, pitching for the Boston Braves against the Brooklyn Dodgers on April 15, 1947, got Robinson—in his first at-bat as the first black player in modern big-league history—to ground out to third baseman Bob Elliott in the first inning.

JOE SCHULTZ
The first—and only—manager of the American League's Seattle Pilots, who moved to Milwaukee and became the Brewers after one season, 1969, in Seattle.

JIMMY SEBRING
Right fielder for the Pittsburgh Pirates who hit the first home run in World Series competition, connecting against Cy Young of the Boston Red Sox in the seventh inning of Game 1 of the 1903 Series.

BOBBY SHANTZ
Pitcher who was the first choice of the Washington Senators (second club) in the American League expansion draft of 1960. Shantz was selected off the New York Yankees' roster.

SHIBE PARK
Philadelphia stadium that was the site of the first night All-Star Game in major league history, July 13, 1943.

Boston pitcher Bill Rohr's 1967 debut was memorable as he held the Yankees hitless until Elston Howard singled with two out in the ninth inning.

Yankee slugger Babe Ruth trots home after hitting the first home run in All-Star Game history in 1933 at Chicago's Comiskey Park.

BILL SINGER
Facing the Chicago White Sox on April 7, 1977, the Toronto Blue Jays' Singer threw the first pitch in the first American League game played in Canada.

ELMER SMITH
Cleveland Indians' right fielder who was the first player to hit a bases-loaded home run in World Series play. Smith walloped his grand slam against the Brooklyn Dodgers in the first inning of Game 5 of the 1920 Series.

KARL SPOONER
One of only nine players to pitch shutouts in their first two big-league games, Spooner made perhaps the most dramatic debut by striking out a total of 27 batters. Called up by the Brooklyn Dodgers from Fort Worth late in the 1954 season, Spooner shut out the New York Giants, 3-0, on three hits September 22 and blanked the Pittsburgh Pirates, 1-0, on four hits September 26. Spooner, who struck out 15 Giants and 12 Pirates, went 8-6 in 1955 and then bowed out of the majors at age 24 because of arm trouble.

DON SUTTON
The winning pitcher in the first major league game played on artificial turf, hurling the Los Angeles Dodgers past the Houston Astros in an April 18, 1966, game at the Astrodome.

IRA THOMAS
Detroit Tigers' player who notched the first pinch hit in World Series history, singling against the Chicago Cubs in the ninth inning of Game 1 of the 1908 Series.

HANK THOMPSON
An infielder-outfielder, he was the first black player for two major league teams—the St. Louis Browns (1947) and the New York Giants (1949). When Thompson made his debut with the Giants, another black, Monte Irvin, appeared in the same game for New York. Thompson, though, started at second base; Irvin was used as a late-inning pinch-hitter.

HECTOR TORRES
Playing for the Toronto Blue Jays against the New York Yankees on June 27, 1977, Torres hit the first bases-loaded home run in Canada in American League history.

GUS TRIANDOS
The first man to catch no-hitters in both major leagues. Triandos caught for Baltimore in 1958 when the Orioles' Hoyt Wilhelm pitched a no-hit game against the New York Yankees, and he caught for Philadelphia in 1964 when the Phillies' Jim Bunning threw a perfect game against the New York Mets.

ARKY VAUGHAN
Shortstop for the Pittsburgh Pirates who in 1941 became the first player to hit two home runs in an All-Star Game.

LUKE WALKER
Pittsburgh Pirates' pitcher who delivered the first pitch in a World Series night game, October 13, 1971, against the Baltimore Orioles.

MOSES (FLEET) WALKER
The first black player in major league history. Walker, a catcher, made his debut on May 1, 1884, when he caught for Toledo against Louisville in an American Association game.

BUCKY WALTERS
Cincinnati Reds' pitcher who won big-league baseball's first televised game, beating the Brooklyn Dodgers on a two-hitter on August 26, 1939.

JACK WARHOP
Pitching for the New York Yankees against the Boston Red Sox on May 6, 1915, he surrendered the first home run of Babe Ruth's major league career.

GARY WASLEWSKI
Pitcher for the St. Louis Cardinals who was the loser in the first big-league game played in Canada, beaten by the Montreal Expos on April 14, 1969.

EDDIE WATT
Baltimore Orioles' reliever who was the losing pitcher against the Pittsburgh Pirates on October 13, 1971, in the first night game in World Series history.

ROY WEATHERLY
Cleveland Indians' center fielder who was the first man to bat in an American League night game, May 16, 1939, in Philadelphia.

BILLY WERBER
Cincinnati third baseman who was the first batter in major league baseball's first televised game, the Reds' August 26, 1939, game against the Dodgers at Brooklyn.

WALLY WESTLAKE
Playing for the Pittsburgh Pirates on June 18, 1948, he hit a home run off the Philadelphia Phillies' Robin Roberts—the first of a major league-record 505 homers surrendered by Roberts during his career.

ART WILLIAMS
The first black umpire in the National League. Williams umpired in the N.L. from 1973 through 1977.

MAURY WILLS
Los Angeles Dodgers' player who was the first man to bat on an artificial surface in a big-league game, leading off against the Houston Astros on April 18, 1966, at the Astrodome.

CY YOUNG
The losing pitcher in the first World Series game in history. Pitching for the Boston Red Sox on October 1, 1903, Young was a 7-3 loser to the Pittsburgh Pirates. He went the distance, allowing 12 hits.

ROSS YOUNGS
New York Giant who was the first player in World Series competition to collect two hits in one inning. Youngs accomplished the feat against the New York Yankees in 1921, doubling and tripling in the seventh inning of Game 3.

RICHIE ZISK
The first American Leaguer to belt a home run in Canada, connecting for the Chicago White Sox against the Toronto Blue Jays on April 7, 1977.

SEVENTH INNING
Notable lasts

HANK AARON, JOE TORRE
The last members of the Milwaukee Braves to play in an All-Star Game, both playing the entire game for the National League in 1965 at Bloomington, Minn. Torre slugged a two-run homer for the N.L. in the first inning.

BABE ADAMS
Pittsburgh pitcher who was beaten, 1-0, by Boston's Cy Young in Young's 511th and last major league victory, September 22, 1911.

BOB ALLISON
The last player to hit a home run for Washington's original American League franchise, connecting for the Senators on September 28, 1960.

WALTER ALSTON
The last manager of the Brooklyn Dodgers, piloting the team in 1957. Alston also managed the club in the three previous seasons, and he guided the Los Angeles Dodgers from 1958 through 1976.

LUKE APPLING
The last manager of the Kansas City Athletics, succeeding Alvin Dark on August 21, 1967, and guiding the club for the rest of the season.

JIM BIVIN
The last man to pitch to Babe Ruth in a major league game. Bivin, pitching for the Philadelphia Phillies against the Boston Braves in the first game of a May 30, 1935, doubleheader at Baker Bowl, retired Ruth in the first inning on a grounder to first baseman Dolph Camilli. Ruth left the game shortly after his first at-bat and never played again.

TINY BONHAM
Pitcher for the New York Yankees who on September 16, 1945, surrendered the last major league hit by Pete Gray, one-armed outfielder of the St. Louis Browns.

BOSTON BRAVES
Facing the Dodgers at Ebbets Field on September 28, 1952, Boston played Brooklyn to a 5-5 tie in the Braves' last game before moving to Milwaukee in 1953. The 12-inning game was called because of darkness. Boston's last National League victory came on September 27, 1952, when pitcher Virgil

171

Jester notched his third and last big league triumph by beating Joe Black and the Dodgers, 11-3.

LOU BOUDREAU
The last player-manager in the major leagues to lead his team to a pennant. Boudreau, a shortstop, batted .355 with 18 home runs and 106 RBIs for his 1948 Cleveland Indians, American League and World Series champions.

BOBBY BRAGAN
The last manager of the Milwaukee Braves, piloting the club in 1965. Bragan, who took over as the Braves' manager in 1963, continued to manage the club when it moved to Atlanta in 1966—but he was dismissed in August of '66.

BROOKLYN DODGERS
Playing their final game before moving to Los Angeles in 1958, the Dodgers lost to the Phillies, 2-1, on September 29, 1957, at Philadelphia. Seth Morehead, collecting the first of only five career victories in the majors, outdueled Roger Craig, the last pitcher of record in Brooklyn history.

MORDECAI BROWN, CHRISTY MATHEWSON
Future Hall of Famers whose pitching matchup on September 4, 1916, marked the last major league playing appearance for both men. Mathewson, Cincinnati's manager, hurled his only game for the Reds that day and beat Brown and the Chicago Cubs, 10-8, in the second game of a doubleheader. Both pitchers went the distance, with Mathewson yielding 15 hits and Brown allowing 19.

GUY BUSH
Pittsburgh pitcher who surrendered the final two home runs of Babe Ruth's big-league career. Playing for the Boston Braves against the Pirates on May 25, 1935, Ruth slugged three homers in the game—the first off Red Lucas and the last two (No. 713 and No. 714, lifetime) against Bush.

STEVE CARLTON
The last pitcher to collect a hit in the All-Star Game. Carlton, St. Louis Cardinals' pitcher, started for the National League in the 1969 game and hit a run-scoring double off Blue Moon Odom in the third inning.

SYD COHEN
Washington Senators' pitcher who yielded a home run to Babe Ruth of the New York Yankees on September 29, 1934—the 708th and last American League homer for Ruth.

RAY CULP
Philadelphia Phillies' pitcher who surrendered Hank Aaron's 398th and last home run for the Milwaukee Braves on September 20, 1965.

EDDIE DENT
Brooklyn pitcher who beat Boston's Cy Young in Young's final appearance in the majors, an October 6, 1911, National League game.

DICK DRAGO
Pitching for the California Angels against the Milwaukee Brewers on July 20, 1976, he allowed Hank Aaron's 755th and last major league home run.

DAVE DUNCAN
The last player to hit a home run for the Kansas City A's, connecting on October 1, 1967.

STEVE DUNNING
The last American League pitcher to hit a bases-loaded home run. Playing for the Cleveland Indians in a May 11, 1971, game against the Oakland A's, Dunning walloped his grand slam off Diego Segui in the second inning.

RAWLY EASTWICK
Pitching for the Cincinnati Reds against the Atlanta Braves on October 2, 1974, Eastwick gave up Hank Aaron's 733rd and last National League home run.

EBBETS FIELD
Pitching for Brooklyn on September 24, 1957, in the last big-league game at Ebbets Field, Danny McDevitt of the Dodgers blanked Pittsburgh, 2-0. The Pirates' losing pitcher was Bennie Daniels, who was making his debut in the majors.

BOB ELLIOTT
The last member of the Boston Braves to play in an All-Star Game, competing in the 1951 classic in Detroit. Elliott hit a two-run homer for the National League.

LARRY FRENCH
Brooklyn Dodgers' pitcher who in the last appearance of his major league career faced the minimum 27 batters, hurling a one-hit, 6-0 triumph against the Philadelphia Phillies on September 23, 1942. Nick Etten got the lone hit off French, a second-inning single, but was erased in a double play. French, who turned 35 a little more than a month after the regular season concluded, soon went into the Navy and his big-league career was at an end.

MIGUEL FUENTES
Making his eighth and last appearance in the major leagues, reliever Fuentes pitched the final inning in the history of the Seattle Pilots. Fuentes worked the ninth inning against the Oakland A's on October 2, 1969.

Camera Day proved a big attraction at Ebbets Field on August 24, 1957—exactly a month from the day that the last big-league game was played at the Brooklyn ballpark.

JIM GANTNER
Milwaukee player who pinch-ran for the Brewers' Hank Aaron in Aaron's last big-league game, October 3, 1976, against the Detroit Tigers.

JIM GOSGER
The last batter to face Satchel Paige in a major league game. Batting for the Boston Red Sox against the Kansas City A's with two out in the third inning of a September 25, 1965, game, Gosger grounded out against the 59-year-old Paige.

BURLEIGH GRIMES
The last of 17 legalized spitball pitchers in the majors, making his final appearance on September 20, 1934, for the Pittsburgh Pirates against the Brooklyn Dodgers. Grimes pitched one inning, the eighth, and surrendered no hits or walks, striking out one batter (Joe Stripp, the last man he faced in the big leagues).

On February 10, 1920, a rules change barred the spitball. Recognizing that some pitchers were in effect making a living by using the spitter, baseball officials certified 17 hurlers as legalized spitballers—meaning those pitchers could throw the pitch for the remainder of their careers; otherwise, the spitter was outlawed. The 17 pitchers, their 1920 clubs and the years that their big-league careers spanned:

American League
Doc Ayers, Detroit, 1913-21
Ray Caldwell, Cleveland, 1910-21
Stan Coveleski, Cleveland, 1912-28
Urban Faber, Chicago, 1914-33
Hub Leonard, Detroit, 1913-25
Jack Quinn, New York, 1909-33
Allan Russell, Boston, 1915-25
Urban Shocker, St. Louis, 1916-28
Allen Sothoron, St. Louis, 1914-26

National League
Bill Doak, St. Louis, 1912-29
Phil Douglas, New York, 1912-22
Dana Fillingim, Boston, 1915-25
Ray Fisher, Cincinnati, 1910-20
Marv Goodwin, St. Louis, 1916-25
Grimes, Brooklyn, 1916-34
Clarence Mitchell, Brooklyn, 1911-32
Dick Rudolph, Boston, 1910-27

CHARLEY GRIMM
The last manager of the Boston Braves. Grimm replaced Tommy Holmes early in the 1952 season, the Braves' final year in Boston, and then managed the Milwaukee Braves from 1953 until mid-June of 1956.

BUMP HADLEY
Washington Senators' pitcher who gave up Ty Cobb's final major league hit. Cobb, pinch-hitting for Philadelphia A's shortstop Joe Boley, doubled off Hadley on September 3, 1928.

175

CARROLL HARDY
Boston player who went in defensively for Ted Williams in the ninth inning of a September 28, 1960, game against the Baltimore Orioles after the Red Sox's left fielder had homered an inning earlier in his last major league at-bat.

GAIL HARRIS
The last player to hit a home run for the New York Giants, connecting in the second game of a doubleheader on September 21, 1957. Harris slugged two homers in that game.

RORIC HARRISON
The last American League pitcher to hit a regular-season home run, connecting for the Baltimore Orioles against Ray Lamb of the Cleveland Indians in the second game of an October 3, 1972, doubleheader.

Ken Holtzman is the last A.L. pitcher to hit a home run, belting one for the Oakland A's in the 1974 World Series.

JIM HICKMAN
The last player to hit a home run at New York's Polo Grounds, connecting for the New York Mets against the Philadelphia Phillies on September 18, 1963.

GIL HODGES
The last representative of the Brooklyn Dodgers to play in an All-Star Game, pinch-hitting in the bottom of the ninth inning in 1957 for Brooklyn teammate Clem Labine (who had pitched the top of the ninth). Gino Cimoli of the Dodgers pinch-hit in the eighth for the National League in the game played at St. Louis.

FRANK HOWARD
The last representative of Washington's second American League franchise to play in an All-Star Game, appearing in the 1971 game at Detroit, he also was the last to homer for them.

BILLY HUNTER
The last player to hit a home run for the St. Louis Browns, connecting on September 26, 1953.

JIM (CATFISH) HUNTER
The last representative of the Kansas City Athletics to appear in an All-Star Game, pitching the final five innings for the American League in the 15-inning game played at Anaheim in 1967. He was the loser as the N.L. won, 2-1.

RANSOM JACKSON
The last player to hit a home run for the Brooklyn Dodgers, connecting on September 28, 1957.

HENRY JOHNSON
New York Yankees' pitcher who retired Ty Cobb of the Philadelphia Athletics in Cobb's final major league at-bat. Pinch-hitting for A's third baseman Jimmie Dykes against Johnson on September 11, 1928, Cobb popped out to New York shortstop Mark Koenig.

EDDIE JOOST
The last manager of the Philadelphia Athletics, guiding the club in 1954.

RIP JORDAN
Pitching for the Washington Senators in the fifth and last game of his big-league career, Jordan surrendered Babe Ruth's final home run as a member of the Boston Red Sox on September 27, 1919. The homer was the 49th of Ruth's major league career.

KANSAS CITY ATHLETICS
Jim (Catfish) Hunter was the last pitcher of record for the Kansas City A's, dropping a 4-3 decision to the Yankees at New York on October 1, 1967. Mel Stottlemyre was the winning pitcher against the A's, who were playing their final game before moving to Oakland in 1968.

BOB KLINE
Pitcher for the Boston Red Sox who was defeated by Babe Ruth of the New York Yankees in Ruth's last big-league pitching appearance, October 1, 1933.

GARY KOLB
St. Louis player who ran for the Cardinals' Stan Musial on September 29, 1963, after Musial singled in his last at-bat in the majors. Musial collected the hit—the 3,630th of his big-league career—off Cincinnati's Jim Maloney in the sixth inning of the season finale.

HARVEY KUENN
The last batter in two of Sandy Koufax's four career no-hitters with the Los Angeles Dodgers. Kuenn, San Francisco's left fielder on May 11, 1963, grounded back to Koufax for the final out in the Dodger pitcher's no-hitter against the Giants; pinch-hitting for Chicago pitcher Bob Hendley on September 9, 1965, he struck out to end Koufax's perfect game against the Cubs.

PETE LaCOCK
Pinch-hitting for the Chicago Cubs against the St. Louis Cardinals on September 3, 1975, LaCock collected the last big-league hit given up by Bob Gibson—a bases-loaded home run.

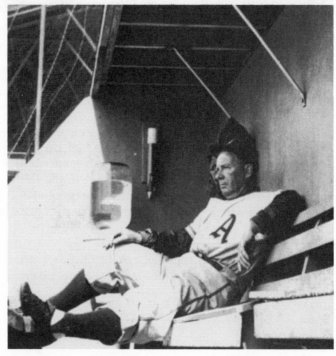

Owner Connie Mack (left) signs Eddie Joost (right) as the Athletics' manager for 1954—the A's last season in Philadelphia.

Joost succeeded Jimmie Dykes, who managed the club from 1951 through 1953 after taking over for Mack.

LAST OUTS IN PERFECT GAMES

June 12, 1880   John Richmond, Worcester (N.L.), 1-0.
Losing pitcher—Jim McCormick, Cleveland.
LAST OUT—Left fielder Ned Hanlon.

June 17, 1880   John Montgomery (Monte) Ward, Providence (N.L.), 5-0.
Losing pitcher—Jim (Pud) Galvin, Buffalo.
LAST OUT—Galvin.

May 5, 1904   Cy Young, Boston (A.L.), 3-0.
Losing pitcher—Rube Waddell, Philadelphia.
LAST OUT—Waddell.

October 2, 1908   Addie Joss, Cleveland (A.L.), 1-0.
Losing pitcher—Ed Walsh, Chicago.
LAST OUT—John Anderson, pinch-hitting for Walsh.

June 23, 1917   Ernie Shore, Boston (A.L.), 4-0.
(first game)   Losing pitcher—Doc Ayers, Washington.
LAST OUT—Mike Menosky, pinch-hitting for Ayers.

April 30, 1922   Charley Robertson, Chicago (A.L.), 2-0.
Losing pitcher—Herman Pillette, Detroit.
LAST OUT—John Bassler, pinch-hitting for Pillette.

October 8, 1956   Don Larsen, New York (A.L.), 2-0, World Series.
Losing pitcher—Sal Maglie, Brooklyn.
LAST OUT—Dale Mitchell, pinch-hitting for Maglie.

May 26, 1959   Harvey Haddix, Pittsburgh (N.L.), 0-1, lost in 13th inning
on one hit.
Winning pitcher—Lew Burdette, Milwaukee.
LAST BATTER—First baseman Joe Adcock, Milwaukee.
Adcock hit a run-scoring double in the 13th inning.

June 21, 1964   Jim Bunning, Philadelphia (N.L.), 6-0.
(first game)   Losing pitcher—Tracy Stallard, New York.
LAST OUT—John Stephenson, pinch-hitting for relief
pitcher Tom Sturdivant.

Sept. 9, 1965   Sandy Koufax, Los Angeles (N.L.), 1-0.
Losing pitcher—Bob Hendley, Chicago.
LAST OUT—Harvey Kuenn, pinch-hitting for Hendley.

May 8, 1968   Jim (Catfish) Hunter, Oakland (A.L.), 4-0.
Losing pitcher—Dave Boswell, Minnesota.
LAST OUT—Rich Reese, pinch-hitting for relief pitcher
Ron Perranoski.

May 15, 1981   Len Barker, Cleveland (A.L.), 3-0.
Losing pitcher—Luis Leal, Toronto.
LAST OUT—Ernie Whitt, pinch-hitting for catcher Buck
Martinez.

Sept. 30, 1984   Mike Witt (California A.L.), 1-0
Losing pitcher—Charlie Hough, Texas.
LAST OUT—Marvis Foley, pinch-hitting for shortstop
Curtis Wilkerson.

Sept.16, 1988   Tom Browning (Cincinnati N.L.), 1-0
Losing pitcher—Tim Belcher, Los Angeles
LAST OUT—Tracy Woodson, pinch-hitting for Belcher.

July 28, 1991   Dennis Martinez (Montreal N.L.), 2-0
Losing pitcher—Mike Morgan, Los Angeles
LAST OUT—Chris Gwynn, pinch-hitting for Morgan.

LAST TEAMS

Many notable players ended their major league careers on teams with whom
they are seldom associated. Included among such players are:

Player	Last Club	Final Year
Hank Aaron	Milwaukee Brewers	1976
Joe Adcock	California Angels	1966
Grover Alexander	Philadelphia Phillies	1930
Richie Allen	Oakland A's	1977
Felipe Alou	Milwaukee Brewers	1974
Jesus Alou	Houston Astros	1979
Matty Alou	San Diego Padres	1974
Luis Aparicio	Boston Red Sox	1973
Richie Ashburn	New York Mets	1962
Earl Averill	Boston Braves	1941
Chief Bender	Chicago White Sox	1925
Wally Berger	Philadelphia Phillies	1940
Yogi Berra	New York Mets	1965
Bobby Bonds	Chicago Cubs	1981
Jim Bottomley	St. Louis Browns	1937
Lou Boudreau	Boston Red Sox	1952

Jim Bunning, the father of six at the time, celebrated Father's Day in 1964 by pitching a perfect game against the Mets, getting John Stephenson on a strikeout to end the game.

Jim (Catfish) Hunter receives a victory ride after striking out Minnesota's Rich Reese for the final out in his perfect game.

Ken Boyer	Los Angeles Dodgers	1969
Roger Bresnahan	Chicago Cubs	1915
Ken Brett	Kansas City Royals	1981
Lew Burdette	California Angels	1967
Jesse Burkett	Boston Red Sox	1905
Johnny Callison	New York Yankees	1973
Dolph Camilli	Boston Red Sox	1945
Max Carey	Brooklyn Dodgers	1929
Phil Cavarretta	Chicago White Sox	1955
Orlando Cepeda	Kansas City Royals	1974
Frank Chance	New York Yankees	1914
Ben Chapman	Philadelphia Phillies	1946
Jack Chesbro	Boston Red Sox	1909
Ty Cobb	Philadelphia A's	1928
Rocky Colavito	New York Yankees	1968
Jocko Conlan	Chicago White Sox	1935
Stan Coveleski	New York Yankees	1928
Mike Cuellar	California Angels	1977
Kiki Cuyler	Brooklyn Dodgers	1938
Al Dark	Milwaukee Braves	1960
Tommy Davis	Kansas City Royals	1976
Willie Davis	San Diego Padres	1976
Dizzy Dean	St. Louis Browns	1947
Paul Dean	St. Louis Browns	1943
Ed Delahanty	Washington Senators	1903
Paul Derringer	Chicago Cubs	1945
Hugh Duffy	Philadelphia Phillies	1906
Del Ennis	Chicago White Sox	1959
Johnny Evers	Boston Braves	1929
Roy Face	Montreal Expos	1969
Ron Fairly	California Angels	1978
Wes Ferrell	Boston Braves	1941
Curt Flood	Washington Senators	1971
Nellie Fox	Houston Astros	1965
Jimmie Foxx	Philadelphia Phillies	1945
Larry French	Brooklyn Dodgers	1942
Bob Friend	New York Mets	1966
Lefty Gomez	Washington Senators	1943
Goose Goslin	Washington Senators	1938
Hank Greenberg	Pittsburgh Pirates	1947
Burleigh Grimes	Pittsburgh Pirates	1934
Dick Groat	San Francisco Giants	1967
Don Gutteridge	Pittsburgh Pirates	1948
Harvey Haddix	Baltimore Orioles	1965
Granny Hamner	Kansas City A's	1962

Tommy Harper	Oakland A's	1975
Bucky Harris	Detroit Tigers	1931
Gabby Hartnett	New York Giants	1941
Bob Hazle	Detroit Tigers	1958
Harry Heilmann	Cincinnati Reds	1932
Billy Herman	Pittsburgh Pirates	1947
Gil Hodges	New York Mets	1963
Tommy Holmes	Brooklyn Dodgers	1952
Rogers Hornsby	St. Louis Browns	1937
Willie Horton	Seattle Mariners	1980
Elston Howard	Boston Red Sox	1968
Frank Howard	Detroit Tigers	1973
Waite Hoyt	Brooklyn Dodgers	1938
Randy Hundley	San Diego Padres	1975
Ron Hunt	St. Louis Cardinals	1974
Monte Irvin	Chicago Cubs	1956
Julian Javier	Cincinnati Reds	1972
Deron Johnson	Boston Red Sox	1976
George Kell	Baltimore Orioles	1957
George Kelly	Brooklyn Dodgers	1932
Harmon Killebrew	Kansas City Royals	1975
Ralph Kiner	Cleveland Indians	1955
Ted Kluszewski	Los Angeles Angels	1961
Harvey Kuenn	Philadelphia Phillies	1966
Nap Lajoie	Philadelphia A's	1916
Don Larsen	Chicago Cubs	1967
Fred Lindstrom	Brooklyn Dodgers	1936
Dick Littlefield	Milwaukee Braves	1958
Mickey Lolich	San Diego Padres	1979
Al Lopez	Cleveland Indians	1947
Sherry Magee	Cincinnati Reds	1919
Sal Maglie	St. Louis Cardinals	1958
Heinie Manush	Pittsburgh Pirates	1939
Juan Marichal	Los Angeles Dodgers	1975
Roger Maris	St. Louis Cardinals	1968
Billy Martin	Minnesota Twins	1961
Eddie Mathews	Detroit Tigers	1968
Christy Mathewson	Cincinnati Reds	1916
Carl Mays	New York Giants	1929
Willie Mays	New York Mets	1973
Sam McDowell	Pittsburgh Pirates	1975
Stuffy McInnis	Philadelphia Phillies	1927
Denny McLain	Atlanta Braves	1972
Roy McMillan	New York Mets	1966
Dave McNally	Montreal Expos	1975

Dizzy Dean's last appearance in the majors came in 1947 with St. Louis—the Browns, that is. Dean, a former Cardinal great, faced the Chicago White Sox as a publicity stunt in the '47 season finale—and pitched four scoreless innings.

Harmon Killebrew hit the last 14 of his 573 career home runs for the Kansas City Royals, with whom he finished his career in 1975.

Bob Meusel	Cincinnati Reds	1930
Bing Miller	Boston Red Sox	1936
Art Nehf	Chicago Cubs	1929
Don Newcombe	Cleveland Indians	1960
Hal Newhouser	Cleveland Indians	1955
Lefty O'Doul	New York Giants	1934
Claude Osteen	Chicago White Sox	1975
Mickey Owen	Boston Red Sox	1954
Camilo Pascual	Cleveland Indians	1971
Roger Peckinpaugh	Chicago White Sox	1927
Herb Pennock	Boston Red Sox	1934
Joe Pepitone	Atlanta Braves	1973
Jim Perry	Oakland A's	1975
Johnny Pesky	Washington Senators	1954
Billy Pierce	San Francisco Giants	1964
Vada Pinson	Kansas City Royals	1975
Eddie Plank	St. Louis Browns	1917
Wally Post	Cleveland Indians	1964
Boog Powell	Los Angeles Dodgers	1977
Pete Reiser	Cleveland Indians	1952
Sam Rice	Cleveland Indians	1934
Robin Roberts	Chicago Cubs	1966
Frank Robinson	Cleveland Indians	1976
Red Ruffing	Chicago White Sox	1947
Babe Ruth	Boston Braves	1935
Ron Santo	Chicago White Sox	1974
Hank Sauer	San Francisco Giants	1959
Ray Schalk	New York Giants	1929
Curt Simmons	California Angels	1967
George Sisler	Boston Braves	1930
Moose Skowron	California Angels	1967
Enos Slaughter	Milwaukee Braves	1959
Duke Snider	San Francisco Giants	1964
Warren Spahn	San Francisco Giants	1965
Tris Speaker	Philadelphia A's	1928
Casey Stengel	Boston Braves	1925
Junior Stephens	Chicago White Sox	1955
Dick Stuart	California Angels	1969
Bobby Thomson	Baltimore Orioles	1960
Virgil Trucks	New York Yankees	1958
Bob Turley	Boston Red Sox	1963
Mickey Vernon	Pittsburgh Pirates	1960
Joe Vosmik	Washington Senators	1944
Rube Waddell	St. Louis Browns	1910
Dixie Walker	Pittsburgh Pirates	1949

Bucky Walters	Boston Braves	1950
Paul Waner	New York Yankees	1945
Vic Wertz	Minnesota Twins	1963
Zack Wheat	Philadelphia A's	1927
Hoyt Wilhelm	Los Angeles Dodgers	1972
Billy Williams	Oakland A's	1976
Ken Williams	Boston Red Sox	1929
Hack Wilson	Philadelphia Phillies	1934
Jimmy Wynn	Milwaukee Brewers	1977
Rudy York	Philadelphia A's	1948
Cy Young	Boston Braves	1911

COOKIE LAVAGETTO
The last manager for Washington's first American League franchise, piloting the Senators in 1960. Lavagetto, who took over as the Senators' manager on May 7, 1957, continued to manage the club when it moved to Minnesota in 1961—but he lasted only 74 games at the Twins' helm.

HAL LEE
Boston Braves' player who replaced Babe Ruth in left field against the Philadelphia Phillies on May 30, 1935, when Ruth—making his last big-league appearance—left the first game of a doubleheader shortly after batting in the first inning.

JIM LEMON
The last representative of Washington's first American League franchise to play in an All-Star Game, participating in the first game in 1960 at Kansas City.

EMIL LEVSEN
Cleveland pitcher who was the last major leaguer to hurl two complete-game victories in one day. Levsen and the Indians beat the Boston Red Sox, 6-1 and 5-1, on August 28, 1926.

LOU LIMMER
The last player to hit a home run for the Philadelphia A's, connecting on September 25, 1954. The homer was the last of 19 for Limmer in the major leagues.

MARTY MARION
The last manager of the St. Louis Browns. Marion, who took over the job during the 1952 season, managed the Browns for all of 1953 (their final year).

EDDIE MATHEWS
The last player to hit a home run for the Boston Braves, connecting on

Paul Waner managed only one hit as a New York Yankee—and it was the 3,152nd and last of his major league career.

September 27, 1952. The homer was one of three Mathews slugged that day.

JON MATLACK
New York Mets' pitcher who surrendered Roberto Clemente's 3,000th and last regular-season major league hit (a double) in a September 30, 1972, game against the Pittsburgh Pirates.

WILLIE MAYS
The last member of the New York Giants to play in an All-Star Game, hitting a single and triple in four at-bats for the National League in 1957 at St. Louis.

MILWAUKEE BRAVES
Playing the Dodgers on October 3, 1965, in Los Angeles, the Milwaukee Braves lost their final National League game, 3-0. Bob Miller was the winning pitcher, while Bob Sadowski took the loss for the Atlanta-bound Braves.

HAL NEWHOUSER
The last major league pitcher to face one-armed Pete Gray of the St. Louis Browns. Pitching to Gray in the eighth inning of a September 30, 1945, game between the Detroit Tigers and the Browns, Newhouser induced the outfielder to hit into a fielder's choice.

Gray played 77 games (all in 1945) in the majors, batting .218 with no homers and 13 runs batted in.

Pittsburgh's Roberto Clemente displays the ball he hit on September 30, 1972, for his 3,000th and last regular-season hit in the majors. Clemente died three months later in a plane crash.

Pete Gray of the St. Louis Browns displays his batting form in 1945.

NEW YORK GIANTS

Playing the Pirates at the Polo Grounds on September 29, 1957, New York lost to Pittsburgh, 9-1, in the Giants' last game before relocating in San Francisco in 1958. Bob Friend was the winning pitcher, beating Johnny Antonelli.

GENE OLIVER

The last player to hit a home run for the Milwaukee Braves, connecting on October 2, 1965.

Playing the outfield took ingenuity but the one-armed Gray found just the right technique.

SATCHEL PAIGE

The last representative of the St. Louis Browns to play in an All-Star Game, pitching the eighth inning of the 1953 game for the American League. In the seventh inning, Billy Hunter of the Browns ran for Mickey Mantle in the game played at Cincinnati.

BEN PASCHAL

The last man to pinch-hit for Babe Ruth. Paschal batted for Ruth in the sixth

The New York Giants and Pittsburgh Pirates head for the locker rooms at the Polo Grounds on September 29, 1957, after the Giants played their final game as a New York-based club.

inning of the 1927 season opener after Ruth had gone 0-for-3 (striking out twice), and he delivered a single.

PHILADELPHIA ATHLETICS
Playing their final game before moving to Kansas City in 1955, the A's defeated the New York Yankees, 8-6, at Yankee Stadium on September 26, 1954. Art Ditmar posted his first major league pitching victory, while Tommy Byrne took the loss for the Yankees.

With nothing at stake in the season finale against the A's, the Yankees played three men out of position. Yogi Berra was at third base for the only time in his big-league career; Bill Skowron played second base (which he did only one other time in the majors), and Mickey Mantle was at shortstop for one of only seven times in the big leagues.

JOE PIGNATANO
New York Mets' catcher who hit into a triple play in his last at-bat in the major leagues. Batting with Sammy Drake on second base and Richie Ashburn on first in the eighth inning of a September 30, 1962, game against the Chicago Cubs, Pignatano popped the ball into short right field. Second baseman Ken Hubbs made a spectacular catch, and throws from Hubbs to first baseman Ernie

Banks and from Banks to shortstop Andre Rodgers caught Ashburn and Drake off base. All three Mets involved in the play—Pignatano, Ashburn and Drake—were playing in their last major league game.

POLO GROUNDS
Facing the New York Mets on September 18, 1963, Chris Short of the Philadelphia Phillies was a 5-1 winner in the last major league game in Polo Grounds history. The losing pitcher was Craig Anderson.

BILL RIGNEY
The last manager of the New York Giants, leading the club in 1957. Rigney also managed the team in 1956, and he piloted the San Francisco Giants from 1958 until mid-June of 1960.

DAVE ROBERTS
Pitching for the Detroit Tigers against the Milwaukee Brewers on October 3, 1976, he was the last man to face Hank Aaron in the major leagues. Roberts gave up a sixth-inning single to Aaron in the Milwaukee designated hitter's final at-bat.

EDDIE ROBINSON
The last member of the Philadelphia Athletics to play in an All-Star Game, pinch-hitting in the eighth inning of the 1953 classic at Cincinnati. Gus Zernial of the A's started the game in left field for the American League, going 1-for-2 before being replaced.

PETE ROSE
The major leagues' last player-manager, having served in that capacity for the National League's Cincinnati Reds from August 16, 1984, through the 1986 season.

Don Kessinger was the American League's last player-manager, his dual role coming in 1979 with the Chicago White Sox. Kessinger managed the White Sox from the start of the '79 season until August 2, when he resigned.

LEE ROSS
Philadelphia A's pitcher who on August 20, 1938, gave up a bases-loaded home run to Lou Gehrig of the New York Yankees—the last of a major league-record 23 grand slams by Gehrig.

ST. LOUIS BROWNS
About 6 1/2 months away from taking the field as the Baltimore Orioles, the Browns played their last game on September 27, 1953, in St. Louis against the Chicago White Sox. Billy Pierce was the winning pitcher and Duane Pillette was charged with the defeat as the White Sox prevailed, 2-1, in 11 innings.

SEATTLE PILOTS
An expansion team that spent only one season in Seattle before shifting to Milwaukee and becoming the Brewers, the Pilots played their final game on October 2, 1969—and lost to the Oakland A's, 3-1. Steve Barber took the loss in the game played at Seattle, while Jim Roland was the winning pitcher.

DUKE SNIDER
The last player to hit a home run at Brooklyn's Ebbets Field, connecting on September 22, 1957. Snider hit two homers that day.

MIKE SQUIRES, BENNY DISTEFANO
The last two lefthanded-throwing catchers in the big leagues. Squires, normally a first baseman, caught in two games for the Chicago White Sox in 1980. Distefano, a first baseman-outfielder, saw duty as a catcher in three games for the 1989 Pittsburgh Pirates.

WILLIE STARGELL
Playing for the Pittsburgh Pirates against the Chicago Cubs on September 3, 1966, Stargell slugged the last of a major league-record 505 home runs surrendered by Robin Roberts.

BILL TERRY
New York Giants' first baseman who was the last National Leaguer to bat .400 in one season, hitting .401 in 1930.

WASHINGTON SENATORS (FIRST A.L. CLUB)
The American League's original-franchise Washington Senators played their last game on October 2, 1960, dropping a 2-1 decision to the Baltimore Orioles at Washington. Milt Pappas was the winning pitcher; Pedro Ramos took the loss for the Senators, who became the Minnesota Twins in 1961.

WASHINGTON SENATORS (SECOND A.L. CLUB)
The American League's second Washington Senators played their final game on September 30, 1971—and it turned into a 9-0 forfeit. With the Senators leading the New York Yankees, 7-5, with two out in the ninth inning at Washington, souvenir hunters swarmed the field—and the game could not be resumed. Since a forfeit results in no pitchers of record, Jim Shellenback—a 6-3 loser to the Yankees' Mel Stottlemyre the night before—was the last Washington pitcher to get a decision. The franchise became the Texas Rangers in 1972.

STEVE WHITAKER
The last player to hit a home run for the Seattle Pilots, connecting on October 2, 1969.

TED WILLIAMS

The last major leaguer to record a season batting average of .400, hitting .406 for the American League's Boston Red Sox in 1941. Nearly thirty years later, Williams was the last manager for Washington's second American League franchise, heading the Senators until 1971. Williams, who became the Senators' manager in 1969, moved with the club to Texas—but he managed the Rangers for only one season, 1972.

TAFT WRIGHT

Right fielder for the Chicago White Sox who grounded out for the final out when Bob Feller of the Cleveland Indians pitched a no-hitter on opening day in 1940.

CARL YASTRZEMSKI

The last player to collect a hit off Satchel Paige in a major league game. Becoming the oldest player in big-league history at age 59, Paige started and pitched three innings for the Kansas City A's against the Boston Red Sox on September 25, 1965—and allowed only one hit, a two-out double by Yastrzemski in the first inning. Paige made only 28 pitches, walking no one and striking out one batter (opposing pitcher Bill Monbouquette). Leading 1-0, Paige was replaced by Diego Segui at the start of the fourth inning. Boston won, 5-2, with Monbouquette notching the victory and Don Mossi being saddled with the loss.

Satchel Paige (29) leaves the mound with Manager Haywood Sullivan on September 25, 1965, after working three innings for the Kansas City A's at age 59. Paige allowed only one hit, a first-inning double by Boston's Carl Yastrzemski.

EIGHTH INNING
Promotions, innovations and gimmicks

YELLOW BASEBALL
In the first game of a doubleheader at Ebbets Field on August 2, 1938, St. Louis and Brooklyn experimented with a yellow baseball throughout the contest to see if it would be easier to follow than a white ball. Terry Moore of the Cardinals was the first to bat against the yellow ball, and St. Louis' Johnny Mize hit the only home run of the game. The Dodgers won, 6-2, behind the pitching of Freddie Fitzsimmons. A conventional white ball was used in the nightcap (use of a yellow ball never gained support in the majors), and Brooklyn prevailed, 9-3.

SMALL STRIKE ZONE
Eddie Gaedel, a 26-year-old midget, pinch-hit for the St. Louis Browns in the second game of an August 19, 1951, doubleheader against Detroit at Sportsman's Park. Bill Veeck, owner of the Browns, used Gaedel as part of a promotional stunt. However, Gaedel was released the next day when American League President Will Harridge refused to approve his contract (Harridge said the use of a midget was not in the best interests of baseball.)

Gaedel, standing 3 feet, 7 inches and wearing uniform number 1/8, batted for right fielder Frank Saucier to lead off the Browns' first inning.

Supporting Cast:
• **Bob Cain.** Detroit pitcher who walked Gaedel on four pitches.
• **Jim Delsing.** St. Louis player who ran for Gaedel after his inning-opening walk.
• **Ed Hurley.** The home-plate umpire when Gaedel went to bat.
• **Bob Swift.** Cain's batterymate for the Tigers.
• **Zack Taylor.** Manager of the Browns who was questioned by Hurley about the legality of Gaedel's participation in an American League game. Taylor produced an official, signed contract, and Gaedel became the smallest player in major league history.

GAEDEL MAKES 'COMEBACK'
Nearly 10 years after appearing as a pinch-hitter for the St. Louis Browns, midget Eddie Gaedel was back in the news at a big-league ballpark. Bill Veeck, owner of the Chicago White Sox, took note of fans' constant complaints about vendors blocking their view and he hired Gaedel and seven other midgets in

"Ball," says umpire Ed Hurley as Bob Swift catches the high pitch to Eddie Gaedel.

When midget Eddie Gaedel popped out of a cake between games of the August 19, 1951, doubleheader at Sportsman's Park, Browns' fans laughed at Bill Veeck's latest stunt. Little did they know, however, that the best was yet to come.

198

Before taking his place in baseball history by stepping to the plate, Gaedel received a little help from Browns Manager Zack Taylor and words of encouragement from coach Johnny Tobin (right).

1961 to work as vendors in the box-seat sections of Comiskey Park on opening day.

As another first-game highlight, Veeck asked John F. Kennedy to throw out the first ball in '61. And Kennedy did. One not-so-small point, though: This JFK was a fan from suburban Oak Lawn, not the President of the United States.

BURYING THE PENNANT
On September 23, 1949, with the Cleveland Indians out of the American League pennant race after winning the A.L. flag and World Series the year before, Owner Bill Veeck held a pregame ceremony during which he buried the 1948 pennant at Municipal Stadium. Wearing a top hat, Veeck guided a horse-drawn hearse at the head of the funeral procession to the gravesite behind the center-field fence. Cleveland Manager Lou Boudreau and his coaches served as pallbearers, and Rudie Schaffer, the club's business manager, read the last rites from the "bible of baseball"—The Sporting News. The cardboard tombstone read simply, "1948 Champs." The Indians went on to lose that night, 5-0, to the Detroit Tigers.

CHARLIE FINLEY
The Kansas City Athletics played at a .405 clip (458 victories, 672 losses) during Finley's seven-year reign (1961-67) as owner of the Kansas City club—but things seldom were dull at Municipal Stadium. With a subpar on-field product, Finley tried to compensate with attractions aimed at luring fans to the ballpark.

The funeral procession approaches the gravesite behind the center-field fence at Cleveland's Municipal Stadium. In uniform at the head of the casket are coach Bill McKechnie and Manager Lou Boudreau (wearing jacket). Indians Vice President Hank Greenberg is third from the left.

Saying that the dimensions of Yankee Stadium gave a distinct advantage to New York hitters and helped make the Yankees a powerhouse, Finley built a "Pennant Porch" at Municipal Stadium, to rival the right-field configuration at New York. The A's owner moved the right-field foul pole from 338 feet to 325 (the big-league minimum for recently constructed ballparks), then angled the fence to a point that was 296 feet from the plate—the same distance as Yankee Stadium's "porch." The structure was up for two exhibition games before Commissioner Ford Frick and American League President Joe Cronin ordered it dismantled. In its place, Finley put up a "One-Half Pennant Porch" that was 325 feet down the line. Foiled in his effort to help A's hitters with dramatically shorter distances (a bleacher roof that also cut the right-field

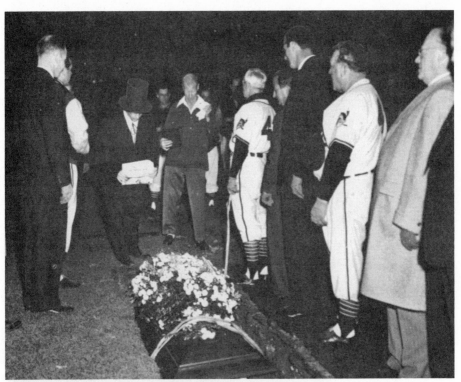

With heavy hearts and respect befitting the sad occasion, Indians players, coaches, managers, officials and Owner Bill Veeck (center) listened to club business manager Rudie Schaffer read the last rites from The Sporting News, the "bible of baseball."

A young fan pays his last respects to the memory of a season lost.

Kansas City's Ken Harrelson emerges from a chauffeured limousine that delivered the starting

The Pennant Porch complete with sheep grazing beyond the right-field wall.

lineup in one of Charlie Finley's promotional stunts.

distance to 296 feet was banned, too), Finley took another tack. He erected a 40-foot-high screen in right field in an attempt to stymie opposing power hitters. That didn't last, either.

Not all of Finley's stunts were aimed at influencing what occurred on the field; entertainment was emphasized. Finley introduced "Harvey," a mechanical rabbit who popped out of the ground and delivered baseballs to the home-plate umpire. The A's owner brought sheep to Municipal Stadium—and a shepherd to tend them. The sheep grazed between the right-field fence and the outer wall, keeping the grass short. There also was Charlie O., a mule who served as a team mascot, and a children's zoo in the picnic area down the left-field line.

Finley also installed a clock to time pitchers (to make sure a game kept moving), and he hired a woman commentator—a television weather reporter from Chicago—to work on the A's radio team. Kansas City's starting lineup once rode into Municipal Stadium as a "mule train," and on another occasion A's players arrived via limousines. And when Kansas City's Rocky Colavito was closing in on his 300th career homer in the majors, Finley parked a Brink's truck beyond the left-field wall so he could reward Colavito when he reached the milestone. Colavito hit No. 300 on the road, though, and a belated presentation was made in Kansas City.

Harvey popped out of the ground to deliver balls to the umpire and Charlie O. the mule
was a frequent companion of Charlie O. the man.

Whatever the promotion or gimmick, Finley still had trouble attracting fans
(the A's best season attendance during Finley's years in Kansas City was
773,929, in 1966). And by 1968, Finley and the A's were off to Oakland.

BROADCASTING FROM ASTRODOME ROOF
On April 28, 1965, broadcaster Lindsey Nelson of the New York Mets called
the Mets-Astros game from a gondola 208 feet above second base at Houston's
Astrodome. Nelson and Joel Nixon, the executive producer of the Mets'
broadcasts, ascended in the gondola to the apex of the dome—and they were
there about 4 hours (the game lasted 3 hours, 24 minutes). Astrodome ground
rules specified that a ball hitting any part of the roof was in play, so Nelson and
Nixon were included in the ground rules. The two men had walkie-talkie
contact to the Mets' radio booth and a direct telephone line to their director,
Joe Gallagher. Nelson described the play-by-play only in the seventh and
eighth innings, but provided color commentary to announcing partners Ralph
Kiner and Bob Murphy the rest of the time. Nelson took only a scorecard and
binoculars with him, but didn't keep score in fear a dropped pen might become

After the Pennant Porch came a 40-foot right-field screen, being surveyed by A's players (left to right) Manny Jimenez, Bill Bryan, Wayne Causey and Jim Dickson.

One of Finley's more memorable gimmicks was bringing in the A's starting lineup by mule train. Leading the procession is Ken Harrelson, followed by Wayne Causey, Rene Lachemann, Ed Charles, Bert Campaneris, Nelson Mathews and Jim Landis.

a dangerous missile to the players below. The game, won by Houston, 12-9, was the seventh regular-season contest in Astrodome history.

PITCHER-AN-INNING STUNT
St. Louis hurler Dick Starr completed a pitcher-an-inning gimmick for the Browns on the final day of the 1949 season. Ned Garver, Joe Ostrowski, Cliff Fannin, Tom Ferrick, Karl Drews, Bill Kennedy, Al Papai, Red Embree and Starr faced the Chicago White Sox in the opener of a doubleheader—and the White Sox won, 4-3. Kennedy took the loss.

The Browns had another attraction in the second game, announcing the major league debut of Eddie Albrecht, a 20-year-old pitcher from St. Louis County. Albrecht, up from Pine Bluff of the Class C Cotton States League (where he won 29 games in '49), started against Chicago and was a 5-3 winner, allowing only one hit in five innings before the game was called because of darkness. The game was one of only three for Albrecht in his big-league career.

NIGHTCLUB SINGER BELTS BALL
During a July 31, 1935, game at Cincinnati's Crosley Field, nightclub singer Kitty Burke grabbed a bat from the Reds' Babe Herman and stepped to the plate for an unofficial at-bat against Paul Dean of the St. Louis Cardinals. The incident occurred with one out in the eighth inning, St. Louis leading, 2-1, and the Reds' Sammy Byrd on first base. Burke motioned to Dean to pitch, and he threw hard the first time. Dean then made an underhand toss, and Burke grounded back to the mound. After being "thrown out" at first base, Burke returned to the crowd (a larger turnout than the Reds' security force could handle was lured to the sixth night game in Cincinnati history, with fans spilling onto the field and making plays impossible in foul territory). Burke's desire to bat stemmed from a kidding-around session involving the Cards' Joe Medwick, with the singer insisting she could hit a pitched ball.

'GOOD OLD JOE EARLEY' NIGHT
In 1948, a Cleveland fan named Joe Earley wrote a letter to a newspaper suggesting that he—as an average follower of the Indians—deserved a night in his honor, claiming players weren't the only ones worthy of such tributes. When Bill Veeck, owner of the Indians, heard about the letter, he thought the idea would make a great promotion—and he was right, as a crowd of 60,405 for "Good Old Joe Earley" Night proved on September 28. Earley, a 26-year-old veteran of World War II who worked as a night guard at an auto plant, and his wife were called to an on-field microphone at the start of pregame festivities. Earley was presented with a new convertible, clothes luggage, books and numerous appliances. In addition, livestock, poultry and other gifts were given to fans, and Veeck spent $30,000 to have orchids flown in from Hawaii to be presented to the first 20,000 women entering the stadium.

Good Old Joe Earley and his wife were well rewarded by Bill Veeck.

'PITCHER' STAN MUSIAL

Frankie Baumholtz of the Chicago Cubs was the only man to bat against Musial in a major league game. Musial made the lone pitching appearance of his big-league career on September 28, 1952, facing Baumholtz in a season-ending stunt at Sportsman's Park that matched the National League's top two hitters in the '52 batting-crown race. Musial, who led Baumholtz .336 to .326, came in from center field to pitch in the first inning of the Cardinals-Cubs game after St. Louis starter Harvey Haddix walked leadoff batter Tommy Brown (Haddix went to right field, and right fielder Hal Rice switched to center). Baumholtz, a lefthanded hitter, batted righthanded against Musial and grounded to Solly Hemus at third base. Hemus, the Cardinals' regular shortstop, bobbled the ball, allowing Baumholtz to reach first base on the error. Musial then returned to center field, Rice went back to right and Haddix resumed his pitching duties. Musial went 1-for-3 during the game, keeping his title-winning average at .336; Baumholtz's 1-for-4 day dropped his figure to .325. The Cubs won, 3-0.

JERSEY CITY DODGERS

The Brooklyn Dodgers played seven home games in 1956 and eight in 1957 at Roosevelt Stadium in Jersey City, N.J. By playing the 15 home games away from Brooklyn, the Dodgers seemingly were threatening to move from the

Cardinal great Stan Musial delivers a pitch to Chicago's Frankie Baumholtz, normally a lefthanded batter, during the final game of the 1952 season at Sportsman's Park in St. Louis. Bill Sarni is St. Louis' catcher.

borough unless its civic leaders helped to provide a new stadium to replace aging—and small—Ebbets Field. The big-league contests were the first in Jersey City since the New York Giants played two games there (but not in Roosevelt Stadium) to open the 1889 season.

Players and teams involved in firsts, lasts and other notable occurrences at Roosevelt Stadium included:

• **Harry Anderson.** Philadelphia player who hit the final major league home run at Roosevelt Stadium, connecting for the Phillies on September 3, 1957.

• **Richie Ashburn.** The first man to bat in a big-league game at Roosevelt Stadium, leading off for the Phils on April 19, 1956.

• **Roy Campanella.** Brooklyn catcher who collected his 1,000th hit in the majors in the first big-league game at Roosevelt Stadium, doubling in the 10th inning.

• **Gino Cimoli.** Brooklyn left fielder who made his major league debut in the Dodgers' first game at Jersey City.

• **Murry Dickson.** The losing pitcher for Philadelphia in the first big-league game at Roosevelt Stadium when the Dodgers defeated the Phillies, 5-4, in 10 innings.

• **Don Drysdale.** Dodger pitcher who hurled the first of his 49 big-league shutouts at Roosevelt Stadium, beating the Chicago Cubs, 4-0, on June 5, 1957. He also was the losing pitcher in the last major league game at Jersey City, dropping a 3-2, 12-inning decision to Philadelphia on September 3, 1957. (The defeat left Brooklyn with an 11-4 record in the Jersey City "experiment.")

• **Dick Farrell.** Philadelphia pitcher who was the winner of the final major

league game at Roosevelt Stadium.
• **Carl Furillo.** The first Brooklyn player to hit a home run at Jersey City, connecting on July 25, 1956.
• **Clem Labine.** The Dodgers' winning pitcher in the first big-league game at Roosevelt Stadium.
• **Eddie Mathews.** Playing for the Milwaukee Braves, he was the only visiting player to hit two home runs at Roosevelt Stadium. He belted one in 1956 and one in '57.
• **Wally Moon.** St. Louis Cardinal who slugged the first major league homer at Jersey City, accomplishing the feat on May 16, 1956.
• **Charlie Neal.** Brooklyn second baseman who collected his first big-league hit at Roosevelt Stadium on April 19, 1956.
• **Don Newcombe.** Brooklyn pitcher who was the biggest winner and loser at Roosevelt Stadium, compiling a 4-3 record.
• **New York Giants.** The only National League team to defeat the Dodgers twice at Roosevelt Stadium. Johnny Antonelli's two-hit pitching and Willie Mays' home run beat the Dodgers, 1-0, on August 15, 1956, and the Giants scored an 8-5 victory over Brooklyn on August 7, 1957. Newcombe lost both games.
• **Philadelphia Phillies.** The only visiting team to play three games against Brooklyn at Roosevelt Stadium. Besides losing the first big-league game at the park and winning the last game there, the Phils also played the Dodgers on April 22, 1957, at Roosevelt Stadium—and Brooklyn prevailed, 5-1.
• **Duke Snider.** The lone Brooklyn player to hit two home runs at Roosevelt Stadium. Both were hit in 1956.

COUNTY STADIUM—HOME OF SOX
The Chicago White Sox played a total of 20 home games (winning eight) in 1968 and 1969 at Milwaukee's County Stadium. Milwaukee had been without major league baseball since the Braves left the city at the end of the 1965 season. In 1970, the Seattle Pilots moved to Milwaukee and became the Brewers.

ALL-ROOKIE LINEUP FAILS
Jay Dahl was the starting pitcher for Houston in the all-rookie lineup that the Colts fielded against the New York Mets on September 27, 1963, at Colt Stadium. Others in the Colts' lineup: Brock Davis, left field; Jimmy Wynn, center field; Aaron Pointer, right field; Rusty Staub, first base; Joe Morgan, second base; Glenn Vaughan, third base; Sonny Jackson, shortstop, and Jerry Grote, catcher. The Mets won, 10-3, over Dahl, whose three-inning stint marked his lone appearance in the majors.

FANS MANAGE BROWNS
Owner Bill Veeck of the St. Louis Browns let 1,115 fans—so-called "grandstand managers"—guide his club during an August 24, 1951, game against the Philadelphia Athletics. As part of a Veeck promotion, the managers sat behind the Browns' dugout and decided strategy by flashing "Yes" or "No" cards after

Houston's all-rookie lineup on September 27, 1963, included (front row, left to right) Jay Dahl, Jerry Grote; (second row) Glenn Vaughan, Sonny Jackson, Joe Morgan, Rusty Staub; (back row) Brock Davis, Aaron Pointer and Jim Wynn.

coaches posed questions at key junctures. The grandstanders chose to bench catcher Matt Batts and first baseman Ben Taylor, replacing them with Sherm Lollar and Hank Arft. Lollar had three hits (including what proved a game-winning home run) and two runs batted in, and Arft contributed two RBIs. After five of the first six A's hit safely in the first inning, the fans were asked, "Shall We Warm Up a New Pitcher?" The response was no, and St. Louis starter Ned Garver allowed only two hits the rest of the way in a 5-3 triumph. While the strategy-deciding process may have appeared time consuming, the game was played in 2 hours, 11 minutes.

DISCO DEMOLITION NIGHT

More than 50,000 fans—many of them teen-agers—showed up at Comiskey Park on July 12, 1979, for Disco Demolition Night. Between games of a doubleheader between the Detroit Tigers and Chicago White Sox, disco records were to be burned—much to the delight of rock fans who paid 98 cents (disc jockey Steve Dahl of 98 WLUP-FM helped arrange the festivities) to get into the park. Many fans started to sling the records Frisbee-style onto the field during the first game, a contest that was delayed a number of times and finally won by Detroit, 4-1. During the record-burning, an estimated 5,000 fans raced onto the field and wouldn't return to their seats despite an appeal from Bill Veeck, owner of the White Sox. Umpire-in-chief Dave Phillips determined the crowd was too difficult to control—furthermore, the field had become a

When strategy questions were posed at key junctures of an August 24, 1951, game between the St. Louis Browns and the Philadelphia Athletics, the majority ruled as 1,115 "grandstand managers" answered with a yes or no. The promotion was another in the large arsenal of Browns Owner Bill Veeck.

mess—and he called off the second game. Later, American League President Lee MacPhail ordered the game forfeited to Detroit.

FLAGPOLE SITTER SITS AND SITS
Cleveland fan Charley Lupica took up residence on a platform atop a flagpole on May 31, 1949, vowing not to come down until his beloved Indians moved into first place in the American League. On September 25, Owner Bill Veeck of the Indians had the platform moved to Municipal Stadium for a ceremony during which Lupica gave up his fruitless, 117-day vigil. The Indians, 1948 World Series champions who were in seventh place when Lupica's stunt began, were in fourth place when Lupica came down and they finished third.

FEATHERED FRIEND
The man who entertains baseball fans as The Chicken (formerly the San Diego Chicken) is Ted Giannoulas.

BERT CAMPANERIS—MR. VERSATILITY
Playing against the California Angels on September 8, 1965, Kansas City's Campaneris became the first man in major league history to play all nine

Bill Veeck's 1979 Disco Demolition promotion backfired when White Sox fans became unruly and forced the forteiture of the second game of the team's doubleheader against Detroit.

Cleveland fan Charley Lupica finally left his flagpole on September 25, after his beloved Indians had been eliminated from the 1949 American League pennant race.

positions in one game. In order, Campaneris played a full inning at shortstop (his normal position), second base, third base, left field, center field, right field (where he made his only error of the game), first base and pitcher. Campaneris then caught part of the ninth inning for the A's before leaving the game because of an injury.

Supporting Cast:
• **Bill Bryan.** A's catcher who caught pitcher Campaneris in the eighth when Campaneris allowed one run on one hit and two walks.
• **Jose Cardenal.** The first California player to bat against Campaneris. Cardenal, Campaneris' second cousin, popped out.
• **Ed Kirkpatrick.** California baserunner who was tagged out by catcher Campaneris in a home-plate collision in the ninth. The play forced Campaneris out of the game with a shoulder injury.
• **Rene Lachemann.** A's player who replaced Campaneris behind the plate in the ninth.
• **Aurelio Monteagudo.** A's pitcher who had Campaneris for a batterymate in the ninth inning of the game that the Angels won, 5-3, in 13 innings.

CESAR TOVAR MATCHES CAMPANERIS
Tovar, Minnesota infielder-outfielder, became the second major leaguer in

Bert Campaneris had his good and bad moments when he displayed his versatility in a September 8, 1965, promotion in Kansas City. Campaneris pitched the eighth inning and caught the ninth until a collision with California's Ed Kirkpatrick forced his to leave the game.

Minnesota's Cesar Tovar duplicated Campaneris' feat in a September 22, 1968, game against Oakland.

history to play all nine positions in one game. Tovar's performance, which started with an inning of pitching, came in the Twins' 2-1 triumph over the Oakland A's on September 22, 1968.

Supporting Cast:
• **Bert Campaneris.** The first big leaguer to accomplish the all-positions playing feat (1965), Campaneris led off the game against Tovar and fouled out. Reggie Jackson then struck out, Danny Cater walked and Sal Bando fouled out.
• **Tom Hall.** Minnesota pitcher who replaced Tovar, hurling 6 1/3 innings of relief and earning the victory.
• **Jerry Zimmerman.** Twins' catcher who caught Tovar in the first inning.

215

Players often are easily identified by their uniform numbers—but not always. Joe DiMaggio wore No. 9 at the outset of his career with the New York Yankees before switching to No. 5.

NINTH INNING
Numbers

0

Number of grand slams hit by Roger Maris during his record 61-home run year of 1961.

0

Number of intentional walks received by Roger Maris during his 61-home run year of 1961. Pitchers were reluctant to give up free passes to Maris because the Yanks' next batter in the lineup wa Mantle, who hit 54 homers that season.

0

The number of changes in the alignment of the major leagues from 1903 through 1952. In each of those 50 years, the American League consisted of Boston, Chicago, Cleveland, Detroit, New York, Philadelphia, St. Louis and Washington; the National League was made up of Boston, Brooklyn, Chicago, Cincinnati, New York, Philadelphia, Pittsburgh and St. Louis.

1/8

Uniform number worn by midget Eddie Gaedel when he batted for the St. Louis Browns in 1951, thereby becoming the smallest player in big-league history.

1

The number of World Series home runs hit by the St. Louis Browns. First baseman George McQuinn connected for the Browns in Game 1 of the 1944 Series against the St. Louis Cardinals (the '44 Series marked the Browns' only appearance in postseason play).

2

Number of grand slams hit by Babe Ruth during his 60-home run year of 1927.

2

Fewest pitchers used by one team in a World Series. The Philadelphia Athletics used only Chief Bender and Jack Coombs in defeating the Chicago Cubs, four games to one, in the 1910 Series.

2 3/4

The maximum number of inches in diameter of a bat at its thickest part.

3

Oakland's designated runner Herb Washington's uniform number in 1974-75.

George McQuinn gave St. Louis Browns fans something to cheer about when he homered in the 1944 World Series.

3
Number of pitchers who gave up hits in four games to Joe DiMaggio during his 56-game hitting streak in 1941. Thornton Lee and Johnny Rigney of the Chicago White Sox and Eldon Auker of the St. Louis Browns were the three.

3.20
The highest earned-run average figure that was the lowest in a league for a season. Early Wynn of the 1950 Cleveland Indians led the American League with the 3.20 ERA.

4
The number of decades in which these players competed in the major leagues:

Player	First Club	Last Club
Jim O'Rourke	Boston, N.L., 1876	New York, N.L., 1904
Dan Brouthers	Troy, N.L., 1879	New York, N.L., 1904
Jack O'Connor	Cincinnati, A.A., 1887	St. Louis, A.L., 1910
Deacon McGuire	Toledo, A.A., 1884	Detroit, A.L., 1912
Kid Gleason	Philadelphia, N.L., 1888	Chicago, A.L., 1912
John Ryan	Louisville, A.A., 1889	Washington, A.L., 1913
Eddie Collins	Philadelphia, A.L., 1906	Philadelphia, A.L., 1930
Jack Quinn	New York, A.L., 1909	Cincinnati, N.L., 1933
Bobo Newsom	Brooklyn, N.L., 1929	Philadelphia, A.L., 1953
Mickey Vernon	Washington, A.L., 1939	Pittsburgh, N.L., 1960
Ted Williams	Boston, A.L., 1939	Boston, A.L., 1960
Early Wynn	Washington, A.L., 1939	Cleveland, A.L., 1963
Tim McCarver	St. Louis, N.L., 1959	Philadelphia, N.L., 1980
Willie McCovey	San Francisco, N.L., 1959	San Francisco, N.L., 1980
Jim Kaat	Washington, A.L., 1959	St. Louis, N.L., 1983
Bill Buckner	Los Angeles, N.L., 1969	Boston, A.L., 1990
Jerry Reuss	St. Louis, N.L., 1969	Pittsburgh, N.L., 1990
Rick Dempsey	Minnesota, A.L., 1969	*Milwaukee, A.L., 1991
Carlton Fisk	Boston, A.L., 1969	*Chicago, A.L., 1991
Nolan Ryan	New York, N.L., 1966	*Texas, A.L., 1991

*Active through 1991.

4
The lowest victory total for a Cy Young Award-winning pitcher. Mark Davis won the honor in the National League in 1989, a year in which he compiled a 4-3 record for the San Diego Padres and collected 44 saves.

4:11
The time of the afternoon when Bobby Thomson hit his three-run, pennant-

Minnie Minoso appeared in big-league games in five decades, while Early Wynn was a four-decade player in the majors.

clinching home run for the New York Giants on October 3, 1951.

4-2
The score by which the Mudville nine lost in Ernest Thayer's "Casey at the Bat."

4.74
The 1960 earned-run average of Boston Red Sox pitcher Ike Delock, who, ironically, compiled a .474 won-lost percentage that year. Delock had a 9-10 record and allowed 68 earned runs in 129 innings for the twin "474" figures.

5
The number of decades in which these players competed in the major leagues:

Player	First Club	Last Club
Nick Altrock	Louisville, N.L., 1898	Washington, A.L., 1933
Minnie Minoso	Cleveland, A.L., 1949	Chicago, A.L., 1980

5
Number of outs accounted for by Brooklyn Dodgers pitcher Clarence Mitchell in his two at-bats during the fifth game of the 1920 World Series. Mitchell lined into the only triple play in Series history in the fifth inning, and he grounded into a double play in the eighth.

5
The number of Delahanty brothers who played in the majors. The brothers with their first and last seasons in the big leagues: Edward J., 1888, 1903 Thomas J., 1894, 1897; James C., 1901, 1912; Frank G., 1905, 1908, and Joseph N., 1907, 1909. Ed, a .346 lifetime hitter, is a member of the Hall of Fame.

5, 5 1/4
The minimum and maximum weight, in ounces, of a baseball.

6
Number of hits a team could possibly get in one inning without scoring a run. The first three batters load the bases with infield singles. The opposing pitcher picks the runners off third and second. Two more infield singles reload the bases and the final batter hits a ball that strikes a baserunner. The runner is out while the batter is credited with a hit.

6
The most hits given up by a pitcher to Joe DiMaggio during his 56-game hitting streak of 1941. Thornton Lee of the Chicago White Sox gave up the six hits in a span of four games.

221

Hall of Famer Ed Delahanty obviously was the best of the five Delahanty brothers, but Jim Delahanty had his moments. In fact, Jim batted .339 for the Detroit Tigers in 1911.

6

The number of World Series sweeps (1927, 1928, 1932, 1938, 1939 and 1950) by the New York Yankees. The Yankees and the Cincinnati Reds (1976, 1990) are the only teams with more than one Series sweep to their credit.

7

Uniform number of Cesar Gutierrez when the Detroit Tigers' shortstop became the first player in modern major league history to get seven hits in seven at-bats in a game. Gutierrez collected six singles and a double in the 12-inning second game of a June 21 doubleheader in 1970.

7

The number of times Roger Maris hit two home runs in a game during his 61-homer year of 1961.

8

The number of times Babe Ruth hit two home runs in a game during his 60-homer year of 1927.

8

The number of major league players who have turned unassisted triple plays.

8

The number of Chicago White Sox players who were barred for life in 1920 by Commissioner Kenesaw Mountain Landis for allegedly fixing the 1919 World Series. Although the players—Ed Cicotte, Joe Jackson, Claude (Lefty) Williams, Oscar (Happy) Felsch, Buck Weaver, Swede Risberg, Chick Gandil and Fred McMullin—later were acquitted by the courts, Landis refused to allow them back into baseball.

9:07

The time of night when Hank Aaron of the Atlanta Braves hit his 715th major league home run, breaking Babe Ruth's all-time record.

11

The most pitchers used by one team in a World Series. The Boston Red Sox used 11 hurlers in losing four out of the seven games played against the St. Louis Cardinals in 1946.

11

The largest number enshrined in baseball's Hall of Fame in one year. The following entered the Hall in 1946: Jesse Burkett, Frank Chance, Jack Chesbro, Johnny Evers, Clark Griffith, Tom McCarthy, Joe McGinnity, Eddie Plank, Joe Tinker, Rube Waddell and Ed Walsh. All were named by the committee on old-timers; none were elected by the Baseball Writers' Association of America.

Joe Jackson and Swede Risberg were two of the eight so-called "Black Sox" of 1919 who were barred from the major leagues. Also banned were Claude (Lefty) Williams and Ed Cicotte (left and right, respectively, in photo), who flank Bill James. James was not involved in the scandal.

12

The number of home runs hit by Roger Maris off lefthanded pitchers in his 61-homer season of 1961.

12:32

Time of the afternoon in which Bob Watson of the Houston Astros scored the millionth run in major league history. Watson scored from second base on a three-run homer by teammate Milt May at San Francisco's Candlestick Park on May 4, 1975. Jose Cruz scored from first on the play. May hit his home run off Giants hurler John Montefusco.

12

The uniform number worn by Ralph Branca in 1952. The Brooklyn Dodgers' pitcher had forsaken No. 13 after giving up Bobby Thomson's pennant-winning homer in 1951. Branca resumed wearing No. 13 in 1953.

14

The uniform number worn by Pete Gray when the one-armed outfielder played for the St. Louis Browns in 1945.

15

The number of home runs hit by Joe DiMaggio during his 56-game hitting streak in 1941.

15

The width and length, in inches, of the bags at first, second and third base.

15

The lowest stolen base total to lead a league. Dominic DiMaggio of the Boston Red Sox stole only 15 bases in 1950, but still led the American League.

16

The most Gold Glove fielding awards won by any player. Pitcher Jim Kaat won 14 in the American League and two in the National League from 1962 through 1977, while Brooks Robinson won the award at third base in the American League from 1960 through 1975.

17

The width, in inches, of home plate.

17

Uniform number worn by Andy Messersmith when he signed as a free agent with the Atlanta Braves in 1976. When Messersmith, who wore number 47 for the Los Angeles Dodgers the year before, came to the Braves, Owner Ted

Ralph Branca, wearing his familiar No. 13, defied superstition on Friday, April 13, 1951, by flaunting the number and holding a black cat . . .

Turner gave him uniform No. 17 because, in Turner's words, "That is the channel at my TV station (Turner owned WTBS, a so-called superstation that broadcasts via satellite and cable out of Atlanta). Super 17, that's Andy." But

. . . but the Brooklyn pitcher changed his tune during spring training of 1952. Having yielded Bobby Thomson's pennant-winning homer the previous October, Branca was ready to discard his old uniform top.

Turner carried things a bit further and, instead of putting Messersmith's name on the back of his uniform, he gave his new pitcher the nickname "Channel." Shortly after, in June of '76, National League President Chub Feeney lectured Turner on his uniform advertising ploy and made Turner remove the word "Channel" from Messersmith's uniform.

17

Largest number of players involved in one major league trade. The deal, between the Baltimore Orioles and New York Yankees, started on November 18, 1954, when Baltimore sent pitcher Bob Turley, pitcher Don Larsen and shortstop Billy Hunter to New York for pitcher Harry Byrd, pitcher Jim McDonald, outfielder Gene Woodling, catcher Hal Smith, shortstop Willie Miranda and catcher-first baseman Gus Triandos. The deal was completed on December 1 when the Orioles sent pitcher Mike Blyzka, catcher Darrell Johnson, first baseman Dick Kryhoski, outfielder Jim Fridley and outfielder Ted Del Guercio to the Yankees for pitcher Bill Miller, third baseman Kal Segrist and second baseman Don Leppert.

18

Uniform number of Don Larsen when he pitched his perfect World Series game in 1956.

18 1/3

The most innings worked by a relief pitcher in one major league game, with Zip Zabel of the Chicago Cubs setting the record on June 17, 1915, against Brooklyn. Zabel allowed nine hits and only one walk, emerging as the winning pitcher in the Cubs' 4-3, 19-inning triumph.

19

The number of home runs Babe Ruth hit off lefthanded pitchers during his 60-homer year of 1927.

22

The record number of World Series titles won by the American League's New York Yankees.

28

The number of home runs hit by Babe Ruth at Yankee Stadium during his 60-home run year of 1927.

29

The number of World Series titles won by A.L. clubs other than the Yankees.

29

The uniform number worn by Satchel Paige when he threw three scoreless

When Atlanta's Ted Turner, owner of WTBS, Channel 17, signed Andy Messersmith to a Braves contract in 1976, he had a uniform ready for his new pitcher. However, N.L. President Chub Feeney didn't approve.

The famed Green Monster (the left-field wall) in Boston's Fenway Park long has provided an inviting target for American League hitters.

innings for the Kansas City A's in 1965, Satch's final appearance in the major leagues.

30
The number of home runs hit by Roger Maris at Yankee Stadium during his 61-homer year of 1961.

31
The number of home runs hit by Roger Maris on the road during his 61-homer year of 1961.

32
The number of home runs hit by Babe Ruth on the road during his 60-homer year of 1927.

33
The record number of World Series appearances by the New York Yankees.

33
The number of different pitchers who gave up home runs to Babe Ruth during his 60-homer year of 1927.

37

Height, in feet, of the famous left-field wall in Boston's Fenway Park. The wall is nicknamed the "Green Monster."

39

The most home runs hit at one ballpark by a player in one season. Hank Greenberg of the Detroit Tigers hit 39 at Detroit's Briggs Stadium in 1938.

40

Height, in feet, of the left-field screen in the Los Angeles Memorial Coliseum, the Dodgers' first California home.

41

The number of home runs hit by Babe Ruth off righthanded pitchers during his 60-homer year of 1927.

42

The major league-record number of times Rickey Henderson was caught stealing in 1982, when the Oakland A's speedster set a modern major league record of 130 stolen bases.

42

The maximum length, in inches, of a bat.

43

Height, in inches, of St Louis Browns' midget Eddie Gaedel.

44

Uniform number worn by Hank Aaron when he hit his major league record-setting 715th home run. Ironically, the pitcher he victimized that night, Los Angeles Dodgers hurler Al Downing, was also wearing No. 44.

46

The number of different pitchers who gave up home runs to Roger Maris during his 61-homer year of 1961.

49

The number of home runs hit by Roger Maris off righthanded pitchers during his 61-homer year of 1961.

50

The most home runs allowed by a pitcher during one season. Bert Blyleven of the Minnesota Twins allowed 50 in 1986.

Montreal's Ron Hunt often found a painful route to first base during the 1971 season.

50

The length, in days, of the 1981 players' strike.

50

The major league-record number of times Ron Hunt of the Montreal Expos was hit by a pitch in 1971. The Pittsburgh Pirates were the only team that did not hit him. Jim Bunning of the Philadelphia Phillies was the first to hit Hunt (April 10) and Milt Pappas of the Chicago Cubs was the last (September 29). Nolan Ryan of the New York Mets hit him the most times overall, four.

53

The number of players to play for the Seattle Pilots in 1969—the club's only year of existence.

53

One of only three numbers between 0 and 61 that has never been totaled by a major league home run hitter during a season. The other two numbers are 55 and 57.

54

The number of hits a team could possibly get during a nine-inning game and still be shut out.

56

The number of singles collected and runs scored by Joe DiMaggio during his 56-game hitting streak of 1941.

56

The day-by-day batting performance of Joe DiMaggio during his major league-record 56-game hitting streak:

Opposing Pitcher and Club	AB.	R.	H.	2B.	3B.	HR.	RBI.
May 15—Smith, Chicago	4	0	1	0	0	0	1
16—Lee, Chicago	4	2	2	0	1	1	1
17—Rigney, Chicago	3	1	1	0	0	0	0
18—Harris (2), Niggeling (1), St. Louis	3	3	3	1	0	0	1
19—Galehouse, St. Louis	3	0	1	1	0	0	0
20—Auker, St. Louis	5	1	1	0	0	0	1
21—Rowe (1), Benton (1), Detroit	5	0	2	0	0	0	1
22—McKain, Detroit	4	0	1	0	0	0	1
23—Newsome, Boston	5	0	1	0	0	0	2
24—Johnson, Boston	4	2	1	0	0	0	2
25—Grove, Boston	4	0	1	0	0	0	0
27—Chase (1), Anderson (2), Carrasquel (1), Washington	5	3	4	0	0	1	3
28—Hudson, Washington (Night)	4	1	1	0	1	0	0

Lou Gehrig's uniform No. 4 was retired by the New York Yankees.

29—Sundra, Washington	3	1	1	0	0	0	0
30—Johnson, Boston	2	1	1	0	0	0	0
30—Harris, Boston	3	0	1	1	0	0	0
June 1—Milnar, Cleveland	4	1	1	0	0	0	0
1—Harder, Cleveland	4	0	1	0	0	0	0
2—Feller, Cleveland	4	2	2	1	0	0	0
3—Trout, Detroit	4	1	1	0	0	1	1
5—Newhouser, Detroit	5	1	1	0	1	0	1
7—Muncrief (1), Allen (1), Caster (1), St. Louis	5	2	3	0	0	0	1
8—Auker, St. Louis	4	3	2	0	0	2	4
8—Caster (1), Kramer (1), St. Louis	4	1	2	1	0	1	3
10—Rigney, Chicago	5	1	1	0	0	0	0
12—Lee, Chicago (Night)	4	1	2	0	0	1	1
14—Feller, Cleveland	2	0	1	1	0	0	1
15—Bagby, Cleveland	3	1	1	0	0	1	1
16—Milnar, Cleveland	5	0	1	1	0	0	0
17—Rigney, Chicago	4	1	1	0	0	0	0
18—Lee, Chicago	3	0	1	0	0	0	0
19—Smith (1), Ross (2), Chicago	3	2	3	0	0	1	2
20—Newsom (2), McKain (2), Detroit	5	3	4	1	0	0	1
21—Trout, Detroit	4	0	1	0	0	0	1
22—Newhouser (1), Newsom (1), Detroit	5	1	2	1	0	1	2
24—Muncrief, St. Louis	4	1	1	0	0	0	0
25—Galehouse, St. Louis	4	1	1	0	0	1	3
26—Auker, St. Louis	4	0	1	1	0	0	1
27—Dean, Philadelphia	3	1	2	0	0	1	2
28—Babich (1), Harris (1), Philadelphia	5	1	2	1	0	0	0
29—Leonard, Washington	4	1	1	1	0	0	0
29—Anderson, Washington	5	1	1	0	0	0	1
July 1—Harris (1), Ryba (1), Boston	4	0	2	0	0	0	1
1—Wilson, Boston	3	1	1	0	0	0	1
2—Newsome, Boston	5	1	1	0	0	1	3
5—Marchildon, Philadelphia	4	2	1	0	0	1	2
6—Babich (1), Hadley (3), Philadelphia	5	2	4	1	0	0	2
6—Knott, Philadelphia	4	0	2	0	1	0	2
10—Niggeling, St. Louis (Night)	2	0	1	0	0	0	0
11—Harris (3), Kramer (1), St. Louis	5	1	4	0	0	1	2
12—Auker (1), Muncrief (1), St. Louis	5	1	2	1	0	0	1
13—Lyons (2), Hallett (1), Chicago	4	2	3	0	0	0	0
13—Lee, Chicago	4	0	1	0	0	0	0
14—Rigney, Chicago	3	0	1	0	0	0	0

15—Smith, Chicago	4	1	2	1	0	0	2
16—Milnar (2), Krakauskas (1), Cleve	4	3	3	1	0	0	0

Totals for 56 games	223	56	91	16	4	15	55

Stopped July 17 at Cleveland, New York won, 4 to 3. First inning, Alfred J. Smith pitching, thrown out by Keltner; fourth inning, Smith pitching, received base on balls; seventh inning, Smith pitching, thrown out by Keltner; eighth inning, James C. Bagby, Jr., pitching, grounded into double play.

60
60 Babe Ruth's 60 home runs in 1927:

HR No.	Game No.	Date		Opposing Pitcher and Club	City
1	4	April	15	Howard J. Ehmke (R), Phila.	New York
2	11	April	23	George E. Walberg (L), Phila.	Phila.
3	12	April	24	Hollis Thurston (R), Wash.	Washington
4	14	April	29	Bryan W. Harriss (R), Boston	Boston
5	16	May	1	John P. Quinn (R), Phila.	New York
6	16	May	1	George E. Walberg (L), Phila.	New York
7	24	May	10	Milton Gaston (R), St. Louis	St. Louis
8	25	May	11	Ernest Nevers (R), St. Louis	St. Louis
9	29	May	17	H. Warren Collins (R), Detroit	Detroit
10	33	May	22	Benj. J. Karr (R), Cleveland	Cleveland
11	34	May	23	Hollis Thurston (R), Wash.	Washington
12	37	May	28*	Hollis Thurston (R), Wash.	New York
13	39	May	29	Daniel MacFayden (R), Boston	New York
14	41	May	30‡	George E. Walberg (L), Phila.	Phila.
15	42	May	31*	John P. Quinn (R), Phila.	Phil.
16	43	May	31†	Howard J. Ehmke (R), Phila.	Phila.
17	47	June	5	Earl O. Whitehill (L), Detroit	New York
18	48	June	7	Alphonse T. Thomas (R), Chi.	New York
19	52	June	11	Garland M. Buckeye (L), Cleve.	New York
20	52	June	11	Garland M. Buckeye (L), Cleve.	New York
21	53	June	12	George E. Uhle (R), Cleveland	New York
22	55	June	16	Jonathan T. Zachary (L), St. L.	New York
23	60	June	22*	Harold J. Wiltse (L), Boston	Boston
24	60	June	22*	Harold J. Wiltse (L), Boston	Boston
25	70	June	30	Bryan W. Harriss (R), Boston	New York
26	73	July	3	Horace O. Lisenbee (R), Wash.	Washington
27	78	July	8+	Donald Hankins (R), Detroit	Detroit
28	79	July	9*	Kenneth Holloway (R), Detroit	Detroit
29	79	July	9*	Kenneth Holloway (R), Detroit	Detroit
30	83	July	12	Joseph B. Shaute (L), Cleve.	Cleveland

Orioles President Jerry Hoffberger presents a framed uniform No. 20, retired by the Baltimore club, to Frank Robinson before the 1972 season. Robinson spent '72 with the Los Angeles Dodgers.

31	94	July	24	Alphonse T. Thomas (R), Chi.	Chicago
32	95	July	26*	Milton Gaston (R), St. Louis	New York
33	95	July	26*	Milton Gaston (R), St. Louis	New York
34	98	July	28	Walter C. Stewart (L), St. L.	New York
35	106	Aug.	5	George S. Smith (R), Detroit	New York
36	110	Aug.	10	Jonathan T. Zachary (L), Wash.	Washington
37	114	Aug.	16	Alphonse T. Thomas (R), Chi.	Chicago
38	115	Aug.	17	George W. Connally (R), Chi.	Chicago
39	118	Aug.	20	J. Walter Miller (L), Cleveland	Cleveland
40	120	Aug.	22	Joseph B. Shaute (L), Cleve.	Cleveland
41	124	Aug.	27	Ernest Nevers (R), St. Louis	St. Louis
42	125	Aug.	28	J. Ernest Wingard (L), St. Louis	St. Louis
43	127	Aug.	31	Tony Welzer (R), Boston	New York
44	128	Sept.	2	George E. Walberg (L), Phila.	Phila.
45	132	Sept.	6*	Tony Welzer (R), Boston	Boston
46	132	Sept.	6*	Tony Welzer (R), Boston	Boston
47	133	Sept.	6†	Jack Russell (R), Boston	Boston
48	134	Sept.	7	Daniel MacFayden (R), Boston	Boston
49	134	Sept.	7	Bryan W. Harriss (R), Boston	Boston
50	138	Sept.	11	Milton Gaston (R), St. Louis	New York
51	139	Sept.	13*	G. Willis Hudlin (R), Clev.	New York
52	140	Sept.	13†	Joseph B. Shaute (L), Clev.	New York
53	143	Sept.	16	Ted Blankenship (R), Chicago	New York
54	147	Sept.	18†	Theodore A. Lyons (R), Chi.	New York
55	148	Sept.	21	Samuel B. Gibson (R), Detroit	New York
56	149	Sept.	22	Kenneth E. Holloway (R), Det.	New York
57	152	Sept.	27	Robert M Grove (L), Phila.	New York
58	153	Sept.	29	Horace O. Lisenbee (R), Wash.	New York
59	153	Sept.	29	Paul Hopkins (R), Washington	New York
60	154	Sept.	30	Jonathan T. Zachary (L), Wash.	New York

*First game of doubleheader. †Second game of doubleheader.
‡Afternoon game of split doubleheader.

61
The game-by-game home run performance of Roger Maris in 1961:

HR No.	Game No.	Date		Opposing Pitcher and Club	City
1	11	April	26	Paul Foytack (R), Detroit	Detroit
2	17	May	3	Pedro Ramos (R), Minnesota	Minneapolis
3	20	May	6	Eli Grba (R), Los Angeles	Los Angeles
4	29	May	17	Peter Burnside (L), Washington	New York
5	30	May	19	James Perry (R), Cleveland	Cleveland

6	31	May 20	Gary Bell (R), Cleveland	Cleveland
7	32	May 21	Charles Estrada (R), Baltimore	New York
8	35	May 24	D. Eugene Conley (R), Boston	New York
9	38	May 28	Calvin McLish (R), Chicago	New York
10	40	May 30	D. Eugene Conley (R), Boston	Boston
11	40	May 30	Miguel Fornieles (R), Boston	Boston
12	41	May 31	Billy Muffett (R), Boston	Boston
13	43	June 2	Calvin McLish (R), Chicago	Chicago
14	44	June 3	Robert Shaw (R), Chicago	Chicago
15	45	June 4	Russell Kemmerer (R), Chicago	Chicago
16	48	June 6	Edwin Palmquist (R), Minnesota	New York
17	49	June 7	Pedro Ramos (R), Minnesota	New York
18	52	June 9	Raymond Herbert (R), Kan. City	New York
19	55	June 11†	Eli Grba (R), Los Angeles	New York
20	55	June 11†	John James (R), Los Angeles	New York
21	57	June 13	James Perry (R), Cleveland	Cleveland
22	58	June 14	Gary Bell (R), Cleveland	Cleveland
23	61	June 17	Donald Mossi (L), Detroit	Detroit
24	62	June 18	Jerry Casale (R), Detroit	Detroit
25	63	June 19	James Archer (L), Kansas City	Kansas City
26	64	June 20	Joseph Nuxhall (L), Kansas City	Kansas City
27	66	June 22	Norman Bass (R), Kansas City	Kansas City
28	74	July 1	David Sisler (R), Washington	New York
29	75	July 2	Peter Burnside (L), Washington	New York
30	75	July 2	John Klippstein (R), Washington	New York
31	77	July 4†	Frank Lary (R), Detroit	New York
32	78	July 5	Frank Funk (R), Cleveland	New York
33	82	July 9*	William Monbouquette (R), Bos.	New York
34	84	July 13	Early Wynn (R), Chicago	Chicago
35	86	July 15	Raymond Herbert (R), Chicago	Chicago
36	92	July 21	William Monbouquette (R), Bos.	Boston
37	95	July 25*	Frank Baumann (L), Chicago	New York
38	95	July 25*	Don Larsen (R), Chicago	New York
39	96	July 25†	Russell Kemmerer (R), Chicago	New York
40	96	July 25†	Warren Hacker (R), Chicago	New York
41	106	Aug. 4	Camilo Pascual (R), Minnesota	New York
42	114	Aug. 11	Peter Burnside (L), Washington	Washington
43	115	Aug. 12	Richard Donovan (R), Wash.	Washington
44	116	Aug. 13*	Bennie Daniels (R), Washington	Washington
45	117	Aug. 13†	Marion Kutyna (R), Washington	Washington
46	118	Aug. 15	Juan Pizarro (L), Chicago	New York
47	119	Aug. 16	W. William Pierce (L), Chicago	New York
48	119	Aug. 16	W. William Pierce (L), Chicago	New York
49	124	Aug. 20	James Perry (R), Cleveland	Cleveland
50	125	Aug. 22	Kenneth McBride (R), L. Angeles	Los Angeles

Joe DiMaggio matches Willie Keeler's 44-game batting streak on the way to establishing the major league record of hitting safely in 56 consecutive games.

51	129	Aug. 26	Jerry Walker (R), Kansas City	Kansas City
52	135	Sept. 2	Frank Lary (R), Detroit	New York
53	135	Sept. 2	Henry Aguirre (L), Detroit	New York
54	140	Sept. 6	Thomas Cheney (R), Washington	New York
55	141	Sept. 7	Richard Stigman (L), Cleveland	New York
56	143	Sept. 9	James Grant (R), Cleveland	New York
57	151	Sept. 16	Frank Lary (R), Detroit	Detroit
58	152	Sept. 17	Terrence Fox (R), Detroit	Detroit
59	155	Sept. 20	Milton Pappas (R), Baltimore	Baltimore
60	159	Sept. 26	John Fisher (R), Baltimore	New York
61	163	Oct. 1	E. Tracy Stallard (R), Boston	New York

*First game of doubleheader. †Second game of doubleheader.

65
The weight, in pounds, of St. Louis Browns midget pinch-hitter Eddie Gaedel.

72
The major league-record number of times Babe Ruth hit two or more home runs in one game during his regular-season career. He did it another four times in the World Series, for a total of 76.

83
The total number of major leaguers who have had their numbers retired (Rod Carew, Casey Stengel and Hank Aaron have had their numbers retired by two clubs):

No. Player/Team
1-Richie Ashburn/Phillies
1-Bobby Doerr/Red Sox
1-Fred Hutchinson/Reds
1-Billy Martin/Yankees
1-Billy Meyer/Pirates
1-Pee Wee Reese/Dodgers
2-Nellie Fox/White Sox
2-Charlie Gehringer/Tigers
3-Earl Averill/Indians
3-Harold Baines/White Sox
3-Harmon Killebrew/Twins
3-Babe Ruth/Yankees
3-Bill Terry/Giants
4-Luke Applying/White Sox
4-Joe Cronin/Red Sox
4-Lou Gehrig/Yankees
4-Ralph Kiner/Pirates

4-Mel Ott/Giants
4-Duke Snider/Dodgers
4-Earl Weaver/Orioles
5-Johnny Bench/Reds
5-Lou Boudreau/Indians
5-Joe DiMaggio/Yankees
5-Hank Greenberg/Tigers
5-Brooks Robinson/Orioles
6-Steve Garvey/Padres
6-Al Kaline/Tigers
6-Stan Musial/Cardinals
7-Mickey Mantle/Yankees
8-Yogi Berra/Yankees
8-Bill Dickey/Yankees
8-Willie Stargell/Pirates
8-Carl Yastrzemski/Red Sox
9-Roger Maris/Yankees
9-Bill Mazeroski/Pirates
9-Minnie Minoso/White Sox
9-Ted Williams/Red Sox
10-Dick Howser/Royals
10-Phil Rizzuto/Yankees
11-Luis Aparicio/White Sox
11-Carl Hubbell/Giants
14-Ernie Banks/Cubs
14-Ken Boyer/Cardinals
14-Gil Hodges/Mets
15-Thurman Munson/Yankees
16-Whitey Ford/Yankees
16-Ted Lyons/White Sox
17-Dizzy Dean/Cardinals
18-Mel Harder/Indians
19-Bob Feller/Indians
19-Jim Gilliam/Dodgers
19-Billy Pierce/White Sox
20-Lou Brock/Cardinals
20-Frank Robinson/Orioles
20-Mike Schmidt/Phillies
20-Pie Traynor/Pirates
21-Roberto Clement/Pirates
21-Warren Spahn/Braves
22-Jim Palmer/Orioles
24-Walter Alston/Dodgers
24-Willie Mays/Giants
26-Billy Williams/Cubs

27-Juan Marichal/Giants
29-Rod Carew/Twins
29-Rod Carew/Angels
32-Steve Carlton/Phillies
32-Elston Howard/Yankees
32-Sandy Koufax/Dodgers
32-Jim Umbricht/Astros (Colt .45s)
33-Eddie Murray/Orioles
33-Honu Wagner/Pirates
35-Phil Niekro/Braves
36-Robin roberts/Phillies
37-Casey Stengel/Yankees
37-Casey Stengel/Mets
39-Roy Campanella/Dodgers
40-Danny Murtaugh/Pirates
40-Don Wilson/Astros
41-Eddie Mathews/Braves
41-Tom Seaver/Mets
42-Jackie Robinson/Dodgers
44-Hank Aaron/Braves
44- Hank Aaron/Brewers
44-Willie McCovey/Giants
45-Bob Gibson/Cardinals
53-Don Drysdale/Dodgers
(The list excludes the Angels' number 26, retired in honor of the club's "26th man," Owner Gene Autry.)

96
Uniform number worn by Bill Voiselle starting in 1947 after he was traded from the New York Giants to the Boston Braves. Voiselle was from the town of Ninety Six, S.C., and his uniform number reflected that fact.

96
The number of home runs that Frank (Home Run) Baker hit in a big-league career that began in 1908 and ended in 1922. Baker never slugged more than 12 homers in one season.

97
The number of pitches thrown by Don Larsen of the New York Yankees in his 1956 World Series perfect game.

98.2
The highest percentage of votes received by a player elected to the Baseball Hall of Fame. Ty Cobb collected votes on 222 of the 226 ballots cast when he was elected in 1936.

Pitcher Bill Voiselle of the Boston Braves was from Ninety Six, S.C.—and obviously proud of it.

103
The most wins achieved in a season by the New York Yankees in the 10-year period between 1949 and 1958. The Yankees won 103 games in 1954, but finished second to Cleveland's 111 wins that season. Ironically, they won the pennant in each of the other nine years, but never won as many as 100 games in any season.

108
The number of double stitches in a regulation baseball.

158
The number of lifetime home runs Roger Maris had after he hit his record 61st of 1961.

186
The distance, in feet, from the playing field to the highest point of the ceiling in Minnesota's Metrodome.

208
The distance, in feet, from the playing field to the highest point of the ceiling in Houston's Astrodome.

250
The distance, in feet, from the playing field to the highest point of the ceiling in Seattle's Kingdome.

251
The distance, in feet, from home plate to the left-field foul pole in the Los Angeles Memorial Coliseum, the Dodgers' first California home.

257
The distance, in feet, from home plate to the right-field foul pole in New York's Polo Grounds.

275
The number of career home runs hit by single-season homer king Roger Maris, who hit 61 in 1961.

279
The distance, in feet, from home plate to the left-field foul pole in New York's Polo Grounds.

297
The distance, in feet, from home plate to the right-field foul pole in Brooklyn's Ebbets Field.

The configuration of the Los Angeles Memorial Coliseum (packed for Game 3 of the 1959 World Series) wasn't meant for baseball, as evidenced by the 251-foot distance from home plate to the left-field flagpole. The left-field screen became a favorite home-run target.

300
The distance, in feet, from home plate to the right-field foul pole in the Los Angeles Memorial Coliseum, the Dodgers' first California home. However, right field proved a tough area in which to hit a home run because the fence curved out dramatically from the foul pole.

323
The highest number of home runs hit by one player in one park during a career. Mel Ott had 323 homers for the New York Giants at the Polo Grounds.

348
The distance, in feet, from home plate to the left-field foul pole in Brooklyn's Ebbets Field.

416
The number of lifetime home runs Babe Ruth had after he hit his 60th of the 1927 season.

483
The distance, in feet, from home plate to the deepest part of center field in New York's Polo Grounds.

The 483-foot marker in deepest center field at the Polo Grounds is barely visible as players stand at attention for flag-raising ceremonies.

500-HOMER CLUB

Twelve players in major league history have hit 500 or more lifetime home runs. The first, 500th and last victims of each follow:

	Hank Aaron (755)	Babe Ruth (714)	Willie Mays (660)
First Victim	Vic Raschi St. Louis, N.L. April 23, 1954 At St. Louis	Jack Warhop New York, A.L. May 6, 1915 At New York	Warren Spahn Boston, N.L. May 28, 1951 At New York
500th Victim	Mike McCormick San Francisco, N.L. July 14, 1968 At Atlanta	Willis Hudlin Cleveland, A.L. August 11, 1929 At Cleveland	Don Nottebart Houston, N.L. Sept. 13, 1965 At Houston
Last Victim	Dick Drago California, A.L. July 20, 1976 At Milwaukee	Guy Bush Pittsburgh, N.L. May 25, 1935 At Pittsburgh	Don Gullett Cincinnati, N.L. August 17, 1973 At New York

	Frank Robinson (586)	Harmon Killebrew (573)	Reggie Jackson (563)
First Victim	Paul Minner Chicago, N.L. April 28, 1956 At Cincinnati	Billy Hoeft Detroit, A.L. June 24, 1955 At Washington	Jim Weaver California, A.L. Sept. 17, 1967 At California
500th Victim	Fred Scherman Detroit, A.L. September 13, 1971 At Baltimore	Mike Cuellar Baltimore, A.L. August 10, 1971 At Minnesota	Bud Black Kansas City, A.L. Sept. 17, 1984 At California
Last Victim	Sid Monge California, A.L. July 6, 1976 At California	Ed Bane Minnesota, A.L. Sept. 18, 1975 At Minnesota	Mike Witt California, A.L. August 17, 1987 At California

	Mike Schmidt (548)	Mickey Mantle (536)	Jimmie Foxx (534)
First Victim	Balor Moore Montreal, N.L. September 16, 1972 At Philadelphia	Randy Gumpert Chicago, A.L. May 1, 1951 At Chicago	Urban Shocker New York, A.L. May 31, 1927 At Philadelphia
500th Victim	Don Robinson Pittsburgh, N.L. April 18, 1987 At Pittsburgh	Stu Miller Baltimore, A.L. May 14, 1967 At New York	George Caster Philadelphia, A.L. Sept. 24, 1940 At Philadelphia
Last Victim	Jim Deshaies Houston, N.L. May 2, 1989 At Philadelphia	Jim Lonborg Boston, A.L. Sept. 20, 1968 At New York	Johnny Lanning Pittsburgh, N.L. September 9, 1945 At Pittsburgh

	Ted Williams (521)	Willie McCovey (521)	Eddie Mathews (512)
First Victim	Bud Thomas Philadelphia, A.L. April 23, 1939 At Boston	Ron Kline Pittsburgh, N.L. August 2, 1959 At San Francisco	Ken Heintzelman Philadelphia, N.L. April 19, 1952 At Philadelphia
500th Victim	Wynn Hawkins Cleveland, A.L. June 17, 1960 At Cleveland	Jamie Easterly Atlanta, N.L. June 30, 1978 At Atlanta	Juan Marichal San Fran., N.L. July 14, 1967 At San Francisco
	Jack Fisher Baltimore, A.L. September 28, 1960 At Boston	Scott Sanderson Montreal, N.L. May 3, 1980 At Montreal	Sammy Ellis California, A.L. May 27, 1968 At California

	Ernie Banks (512)	Mel Ott (511)
First Victim	Gerry Staley St. Louis, N.L. September 20, 1953 At St. Louis	Hal Carlson Chicago, N.L. July 18, 1927 At New York

	Pat Jarvis	Johnny Hutchings
500th	Atlanta, N.L.	Boston, N.L.
Victim	May 12, 1970	August 1, 1945
	At Chicago	At New York

	Jim McGlothlin	Oscar Judd
Last	Cincinnati, N.L.	Philadelphia, N.L.
Victim	August 24, 1971	April 16, 1946
	At Chicago	At New York

600-HOMER CLUB

Only three players have hit 600 or more major league home runs. The players and their 600th victims follow:

Player, Club	Victim, Club	Date, Place
Babe Ruth, New York, A.L.	George Blaeholder, St. Louis	August 21, 1931 At St. Louis
Willie Mays, San Francisco, N.L.	Mike Corkins, San Diego	September 22, 1969 At San Diego
Hank Aaron, Atlanta, N.L.	Gaylord Perry, San Francisco	April 27, 1971 At Atlanta

Harmon Killebrew entered the 500-homer club on August 10, 1971, and added another for good measure.

Willie Mays (right) trots home after slugging career homer No. 600 in a 1969 game against the San Diego Padres.

Red Barber interviews Dodgers Manager Leo Durocher (center) after W2XBS presented the first telecast of a big-league game in 1939. Reds Manager Bill McKechnie (1) also was interviewed.

672

The highest number of at-bats compiled by one player during a season without hitting a home run. Rabbit Maranville of the Pittsburgh Pirates reached this figure in 1922.

691

The major league-record number of games in which Hank Aaron hit one or more home runs in his regular-season career. In addition, he hit homers in eight post-season and All-Star Games.

Baseball comedian Max Patkin apparently is puzzled over what uniform number he should wear.

700-HOMER CLUB
The only two players to hit 700 big-league home runs, and their 700th victims:

Player, Club	Victim, Club	Date, Place
Babe Ruth, New York, A L.	Tommy Bridges, Detroit	July 13, 1934 At Detroit
Hank Aaron, Atlanta, N.L	Ken Brett, Philadelphia	July 21, 1973 At Atlanta

712
The number of games canceled in the major leagues during the 1981 players' strike. There were 328 games canceled in the N.L. and 384 in the A.L.

755
The record number of career home runs hit by Hank Aaron. Including All-Star Games and post-season contests, Aaron hit 763.

W2XBS
The experimental television station in New York which aired the first televised major league game on August 26, 1939 from Ebbets Field, between the Cincinnati Reds and Brooklyn Dodgers. The Reds won the game, 5-2. Only three commercials were shown during the game: Ivory Soap, Mobil Oil and Wheaties. The contest was the first game of a doubleheader played between the two teams that day.

?
The uniform "number" of baseball comedian Max Patkin.

TENTH INNING
Touching other bases

AND IN RIGHT FIELD . . .
In the "Who's on First?" comedy sketch that Bud Abbott and Lou Costello made famous, the name of one player—the right fielder—was routinely omitted. Names in the rest of the lineup:
* **First baseman**—Who.
* **Second baseman**—What.
* **Third baseman**—I Don't Know.
* **Shortstop**—I Don't Care.
* **Left fielder**—Why.
* **Center fielder**—Because.
* **Catcher**—Today.
* **Pitcher**—Tomorrow.

EARL AVERILL
Cleveland outfielder who hit a line drive off the foot of pitcher Dizzy Dean of the St. Louis Cardinals in the 1937 All-Star Game at Washington. Averill was thrown out, but Dean suffered a broken toe on the play.

Dean, 26 years old at the time of the toe injury, apparently tried to come back too soon after the fracture and put stress on his arm. Having entered the 1937 All-Star Game with a 12-7 season record and a 133-72 career mark in the majors, the sore-armed Dean won only 17 more games in the big leagues (losing three of his four post-All-Star decisions in '37 to begin the slip from stardom).

BOBBY BRAGAN
Pittsburgh manager who after being thrown out of a July 31, 1957, game at Milwaukee returned to the field later in the game sipping an orange drink. Bragan, who offered a sip to the umpiring crew, had intended to be munching on a hot dog as well (but the sandwich never arrived after Bragan ordered it). National League President Warren Giles fined and reprimanded Bragan for "repeated farcical acts," and two days after the incident the Pirates dismissed the manager.

TOM BROWN
The only man to play major league baseball and also appear in football's Super Bowl. Brown, from the University of Maryland, was a first baseman-outfielder who played in 61 games for Washington in 1963 and batted .147 with one home run. He then played with Green Bay of the National Football League from 1964

The comedy team of Bud Abbott and Lou Costello brought baseball into its act and smiles to faces in the audience.

Pittsburgh Manager Bobby Bragan's orange drink-sipping routine in 1957 may have cost him his job.

through 1968, starting at safety for the Packers in Super Bowls I and II, and finished his NFL career with the Washington Redskins in 1969.

STEVE CARLTON
The only man to win the Cy Young Award while pitching for a last-place team. Carlton was honored after compiling a 27-10 record for the 1972 Philadelphia Phillies, whose 59-97 mark (.378) was the worst in the National League.

RAY CHAPMAN
Cleveland shortstop who was fatally injured when struck by a pitch from the Yankees' Carl Mays on August 16, 1920, at the Polo Grounds. Chapman led off the fifth inning for the Indians and was hit in the head by Mays' first pitch of the inning. Chapman was rushed to New York's St. Lawrence Hospital, where he died the next morning of massive head injuries at age 29.

257

Rocky Colavito (left), who shared American League home run honors in 1959, and 1959 batting champion Harvey Kuenn talk things over after being traded for each other prior to the 1960 season.

Harry Lunte, who played in only 54 regular-season games in his big-league career, is the man who replaced Chapman in the game.

HAL CHASE
Of the 51 men receiving votes in the first Hall of Fame balloting in 1936, only eight have failed to make it to Cooperstown over the years—and Chase is one of them. Five of the 51 were elected the first year, and 38 more eventually were inducted. Unable to win election: Chase (11 votes in '36), Johnny Kling (8), Lou Criger (7), Joe Jackson (2), Bill Bradley (1), Nap Rucker (1), Jake Daubert (1) and Kid Elberfeld (1).

TY COBB
The leading vote-getter among the five first-year Hall of Fame inductees when balloting for the shrine began in 1936. Needing 75 percent of the 226 ballots cast for election to the Hall of Fame, Cobb received 222 votes.

Other first-time Hall choices and their vote totals: Babe Ruth and Honus Wagner, 215; Christy Mathewson, 205, and Walter Johnson, 189.

ROCKY COLAVITO, HARVEY KUENN
Colavito, Cleveland outfielder who shared the American League homer championship in 1959, and Kuenn, Detroit outfielder who won the '59 A.L. batting title, were dealt away two days before their clubs were to open the 1960 season—and they were traded for each other. The stunning swap took on added drama since the Tigers and Colavito—one of the most popular players in Cleveland history—were scheduled to begin the '60 season with two games against the Indians in Cleveland. With 52,756 fans on hand for the opener, Detroit beat the Indians, 4-2, in 15 innings—but Colavito had a dismal "homecoming," going 0-for-6 and striking out four times. Kuenn went 2-for-7. Colavito rebounded the next day, though, slugging a three-run homer in Detroit's 64 triumph. Kuenn was sidelined because of a pulled muscle.

GENE CONLEY
Played for the 1957 World Series champion Milwaukee Braves, and for the 1959, 1960 and 1961 National Basketball Association champion Boston Celtics.

GENE CONLEY
Pitcher who jumped the Boston Red Sox's team bus in midtown Manhattan on July 26, 1962, after absorbing a 13-3 loss to the New York Yankees. Gone from the club for four days, Conley tried to book a flight to Israel during his absence without leave—but he was foiled because he didn't have a passport. Teammate Pumpsie Green, an infielder, also left the bus (which was tied up in traffic), and he and Conley reportedly lived it up in New York that night. Green returned to the Red Sox in 48 hours.

The familiar face belongs to Dodger Chuck Connors, alias The Rifleman, prior to the start of his successful acting career.

CHUCK CONNORS

Better known as "The Rifleman" of television fame and as an actor in many other roles, Connors also was a major league baseball player in 1949 and 1951. After appearing in one game for the Brooklyn Dodgers in '49, Connors played 66 games for the Chicago Cubs in '51 and batted .239 in 201 at-bats. The first baseman hit two home runs for the Cubs, connecting off Dave Koslo of the New York Giants on July 18 and against Sal Maglie of the Giants on August 26.

COPACABANA

Observing Billy Martin's 29th birthday on May 15, 1957, six New York Yankees—Hank Bauer, Mickey Mantle, Whitey Ford, Yogi Berra, Johnny Kucks and Martin—partied at the Copacabana nightclub in New York beyond midnight. The revelry ended when Bauer was accused of striking a patron. Bauer was later cleared of the charges, but the Yankees fined all six players for their roles in the disturbance—and they traded Martin to Kansas City a month after the incident.

JIMMIE DYKES, JOE GORDON

Major league managers who in an unprecedented move exchanged jobs on August 3, 1960. The "trade" sent Dykes from sixth-place Detroit to fourth-place Cleveland and Gordon from the Indians to the Tigers. The possibility of such a swap was raised in trade talks earlier in the season when Detroit General Manager Bill DeWitt told Cleveland General Manager Frank Lane "While we're talking about deals, let's talk about a big one. Let's talk about trading managers." DeWitt's remark seemed facetious; besides, Cleveland was playing well at the time and Lane wasn't inclined to make a change. When the season ended, the Indians and Tigers found themselves in the same spots in the American League standings as they were when the "trade" was made.

BOB FELLER

On Mother's Day, May 14, 1939, Feller's parents traveled from Van Meter, Iowa, to Chicago to see their son pitch for the Cleveland Indians against the White Sox. While Bob beat the White Sox, 9-4, it wasn't a great Mother's Day for Mrs. Feller. Sitting along the first-base line, Mrs. Feller was struck in the head in the third inning by a foul ball off the bat of Chicago third baseman Marv Owen. The ball broke her glasses, and Mrs. Feller suffered a cut above her right eye that required six stitches. After going into the stands to check on his mother, Feller returned to the mound and struck out Owen.

JIMMIE FOXX

The only major leaguer to win Most Valuable Player awards for two teams in the same league. Foxx was the American League's MVP as a member of the Philadelphia Athletics in 1932 and 1933, and he won the honor in 1938 while with the Boston Red Sox.

A thoughtful Jimmie Dykes watches action duiring the 1960 Cleveland-Baltimore game that marked his managerial debut with the Indians. Only three days earlier, Dykes, manager of Detroit, and Joe Gordon, Cleveland manager, were "traded" for each other in an unprecedented move.

CHICK FULLIS

The man who replaced Joe Medwick for the St. Louis Cardinals in the bottom of the sixth inning of Game 7 of the 1934 World Series at Detroit after Medwick was pelted with fruit, vegetables, bottles and other debris. Medwick had slid hard into Detroit third baseman Marv Owen in the top of the sixth, and Tiger fans—unhappy about their club's 9-0 deficit—showed their displeasure with St. Louis' left fielder when he returned to his defensive position. To quell the disturbance over the Medwick-Owen incident Commissioner Kenesaw Mountain Landis ordered Medwick out of the game (and the Cardinals sent in Fullis). St. Louis went on to wrap up the Series, winning, 11-0, behind a 17-hit attack and Dizzy Dean's six-hit pitching.

EDDIE GRANT MEMORIAL

The plaque in center field at the Polo Grounds that honored a former major league infielder who was killed in World War I. Grant, a Harvard graduate who played for Cleveland, the Phillies and Cincinnati before closing out his 10-year career in the majors with the New York Giants, retired from baseball in 1916 and entered law practice. A year later he enlisted in officers' training school. On October 5, 1918, a little more than a month before the end of the war, Grant was killed at age 35 in the Argonne Forest of France. On May 30, 1921, Grant's two sisters were at the Polo Grounds to help unveil the plaque.

Game 7 of the 1934 World Series started getting out of hand when St. Louis' Joe Medwick slid hard into third baseman Marv Owen in the sixth inning, igniting the wrath of Detroit fans.

PUMPSIE GREEN
The player who completed the integration of the pre-expansion era's 16 major league teams. The Boston Red Sox were the last club to use a black player, bringing up Green, an infielder, in 1959 (and Green made his debut July 21).

HANK GREENBERG
The first of only three major leaguers to win Most Valuable Player awards at different positions. Greenberg was the American League's MVP as a first baseman for Detroit in 1935 and as a outfielder for the Tigers in 1940.

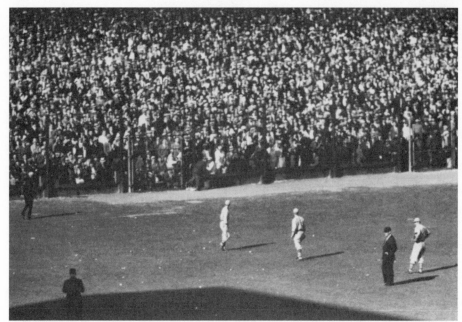

When Medwick took his position in left field, unhappy Detroit fans showered him with debris. Commissioner Kenesaw Mountain Landis conferred with Medwick and St. Louis Manager Frankie Frisch (left) and eventually told Frisch to remove Medwick from the game.

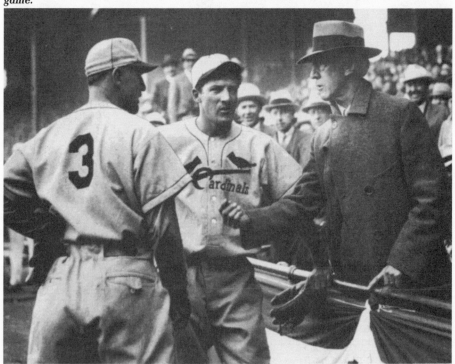

Stan Musial captured the National League's MVP honor in 1943 and 1948 as an outfielder for St. Louis and in 1946 as a first baseman for the Cardinals. Robin Yount was voted the A.L.'s MVP in 1982 as a shortstop for Milwaukee and in 1989 as a outfielder for the Brewers.

BUMP HADLEY
New York Yankees hurler who on May 25, 1937, hit Detroit's Mickey Cochrane with a fifth-inning pitch that fractured Cochrane's skull and ended the playing career of the Tigers' 34-year-old player-manager. Ray Hayworth replaced his injured pilot, taking over as the Tigers' catcher against the Yankees.

BOB HAZLE
Called up from Class AAA Wichita (where he was batting only .279), Hazle earned the nickname "Hurricane" by hitting .403 in 41 games for Milwaukee in 1957 and helping the Braves to the National League pennant. The outfielder's only other big-league experience consisted of six games in 1955 and 63 games in 1958.

BOBBY HOFMAN
Utility player for the New York Giants whose ninth-inning line drive on the final day of the 1955 season brought Leo Durocher's managerial career with the Giants to a stunning finish. Durocher, having announced his resignation and acceptance of a television job, saw his club trailing Philadelphia, 3-1, entering the bottom of the ninth inning at the Polo Grounds. Two Giants reached base with no one out, and Hofman was the batter. Hofman lined a Jack Meyer pitch to shortstop Ted Kazanski for one out, and Kazanski's throw to Bobby Morgan doubled off Joey Amalfitano at second. Morgan's throw to Marv Blaylock at first caught Whitey Lockman off the bag, completing a triple play for the Phillies.

CAL HUBBARD
The only man inducted into both the Baseball Hall of Fame in Cooperstown, N.Y., and the Pro Football Hall of Fame in Canton, Ohio. Hubbard was a standout lineman for nine seasons (1927-33, 1935-36) in the National Football League, an American League umpire for 16 years (1936-51) and then a supervisor of umpires.

VIC JANOWICZ, BO JACKSON
The only Heisman Trophy winners to play big-league baseball. Janowicz, winner of college football's most prestigious award in 1950 while playing for Ohio State, was a catcher-third baseman for the Pittsburgh Pirates in 1953 and 1954. Jackson, the Heisman recipient in 1985 at Auburn, has been a major leaguer since 1986 when he broke in as an outfielder with the Kansas City Royals.

The plaque on the monument that stood in center field at the old Polo Grounds told the story of former major leaguer Eddie Grant.

NELLY KELLY
The name of the girl featured in the song, "Take Me Out to the Ball Game."

LERRIN LaGROW
Detroit pitcher at whom Oakland's Bert Campaneris hurled his bat in Game 2 of the 1972 American League Championship Series. Campaneris was 3-for-3 at the plate as he went to bat in the seventh inning, and the A's (up 1-0 in the series) led the game, 5-0. LaGrow's first pitch in the seventh struck Campaneris' left ankle. After falling to the ground, Campaneris got up and flung his bat toward the Tigers' pitcher. As the bat sailed over LaGrow's head, both benches emptied. Campaneris and LaGrow were ejected. The A's advanced to the World Series and Campaneris, suspended for the rest of the Championship Series, was permitted to play. However, Commissioner Bowie Kuhn suspended Campaneris for the first seven games of the 1973 season.

Dal Maxvill pinch-ran and went in to play shortstop for Oakland's Campaneris, and John Hiller replaced LaGrow on the mound for the Tigers.

NAP LAJOIE
The player who collected the most votes among those who did not make the Hall of Fame in 1936, the first year of balloting. Needing 75 percent of the 226 votes cast for election to the Hall, Lajoie garnered 64.6 percent (146 votes). He was elected to Cooperstown in 1937.

PHIL LINZ
Reserve infielder for the New York Yankees whose harmonica playing on the team bus on August 20, 1964, angered Manager Yogi Berra. The Yankees had just lost their fourth straight game to the Chicago White Sox, falling 4 1/2 games out of first place. Berra told Linz to quit playing the harmonica, but Linz played on—until the manager confronted him. Linz flipped the instrument toward Berra, who swatted it. Frank Crosetti, Yankee coach, called the incident the "first case of open defiance by a player" in his 33 years with the club. New York went on to win the '64 American League pennant.

DICK LITTLEFIELD
Pitcher who was the player the Brooklyn Dodgers acquired in exchange for Jackie Robinson in a December 13, 1956, trade with the New York Giants. (Robinson subsequently retired, voiding the deal.)

ROGER MARIS
The American League's Most Valuable Player in the season preceding Maris' 61-homer, MVP year of 1961 was . . . Maris. Obtained in December of 1959 from the Kansas City A's, Maris won A.L. MVP honors for the New York Yankees in 1960 by hitting 39 home runs, driving in 112 runs and batting .283. In fact, Maris had more overall MVP points (225 to 202) and first-place votes (8 to 7)

Cal Hubbard, pictured as the captain of the Green Bay Packers in 1933 and later during his days as an American League umpire, has a special niche in sports. He's the only man ever to be elected to both the Baseball Hall of Fame and the Pro Football Hall of Fame.

in 1960 than he did in 1961.

CARLOS, LEE MAY
The only brothers to win The Sporting News' Rookie Player of the Year honor. Carlos, playing for the Chicago White Sox, captured the award in the American League in 1969; Lee, as a member of the Cincinnati Reds, won the National League honor in 1967.

DAVE MAY
The player the Atlanta Braves received from the Milwaukee Brewers for Hank Aaron on November 2, 1974. (In addition to May, an outfielder, the Brewers also sent minor league pitcher Roger Alexander to Atlanta in the trade.)

WILLIE MAYS
The major leaguer with the longest stretch, 11 years, between winning Most Valuable Player honors. Mays won the award with the New York Giants in 1954 and with the San Francisco Giants in 1965.

GIL McDOUGALD
New York Yankee player whose first-inning line drive on May 7, 1957, struck Cleveland pitcher Herb Score in the right eye. Score, a month away from his 24th birthday, was relieved by Bob Lemon (who worked the final 8 1/3 innings and beat the Yankees, 2-1).

Score, a standout pitcher for the Indians in 1955 (his rookie year) and 1956 (when he won 20 games), was nowhere as effective after the injury—although he blamed arm troubles, not the eye mishap, for his decline. Apparently headed for greatness, Score had led the American League in strikeouts in his first two seasons and posted a major league record of 38-20 through May 7, 1957. In 512 2/3 career innings, he had struck out 547 batters, allowed only 338 hits and recorded a 2.63 earned-run average. After the eye injury, Score compiled a 17-26 record in a big-league career that ended in 1962 with the Chicago White Sox (to whom he was traded in 1960).

GIL McDOUGALD, MINNIE MINOSO
American League Rookie of the Year selections in 1951—the season in which Mickey Mantle broke into the majors with the New York Yankees. Minoso, an outfielder with the Chicago White Sox, won The Sporting News' rookie honor; McDougald, an infielder with the Yankees, took the Baseball Writers' Association award.

Like Mantle, Willie Mays of the New York Giants broke into the big leagues in '51. Mays, though, won both The Sporting News' honor and the writers' award as the top rookie in the National League.

The harmonica-playing exploits of Yankee Phil Linz proved a hit with the fans, but the timing of the music puzzled Manager Yogi Berra.

MINNESOTA TWINS
The Twins-Senators games of August 27-28, 1963, were called off because of a civil-rights march on Washington, and an all-morning rain prevented batting practice before the August 29 doubleheader between the teams. So, without benefit of batting practice for about three days, the Twins went out and . . . hit eight home runs (tying a major league record) while winning the opener, 14-2. Minnesota then slugged four homers in the nightcap, beating Washington, 10-1.

RANDY MOFFITT
Owner of 43 pitching victories and 96 saves in a 12-year major league career that ended in 1983 and brother of longtime tennis star Billie Jean King.

DICK NEN
Dodger rookie (up from Class AAA Spokane) whose ninth-inning, game-tying home run in the finale of a three-game series at St. Louis on September 18, 1963, proved a key moment in that season's National League pennant race. The Cardinals, who entering the series had crept within one game of first-place Los Angeles by winning 19 of their previous 20 games, dropped the first two games at old Busch Stadium. With Bob Gibson pitching, though, St. Louis took a 5-1 lead into the eighth inning of the third game. However, the Dodgers rallied for three runs in the eighth; then, in the ninth, Nen homered off Ron Taylor in his second big-league at-bat to tie the score, 5-5 (Nen lined out as a pinch-hitter in the eighth, then took over at first base). Los Angeles went on to win, 6-5, in 13 innings, and Nen's homer seemingly demoralized the Cardinals. Starting the series with hopes of seizing the league lead or at least tying for first, the Cards instead fell four games back and finished six games behind.

Nen played only seven games of his 367-game major league career with Los Angeles and had only one hit as a Dodger—this home run.

DON NEWCOMBE
The winner of the major leagues' first Cy Young Award (an honor that had only one yearly recipient from its inception in 1956 through 1966). Newcombe was honored in '56 after posting a 27-7 record for Brooklyn, recording a 3.06 earned-run average for the Dodgers and pitching five shutouts.

HAL NEWHOUSER
The only pitcher in major league history to win two straight Most Valuable Player awards, earning the American League's MVP honor in 1944 and 1945 as a member of the Detroit Tigers. Newhouser compiled a 29-9 record in '44, registered a 2.22 earned-run average and threw six shutouts. In '45, he went 25-9, fashioned a 1.81 ERA and tossed eight shutouts.

Catcher Jim Hegan comforts Herb Score after the Cleveland pitcher was struck by a line drive off the bat of Gil McDougald on May 7, 1957. Indians third baseman Al Smith heads for the mound to lend assistance. Teammates carry Score off the field during the game at Cleveland's Municipal Stadium.

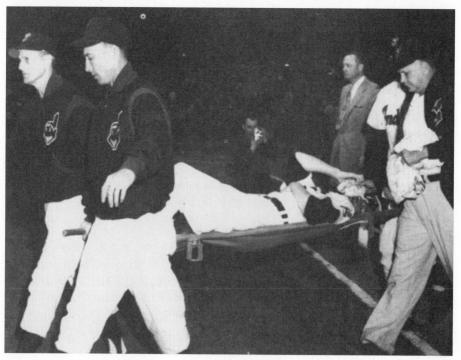

Almost 2 1/2 months after being injured, Score (left) indicates he's all right during a chat with the Yankees' McDougald. Score never regained his pitching effectiveness, however.

JACK NORWORTH
In 1908, he wrote the lyrics to "Take Me Out to the Ball Game." Norworth didn't see his first big-league game, though, until more than 30 years after writing the lyrics.

GAYLORD, JIM PERRY
The only brothers to win the Cy Young Award. Gaylord, the only pitcher to win the award in both major leagues, was honored in 1972 with the Cleveland Indians of the American League and in 1978 with the San Diego Padres of the National League. Jim was a Cy Young Award recipient in 1970 for the A.L.'s Minnesota Twins.

For pitcher Randy Moffitt and tennis standout Billie Jean King, athletic talent was all in the family.

Jack Norworth had no connection with baseball other than the lyrics he wrote to 'Take Me Out to the Ball Game.'

FRANK ROBINSON
The only man to be named the Most Valuable Player in both major leagues. Playing for the Cincinnati Reds in 1961, Robinson was the MVP in the National League; as a member of the Baltimore Orioles in 1966, he was the American League's MVP.

BABE RUTH
Voted the greatest baseball player of all time by the Baseball Writers' Association of America in a poll taken during professional baseball's centennial year, 1969.

BOB SCHRODER
San Francisco player who pinch-hit (and struck out) for pitcher Juan Marichal on August 22, 1965, when Marichal was ejected in the third inning of a game against Los Angeles for hitting Dodger catcher John Roseboro on the head with his bat. Marichal was incensed because he thought Roseboro intentionally threw close to his head when returning a ball to Los Angeles pitcher Sandy Koufax.

Jeff Torborg replaced the injured Roseboro as the Dodgers' catcher, and Ron Herbel came on to pitch for the Giants in the fourth inning. Herbel worked 5 1/3 innings and was a 4-3 winner.

BERT SHEPARD
Pitcher whose big-league career consisted of one appearance—and that came after amputation of his right leg below the knee (as a result of injuries suffered when his plane was shot down during World War II). Pitching on an artificial leg against the Boston Red Sox in the second game of an August 4, 1945, doubleheader at Washington's Griffith Stadium, Shepard worked 5 1/3 innings of relief for the Senators and allowed only three hits and one run. He walked one batter and struck out two as the Red Sox prevailed, 15-4.

CHARLEY SMITH
Infielder who was the player the New York Yankees obtained from St. Louis in the December 8, 1966, trade that sent Roger Maris to the Cardinals.

HARRY STEINFELDT
The Chicago Cubs' "forgotten" third baseman during the heyday of the club's Tinker-to-Evers-to-Chance infield combination. Obtained from Cincinnati before the 1906 National League season, Steinfeldt batted .327 for the '06 Cubs and helped the team to a major league-record 116 victories. During Steinfeldt's five years with the club (1906-1910), the Cubs won four pennants and two World Series titles.

When Joe Tinker, Johnny Evers and Frank Chance played their first game as a

Despite amputation of his right leg below the knee, pitcher Bert Shepard still managed to make an appearance in the major leagues.

The Cubs won four pennants from 1906-1910, and the team's infield of (left to right) Harry Steinfeldt, Joe Tinker, Johnny Evers and Frank Chance contributed heavily.

shortstop-second base-first base unit for the Cubs on September 13, 1902, Germany Schaefer was the third baseman. In the double-play combination's final appearance as a unit with Chicago on April 12, 1912, Ed Lennox was at third base.

MONTY STRATTON

Pitcher whose major league career ended when he was 26 years old after a hunting accident in November of 1938 forced the amputation of his right leg.

Stratton had led the Chicago White Sox in victories in 1937 and 1938, compiling 15-5 and 15-9 records. He later pitched in the minors, winning 18 games in 1946 for Sherman of the Class C East Texas League.

DR. DAVID F. TRACY

After compiling records of 59-95, 59-94 and 53-101 in 1947, 1948 and 1949, the St. Louis Browns hired Tracy, a New York psychologist and hypnotist, to help the team overcome its losers' complex in 1950. The Browns let Tracy go May 31 . . . when they were 8-25 and last in the American League.

TRADES
Major league deals involving two or more future baseball Hall of Famers:

1894—Dan Brouthers, Brooklyn Bridegrooms
Willie Keeler, Brooklyn Bridegrooms
for
Billy Shindle,-Baltimore Orioles
George Treadway, Baltimore Orioles

1900—Christy Mathewson, Cincinnati Reds
for
Amos Rusie, New York Giants

1916—Christy Mathewson, New York Giants
Edd Roush, New York Giants
Bill McKechnie, New York Giants
for
Buck Herzog, Cincinnati Red
Red Killefer, Cincinnati Reds

Christy Mathewson

1918—Burleigh Grimes, Pittsburgh Pirates
Chuck Ward, Pittsburgh Pirates
Al Mamaux, Pittsburgh Pirates
for
Casey Stengel, Brooklyn Dodgers
George Cutshaw, Brooklyn Dodgers

1923—Dave Bancroft, New York Giants
Casey Stengel, New York Giants
Bill Cunningham, New York Giants
for
Joe Oeschger, Boston Braves
Billy Southworth, Boston Braves

Casey Stengel

1926—Frankie Frisch, New York Giants
Jimmy Ring, New York Giants
for
Rogers Hornsby, St. Louis Cardinals

1927—George Kelly, New York Giants
for
Edd Roush, Cincinnati Reds

1930—Goose Goslin, Washington Senators
for
Heinie Manush, St. Louis Browns
Alvin Crowder, St. Louis Browns

1931—Burleigh Grimes, St. Louis Cardinals
for
Hack Wilson, Chicago Cubs
Bud Teachout, Chicago Cubs

1963—Luis Aparicio, Chicago White Sox
Al Smith, Chicago White Sox
for
Hoyt Wilhelm, Baltimore Orioles
Pete Ward, Baltimore Orioles
Ron Hansen, Baltimore Orioles
Dave Nicholson, Baltimore Orioles

Frankie Frisch

TED TURNER

Owner of the Atlanta Braves who during the 1977 season appointed himself as the club's manager—but he lasted only one day on the job. After the Braves had lost 16 straight games, Turner dispatched Manager Dave Bristol on a scouting mission to look at Atlanta's minor-league clubs. Turner, saying he wanted to know firsthand about managing and why the Braves were playing so badly, observed the goings-on and signed the lineup card at Pittsburgh on May 11. Actually, coach Vern Benson (with some advice from other coaches and Turner) managed the club; regardless, the Braves' streak reached 17 in a 2-1 loss. Turner was forced to step down as manager the next day when National League President Chub Feeney—with support from Commissioner Bowie Kuhn—turned down his on-field contract, saying it wasn't in the best interests of baseball. While Bristol was about to get his job back, Benson was in complete control as manager on May 12 when the Braves beat the Pirates, 6-1, and snapped their losing streak.

ALBERT VON TILZER

In 1908, he wrote the music to "Take Me Out to the Ball Game."

ARCH WARD

The sports editor of the Chicago Tribune who in 1933 came up with the idea of a major league All-Star Game.

Monty Stratton (left) and Jimmy Stewart, the man who portrayed Stratton in a motion picture, take a timeout at the movie studio's practice field.

CHARLIE WILLIAMS
Pitcher who was the player the San Francisco Giants received in the May 11, 1972, trade that sent Willie Mays to the New York Mets.

DEWEY WILLIAMS
Suspended for touching an umpire during the 1948 season, the Cincinnati Reds' reserve catcher served the suspension in uniform—but he never left the clubhouse. With Ray Mueller (another catcher) on the disabled list, Ray Lamanno was the Reds' only available catcher during Williams' forced layoff. Cincinnati received permission, though, to have Williams at the ready in the event Lamanno suffered an injury. An additional day would have been added to the suspension for each game in which Williams appeared, but his presence wasn't necessary.

Dr. David Tracy, a psychologist and hypnotist employed by the St. Louis Browns, peers at his "patients" and huddles with Manager Zack Taylor. Tracy was dismissed six weeks into the 1950 season.

Rogers Hornsby was involved in the 1926 trade that also included fellow Hall of Famer Frankie Frisch.

Owner Ted Turner (center) cheers on the Atlanta Braves during his one-game stint as manager in 1977. Coach Chris Cannizzaro (left) and catcher Vic Correll watch the action.

TED WILLIAMS
Outfielder for the Boston Red Sox who won Triple Crowns in 1942 and 1947—but didn't win the American League's Most Valuable Player honor either season. Joe Gordon of the New York Yankees was the American League's MVP in '42, and Joe DiMaggio of the Yankees was the A.L.'s MVP in '47.

GAME TWO

United States President William Howard Taft became the first Chief Executive to throw out the first ball at a major league season opener, setting the stage for the Senators-Philadelphia A's Washington inaugural in 1910.

FIRST INNING
Wild, wacky and
one-for-the-book moments
from "opening day"

HANK AARON
The major leagues' all-time home run leader, he hit only one opening-day homer in his nine seasons with the Atlanta Braves—the April 4, 1974, smash at Cincinnati's Riverfront Stadium that tied him with Babe Ruth (714 homers) on the career list.

Aaron hit only one other opening-day home run in the big leagues, connecting for the Milwaukee Braves against the Chicago Cubs on April 17, 1956, in Milwaukee. He finished his 23-season career in the majors with 755 homers.

ATLANTA BRAVES
National League team that lost nine straight opening-day games from 1972 through 1980, tying the big-league record for beginning-of-the-season futility that had been established by the New York Giants at the turn of the century. The Giants' string of losses in season openers began in 1893 and ran through 1901.

ATLANTA BRAVES, MILWAUKEE BREWERS
Co-holders of the modern major league record for consecutive victories at the beginning of a season. The Braves won 13 games at the outset of the 1982 season and went on to capture the National League West championship, while the Brewers started out 13-0 in 1987 on the way to a third-place finish in the American League East.

EARL AVERILL
The only member of baseball's Hall of Fame to hit a home run in his first big-league at-bat on opening day. Playing for the Indians in an April 16, 1929, game at Cleveland, center fielder Averill broke into the majors by homering in the first inning off Detroit's Earl Whitehill. Cleveland went on to a 5-4 victory in 11 innings, and Averill went on to an outstanding career (238 homers, a .318 lifetime batting average).

Hoyt Wilhelm is the only other Hall of Famer who homered in his first major league at-bat, regardless of the juncture of the season. Pitcher Wilhelm connected for the New York Giants in an April 23, 1952, game against the Boston Braves (and never hit another homer in a big-league career that spanned 21 seasons).

GEORGE BELL
The only player in big-league history to hit three home runs in a season-opening game. Playing for the Toronto Blue Jays, Bell cracked three homers off Royals starter Bret Saberhagen in an April 4, 1988, game in Kansas City.

YOGI BERRA, GARY CARTER
The only players in big-league history to smash home runs in four consecutive season-opening games. Berra clubbed homers for the New York Yankees on each opening day from 1955 through 1958, while Carter homered for Montreal in all of the Expos' season openers from 1977 through 1980.

BERT BLYLEVEN
Pitcher who at the age of 30 had started season openers for four major league clubs. Blyleven was the opening-day starter for the Minnesota Twins from 1972 through 1976, for the Texas Rangers in 1977, for the Pittsburgh Pirates in 1979 and 1980 and, five days past his 30th birthday, for the Cleveland Indians in 1981.

Blyleven was the opening-day pitcher for Cleveland again in 1985, for Minnesota again in 1987 and for the California Angels in 1990.

BOSTON BRAVES
Winners of their 1946 season opener, but one aspect of the 5-3 triumph over Brooklyn didn't sit too well with more than 300 of the 18,261 spectators at Braves Field. Shortly before the April 16 opening-day game, Braves management decided to spruce up the stands with a fresh coat of paint. Cold and damp weather prevented the paint from drying by game time in some sections of the grandstand, though, and a throng of customers showed up at the club offices after the game complaining about paint stains on clothing. The following day, the Braves ran a notice in the Boston newspapers offering apologies to fans and agreeing to pay cleaning bills.

BOSTON RED SOX
The only team to hit three consecutive home runs in an opening-day major league game. In the second inning of an April 19, 1948, game at Boston's Fenway Park, Stan Spence, Vern Stephens and Bobby Doerr homered in succession for the Red Sox off Philadelphia pitcher Phil Marchildon. The homers weren't enough, however, as Boston fell, 5-4, to the A's in 11 innings.

PETE BURNSIDE
The winning pitcher in the longest opening-day game in big-league history.

Jubilant Atlanta fans had plenty of reason to celebrate in 1982 when the Braves dispatched Cincinnati for their 13th straight victory.

Working four innings of relief for the Tigers in their April 19, 1960, opener in Cleveland, Burnside was credited with the victory as Detroit downed the Indians, 4-2, in 15 innings. Jim (Mudcat) Grant, who pitched 3 1/3 innings in a relief role, took the loss for Cleveland.

CHICAGO, CINCINNATI
Cities whose National League teams have played a major league-record number of opening-day games against each other. A Chicago-Cincinnati matchup has been the first game of the N.L. season for both clubs 30 times. (Such a pairing has proved the initial game of the season for the Cubs 32 times. In 1951 and 1953, the Cubs opened play against the Reds—but Cincinnati had started its season a day earlier against Pittsburgh and Milwaukee, respectively.)

CHICAGO CUBS
National League club that, in 10 opening-day games from 1944 through 1953, employed 10 different starting pitchers. In order, the Cubs called on Hank Wyse, Paul Derringer, Claude Passeau, Hank Borowy, Russ Meyer, Dutch

Leonard, Johnny Schmitz, Frank Hiller, Paul Minner and Bob Rush. Chicago won seven of the 10 games, with Wyse, Derringer, Schmitz, Hiller and Rush notching victories and Passeau and Minner getting no-decisions in games won by Chicago relievers Ray Prim and Joe Hatten. Borowy, Meyer and Leonard were charged with losses in their season-opening starts.

CINCINNATI REDS

National League team that opened the season at home for 76 consecutive years, 1890 through 1965, a major league record. The Reds compiled a 32-44 mark in those opening-day games before starting the 1966 season at Philadelphia following the rainout of a scheduled three-game series at Crosley Field against the New York Mets. Cincinnati, the city that fielded baseball's first professional team in 1869, resumed its opening-at-home tradition in 1967, and through 1991 the Reds had played only two season openers—the '66 game and the '90 inaugural—outside Cincinnati in 101 years. Scheduled to begin play at home in '90, the Reds instead opened on the road (at Houston) when a spring-training lockout forced a one-week delay in the start of the season.

CINCINNATI REDS

The only major league club to hit home runs in 10 straight opening-day games, connecting in season openers from 1963 through 1972. Fourteen Reds accounted for a total of 17 homers in those games, with Deron Johnson, Tony Perez and Bobby Tolan leading the way with two each.

JOHN CLARKSON, WALTER JOHNSON

The only pitchers in major league history to win five consecutive opening-day games for one team. Clarkson won season-opening starts for Boston's National League club from 1888 through 1892, and Johnson was victorious for the American League's Washington Senators in openers from 1913 through 1917.

DAIN CLAY, HOD LISENBEE

Cincinnati players whose combined efforts on opening day in 1945 proved noteworthy in the Reds' 7-6, 11-inning triumph over Pittsburgh. Clay, the Reds' center fielder, cracked a bases-loaded home run off the Pirates' Fritz Ostermueller in the fifth inning of the April 17 season opener and delivered a game-winning single in the 11th. The grand slam was Clay's only homer of the year—he had a major league-leading 656 at-bats in '45—and the first of only three home runs in his four-season big-league career. Lisenbee, a 43-year-old relief pitcher, worked two hitless innings and was credited with the victory— his 37th and last triumph in an eight-year career in the majors.

HARRY COVELESKI

The only pitcher in big-league history to collect four hits in an opening-day game. Detroit's Coveleski hit two singles, a double and a triple April 12, 1916, at Chicago, and pitched a three-hitter as the Tigers bested the White Sox, 4-0.

FRANK (POP) DILLON, JIM GREENGRASS
The only players in big-league history to hit four doubles in an opening-day game. Dillon, playing for the Tigers in an April 25, 1901, game in Detroit, collected his doubles in a 14-13 victory over the Milwaukee Brewers. Greengrass' four-double spree came on April 13, 1954, and helped the Cincinnati Reds to a 9-8 triumph against another Milwaukee team—the Braves—at Crosley Field. (Because seats were set up on the field at Cincinnati to accommodate an overflow crowd, ground-rule doubles were plentiful in the '54 opener. In fact, there were 12 ground-rule doubles in the game and 13 doubles overall.)

DON DRYSDALE
The only pitcher in major league history with two lifetime home runs on opening day. On April 11, 1959, at Wrigley Field, Drysdale provided the Los Angeles Dodgers with their only run in a 6-1 loss to the Chicago Cubs when he homered off Bob Anderson. Six years later (April 12, 1965), Drysdale slugged a two-run homer off New York's Al Jackson as Los Angeles scored a 6-1 victory over the Mets at Shea Stadium.

CHUCK ESSEGIAN
Playing his first regular-season game after establishing a World Series record the previous fall with two pinch-hit home runs for the Los Angeles Dodgers, he got the Dodgers' 1960 season off to a dramatic start on April 12. Cast in his familiar role of pinch-hitter, Essegian went to the plate with the score tied, 2-2, and two out in the 11th inning at the Los Angeles Memorial Coliseum and drilled a game-winning homer off Cubs reliever Don Elston. The Dodgers' 3-2 victory over Chicago featured a complete-game, 14-strikeout performance by Dodgers pitcher Don Drysdale and came before a season-opening crowd of 67,550.

AL EVANS
Reflecting the personnel changes that gripped major league baseball during World War II and the postwar period, catcher Evans was the lone player to start for the Washington Senators on opening day in both 1945 and 1946. In its '45 season opener, Washington started Joe Kuhel at first base, George Myatt at second base, Harlond Clift at third base, Gil Torres at shortstop, George Case in left field, Walt Chipple in center field, George Binks in right field, Evans behind the plate and Dutch Leonard on the mound. The Senators' first-day lineup in '46 had Mickey Vernon at first, Jerry Priddy at second, Sherry Robertson at third, Cecil Travis at short, Jeff Heath in left, Stan Spence in center, Buddy Lewis in right, Evans catching and Roger Wolff pitching.

BOB FELLER, LEON (RED) AMES
Pitchers who, respectively, tossed the only complete-game no-hitter on opening day in big-league history and threw no-hit ball through nine innings in a season

Cleveland Indians great Bob Feller receives a pat on the back from teammate Hal Trosky after completing his 1940 opening-day no-hitter against the Chicago White Sox.

opener only to lose in extra innings. Cleveland's Feller held the White Sox hitless in a 1-0 Indians triumph on April 16, 1940, at Chicago. Ames, working for the New York Giants, yielded his first hit to Brooklyn in the 10th inning of an April 15, 1909, opener that was 0-0 through 12 innings. Brooklyn wound up with seven hits and a 3-0, 13-inning victory over Ames at New York.

4-0
The opening-day record in 1969 of the four expansion teams that entered the major leagues that year. The Montreal Expos won their first National League game, beating the New York Mets, 11-10, while the San Diego Padres broke into the N.L. with a 2-1 victory over the Houston Astros. The American League's two new clubs, the Seattle Pilots and Kansas City Royals, won over California and Minnesota, respectively. The Pilots slipped past the Angels, 4-3, and the Royals edged the Twins by the same score in a 12-inning game.

The six other modern expansion teams went 3-3 in their franchise-opening games. Opening-day winners in their first seasons were the Los Angeles Angels (1961), Houston Colt .45s (1962) and Toronto Blue Jays (1977); losers their first time out were the second Washington Senators team ('61), the New York Mets ('62) and the Seattle Mariners ('77).

14-3, 16-7
If getting off on the right foot is crucial, then the Houston Astros may have had misgivings about the 1982 and 1983 seasons—as evidenced by these 11- and nine-run losses that the National League team suffered at the beginning of '82 and '83. The Astros lost to the St. Louis Cardinals in their April 6, 1982, season opener as the Cards broke loose for 18 hits and 14 runs. Then, on April 5, 1983, the Los Angeles Dodgers went on a 15-hit, 16-run spree against Houston. Adding insult to injury, both first-game trouncings came in Houston's home ball park, the Astrodome.

The Astros went on to finish fifth in the National League West in '82 with a 77-85 record, but they ended up third in the West Division in '83 with an 85-77 mark.

NELLIE FOX
The last player to get five hits in a season-opening major league game. Playing for the White Sox on April 10, 1959, at Detroit, Fox rapped three singles and a double before connecting for a game-winning home run in the 14th inning as Chicago downed the Tigers, 9-7. Fox, who had seven at-bats in the contest, slugged his homer with a man on base.

LOU GEHRIG, TED WILLIAMS
Gehrig's 17-year big-league playing career ended two weeks into the 1939 season and Williams' 19-season stay in the majors began in '39, so chances that

the future Hall of Famers played against each other might appear slim. However, Yankee first baseman Gehrig and Red Sox outfielder Williams did go head-to-head—once. While storms postponed the scheduled Yankees-Red Sox season opener on April 18, 1939, at Yankee Stadium and also wiped out April 19 action, the teams finally got their seasons under way on April 20 in New York, and the Yanks' Red Ruffing outdueled Boston's Lefty Grove, 2-0. Williams cracked a double in four at-bats in his major league debut; Gehrig went 0 for 4, lining into two double plays, but stretched his consecutive game streak to 2,123. Gehrig played in only seven more games that spring before leaving the New York lineup for good.

AL (LEFTY) GERHEAUSER
The last man to make his major league debut as a starting pitcher in an opening-day game. Gerheauser was the Phillies' starter in the club's 1943 opener, played April 24 at Brooklyn. He allowed seven hits and five runs in four innings, striking out two and walking three, as Philadelphia lost to the Dodgers, 11-4. Gerheauser went on to post a 10-19 record in '43 and a 25-50 mark in five big-league seasons.

PETE GRAY
One-armed outfielder whose big-league debut came on opening day, 1945, at Sportsman's Park in St. Louis. Playing for the Browns, Gray went 1 for 4 at the plate against Detroit—he singled off reliever Les Mueller—as St. Louis defeated the Tigers, 7-1, in an April 17 game. The '45 season was Gray's only year in the majors, and he wound up hitting .218 in 77 games.

GUY HECKER
He made his major league debut on opening day, 1882, as a first baseman—and collected four hits. Then, in the next four years, he served as the season-opening pitcher for his big-league club. Hecker's team was Louisville and his league was the American Association, which at the time was a "major league." Hecker singled four times on May 2, 1882—the first day of play in the Association's 10-year history—as Louisville lost, 9-7, at St. Louis. In his opening-day pitching starts from 1883 through 1886, Hecker fashioned a 3-1 record for Louisville.

Getting four hits in a major league debut on opening day was achieved five other times in "pre-modern" baseball history—and one of those performances also came on the American Association's first afternoon of action. Charlie Morton of Pittsburgh broke into the majors with four hits in a May 2, 1882, Association opener at Cincinnati.

SPOOK JACOBS, DELINO DeSHIELDS
The only players in modern big-league history to collect four hits in an opening-day game that marked their debuts in the majors. Jacobs, a second

baseman, broke into the major leagues with a four-hit effort for the Philadelphia Athletics on April 13, 1954. DeShields, also a second baseman, drilled four hits for the Montreal Expos in his big-league debut, which came on April 9, 1990.

SPUD JOHNSON
He went 9 for 9 at the plate in his first two opening-day games in the majors, breaking into the big leagues with four hits in four at-bats for Columbus of the American Association in its April 18, 1889, game against Baltimore and then going 5 for 5 in Columbus' April 17, 1890, contest against Toledo. (No other player in major league history has totaled nine hits in two straight season openers.) Johnson, who played only three years in the major leagues, was 2 for 4 for Cleveland in that National League club's April 22, 1891, season opener against Cincinnati, giving him 11 hits in 13 at-bats (.846) on opening day.

WALTER JOHNSON
The Washington great who pitched seven opening-day shutouts in his 21-season major league career, all of which was spent with the Senators. Johnson was the Senators' starting pitcher 14 times overall on opening day, and he fashioned a 9-5 record in those games.

Johnson's best opening-day performance was his first, which came on April 14, 1910, in Washington. Johnson tossed a one-hitter that day in the Senators' 3-0 American League victory over the Philadelphia A's. On the same afternoon in Chicago, Frank Smith of the White Sox allowed the Browns only one hit as the Sox beat St. Louis, 3-0, in another A.L. opener.

MIKE (KING) KELLY
The first player in major league history to hit a home run on opening day, connecting on the first afternoon of play in the National League's fifth season. Kelly's homer, which came with Cap Anson on base in the second inning, helped the Chicago White Stockings to a 4-3 triumph over the Red Stockings on May 1, 1880, at Cincinnati. The second homer in opening-day history was struck in the same game—by Cincinnati's player-manager, John Clapp, who socked a two-run shot in the eighth inning.

SANDY KOUFAX
Winner of three Cy Young Awards, recipient of one Most Valuable Player honor and author of four no-hitters in the majors—but an opening-day pitcher in the big leagues only once. Koufax's lone season-opening start came on April 14, 1964, at Dodger Stadium, and the lefthander pitched Los Angeles to a 4-0 victory over St. Louis. Koufax held the Cardinals to six hits.

ERNIE KOY, EMMETT MUELLER
Principals in the lone instance in history when two players hit home runs in

their first major league at-bats in the same game. On opening day of the 1938 season at Philadelphia's Baker Bowl, Brooklyn left fielder Koy made his big-league debut at the plate with two out in the top of the first inning and rapped a bases-empty homer off Phillies pitcher Wayne LaMaster. Then, leading off the bottom of the first against the Dodgers' Van Lingle Mungo, Phils second baseman Mueller tied the score, 1-1, with a home run in his first time up in the majors. Koy went 3 for 5 overall for the Dodgers, who won, 12-5; Mueller was 2 for 3 for Philadelphia.

SIXTO LEZCANO
The only player in big-league history to hit bases-loaded home runs in two opening-day games—and he slugged only three grand slams in his 12-year major league career. As a member of the Milwaukee Brewers, Lezcano socked bases-full homers on the first day of the season in 1978 and 1980.

Lou Gehrig, the majors' all-time leader in grand slams with 23, never hit a bases-loaded homer on opening day. In fact, the longtime Yankee star never hit a grand slam in the month of April.

Phillies second baseman Emmett Mueller and Brooklyn outfielder Ernie Koy celebrated their 1938 major league arrivals by hitting first-inning home runs in the same game on their first big-league at-bats.

HERMAN LONG
The first player in major league history to slug two home runs in an opening-day game, connecting for Boston of the National League on April 19, 1890, in a 15-9 victory over Brooklyn.

ROGER MARIS
Acquired from the Kansas City Athletics in December 1959, the majors' future single-season home run champion made his debut with the New York Yankees on opening day, 1960—and slugged two homers at Boston's Fenway Park. Maris, in fact, went 4 for 5 with four runs batted in as the Yankees downed the Red Sox, 8-4, in an April 19 game.

BILLY MARTIN, RUSS MORMAN
The only men to collect two hits in one inning in their first major league games—and Martin performed his feat in his first two trips to the plate in the majors as the Yankees battled the Red Sox in a 1950 season opener. After replacing Jerry Coleman at second base for New York in the sixth inning of an April 18 game at Boston, Martin made his first big-league plate appearance in the eighth inning and doubled home a run against Boston starter Mel Parnell. Martin batted again in the eighth—the Yankees enjoyed a nine-run inning—and delivered a two-run single off Al Papai. New York, which had trailed, 9-0, after four innings, won the slugfest, 15-10. Morman homered and singled for the Chicago White Sox in the fourth inning of his first big-league game, an August 3, 1986, contest against the Detroit Tigers at Comiskey Park. He had singled in his first major league at-bat in the second inning.

JOHN MAYBERRY
The last of only five players in big-league history to collect four or more hits in consecutive season-opening games. Mayberry went 4 for 4 for Toronto in the Blue Jays' 1979 opener, played April 5 in Kansas City. In the Jays' first game of 1980, contested April 9 in Seattle, Mayberry socked two home runs and had four hits overall in five at-bats. Despite Mayberry's slugging, Toronto lost its '79 and '80 openers by scores of 11-2 and 8-6.

Also getting four or more hits in consecutive opening-day major league games were: Spud Johnson, Columbus, American Association, 1889 and 1890; Joe Gedeon, St. Louis Browns, 1918 and 1919; Buck Weaver, Chicago White Sox, 1919 and 1920, and Ira Flagstead, Boston Red Sox, 1925 and 1926.

WILLIE MAYS
The only player in major league history to hit home runs in each of his club's first four games of a season. Playing for San Francisco in 1971, Mays homered at San Diego on April 6, 7 and 8 as the Giants won two of three season-opening games from the Padres. In the fourth game of the season, an April 10 contest at St. Louis, Mays connected again as the Giants won for the third time.

JIM McCORMICK, RICK REUSCHEL

The only pitchers in big-league history to lose opening-day games in four consecutive years for the same team. McCormick, pitching for Cleveland of the National League, lost season openers from 1879 through 1882, while Reuschel was a first-day loser for the Chicago Cubs from 1978 through 1981.

MILWAUKEE BREWERS

Members of the American League when the circuit opened its first big-league season in 1901, the Brewers got everyone's attention by mounting a 13-3 lead after 7 1/2 innings in their debut in the majors—and then really made headlines. Negative headlines. Detroit, Milwaukee's opponent in the April 25, 1901, game, scored once in the bottom of the eighth inning and 10 times in the last of the ninth for a stunning 14-13 victory. The Tigers' Frank (Pop) Dillon hit two doubles in the ninth—the second proving to be the game-winning hit—and had four doubles overall that afternoon in Detroit.

The Brewers' opening-day collapse was a hint of things to come. Milwaukee went on to finish last in the American League's maiden season, compiling a 48-89 record. By 1902, Milwaukee was out of the league and St. Louis was in (with the Browns).

MONTREAL EXPOS

An expansion club that began play in 1969, this team has opened the National League season at home only twice—in 1988 and 1989.

BOBBY MURCER

The only player in big-league history to slug a bases-loaded home run on opening day as a pinch-hitter. Playing for the New York Yankees against Texas on April 9, 1981, Murcer was called upon to bat for designated hitter Dennis Werth in the seventh inning and walloped a grand slam off Rangers pitcher Steve Comer. The Yankees beat Texas, 10-3, at Yankee Stadium.

BOBO NEWSOM

Opening-day winning pitcher for the St. Louis Browns in 1938 and 1939 and opening-day losing pitcher against the Browns in 1940 and 1941. In a '38 opener, the Browns' Newsom beat Cleveland, 6-2; in the first game of the '39 season, he pitched the St. Louis club to a 5-1 victory over the Chicago White Sox. Traded to Detroit in May 1939, Newsom started season-opening games for the Tigers in '40 and '41 and lost to the Browns by 5-1 and 8-1 scores.

19-1

The biggest opening-day romp in modern major league history, with the New York Yankees beating the Washington Senators by that 18-run margin at Yankee Stadium in the Yanks' first game of the 1955 season. (The Senators had opened their season two days earlier in Washington with a 12-5 rout of the

Baltimore Orioles.) Whitey Ford pitched a two-hitter for the Yankees in the April 13 game and also contributed three singles and four runs batted in. Mickey Mantle and Bob Cerv also had four RBIs apiece. Yogi Berra, Bill Skowron and Mantle hit homers for the Yanks, who scored two or more runs in every inning from the third through the eighth against the Senators, who employed four pitchers (one of whom, reliever Vince Gonzales, was appearing in his only major league game).

19-17
The highest-scoring season opener (36 total runs) in big-league history. The date was April 19, 1900, and the city was Boston—and the local National League team thrilled the crowd by tying Philadelphia, 17-17, with a nine-run outburst in the bottom of the ninth inning. But Philadelphia, which at one point led, 16-4, scored twice in the 10th inning and emerged as the opening-day winner.

The Cleveland Indians and St. Louis Browns fell one run short of the combined opening-day scoring record when they played a 21-14 season opener (won by Cleveland) on April 14, 1925—but the Indians-Browns game may have been more notable because of slick-fielding George Sisler's four errors at first base for St. Louis than for the day's offensive fireworks.

OPENING-DAY PITCHERS
A team-by-team listing of pitchers most prominent in the opening-day history of baseball's old and current franchises:

NATIONAL LEAGUE

Club	Games Started	Wins	Losses
Atlanta Braves	Phil Niekro-8	Rick Mahler-4	Phil Niekro-6
Boston Braves	Kid Nichols-6 Vic Willis-4 Dick Rudolph-4 Al Javery-4 Johnny Sain-4	John Clarkson-5 Kid Nichols-5 Cy Young-3	Dick Rudolph-3 Al Javery-3 Johnny Sain-3
Brooklyn Dodgers	William Kennedy-6 Nap Rucker-4 Van Mungo-4 Carl Erskine-4	William Kennedy-4 Bill Donovan-2 Leon Cadore-2 Dutch Ruether-2 Jesse Petty-2 Van Mungo-2 Curt Davis-2	Nap Rucker-3

Chicago Cubs	Fergie Jenkins-7	Lon Warneke-4	Rick Reuschel-4
Cincinnati Reds	Mario Soto-6	Mario Soto-4	Art Fromme-3 Bucky Walters-3
Houston Astros	J.R. Richard-5	Larry Dierker-4	Don Wilson-2 J.R. Richard-2 Joe Niekro-2 Nolan Ryan-2
Los Angeles Dodgers	Don Drysdale-7 Don Sutton-7	Don Drysdale-5	F.Valenzuela-3
Milwaukee Braves	Warren Spahn-8	Warren Spahn-3	Warren Spahn-3
Montreal Expos	Steve Rogers-9	Steve Rogers-2	Steve Rogers-4
New York Giants	Carl Hubbell-6	Mickey Welch-4 C. Mathewson-3 Bill Voiselle-3	Amos Rusie-4 Leon Ames-3 Carl Hubbell-3 Larry Jansen-3
New York Mets	Tom Seaver-11	Tom Seaver-6	Roger Craig-2 Al Jackson-2
Philadelphia Phillies	Steve Carlton-14	Robin Roberts-5	Steve Carlton-9
Pittsburgh Pirates	Bob Friend-7	D. Phillippe-3 Howie Camnitz-3 Babe Adams-3 Rip Sewell-3	Frank Killen-4 Wilbur Cooper-3
St. Louis Cardinals	Bob Gibson-10	Flint Rhem-3	Bob Forsch-3
San Diego Padres	Randy Jones-4 Eric Show-4	Clay Kirby-2 Randy Jones-2	Eric Show-2
San Fran. Giants	Juan Marichal-10	Juan Marichal-6	Juan Marichal-2 Gary Lavelle-2

AMERICAN LEAGUE

Club	Games Started	Wins	Losses
Baltimore Orioles	Jim Palmer-6	Jim Palmer-5	Mike Flanagan-2
Boston Red Sox	Cy Young-6	Babe Ruth-3 Wes Ferrell-3	Cy Young-3 Howard Ehmke-3 Bob Stanley-3
California Angels	Mike Witt-5	Nolan Ryan-3	Mike Witt-3
Chicago White Sox	Billy Pierce-7	Billy Pierce-3	Billy Pierce-3
Cleveland Indians	Bob Feller-7	Bob Feller-4	Bob Feller-3
Detroit Tigers	Jack Morris-11	Jack Morris-7	George Mullin-5
Kansas City Athletics	Alex Kellner-2	Alex Kellner-2	Many With 1
Kansas City Royals	Dennis Leonard-4	Bud Black-2	D. Leonard-3
Milwaukee Brewers	Jim Slaton-3 Ted Higuera-3	Ted Higuera-3	Many With 1
Minnesota Twins	Bert Blyleven-6	Gaylord Perry-2 Bert Blyleven-2 Frank Viola-2	Frank Viola-2
New York Yankees	Whitey Ford-7 Mel Stottlemyre-7 Ron Guidry-7	Mel Stottlemyre-4	Ray Caldwell-3 Lefty Gomez-3 Whitey Ford-3 M. Stottlemyre-3
Oakland Athletics	Rick Langford-5	Dave Stewart-3	Rick Langford-3

Philadelphia Athletics	Lefty Grove-4	Chief Bender-2 Eddie Plank-2 Jack Coombs-2 Lefty Grove-2 Chubby Dean-2 Phil Marchildon-2	Joe Bush-3
St. Louis Browns	Urban Shocker-4 Ned Garver-4	Urban Shocker-3 Ned Garver-3	Carl Weilman-2
Seattle Pilots	Marty Pattin-1	Marty Pattin-1	None
Seattle Mariners	Glenn Abbott-3 Mike Moore-3 Mark Langston-3	Many With 1	Mark Langston-3
Texas Rangers	Charlie Hough-6	Charlie Hough-3	Dick Bosman-2
Toronto Blue Jays	Dave Stieb-3 Jimmy Key-3	Jimmy Key-3	D. Lemanczyk-2 Dave Stieb-3
Washington Senators (1)	Walter Johnson-14	Walter Johnson-9	Walter Johnson-5
Washington Senators (2)	Pete Richert-2 Camilo Pascual-2 Dick Bosman-2	Bennie Daniels-1 Dick Bosman-1	Pete Richert-2 C. Pascual-2

NOTE: In instances where there are two numbers in a category, the smaller number represents the modern (1900 or later) record.

MEL OTT

Longtime New York Giants star and one of only 14 players to hit 500 or more home runs in his major league career, he struck his last big-league homer in an opening-day game—an April 16, 1946, clash against the Philadelphia Phillies at the Polo Grounds. Ott, the Giants' player-manager at the time, smashed a first-inning homer—the 511th of his career—off Oscar Judd and New York went on to an 8-4 victory.

Ott, who appeared in only 30 more games in 1946 and in just four in 1947 before ending the playing portion of his career, was the National League's all-time home run king until another Giant—San Francisco's Willie Mays—surpassed him 20 years later. Mays hammered No. 512 on May 4, 1966, and finished with 660 homers in his career (which concluded with nearly two seasons with the New York Mets).

MIKE PARROTT

The starting and winning pitcher for Seattle in the Mariners' 1980 season opener against Toronto—but everything was downhill from there. In fact, Parrott never won again in 1980 despite 26 additional appearances that included 15 more starts. After pitching 6 1/3 innings and gaining the victory in Seattle's 8-6 triumph over the Blue Jays on April 9 at the Kingdome, Parrott lost his next four decisions in April and proceeded to go 0-2 in May, 0-3 in June, 0-2 in July, 0-0 in August (most of which he spent in the minor leagues), 0-4 in September and 0-1 in October. Parrott's 1-16 won-lost record in 1980 was accompanied by a 7.28 earned-run average.

CAMILO PASCUAL

Pitcher who lost opening-day games for both the first and second Washington Senators franchises—in fact, he dropped two season openers for both teams. While with the first Senators club (which moved to Minnesota in 1961 and became the Twins), Pascual lost to the New York Yankees as a starter in 1956 and to the Baltimore Orioles as a reliever in 1957; as a starter for the second Senators team (an expansion club that began play in '61), he lost to the Twins in 1968 and to the Yankees in 1969. Overall, Pascual was 1-4 on opening day for Washington's two modern major league franchises. He pitched a complete game in the Senators' 1960 season opener, beating the Boston Red Sox.

Pascual pitched for the first Senators franchise from 1954 through 1960 and then accompanied the team to Minnesota. After pitching for the Twins from 1961 through 1966, Pascual was traded to Washington and pitched for the second Senators club in 1967, 1968 and 1969. He saw brief duty with the Cincinnati Reds, Los Angeles Dodgers and Cleveland Indians at the end of his career.

HERB PENNOCK

A's pitcher who on opening day, 1915, pitched no-hit ball against the Boston Red Sox for 8 2/3 innings. Boston's Harry Hooper then bounced a single over the lefthander's head, and Pennock had to settle for a one-hit, 2-0 triumph in the April 14 game at Philadelphia.

Two months after his one-hitter against Boston, Pennock was claimed on waivers from Philadelphia by the Red Sox.

GAYLORD PERRY

Pitcher who didn't start an opening-day major league game until he was 31 years old—but wound up as a season-opening pitcher a total of nine times for five clubs. Perry started on opening day for the San Francisco Giants in 1970, for the Cleveland Indians from 1972 through 1975, for the Texas Rangers in 1976, for the San Diego Padres in 1978 and 1979 and, at age 44, for the Seattle Mariners in 1983.

PHILADELPHIA PHILLIES

The only team in modern major league history to win an opening-day game because of a forfeit. In the ninth inning of a cold April 11, 1907, game in New York (snow had to be cleared from the field prior to the contest), many fans left the stands and gathered behind the outfielders and the home-plate umpire. Apparently disinterested in the baseball goings-on—Phillies pitcher Frank Corridon was tossing a one-hitter and holding a 3-0 lead—fans remaining in the stands and those positioned on the field began a cushion-and-snowball exchange and plate umpire Bill Klem, believing the crowd was breaking out of control, proclaimed the game a forfeit, with the Phillies listed as 9-0 winners.

Shortly before the start of the 1907 season, New York's police commissioner decided not to deploy officers inside the ball park. Instead, he asked that owners of entertainment enterprises supply their own security—and the Giants' in-house security staff obviously couldn't handle the New York crowd for the '07 opener.

PHILADELPHIA PHILLIES

The only team in big-league history to play season-opening tie games in consecutive years. The Phillies battled the Dodgers to a 5-5 deadlock in their 1923 season opener at Brooklyn and they tied the Boston Braves, 6-6, in 11 innings in their 1924 opener at Philadelphia. Darkness stopped both games.

LOU PINIELLA

Outfielder who on opening day, 1969, collected the first four hits of his major league career. Hitless in brief appearances with the Baltimore Orioles in 1964 (one at-bat) and Cleveland Indians in 1968 (five at-bats), Piniella lashed a double and three singles in five at-bats for the expansion Kansas City Royals, who were making their American League debut in a game against the Minnesota Twins. Piniella's first-inning double accounted for the first hit in Royals history and his sixth-inning single tied the score, 3-3. The Royals went on to win, 4-3, in 12 innings in an April 8 game at Kansas City that marked the major league managerial debut of the Twins' Billy Martin.

An expansion-draft selection of the American League's other new team of 1969, the Seattle Pilots, Piniella had been traded to the Royals a week before the '69 season opener.

PITTSBURGH PIRATES

After opening the season at home in their first five years of play (1887 through

Outfielder Lou Piniella was a Kansas City Royals rookie on opening day in 1969 when he collected his first four major league hits.

1891) and six of their first seven seasons of existence, the Pirates played their season openers on the road for 60 consecutive years (1894 through 1953), a major league record. Long considered a "cold weather" city in terms of schedule-making (and early-season games therein), Pittsburgh played 24 of its 38 season openers on the road from 1954 through 1991.

PITTSBURGH PIRATES, ST. LOUIS CARDINALS
Participants in the major leagues' first season-opening game played at night. The Pirates and the Cardinals squared off in St. Louis on the evening of April 18, 1950, and the Cards—getting six-hit pitching from Gerry Staley and home runs from Red Schoendienst and Stan Musial—scored a 4-2 victory.

MIKE POWERS
Philadelphia A's catcher whose death two weeks after the beginning of the 1909 season may have been linked to an injury incurred in his club's season-opening game. Powers, 38 years old, made a desperate lunging attempt to catch a foul ball on opening day, April 12, against the Boston Red Sox. After the game, which the A's won, 8-1, in the first major league game played at Philadelphia's new Shibe Park, Powers complained of severe abdominal pain. While acute indigestion was the immediate diagnosis, Powers' condition deteriorated that night when a gangrenous condition set in. The next day, surgeons removed part of Powers' intestines, but the 11-year major leaguer failed to improve. Powers died on April 26, with one doctor speculating that his death resulted from internal injuries suffered on the pop-fly lunge.

Powers appeared in 647 big-league games, playing for Louisville and Washington of the National League and for Philadelphia and New York of the American League.

CARL POWIS
Outfielder who had only two runs batted in during his major league career— but one of the RBIs was a game-winner for Baltimore on opening day, April 15, 1957, at Washington's Griffith Stadium. With the Senators and Orioles tied, 6-6, after 10 innings, Baltimore's Dick Williams doubled in the 11th inning and moved to third on Al Pilarcik's sacrifice. Powis, appearing in his first major league game, lofted a sacrifice fly and Baltimore held on for a 7-6 victory.

Powis played in only 15 big-league games, all for the '57 Orioles, and batted .195 (eight hits in 41 at-bats).

ROBIN ROBERTS
Pitcher who started the most consecutive opening-day games for one team in major league history. Roberts was the Philadelphia Phillies' season-opening pitcher for 12 straight years, 1950 through 1961, and he compiled a 5-6 won-lost record in those starts (with one no-decision).

308

FRANK ROBINSON

The major leagues' all-time leader in opening-day home runs with eight. Robinson belted three homers in season openers for the Cincinnati Reds, three for the Baltimore Orioles and one each for the California Angels and Cleveland Indians.

No other player has walloped opening-day homers for four big-league teams.

BABE RUTH

Baseball legend forever linked to uniform number 3, but he never wore that number—or any number—in the majors until opening day of the 1929 season, his 16th year in the big leagues. While the Cleveland Indians experimented with small numbers on their sleeves in 1916 and made big-league history by introducing numbers on the backs of their home uniforms in their 1929 season opener (played two days before the twice-rained-out New York Yankees initially appeared in numbered uniforms), it was the Yankees who first wore large numbers on their backs on a permanent basis, home and away. The Yankees' numbers for the outset of the '29 season corresponded to the batting order of the team's position players, and they went like this for New York's delayed season-opening game against Boston on April 18 at Yankee Stadium:

Uniform number/Yankees' batting order
1 Earle Combs, center field
2 Mark Koenig, third base
3 Babe Ruth, right field
4 Lou Gehrig, first base
5 Bob Meusel, left field
6 Tony Lazzeri, second base
7 Leo Durocher, shortstop
8 Johnny Grabowski, catcher
14 George Pipgras, pitcher

Fred Heimach, who relieved winning pitcher Pipgras that day in the Yankees' 7-3 victory over the Red Sox, wore number 17 and was the only other New York player to appear in the game.

BABE RUTH

A .422 hitter in 18 opening-day major league games, and his first-game production included five doubles, one triple and seven home runs. Ruth had particularly memorable season openers in 1921, 1932 and 1935. In '21, he began the year with a 5-for-5 performance for the New York Yankees against the Philadelphia A's. He drilled two home runs and a single for the Yanks in the '32 opener against the A's, and in his National League debut on opening day, 1935, he singled and homered for the Boston Braves against New York Giants' pitching standout Carl Hubbell.

When Babe Ruth hit his 60th home run in 1927, he was identifiable only by his good looks and familiar home run trot. But by 1929, the Bambino was wearing the No. 3 that will forever remain part of his baseball mystique.

(below)
He later hauled the uniform out of mothballs for a post-career appearance at Yankee Stadium.

Not only did Ruth excel as a hitter in season inaugurals, he also was the starting and winning pitcher for the Boston Red Sox in his first three opening-day appearances in the majors (1916, 1917 and 1918).

ST. LOUIS BROWNS
Possessing a checkered history in 52 years of American League play, this team went out with a whimper by compiling 64-90 and 54-100 records in the franchise's final two seasons before moving to Baltimore in 1954—but the Browns left with an opening-day roar. In their next-to-last opening-day game, played April 15, 1952, at Detroit, the Browns shut out the Tigers, 3-0, behind the six-hit pitching of Ned Garver. Then, in an April 14, 1953, season opener at St. Louis' Sportsman's Park, the Browns walloped Detroit, 10-0, as Virgil Trucks tossed a four-hitter.

ST. LOUIS BROWNS, NEW YORK METS
Co-holders of the modern major league record for consecutive opening-day games won, nine. The American League's Browns won season openers from 1937 through 1945, while the National League's Mets were victorious on opening day from 1975 through 1983.

ST. LOUIS CARDINALS
The only club in modern major league history to lose as many as four consecutive games at the start of the season and then win a league championship. The 1985 Cardinals lost their first two games of the year to the Mets at New York, then dropped two straight to the Pirates in Pittsburgh. Overall, St. Louis dropped six of its first eight games in '85, but the Cardinals went 99-55 the rest of the way in the regular season and won the National League East by three games over the Mets. St. Louis then defeated the Los Angeles Dodgers, four games to two, in the N.L. Championship Series.

The only other team in big-league history to win a pennant after losing its first four games of the season was Boston's 1897 National League club, which actually went winless in its first six games. Boston began the year with four consecutive defeats, played a tie game and then lost again before winning 93 of its final 127 decisions and capturing the N.L. flag by two games over Baltimore.

Since divisional play was adopted in the majors in 1969, three teams besides the 1985 Cardinals have lost at least four games at the start of a season but rebounded to win division championships. However, all three clubs—the 1969 Minnesota Twins (who started off 0-4), the 1974 Pittsburgh Pirates (0-6) and the 1977 Philadelphia Phillies (0-4)—lost in Championship Series play.

SAN DIEGO PADRES, SAN FRANCISCO GIANTS
National League teams that on April 5, 1983, played the majors' highest-

scoring season opener in more than 50 years, with the Padres seizing a 13-3 lead and holding on for a 16-13 triumph at Candlestick Park. Garry Templeton homered and drove in four runs for San Diego, which got three RBIs apiece from Terry Kennedy and winning pitcher Tim Lollar. Bob Brenly paced the Giants' attack with a home run and four RBIs, and Darrell Evans Max Venable and Chili Davis also hit homers for San Francisco.

MANNY SANGUILLEN
The Pirates' No. 1 catcher for the four previous years, he started in right field in the club's 1973 season opener—Pittsburgh's first regular-season game since the death of Roberto Clemente, the team's longtime right-field star. Clemente, a four-time National League batting champion and lifetime .317 hitter in 18 big-league seasons, was killed in a December 31, 1972, plane crash off the coast of Puerto Rico. Sanguillen went 2 for 4 in the April 6, 1973, opener against St. Louis as the Pirates rallied from a 5-0 deficit and handed the Cardinals a 7-5 loss at Pittsburgh.

By the time the '73 season ended, Richie Zisk had the most playing time in right field for Pittsburgh. Zisk batted .324 with 10 home runs and 54 runs batted in while playing 103 games overall and getting 333 at-bats. He was the everyday right fielder in 1974 and responded by hitting .313 with 17 homers and 100 RBIs. Sanguillen, who wound up playing the outfield in 59 games in '73 (and catching in 89), returned to full-time catching duty for the Pirates in '74.

EDDIE SAWYER
Manager of the Philadelphia Phillies for the previous year and a half, he guided the Phils into the 1960 season—but quit as the club's pilot after one game. Sawyer, who also managed the Phillies in the late 1940s and early 1950s (and was at the helm of the '50 Whiz Kids), saw his 1960 team lose at Cincinnati, 9-4, on opening day. The Phillies were off the next day, April 13. On the morning of April 14, the Phils announced Sawyer had resigned; that night, with coach Andy Cohen running the team, Philadelphia won its home opener over Milwaukee, beating the Braves, 5-4, in 10 innings. Gene Mauch, ticketed to manage Minneapolis of the American Association for the third straight year, was appointed the Phils' manager and took over in game three of the '60 season.

"There wasn't any one thing (that prompted the resignation), just a lot of things," said Sawyer, explaining his actions. The quality of his team probably headed Sawyer's list of reasons; the Phils went on to compile a 59-95 record in '60 and finished last in the National League.

SEALS STADIUM
Site of a 1958 opening-day game in San Francisco that marked the debut of major league baseball on the West Coast. The Dodgers and Giants, longtime Brooklyn and New York franchises, transferred to Los Angeles and San

Pittsburgh catcher Manny Sanguillen became the Pirates' early-season regular right fielder in 1973 after the death of Roberto Clemente. By the time the '73 season came to an end, however, Sanguillen was back behind the plate with Richie Zisk in right.

A packed house at San Francisco's Seals Stadium watched on April 15, 1958, as the Giants and Dodgers participated in opening-day ceremonies for the first major league game on the West Coast.

Francisco, respectively, after the 1957 National League season and met in an April 15, 1958, season opener that the Giants won, 8-0. Playing before 23,448 fans in San Francisco's former minor league ball park, the Giants got six-hit pitching from Ruben Gomez and home runs from Daryl Spencer and rookie Orlando Cepeda in the landmark game.

TOM SEAVER
The major leagues' all-time leader in opening-day pitching starts with 16. Seaver, career winner of more than 300 games while pitching for the New York Mets (two stints), Cincinnati Reds, Chicago White Sox and Boston Red Sox, was the season-opening pitcher for the Mets for 10 straight seasons, 1968 through 1977, and again in 1983. He also drew the first-game assignment for the Reds in 1978, 1979 and 1981, and for the White Sox in 1985 and 1986. Seaver has seven opening-day victories, only two losses and seven no-decisions.

DIEGO SEGUI
He pitched in the first game of both Seattle franchises in the big leagues, working in relief in the Pilots' season-opening game against California in 1969

and starting and losing in the Mariners' 1977 opener against the Angels.

SHEA STADIUM
Site of an April 6, 1974, opening-day major league game in which New York—the Yankees, that is—scored a 6-1 victory. The Yankees, uprooted from Yankee Stadium in 1974 and 1975 because of a massive renovation of their half-century-old ball park, played their home games at the Mets' stadium in those two years and opened the '74 season by beating Cleveland at Shea. Mel Stottlemyre stopped the Indians on seven hits, and Graig Nettles socked a two-run home run for the Yankees. Only 20,744 fans turned out at Shea for the Yanks' American League season opener.

The Mets opened the '74 season on the road, while in 1975 the National League club began the year at Shea Stadium and the Yankees started the season away from home.

JIMMY SHECKARD
The lone player in big-league history to hit three triples in an opening-day

Pitcher Diego Segui made his mark in Seattle baseball history by pitching in the first game for both the Pilots and the Mariners. The Pilots were moved to Milwaukee after one season and became the Brewers.

game, accomplishing the feat for Brooklyn on April 18, 1901, at Philadelphia. Sheckard scored four runs that day as Brooklyn defeated the Phillies, 12-7.

Sheckard's penchant for triples didn't stop on opening day. He went on to lead the National League in three-base hits in 1901 with 21.

LOU STRINGER
Infielder who made his major league debut on opening day, 1941, as the starting shortstop for the Chicago Cubs—and proceeded to make four errors that afternoon. The Cubs opened the season April 15 at Wrigley Field, and Chicago overcame Stringer's miscues and downed the Pittsburgh Pirates, 7-4. Stringer contributed offensively, rapping a single and a double and scoring two runs.

A second baseman in four minor league seasons (1937 through 1940), Stringer was returned to his old position three weeks into the 1941 season after the Cubs traded Billy Herman, their longtime second baseman, to the Brooklyn Dodgers. Stringer ended up playing 137 games at second base for the Cubs in '41.

CLYDE SUKEFORTH
Brooklyn coach who was thrust into the Dodgers' managerial job for the first two games of the 1947 season—and thus was managing Brooklyn when Jackie Robinson became the first black player in modern major league baseball. Robinson made his debut with the Dodgers on April 15, 1947, six days after Commissioner Happy Chandler had suspended Dodgers Manager Leo Durocher for the '47 season because of "conduct detrimental to baseball." Sukeforth handled the team April 15 and again on April 17, fashioning a 2-0 record (the Dodgers scored 5-3 and 12-6 victories over the Boston Braves) before scout Burt Shotton took over the club for the balance of the season.

WILLIAM HOWARD TAFT
The 27th President of the United States—and the first Chief Executive to throw out the first ball at a major league season opener. Taft made his tradition-starting toss on April 14, 1910, in Washington before the Senators-Philadelphia A's game. Washington pitcher Walter Johnson, about to begin his fourth big-league season, caught Taft's throw and then shut out the A's, 3-0. Johnson allowed only one hit, a double by Frank Baker.

RON TAYLOR
Canadian who gave up what proved to be a game-deciding home run in the first major league game involving a Canadian-based team. Pitching in relief for the New York Mets on opening day, 1969, Taylor, a native of Toronto, yielded a three-run homer to Coco Laboy of Montreal in a four-run eighth inning that boosted the expansion Expos into an 11-6 lead. Montreal weathered a four-run Mets rally in the ninth and won, 11-10, at Shea Stadium in an April 8 game.

Because of Brooklyn Manager Leo Durocher's one-season suspension, coach Clyde
Sukeforth (center) was interim manager on opening day in 1947 when Jackie Robinson
(right) became the first black player in modern major league history.

BILL TERRY
The first player in major league history to smash a bases-loaded home run on
opening day. Terry walloped his grand slam for the New York Giants on April
12, 1927, at Philadelphia, and the fifth-inning blast off Hal Carlson helped the
Giants to a 15-7 rout of the Phillies.

FRANK THOMAS
He played in the last game in New York Giants history and the first game in
New York Mets history. On September 29, 1957, at the Polo Grounds, Thomas
played first base for Pittsburgh against New York in the Giants' last game as a

New York-based club (the team moved to San Francisco in 1958). Then, on April 11, 1962, Thomas was the left fielder for the Mets as that expansion club made its debut at St. Louis against the Cardinals.

JOE TORRE
Braves player who hit two home runs in his team's season-opening game in 1965 and duplicated the feat in 1966. Torre turned the trick for the Milwaukee Braves on April 12, 1965, at Cincinnati and repeated the accomplishment exactly a year later in Atlanta when the transplanted Braves made their debut in the Georgia city. His two-homer performance in the '66 opener came against Pittsburgh.

Only one other player in big-league history has enjoyed two two-homer games in season openers—and he also was a member of the Braves. And, like Torre, Eddie Mathews unloaded for Milwaukee at Cincinnati (April 13, 1954) and then at home (Milwaukee, in Mathews' case, on April 15, 1958) against Pittsburgh.

23-2
The score by which Buffalo of the Players League won its season-opening game over Cleveland on April 19, 1890. Buffalo's run total and its 21-run victory margin established opening-day major league records that still stand, and the club proceeded to win its next three games as well. A juggernaut in the making? Guess again. Buffalo finished the season with a 36-96 record.

GALE WADE
The opening-day center fielder for the Chicago Cubs in 1955 and 1956—but a member of the starting lineup in only seven other major league games. Wade, a rookie, started the first three games of the '55 National League season, going 1 for 12 at the plate, and soon was returned to the minor leagues. Recalled, he started four more games for Chicago in September. In 1956, Wade was the Cubs' center fielder for the first two games of the year, contests in which he went 0 for 8, and then saw brief service as a pinch-runner, pinch-hitter and defensive replacement before being reassigned to the minors. Overall, Wade appeared in 19 big-league games—all for the Cubs in '55 and '56—and batted .133 (6 for 45) with one home run.

GERALD (GEE) WALKER
The lone player in major league history to hit for the cycle on opening day. Playing for the Tigers against the Indians on April 20, 1937, at Detroit, outfielder Walker began his assault with a second-inning home run and followed, in order, with a triple, double and single. His 4-for-4 performance helped the Tigers edge Cleveland, 4-3.

New York Gov. Al Smith was the center of attention on April 18, 1923, when he threw out the first ball for the first major league game at Yankee Stadium.

LON WARNEKE

Chicago Cubs pitcher who opened his club's 1934 season on April 17 by tossing a one-hitter against the Reds in Cincinnati and followed up that masterpiece with a one-hitter on April 22 against the Cardinals in St. Louis. Warneke won his consecutive one-hitters by scores of 6-0 and 15-2, allowing a one-out ninth-inning single to Reds outfielder Adam Comorosky in the first game and a fifth-inning double to St. Louis first baseman Rip Collins in his second start of the year.

WASHINGTON

Traditional major league opening-day site that played host to its last season opener on April 5, 1971, when the Senators' Dick Bosman shut out the Oakland A's, 8-0, on six hits before 45,061 fans at Robert F. Kennedy Stadium. Frank

Howard and Mike Epstein each drove in two runs for the Senators, who moved to Arlington, Tex., in 1972 and became the Texas Rangers. Washington, which had lost its last 14 games of the 1970 season, beat Oakland's Vida Blue, who was making his first opening-day start in the big leagues. Blue, sporting a 3-1 career record in the majors entering the game, went on to post 24 victories in '71 and he captured Most Valuable Player and Cy Young Award honors in the American League that year.

Army Master Sgt. Daniel Pitzer, a former prisoner of war in Vietnam, threw out the ceremonial first ball at Washington's last opening-day game.

TED WILLIAMS
Boston Red Sox star who played in 14 opening-day games in his big-league career—and hit safely in all of them. In fact, Williams went 22 for 49 (.449) in season-opening games, with seven doubles, one triple, three home runs, 14 runs batted in and nine runs scored. Williams saw action in 19 major league seasons from 1939 through 1960, with military service cutting into his career.

AL WOODS
The last player to hit a pinch home run in his first major league at-bat in an opening-day game, accomplishing the feat on April 7, 1977. Batting for Toronto right fielder Steve Bowling in the fifth inning of the first game in Blue Jays history, Woods walloped a two-run homer off Chicago White Sox reliever Francisco Barrios. Toronto went on to win, 9-5, at Exhibition Stadium.

Only two other players have hit pinch homers in their first big-league at-bats on opening day—Eddie Morgan of the St. Louis Cardinals in 1936 and Chuck Tanner of the Milwaukee Braves in 1955.

Following is a list of all players who have homered in their first big-league at-bats on opening day:

Mike Griffin, Baltimore, American Association, April 16, 1887
Johnny Bates, Boston, National League, April 12, 1906
Earl Averill, Cleveland, American League, April 16, 1929
*Eddie Morgan, St. Louis, National League, April 14, 1936
Ernie Koy, Brooklyn, National League, April 19, 1938
Emmett Mueller, Philadelphia, National League, April 19, 1938
George Vico, Detroit, American League, April 20, 1948
Wally Moon, St. Louis, National League, April 13, 1954
*Chuck Tanner, Milwaukee, National League, April 12, 1955
*Al Woods, Toronto, American League, April 7, 1977
Will Clark, San Francisco, National League, April 8, 1986

*Pinch-hitter

WRIGLEY FIELD

Site of the last tie game to occur on opening day in the major leagues. In an April 12, 1965, season opener matching the Chicago-Cubs against the St. Louis Cardinals, the visiting Cards struck for five first-inning runs and led, 9-6, entering the bottom of the ninth. However, the Cubs' Ernie Banks drilled a three-run homer off Barney Schultz that sent the game into extra innings. Both teams scored in the 11th inning, after which the 10-10 game was halted because of darkness.

The '65 Cubs-Cardinals opener featured the managerial debut of the Cards' Red Schoendienst. It also marked the first major league appearance of pitcher Steve Carlton, who faced one batter in an 11th-inning relief role for St. Louis. The 20-year-old Carlton walked the Cubs' George Altman and was promptly removed. (Schoendienst went on to manage the Cardinals to two National League pennants and one World Series title, while Carlton proceeded to win 329 games as a member of the Cards, Philadelphia Phillies, San Francisco Giants, Chicago White Sox, Cleveland Indians and Minnesota Twins.)

YANKEE STADIUM

"The House That Ruth Built" was host to its first American League game on April 18, 1923—a season opener that, fittingly, starred Yankee slugger Babe Ruth himself. Ruth, whose gate appeal and accompanying revenue-producing power had led, in large part, to the construction of Yankee Stadium, drilled a three-run home run in the '23 opener at New York, connecting in the third inning off Boston's Howard Ehmke. Pitcher Bob Shawkey and the Yankees went on to a 4-1 victory over the Red Sox before a crowd reportedly exceeding 74,000.

SECOND INNING
The majors'
home run hitting feats
and long-ball oddities

HANK AARON, DICK ALLEN
The only visiting players to hit home runs at both Cincinnati ball parks in 1970, a season in which the Reds played their first 36 home games at Crosley Field and their last 45 in new Riverfront Stadium. Playing for the Atlanta Braves, Aaron socked two homers in both Crosley Field and Riverfront Stadium. Allen, of the St. Louis Cardinals, walloped one homer at Crosley and two at Riverfront.

Six Reds players—Johnny Bench, Lee May, Tony Perez, Pete Rose, Bobby Tolan and Bernie Carbo—homered in each stadium, with Bench leading the way with 15 in each park.

HANK AARON, BABE RUTH, WILLIE MAYS
Major league baseball's top three career home run hitters with totals of 755, 714 and 660, they concluded their long big-league careers in the same cities in which they began them—but with different franchises. Aaron reached the majors in 1954 with the Milwaukee Braves and bowed out in 1976 as a member of the Milwaukee Brewers. Ruth broke into the big leagues in 1914 with the Boston Red Sox and wound up his playing career in 1935 with the Boston Braves. And Mays started out with the New York Giants in 1951 and finished up with the New York Mets in 1973.

HANK AARON, CHARLIE WHITE
Milwaukee Braves rookies who hit their first major league home runs in the same game, April 23, 1954, at St. Louis. Aaron, who hit a bases-empty shot off Cardinals starter Vic Raschi in the fourth inning, went on to slug 754 more homers in his big-league career. White, who connected with no one on base against Cot Deal in the 13th inning, never hit another homer in the majors. The Braves beat the Cards that night, 7-5, in 14 innings.

JOE ADCOCK
Milwaukee Braves slugger who, the day after slamming a landmark home run at the Polo Grounds in New York, was removed for a pinch-hitter in the eighth inning of a 0-0 game with the Giants. On April 29, 1953, Adcock became the

first hitter in a regular-season major league game to reach the Polo Grounds' distant center-field bleachers since the bleachers were remodeled (and the distance to the fence lengthened) in 1923. Adcock's homer against the Giants carried an estimated 475 feet. But, with the bases loaded in the eighth the next afternoon, Milwaukee Manager Charley Grimm sent up George Crowe to bat for Adcock (who was hitless in three at-bats). Sal Maglie induced Crowe to ground out, ending the inning, and New York wound up a 1-0 winner when Bobby Thomson—no stranger to heroics at the Polo Grounds—socked a one-out homer in the ninth off Vern Bickford.

JOE ADCOCK
Drilling home runs against Don Newcombe, Erv Palica, Pete Wojey and Johnny Podres on July 31, 1954, at Brooklyn, Milwaukee's Adcock equaled the major league record of four home runs in one game—a feat that had last been accomplished nearly four years earlier in the same ball park, Ebbets Field, by the Dodgers' Gil Hodges in a game that also involved the Braves (then based in Boston). Adcock embellished his accomplishment with a double off Palica, establishing a big-league record for total bases in one game, 18. The Braves thrashed the Dodgers, 15-7, as Adcock drove in seven runs.

The night before his home run barrage, Adcock singled, doubled and homered against Brooklyn. The day after the four-homer performance, he doubled in two at-bats before leaving the game after being hit in the head by a pitch from Dodgers reliever Clem Labine. Adcock was back in the lineup the next day.

AMERICAN LEAGUE
The league that since 1919 has possessed the majors' single-season home run leader. In 1919, Babe Ruth of the Boston Red Sox belted 29 home runs, breaking the major league season mark of 27 established by Ned Williamson of Chicago's National League club in 1884. Ruth eventually raised his record total to 60 with the New York Yankees until the mark was exceeded in 1961 by another Yankee, Roger Maris. Following is a chronology showing the one-season record-holders for each league since the inception of the N.L. in 1876 and the A.L. in 1901 (capitalized names indicate that the player's total was a major league record):

NATIONAL LEAGUE	YEAR	AMERICAN LEAGUE
GEORGE HALL, Philadelphis, 5	1876	
CHARLEY JONES, Boston, 9	1879	
BUCK EWING, New York, 10	1883	
NED WILLIAMSON, Chicago, 27	1884	
	1901	Nap Lajoie, Philadelphia, 14
	1902	Socks Seybold, Philadelphia, 16
	1919	BABE RUTH, Boston, 29
	1920	BABE RUTH, New York, 54

	1921	BABE RUTH, New York, 59
Rogers Hornsby, St. Louis, 42	1922	
	1927	BABE RUTH, New York, 60
Chuck Klein, Philadelphia, 43	1929	
Hack Wilson, Chicago, 56	1930	
	1961	ROGER MARIS, New York, 61

BALTIMORE ORIOLES

Team whose pitching staff allowed a league-low three home runs to Roger Maris in 1961 when the Yankee outfielder set a major league record with 61 homers. While Oriole pitchers were stingy in the home run department in their battles with Maris, they did figure in two of Maris' dramatic blasts as Milt Pappas gave up No. 59 and Jack Fisher was tagged for No. 60. Baltimore's Chuck Estrada yielded No. 7 to Maris, who found Chicago White Sox pitching the easiest home run mark. Maris drilled 13 homers off White Sox pitchers in '61.

BABE BIRRER

Relief pitcher who worked four scoreless innings for Detroit against Baltimore on July 19, 1955, and won headlines—for his hitting. Birrer went 2 for 2 that afternoon and cracked a three-run homer on each trip to the plate. After taking over for starter Frank Lary in the top of the sixth inning and protecting the Tigers' 5-4 lead, Birrer homered off Orioles reliever George Zuverink with two men on base in the bottom half of the inning and then repeated the long-ball feat against Art Schallock in the eighth. Birrer's second homer accounted for the final three runs of the game as the Tigers trounced the Orioles, 12-4, in Detroit.

Birrer pitched in the majors in 1955, 1956 and 1958, compiling a 4-3 record while appearing in a total of 56 games for Detroit, Baltimore and the Los Angeles Dodgers. In 27 at-bats, he collected seven hits for a .259 average. Birrer's career homer and runs-batted-in totals? HRs: 2. RBIs: 6.

BOSTON RED SOX

The team most frequently victimized by Babe Ruth when the Yankee slugger hit 60 home runs in 1927. Red Sox pitchers gave up 11 homers to Ruth. The Chicago White Sox, on the other hand, were the toughest for Ruth to measure; their pitchers allowed only six homers to the Babe in '27.

CLAY CARROLL

A major league pitcher for 15 seasons, he allowed only two bases-loaded home runs in 1,353 innings of work—and those grand slams were struck by the same player in the same year (Carroll's 14th big-league season) and in the same ball park. Los Angeles' Steve Garvey connected for bases-full homers at Dodger

Slugger Joe Adcock gets a warm reception from the Milwaukee bat boy and teammate Jim Pendleton after crossing the plate on the last of his four home runs against the Brooklyn Dodgers on July 31, 1954.

Adcock doubled in two at-bats the next day against the Dodgers before being struck on the head by a Clem Labine pitch and having to leave the game.

Stadium against St. Louis' Carroll on June 22, 1977, and again on August 28. The homers, Garvey's first two grand slams in the majors, helped the Dodgers to 12-1 and 11-0 victories over the Cardinals.

ORLANDO CEPEDA

Veteran slugger who in 1966 hit one home run at St. Louis' old Busch Stadium, formerly Sportsman's Park, and eight at the new Busch Stadium, which became the Cardinals' home about a month into the '66 season. Cepeda, traded from San Francisco to St. Louis on May 8, 1966, was a member of the Giants when he homered at the old stadium in '66 and played for the Cardinals when he hit eight homers that year at the new ball park. While no one hit as many as two homers at both Busch Stadiums that season, nine players besides Cepeda connected for at least one home run at both St. Louis parks. Those nine were Lou Brock, Curt Flood, Tim McCarver, Mike Shannon and Charley Smith, all of the Cardinals; Willie Stargell and Jim Pagliaroni of the Pittsburgh Pirates; Dick Allen of the Philadelphia Phillies, and Eddie Bressoud of the New York Mets.

CINCINNATI REDS

The victimized team each time a National League club has hit five home runs

Dodgers first baseman Steve Garvey arrives home after slugging his second grand slam of the 1977 season against the Cardinals and pitcher Clay Carroll. Those two slams were the only ones Carroll allowed in 15 major league seasons.

in one inning—and such an outburst has occurred three times.

The New York Giants were the first big-league team to wallop five homers in one inning, with Harry Danning, Frank Demaree, Burgess Whitehead, Manny Salvo and Joe Moore connecting after the first two Giants batters had been retired in the fourth inning of a June 6, 1939, game against the Reds. The homers by Whitehead, pitcher Salvo (his inside-the-park smash was the only homer of his major league career) and Moore came in succession and featured an eight-run inning that gave the Giants a 14-0 lead at the Polo Grounds. New York ended up a 17-3 winner and finished with 20 hits, seven of which were homers.

Ten years later, on June 2, 1949, the Phillies clouted five eighth-inning homers against Cincinnati—Andy Seminick drilled two of them—in a 12-3 victory at Philadelphia. The Phils, who got three home runs from Seminick in the game, scored 10 runs in the eighth, with Del Ennis, Willie Jones and pitcher Schoolboy Rowe also homering in the inning. The Reds were victimized again on August 23, 1961, when San Francisco's Orlando Cepeda, Felipe Alou, Jim Davenport, Willie Mays and John Orsino hit homers in a 12-run ninth-inning explosion at Crosley Field that turned a pitchers' duel into a 14-0 Giants triumph (with Juan Marichal winning, Joey Jay losing).

The fourth and last five-homer inning by a major league team—and the first such inning in American League history—occurred on June 9, 1966, when Minnesota's Rich Rollins, Zoilo Versalles, Tony Oliva, Don Mincher and Harmon Killebrew lashed seventh-inning homers against the Kansas City Athletics. The shots by Oliva, Mincher and Killebrew came in succession, and the five homers produced six runs and a 9-4 Twins win at Bloomington, Minn.

HORACE CLARKE
A 10-year major leaguer who hit only 27 home runs in 1,272 games, but whose first two big-league homers came with the bases loaded. Playing for the New York Yankees, Clarke hit his first homer in the majors off Cleveland's Floyd Weaver on September 21, 1965. The grand slam helped the Yankees to a 9-4 victory at Yankee Stadium. On July 16, 1966, Clarke rapped a bases-full homer off the Athletics' Jack Aker, and the 10th-inning blast enabled New York to score a 9-5 triumph at Kansas City. None of Clarke's subsequent 25 homers came with the bases loaded.

ROCKY COLAVITO
The last American Leaguer to hit four home runs in one game (only three A.L. players have achieved the feat), and his big night on June 10, 1959, was particularly remarkable because it came in a ball park that, previous to Colavito's rampage, had not yielded more than three homers to a team in one major league game. In fact, in more than five seasons of big-league service,

Baltimore's Memorial Stadium had yielded three homers to one club only six times preceding Colavito's heroics. Playing for Cleveland, Colavito slammed a third-inning homer off the Orioles' Jerry Walker, fifth- and sixth-inning shots off Arnold Portocarrero and a ninth-inning drive against Ernie Johnson as the Indians scored an 11-8 victory. Colavito's homers accounted for six RBIs. Cleveland hit six homers overall in the game, with Minnie Minoso and Billy Martin also connecting.

DALE COOGAN
Pittsburgh first baseman who hit his only big-league home run on June 24 1950, at Brooklyn's Ebbets Field—but was playing in the minor leagues by the time that night's Pirates-Dodgers game was completed. Coogan, only 19 years old, drilled a three-run homer off Ralph Branca in the first inning of a wild game that was halted by curfew, stoppage coming in the eighth inning with Brooklyn leading, 19-12. The game—won by the Dodgers, 21-12—was completed on August 1, a night on which the demoted Coogan was playing for Indianapolis of the American Association.

PAT CRAWFORD, LESTER BELL
Players who slugged pinch-hit, bases-loaded home runs in successive innings of a May 26, 1929, Giants-Braves contest, the only game in big-league history in which two pinch grand slams have been struck. With the score tied, 2-2, in the bottom of the sixth inning at the Polo Grounds, Crawford triggered a nine-run New York inning by belting a bases-full home run off Harry Seibold while batting for Giants pitcher Dutch Henry. With the bases loaded in the top of the seventh, Bell was sent up as a pinch-hitter for Boston relief pitcher Art Delaney and promptly smashed a homer off reliever Carl Hubbell. The Giants beat the Braves, 15-8.

JOE CUNNINGHAM
Holder of the modern record for most home runs in a player's first two games in the major leagues, having hit three for the St. Louis Cardinals against Cincinnati and Milwaukee on June 30 and July 1, 1954. Brought up from Rochester of the International League by the Cardinals, Cunningham slammed a three-run, fifth-inning homer off the Reds' Art Fowler on June 30 for his first big-league hit and later contributed a two-run single as the Cards drubbed the Reds, 11-3, at Crosley Field. The next day, at County Stadium, the rookie first baseman homered twice off Warren Spahn—first with the bases empty and then with two men on—and St. Louis bombed the Braves, 9-2. Cunningham drove in a total of nine runs in his first two games in the majors.

TOMMY DAVIS
The first of only four major leaguers to hit home runs at both Colt Stadium, Houston, and Sick's Stadium, Seattle, outdoor ball parks that predated the domed stadiums currently used in those big-league cities. As a member

of the Los Angeles Dodgers, Davis homered once in 1962 and twice in 1964 at Houston's outdoor park (where the National League's expansion Colts played from '62 through '64 before becoming the Astros and moving into the Astrodome). And as a member of the Seattle Pilots (an American League expansion team that played only one season in the Pacific Northwest before moving to Milwaukee), Davis homered against the Chicago White Sox on April 13, 1969, in the third big-league game played at the Pilots' outdoor stadium. It was one of three homers that Davis hit at Sick's Stadium, a ball park that saw just one year of major league service. The American League's Mariners (Seattle's second expansion team) have played in the Kingdome since joining the A.L. in 1977.

Also slugging home runs at both Colt Stadium and Sick's Stadium were Leo Cardenas (two at Colt Stadium, one at Sick's), Frank Howard (three at Colt Stadium, four at Sick's) and Jim Pagliaroni (two at Colt Stadium, five at Sick's).

ED DELAHANTY, BOB HORNER
Two of the 11 major leaguers to hit four home runs in a game—and the only players to accomplish the feat as members of losing teams. Delahanty walloped four homers for the Philadelphia Phillies in a July 13, 1896, game in Chicago, but the Phils lost, 9-8. Adonis Bill Terry yielded all four homers to Delahanty, who also singled in the National League game. Atlanta's Horner slugged three home runs off Montreal's Andy McGaffigan and connected for a ninth-inning shot against Expos reliever Jeff Reardon on July 6, 1986; the Braves, though, were 11-8 losers despite Horner's four homers and six runs batted in. Horner hit bases-empty homers in the second, fourth and ninth innings and blasted a three-run drive in the fifth inning at Atlanta.

JOE DiMAGGIO, JOE GORDON
The last major league players to out-homer a league rival—a rival team, that is. In 1948, DiMaggio pounded 39 home runs for the New York Yankees and Gordon drilled 32 for the Cleveland Indians; the Washington Senators, collectively, hit 31. Cleveland's Ken Keltner equaled the Senators' team total.

The last major leaguer to match the home run production of a team from his league was Ted Williams of the Boston Red Sox. Williams' 43 homers in 1949 equaled the season output of the Chicago White Sox.

EBBETS FIELD, SHIBE PARK
The only ball parks where four-homer games were achieved by as many as two big-league players, with Gil Hodges of the Dodgers (1950) and Joe Adcock of the Milwaukee Braves (1954) enjoying record-equaling home run salvos at Brooklyn's Ebbets Field and Lou Gehrig of the New York Yankees (1932) and Pat Seerey of the Chicago White Sox (1948) hitting four homers in games played at Philadelphia's Shibe Park.

Atlanta first baseman Bob Horner is welcomed back to the Braves' dugout by Manager Chuck Tanner and catcher Ozzie Virgil after hitting the second of his record-tying four homers in a July 6, 1986, game against Montreal.

DARRELL EVANS
The oldest single-season home run champion in major league history. Playing for the Detroit Tigers at age 38, Evans cracked an American League-leading 40 homers in 1985. The homer crown was a first for Evans.

DARRELL EVANS
The only player to wallop 40 or more home runs in a season in both the National League and the American League. Evans smashed 41 homers for the Atlanta Braves in the 1973 N.L. season and clubbed 40 for the A.L.'s Detroit Tigers in 1985.

HOOT EVERS
His game-winning, inside-the-park home run for the Tigers in the ninth inning of a June 23, 1950, game at Detroit against the New York Yankees capped a 10-9 contest in which 11 homers—a major league record—were struck and all 19 runs were scored on homers. The losing Yankees cracked six homers—two by Hank Bauer and one apiece by Yogi Berra, Jerry Coleman, Joe DiMaggio and pinch-hitter Tommy Henrich. Evers, whose ninth-inning drive came with one

Darrell Evans enjoyed a big 1985 season for Detroit, becoming the oldest player in major league history to win a home run title and the only player to hit 40 or more homers in both the American and National leagues.

runner on base, had homered earlier in the game for Detroit. The Tigers also got homers from Vic Wertz, Jerry Priddy and pitcher Dizzy Trout, who socked a grand slam.

The 11-homer record has been equaled six times since the 1950 Tigers-Yankees game.

RON FAIRLY
The top home run hitter in the history of Jarry Park, which served as the Montreal Expos' home field from their inception in 1969 through 1976. Fairly, who joined the Expos in June 1969 and played for Montreal through 1974, hit 58 homers at Jarry Park, all as a member of the Expos. He also played at Jarry Park as a member of the Los Angeles Dodgers and St. Louis Cardinals.

CARLTON FISK
Still active entering 1992, he is the career homer leader in the 91-season history of the Chicago White Sox franchise. Through 1991, Fisk had hit 210 homers for the White Sox, a club he joined in 1981.

Harold Baines, a White Sox player from 1980 to mid-1989, is second on the Sox's homer list with 186.

GEORGE FOSTER
The only major leaguer from a non-domed-stadium team to lead his league in indoor home runs in a season, topping the National League with four at Houston's Astrodome in 1979 while playing for the Cincinnati Reds. Denny Walling had a Houston-high three homers at the Astrodome in '79.

PAUL FOYTACK
The only pitcher in big-league history to allow four consecutive home runs in one inning. Working in relief for the Los Angeles Angels in the second game of a July 31, 1963, doubleheader at Cleveland, Foytack retired the first two Indians batters in the sixth inning before Woodie Held, Pedro Ramos, Tito Francona and rookie Larry Brown rocked the 32-year-old veteran for homers. The home run was the second of the game for Ramos, Cleveland's starting and winning pitcher, while Brown's homer was his first in the majors.

Ten other major league pitchers have been tagged for four homers in an inning, the last of whom was Cincinnati's Mario Soto. In the fourth inning of an April 29, 1986, Reds-Expos game in Cincinnati, Soto yielded home runs to Andre Dawson, Hubie Brooks, Tim Wallach and Mike Fitzgerald (a two-run shot).

LOU GEHRIG
The first American Leaguer to hit four home runs in one game. On June 3, 1932, in Philadelphia, Gehrig socked three homers off the Athletics' George Earnshaw

and another off Roy Mahaffey as the New York Yankees outscored the A's, 20-13. Bidding for a record fifth homer in the ninth inning, Gehrig saw his long smash hauled down by center fielder Al Simmons and settled for a four-homer, six-RBI day. Despite Gehrig's homers, which came in succession, the Yankees needed a six-run ninth inning—highlighted by Tony Lazzeri's grand slam—to ensure the victory.

LOU GEHRIG
New York Yankees star who smashed 14 home runs against the Cleveland Indians in 1936, the most in one season against one club in major league history. Gehrig walloped four of his homers against Lloyd Brown and three off Johnny Allen en route to matching his big-league high of 49 home runs in one season (achieved two years earlier).

GEORGE HALL
The only player to hit all of his lifetime major league home runs in one league-leading season. Hall was the first home run champion in big-league history, hitting five homers for Philadelphia in the National League's first season, 1876. Hall played only one other season of big-league ball, in 1877 with Louisville.

Only two other major leaguers failed to hit another home run after enjoying homer-leading seasons. Cincinnati's Fred Odwell, who managed one homer in his rookie season of 1904, topped the National League with nine in 1905 but was unable to hit a home run in either of his final two big-league seasons, 1906 and 1907. Boston's Dave Brain, who entered the 1907 National League season with 17 career homers, slugged a league-high 10 homers in '07 but failed to connect in 1908, his last year in the big leagues.

TOBY HARRAH, LARRY SHEETS, JIM DWYER
Players who hit bases-loaded home runs in the August 6, 1986, Texas-Baltimore game, the only contest in major league history in which three grand slams have been struck. Texas, paced by Harrah's bases-full homer off Baltimore starting pitcher Ken Dixon in the second inning, took a 6-0 lead into the bottom of the fourth, an inning in which the Orioles scored nine times and became only the fifth team in big-league history to hit two bases-loaded home runs in one inning as Sheets connected off Rangers starter Bobby Witt and Dwyer delivered against Jeff Russell. Baltimore added two more runs in the sixth inning, but Texas regained the lead with a six-run rally in the eighth and scored a 13-11 victory at Baltimore's Memorial Stadium.

CHUCK HINTON
California Angels right fielder who was the first player to hit an American League home run at Milwaukee's County Stadium. Home park for the National League's Milwaukee Braves from 1953 through 1965 and for the American League's Milwaukee Brewers beginning in 1970, County Stadium was first

used for American League regular-season games in 1968 and 1969 when the Chicago White Sox played a total of 20 "home games" there. In the first of those games, contested on May 15, 1968, Hinton hit a ninth-inning homer off Chicago's Wilbur Wood.

GIL HODGES
Of the 11 major leaguers to hit four home runs in one game, the one to collect the most runs batted in during the contest and the first to connect against four different pitchers. Brooklyn's Hodges knocked in nine runs in his four-homer game, rapping two-run homers off Boston's Warren Spahn, Bob Hall and Johnny Antonelli and a three-run shot off Norman Roy on August 31, 1950. Hodges also singled as the Dodgers lambasted the Braves, 19-3, in a night game at Brooklyn.

DICK HUGHES
The only pitcher to surrender three home runs in one inning of a World Series game. Pitching for the St. Louis Cardinals in Game 6 of the 1967 Series, Hughes gave up a leadoff homer to Boston's Carl Yastrzemski in the fourth inning. After retiring the next two Red Sox batters, Hughes yielded consecutive homers to Reggie Smith and Rico Petrocelli in the October 11 game at Fenway Park. Boston's three-homer inning, unmatched in Series history, helped the Red Sox to an 8-4 victory.

DON HURST
Phillies first baseman who in 1929 went 6 for 21 at the plate in a six-game stretch from July 28 through August 2—and all six hits were home runs. Hurst's at-bats/hits figures for the six contests were (in succession): 4-1, 4-2, 4-1, 3-1, 2-0 and 4-1. Hurst was on the way to a 31-homer, 125-runs-batted-in season for Philadelphia.

REGGIE JACKSON
The only player in major league history to slug 100 or more home runs for three franchises. Jackson hit 269 of his 563 career homers while with the A's (one when the club was based in Kansas City, 268 after the team moved to Oakland), 144 for the New York Yankees and 123 for the California Angels. Jackson also homered 27 times as a member of the Baltimore Orioles.

HARRY KELLEY
The most-victimized pitcher during Rudy York's record home run spree in August 1937. Detroit's York, establishing a major league mark for most home runs in a month, blasted 18 homers in August of '37 and connected three times off the Philadelphia Athletics' Kelley, twice against Pete Appleton of the Washington Senators and Bill Trotter of the St. Louis Browns and once each off 11 other American League pitchers. Kelley allowed York's first homer of the month on August 4 and yielded No. 11 and No. 12 to the Tigers' slugger in the

Cardinals pitcher Dick Hughes stares in disbelief as Manager Red Schoendienst approaches the mound to make a pitching change in the sixth game of the 1967 World Series. Boston jumped on Hughes for three fourth-inning home runs.

first game of an August 24 doubleheader.

GEORGE KELLY

The first major leaguer to wallop home runs in three consecutive innings, smashing homers for the New York Giants in the third, fourth and fifth innings of a September 17, 1923, game against the Cubs at Chicago. Kelly's slugging helped the Giants to a 13-6 victory.

Only three other big-league players have hit homers in three straight innings. On July 2, 1930, at New York, Carl Reynolds of the Chicago White Sox homered in each of the first three innings of a game against the Yankees that Chicago dominated, 154. Another White Sox player accomplished the feat on July 18, 1948, as Pat Seerey—en route to a four-homer performance in an 11-inning, 12-11 Chicago victory—smashed home runs in the fourth, fifth and sixth innings against the A's at Philadelphia. And, 30 years later, Larry Parrish turned the trick. Parrish drilled homers for Montreal in the third, fourth and fifth innings of a July 30, 1978, contest in Atlanta. The Expos romped, 19-0.

HARMON KILLEBREW

Minnesota Twins slugger whose 1963 home run total of 45 stands as a big-league high for a player finishing a season with fewer than 100 runs batted in. Killebrew collected 96 RBIs in '63.

Six other big-leaguers have missed the 100-RBI mark despite hitting 40 or more homers in a season. Those six are: Dave Johnson, Atlanta Braves, 1973 (43 homers, 99 RBIs); Mickey Mantle, New York Yankees, 1958 (42, 97) and 1960 (40, 94); Rico Petrocelli, Boston Red Sox, 1969 (40, 97); Hank Aaron, Braves, 1973 (40, 96); Darrell Evans, Detroit Tigers, 1985 (40, 94), and Duke Snider, Brooklyn Dodgers, 1957 (40, 92).

DAVE KINGMAN

The only player to homer for a team in each of the major leagues' four divisions in one season. In fact, Kingman is the only man to play for teams in all four divisions in one year. Kingman started the 1977 season with the National League East's New York Mets, for whom he hit nine home runs in 58 games. In June, he was traded to San Diego of the N.L. West and went on to smack 11 homers for the Padres in 56 games. Sold to the American League West's California Angels in September, Kingman connected for two homers in 10 games before being sold again—this time to the New York Yankees of the A.L. East. As a Yankee, Kingman rapped four home runs in eight games.

CHUCK KLEIN

The first National Leaguer in the 20th Century to slug four home runs in one game and the first major leaguer to achieve the feat in an extra-inning game. Klein's fourth homer of the day, a bases-empty shot off Bill Swift, broke a 6-

6 tie in the 10th inning and sparked the Philadelphia Phillies to a 9-6 triumph over the Pittsburgh Pirates on July 10, 1936. Klein, a Phillies star in the late 1920s and early 1930s before being traded to the Chicago Cubs, had been reacquired by the Phils only seven weeks before his four-homer performance, which occurred in Pittsburgh. Klein drove in six runs against the Pirates.

TED KLUSZEWSKI
Veteran first baseman who hit home runs for the Los Angeles Angels in each of the first two innings of play in the American League expansion team's history. The Angels made their debut on April 11, 1961, in Baltimore and Kluszewski hammered a two-run homer off Orioles starter Milt Pappas in the first inning. Then, in the second inning, he powered a three-run shot off rookie reliever John Papa, who was facing his first batter in the big leagues. The Angels downed the Orioles, 7-2.

HAL LEE, GEORGE PUCCINELLI
Two of the four players who walloped pinch-hit home runs in the July 21, 1930, doubleheader between Brooklyn and St. Louis—and the pinch homers were the first major league hits for Brooklyn's Lee and St. Louis' Puccinelli. In the opening game of the doubleheader at Ebbets Field, Brooklyn scored a 9-8 victory when Harvey Hendrick smashed a pinch three-run homer in the ninth inning. Jim Bottomley had put the Cardinals ahead, 5-4, with a two-run pinch homer in the seventh inning, and the Cards' Puccinelli, hitless in two previous big-league at-bats, had broken a 5-5 tie with a three-run pinch homer in the eighth. Lee, 0 for 16 at the plate in the majors, clubbed a three-run pinch homer in the second inning of the nightcap, but St. Louis romped to a 17-10 victory.

The four pinch homers established a major league record for a doubleheader, a mark that has never been equaled.

MICKEY LOLICH
The only man in big-league history to hit a home run in World Series play but never one in a regular-season game. Pitcher Lolich, who posted a lifetime batting average of .110 (90 for 821) while playing for the Detroit Tigers, New York Mets and San Diego Padres in a 16-season career in the majors, blasted his lone big-league homer in his first at-bat in World Series competition, connecting for the Tigers in the third inning of Game 2 of the 1968 World Series. Lolich's bases-empty smash came off St. Louis Cardinals pitcher Nelson Briles.

LOS ANGELES ANGELS
The winning team in all four 1-0 games decided by home runs in the American League during the 1964 season, with the homers giving Dean Chance three victories and Fred Newman one. Chance, on the way to the '64 Cy Young Award, benefited from a July 11 homer by Joe Adcock against the Chicago

Detroit pitcher Mickey Lolich (center) enjoyed his unlikely role as a home run hitter, posing with teammates Norm Cash (left) and Willie Horton after the Tigers had defeated St. Louis in Game 2 of the 1968 World Series.

White Sox, a July 15 smash by Bob Perry against Detroit and an August 18 drive by Vic Power against the Tigers. Felix Torres' homer on July 17 against the Minnesota Twins made a winner out of Newman, who received two-inning relief help from Bob Lee.

BOBBY LOWE
The first player in major league history to hit four home runs in one game. Playing for Boston's National League team on May 30, 1894, Lowe slammed four consecutive homers off Cincinnati's Elton Chamberlain and led Boston to a 20-11 victory in the second game of a morning-afternoon doubleheader. Lowe smashed two homers in his team's nine-run third inning and also contributed a single in the game, which was played in Boston.

Of the 11 major leaguers to have hit four home runs in a single game, the one with the lowest lifetime homer total. Lowe, who played for Boston, Chicago and Pittsburgh in the National League and for Detroit in the American League, finished his 18 seasons in the big leagues with 70 homers.

MICKEY MANTLE
Holder of the record for most home runs in a season by a major league batting champion. Mantle won the American League batting crown in 1956 with a .353 average and clouted 52 home runs for the New York Yankees that year.

Jimmie Foxx is the only other player in big-league history to hit 50 or more home runs and win a batting title in the same year. He hit 50 homers for the Red Sox in 1938 and led the American League in hitting with a .349 mark.

ROGER MARIS, HACK WILSON
The leading single-season home run hitters in American League and National League history—Maris struck an A.L.-record 61 homers for the New York Yankees in 1961 and Wilson slugged an N.L.-high 56 for the Chicago Cubs in 1930—but neither hit as many as 40 homers in another big-league season. Maris and Wilson hit 39 home runs in their second-best long-ball seasons, and both achieved their No. 2 homer totals in years (1960, 1929) immediately preceding their record accomplishments.

WILLIE MAYS
San Francisco slugger who, two days after Milwaukee's Warren Spahn had pitched a no-hitter against the Giants, jolted Braves pitching for a record-tying four home runs in one game during the first month of the 1961 season. Mays' four-homer spree came on April 30 at Milwaukee's County Stadium and paved the way for a 14-4 Giants victory. Lew Burdette was the victim of Mays' first two homers, in the first and third innings, while Seth Morehead allowed No. 3 (a three-run smash) in the sixth inning and Don McMahon surrendered No. 4 in the eighth inning. Mays, who collected eight runs batted in, was on deck when the Giants were retired in the ninth inning.

The highest-ranking player on the majors' career home run list to have struck four homers in one game. Mays is No. 3 in the big leagues with 660 lifetime homers.

PETE MILNE
New York Giants outfielder who hit one home run in his major league career—a pinch-hit, inside-the-park grand slam. With Brooklyn leading New York, 8-6, in the seventh inning of an April 27, 1949, game at the Polo Grounds, the Giants closed within one run on two walks and Jack Lohrke's single. Walker Cooper's infield hit filled the bases and Milne was called upon to bat for relief pitcher Andy Hansen. Milne, facing Brooklyn reliever Pat McGlothin, lashed a drive to left-center field and Dodgers center fielder Duke Snider dived for the ball. The ball got past Snider, however, and rolled to the wall; Milne circled the bases without a play at the plate. The home run capped the day's scoring as the Giants held on for an 11-8 victory.

Milne played for the Giants in 1948, 1949 and 1950 and appeared in a total of 47 games.

MILWAUKEE BRAVES

The first team in major league history to slug four consecutive home runs in one inning, accomplishing the feat on June 8, 1961, at Cincinnati. In the seventh inning of the Braves-Reds game at Crosley Field, Eddie Mathews (with a man on base), Hank Aaron, Joe Adcock and Frank Thomas rifled consecutive homers. Despite the onslaught, the Braves lost to Cincinnati, 10-8.

The Cleveland Indians and the Minnesota Twins have equaled the Braves' achievement. In the sixth inning of the second game of a July 31, 1963, doubleheader at Cleveland, the Indians' Woodie Held, Pedro Ramos, Tito Francona and Larry Brown stroked consecutive homers against the Los Angeles Angels on the way to a 9-5 victory. And the Twins socked four straight home runs in the 11th inning of a May 2, 1964, game at Kansas City. The homers—by Tony Oliva, Bob Allison, Jimmie Hall and Harmon Killebrew—powered Minnesota to a 7-3 triumph over the Athletics.

MILWAUKEE BREWERS

The only team in major league history to hit bases-loaded home runs in three straight games—and the Brewers got the 1978 season off to a rousing start by accomplishing the feat at County Stadium in the first series of the year. On April 7, 1978, Sixto Lezcano belted a grand slam as Milwaukee opened its season by walloping Baltimore, 11-3, in George Bamberger's debut as the Brewers' manager. On April 8, Gorman Thomas homered with the bases full as the Brewers humbled the Orioles, 16-3. And, on April 9, Cecil Cooper connected with the bases loaded as Milwaukee punished Baltimore, 13-5.

The Brewers hit six home runs overall in the three games against the Orioles and outscored Baltimore, 40-11.

STAN MUSIAL

The majors' career home run leader among players who never won a league homer title. Musial socked 475 home runs for the St. Louis Cardinals, yet he never finished higher than runner-up in a battle for the National League homer crown. Musial belted a career-high 39 homers in 1948, but Ralph Kiner of the Pittsburgh Pirates and Johnny Mize of the New York Giants shared the N.L. championship with 40. In 1949, Musial smacked 36 homers—his second-best season total—but finished a distant second to Kiner, who hit 54.

STAN MUSIAL

Easily the St. Louis Cardinals' career home run leader. His 475 homers for the Cards are 220 ahead of St. Louis' No. 2 man, Ken Boyer.

This aerial view of Milwaukee's County Stadium shows the routes of Willie Mays' four home runs in an April 30, 1961, game between the San Francisco Giants and Milwaukee Braves.

TONY OLIVA
The first player in major league history to hit a home run in the role of designated hitter. The designated-hitter rule was introduced in the American League in 1973, and season-opening games on April 6 included a night contest at Oakland matching the A's against the Minnesota Twins. Oliva, Minnesota's "DH," rapped a two-run homer in the first inning off Jim (Catfish) Hunter and the Twins went on to an 8-3 triumph.

LARRY PARRISH
The most recent of five players to slug three home runs in a game in both the National League and the American League. Parrish had three-homer games for the N.L.'s Montreal Expos in 1977, 1978 and 1980 before connecting for three home runs in one contest for the A.L.'s Texas Rangers in 1985.

Babe Ruth, Johnny Mize, Claudell Washington and Dave Kingman also have recorded three-homer performances in both leagues.

GAYLORD PERRY, NOLAN RYAN
Pitchers who gave up regular-season home runs to Hank Aaron in both the National League and the American League. Perry, who won 314 games in the majors, and Ryan, the big leagues' all-time strikeout king, were not alone in this victimized-by-Aaron category. Mike Cuellar, Pat Dobson, Nelson Briles and Dave Roberts also surrendered regular-season homers to Aaron in both leagues.

Don Larsen also allowed home runs to the majors' career long-ball king as an N.L. and A.L. pitcher, but Aaron was batting as a National Leaguer both times—once in the regular season and once in the World Series.

PHILADELPHIA ATHLETICS
The opposing team that, by finishing with 56 home runs, came closest to Babe Ruth's homer total of 60 in the 1927 American League season. The Yankees' Ruth, while personally out-homering all seven other American League teams, posted a total more than double that of the club figures compiled by Cleveland (26), Boston (28) and Washington (29). New York hit 158 homers overall, with Lou Gehrig's 47 accounting for nearly half of the Yanks' other 98 homers.

PHILADELPHIA PHILLIES
National League team that has accounted for three of the 11 four-homer performances by big-league players. Ed Delahanty was the first Phillies player to accomplish the feat, slugging four home runs against Chicago on July 13, 1896. Forty years later, on July 10, 1936, the Phils' Chuck Klein walloped four homers in a game against Pittsburgh. And, 40 years after Klein's bombardment, Philadelphia's Mike Schmidt—playing against the Cubs on April 17, 1976—drilled four homers in one contest.

BILL PHILLIPS
The only pitcher in big-league history to allow two bases-loaded home runs in one inning. Working for Pittsburgh in an August 16, 1890, National League game against Chicago, Phillips yielded fifth-inning grand slams to third baseman Tom Burns and catcher Malachi Kittredge. The homers highlighted a 13-run Chicago inning in a game that Pittsburgh lost, 18-5.

PINE TAR GAME, PART I
With two out in the top of the ninth inning and Kansas City trailing New York, 4-3, in a July 24, 1983, American League game at Yankee Stadium, Royals' U.L. Washington singled off Yankees reliever Dale Murray. George Brett was the next batter, and Yankees Manager Billy Martin replaced Murray with bullpen ace Goose Gossage. Brett promptly drilled a Gossage delivery into the right-field stands, thrusting the Royals into a 5-4 lead. After Brett circled the bases following his dramatic smash, Martin, acting at coach Don Zimmer's urging, asked the umpires to check Brett's bat. The umpires discovered that pine tar

extended beyond the 18-inch limit allowed above the knob, and they subsequently signaled Brett out. End of game. Apparently. New York 4, Kansas City 3. Brett went into a rage over the no-homer ruling, and the Royals protested the umpires' decision. Kansas City claimed that a clarification of the rules—particularly in regard to "intent"—would lead to a restoration of Brett's home run.

Supporting Cast:
• **Bud Black.** Royals starting pitcher who worked six innings and allowed all four New York runs.
• **Joe Brinkman.** Crew chief of the umpires who worked the Pine Tar Game.
• **Lee MacPhail.** American League president who took the Royals' protest under advisement.
• **Tim McClelland.** Plate umpire and the target of Brett's furious protest. After examining the bat and making the initial measurement of the tar, McClelland conferred with his three associates, at which time Brinkman took charge and made a second measurement.
• **Gaylord Perry.** Royals pitcher who didn't appear in the game, but who sneaked behind the home-plate chaos and spirited away the bat, only to have it intercepted by a uniformed guard.
• **Shane Rawley.** New York's starting pitcher. He yielded 10 hits and three runs in 5 1/3 innings.

On July 28, MacPhail upheld the Royals' protest, saying that the intent of the rules was to penalize a player for using a bat "altered to improve the distance factor." Brett's motive clearly was to get a better grip on his bat, not better distance on the batted ball. MacPhail stressed that the problem was not with the umpires' handling of the situation, but with ambiguous playing rules that needed to be "rewritten and clarified." He ordered a resumption of the game with the Royals ahead, 5-4, with two out in the top of the ninth inning. The continuation would come during the regular season if "practicable," or after the season if the game's outcome would affect either A.L. divisional race.

PINE TAR GAME, PART II
Resumption of the July 24 Royals-Yankees game proved "practicable" on August 18, originally an open date for both clubs. The Yankees were between dates of a home stand, while the Royals were en route to Baltimore. With a gathering of 1,245 fans on hand, George Frazier took the mound for the Yankees. Before Frazier threw a pitch, the Yankees made appeal plays at first and second, claiming Brett had missed first base, at least, on his home run trot 25 days earlier. Crew chief Dave Phillips came prepared, flashing a notarized letter from the July 24 umpiring crew that said Brett had touched every base.

Supporting Cast:
• **Mike Armstrong.** The winning pitcher in the Pine Tar Game, having worked

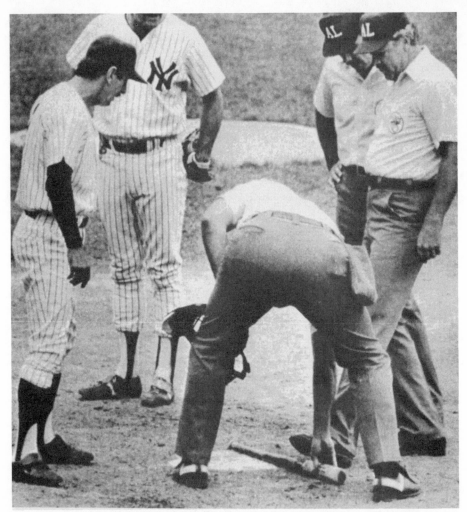

The great Pine Tar controversy began when umpire Tim McClelland, under the watchful eye of Yankees Manager Billy Martin, measured George Brett's bat against home plate to see if the amount of pine tar exceeded the major league rule limit. It did, and Brett and Kansas City Manager Dick Howser reacted vehemently when Brett was declared out and his ninth-inning, game-winning home run was disallowed.

the seventh and eighth innings for Kansas City. Gossage took the loss.

• **Ron Guidry, Don Mattingly.** Guidry, New York's standout lefthanded pitcher, was the Yankees' center fielder when the game resumed; Mattingly, a lefthanded first baseman, was the Yanks' second baseman. New York employed the strategy because of manpower needs, in light of the possibility of extra innings.

• **Hal McRae.** Royals designated hitter who was the first man to bat August 18. He struck out against Frazier, ending the top of the ninth inning.

• **Greg Pryor.** Royals reserve infielder who took over for Brett at third base in

the bottom of the ninth. Brett and Manager Dick Howser had been ejected from the game July 24 because of their heated arguing over the no-homer ruling. •**Dan Quisenberry.** Kansas City reliever who wrapped up the Pine Tar Game in the Yankees' ninth by getting Mattingly to fly to center field, Roy Smalley to fly to left field and Oscar Gamble to ground out to second base.

The game's outcome didn't affect either A.L. divisional race. The Yankees finished third in the East, seven games behind division titlist Baltimore, and the Royals ended up second in the West, 20 games behind Chicago.

BOB RODGERS
The only Angels player to hit home runs in all three home ball parks of the American League's Los Angeles/California franchise. Rodgers collected two homers at Wrigley Field, Los Angeles, which served as the Angels' home in the expansion team's first season of play, 1961. From 1962 through 1965, when the Angels played at Chavez Ravine (Dodger Stadium), Rodgers hit two homers in his home park. And from 1966 until his major league career ended in 1969, Rodgers totaled seven homers at the club's third home, Anaheim Stadium.

BABE RUTH
Renowned slugger who hit all 714 of his major league home runs in the United States (the big leagues' expansion into Canada came 34 years after he retired), but whose lone minor league homer was struck in Canada. On September 5, 1914, Ruth pitched a one-hitter for Providence of the International League and slugged a three-run homer off Ellis Johnson in a 9-0 triumph at Toronto. Ruth, who appeared in 2,503 major league games, played in only 46 minor league contests.

EDDIE SANICKI
Called up from Toronto of the International League by the Philadelphia Phillies in mid-September of 1949, outfielder Sanicki broke into the majors by going 3 for 13 at the plate in the final three weeks of the National League season—and all three of his hits were home runs. On September 14, Sanicki made his first plate appearance in the big leagues a memorable one by drilling a three-run homer off the Pirates' Rip Sewell in Pittsburgh. Five days later in St. Louis, he hit a two-run shot off the Cardinals' Howie Pollet. And on September 28, in Philadelphia, Sanicki slugged a bases-empty home run off Sheldon Jones of the New York Giants. Sanicki, who boasted a .923 slugging percentage in his '49 stint in the majors, also played briefly for the Phillies in 1951.

HANK SAUER
A player with 288 lifetime home runs in the majors, he twice hit three home runs in one game—and Phillies starter Curt Simmons was the victim of both onslaughts, yielding all six homers. Sauer, playing for the Cubs, slammed three

home runs off lefthander Simmons on August 28, 1950, as Chicago prevailed, 7-5, in the first game of a doubleheader at Wrigley Field. On June 11, 1952, again at Wrigley Field, Sauer repeated the three-homer salvo against Simmons and the Cubs edged Philadelphia, 3-2. Simmons was the losing pitcher in both games.

MIKE SCHMIDT
The 10th major leaguer to smack four home runs in one game—and he didn't hit his first homer on the record-tying afternoon of April 17, 1976, until the fifth inning. The Phillies' Schmidt further embellished his performance by connecting for three of his homers off a brother combination and winning the game against the Cubs with a two-run shot in the 10th inning. Philadelphia, which twice in the game had trailed by 11 runs, scored another run in the 10th and held on for an 18-16 triumph at Chicago's windswept Wrigley Field. With his team behind, 13-2, Schmidt went to work in the fifth inning by hammering a two-run homer off Chicago starter Rick Reuschel and then, in the seventh, he solved Reuschel for a bases-empty home run. With Mike Garman pitching for the Cubs in the eighth, the Phillies' third baseman hit a three-run smash. Finally, with the score tied, 15-15, in the 10th, Schmidt connected for a two-run blast off Paul Reuschel, Rick's older brother, capping an eight-RBI, 5-for-6 day (the Phils' standout singled in the fourth inning).

PAT SEEREY
Chicago White Sox player whose power-hitting display in the first game of a July 18, 1948, doubleheader marked the second straight time in major league history that a four-homer performance had been capped by a game-winning, extra-inning home run. Seerey's bases-empty blast off Athletics pitcher Lou Brissie, his fourth homer of the game, gave the White Sox a 12-11 victory in 11 innings at Philadelphia. Seerey, who totaled seven RBIs in the contest, had been obtained from the Cleveland Indians a month and a half earlier.

Before Seerey's dramatic long-ball outburst—which included homers in three consecutive innings—the last four-homer game in the majors had been recorded by the Philadelphia Phillies' Chuck Klein, whose final homer of the day proved decisive in a 10-inning game in 1936.

ART SHAMSKY
Cincinnati Reds outfielder who hammered three home runs in an August 12, 1966, game at Crosley Field against the Pittsburgh Pirates—and he didn't enter the game until the eighth inning. Inserted into the lineup during defensive maneuvering in the top of the eighth, when the Reds trailed the Pirates, 7-6, Shamsky came to bat in the bottom of the inning and laced a two-run home run off Pittsburgh relief pitcher Al McBean. Pittsburgh tied the score, 8-8, in the ninth and seized a 9-8 edge in the 10th when Willie Stargell homered. However, Shamsky countered with a bases-empty shot off Roy Face in the

bottom of the 10th. The Bucs regained the lead in the 11th when Bob Bailey doubled home two runs, but Shamsky continued his dramatics with a two-run homer off Billy O'Dell in the bottom of the 11th. Pittsburgh scored three runs in the 13th, though, and emerged a 14-11 winner in a game that featured 11 homers, a total that tied the big-league record for two teams in one game. Among the home runs—besides Shamsky's three clutch blows—were two by the Pirates' Bailey and one by Pittsburgh's Jerry Lynch, whose 18th and last career pinch homer (still tops in the National League) thrust the Pirates into a tie in the ninth inning.

After sitting out the Reds' August 13 game against Pittsburgh, Shamsky was called upon as a pinch-hitter on August 14 and tagged Vern Law for a two-run homer (and thus equaled a major league record with his fourth consecutive home run).

WILLIE STARGELL, ROBERTO CLEMENTE
Pirate standouts who were the most prolific of the nine players who walloped home runs at both Pittsburgh ball parks in 1970. Stargell hit four homers at Forbes Field, which closed its gates on June 28, 1970, and nine at Three Rivers Stadium, which became the Pirates' new home on July 16. Clemente slammed three homers at both Forbes Field and Three Rivers. No other National Leaguer hit as many as two homers at both stadiums in '70, but seven other players did slug at least one homer at both parks that season. Those seven were Pittsburgh's Richie Hebner, Al Oliver, Bob Robertson and Manny Sanguillen, Willie Smith and Billy Williams of the Chicago Cubs and Jim Wynn of the Houston Astros.

DICK STUART
The first player in major league history to achieve 30-homer seasons in both the National League and the American League. After cracking 35 home runs for the N.L.'s Pittsburgh Pirates in 1961, Stuart drilled 42 homers for the A.L.'s Boston Red Sox in 1963 (and 33 more for Boston in 1964).

Thirteen other players have joined Stuart in recording 30-homer seasons in both leagues: Dick Allen, Bobby Bonds, Jeff Burroughs, Darrell Evans, Frank Howard, Dave Kingman, Greg Luzinski, Fred McGriff, Larry Parrish, Frank Robinson (the only man with four or more 30-homer years in both leagues, totaling seven in the National and four in the American), Reggie Smith, Jason Thompson and Dave Winfield.

ED SUMMERS
A Detroit Tigers pitcher who fashioned a 68-45 record in the majors, he hit two home runs as a big-leaguer—and both came off the same pitcher in the same game. Summers, a lifetime .162 hitter, not only pitched the Tigers to a 10-3 victory over the A's on September 17, 1910, at Detroit, but homered twice that day off Philadelphia's Harry Krause.

Pat Seerey and his bat were the center of attention on July 18, 1948, after the Chicago White Sox player had blasted four home runs in a game against the Philadelphia A's.

JIM TOBIN

The only pitcher in modern major league history to hit three home runs in one game. In a May 13, 1942, contest at Boston against the Chicago Cubs, the Braves' Tobin clubbed bases-empty homers in the fifth and seventh innings and then broke a 4-4 tie in the eighth with his third consecutive home run, a two-run shot. Tobin pitched a five-hitter as Boston won, 6-5.

The day before his three-homer salvo, Tobin was used as a pinch-hitter against the Cubs—and socked a two-run homer.

DEL WILBER

The only player in big-league history to hit three bases-empty home runs in a game in which no other runs were scored by either team. In the second game of an August 27, 1951, doubleheader at Philadelphia, Phillies lefthander Ken Johnson shut out the Reds, 3-0, and batterymate Wilber cracked three homers off Cincinnati's Ken Raffensberger.

Only five other major leaguers have homered three times in a game in which their teams scored only three runs. Clyde McCullough and Hank Sauer accomplished the feat for the Chicago Cubs (McCullough in a 4-3 loss in 1942 and Sauer in a 3-2 victory in 1952), Boog Powell and Eddie Murray turned the trick for the Baltimore Orioles (Powell in a 3-1 triumph in 1964 and Murray in a 4-3 setback in 1980) and Gus Bell hit three solo homers for the Cincinnati Reds in a 5-3 defeat in 1955.

GENE WOODLING
New York Yankees outfielder who in 1951 hit home runs off Cleveland's Early Wynn on June 24, July 24 and August 24.

YANKEES, GIANTS
The only major league teams for whom *two* players have struck 500 home runs. Babe Ruth hit a club-record 659 homers as a Yankee and Mickey Mantle contributed 536 for the Yanks. Willie Mays socked a franchise-record 646 homers for the Giants (187 when the club was based in New York and 459 after the team switched to San Francisco), while Mel Ott smashed 511 home runs for the New York Giants.

RUDY YORK
The only man in the history of the majors to belt two bases-loaded home runs in one game off one pitcher. Playing for the Boston Red Sox against the Browns on July 27, 1946, at St. Louis, York hit a grand slam off Browns reliever Tex Shirley in the second inning and then clubbed another bases-full shot off Shirley in the fifth. Boston thrashed St. Louis, 13-6.

Six other big-leaguers have hit two grand slams in one game, connecting off different pitchers. They are Tony Lazzeri of the New York Yankees (1936), Jim Tabor of the Red Sox (1939), Jim Gentile and Frank Robinson of the Baltimore Orioles (1961, 1970), Tony Cloninger of the Atlanta Braves (1966) and Jim Northrup of the Detroit Tigers (1968).

RICHIE ZISK
The first player to hit home runs in Canada in both the National League and the American League. After hitting four N.L. homers at Montreal's Jarry Park earlier in his career, Zisk connected for the Chicago White Sox at Toronto in an April 7, 1977, game that marked the Blue Jays' A.L. debut. Zisk's smash off Bill Singer at Exhibition Stadium was the first A.L. home run ever hit in Canada.

Slugger Richie Zisk, pictured in 1973 when he played for the Pittsburgh Pirates, went on to become the first player to homer in Canada in both the American and National leagues.

THIRD INNING
Classic achievements and occurences in the All-Star Game

HANK AARON
The last player to hit an All-Star Game home run in his home park. Representing the Atlanta Braves in the 1972 All-Star contest at Atlanta Stadium, Aaron connected off Cleveland's Gaylord Perry with one man on base in the sixth inning. The homer thrust the National League into a 2-1 lead in a game that the N.L. won, 4-3, in 10 innings. A complete list of players who have slugged All-Star Game homers in their home parks follows:

1939/Joe DiMaggio, New York Yankees/Yankee Stadium
1946/Ted Williams, Boston Red Sox (2 homers)/Fenway Park
*1948/Stan Musial, St. Louis Cardinals/Sportsman's Park
1951/Vic Wertz, Detroit Tigers/Briggs Stadium
1951/George Kell, Detroit Tigers/Briggs Stadium
1954/Al Rosen, Cleveland Indians (2 homers)/Cleveland Stadium
1954/Larry Doby, Cleveland Indians/Cleveland Stadium
**1959/Jim Gilliam, Los Angeles Dodgers/Memorial Coliseum
1965/Harmon Killebrew, Minnesota Twins/Metropolitan Stadium
1969/Frank Howard, Washington Senators/Robert F. Kennedy Stadium
1972/Hank Aaron, Atlanta Braves/Atlanta Stadium

*The St. Louis Browns, host team for the 1948 All-Star Game, shared their ball park with the Cardinals.
**Second All-Star Game of the season.

HANK AARON
The first of only three major leaguers to play for the same manager for both National League and American League teams in All-Star Game competition. Aaron played for Alvin Dark as a National Leaguer in 1963 and as an American Leaguer in 1975.

Nolan Ryan pitched for the 1973 A.L. and 1985 N.L. All-Star teams, both of which were managed by Dick Williams. And Dave Winfield played for Sparky Anderson on the 1977 N.L. squad and the 1985 A.L. club.

SPARKY ANDERSON
The only man in All-Star Game history to suffer losses as both a National League and American League manager. Anderson compiled a 3-1 record as a N.L. manager and has a 0-1 mark as an A.L. pilot. His N.L. loss was by a 6-4 score in 1971 and his A.L. defeat was a 6-1 setback in 1985.

Only two other managers have guided N.L. and A.L. clubs in the All-Star Game. Al Dark won his lone game as an N.L. manager and lost his only A.L. managerial assignment. Dick Williams was 1-0 in the N.L. and 0-3 in the A.L.

WALLY BERGER
The only starting player in the 1934 All-Star Game who has not reached the Hall of Fame. Berger, center fielder for the Boston Braves, batted fifth for the National League All-Stars in the '34 game and went 0 for 2. He played 11 seasons in the major leagues, batting a composite .300 for the Braves, New York Giants, Cincinnati Reds and Philadelphia Phillies and socking 242 home runs. Berger was the N.L. homer champion in 1935 and topped the 100-runs-batted-in mark in four big-league seasons.

Starting lineups for the 1934 All-Star Game with American Leaguers or left and National Leaguers on the right:

Charlie Gehringer, second base/ Frankie Frisch, second base
Heinie Manush, left field/ Pie Traynor, third base
Babe Ruth, right field/ Joe Medwick, left field
Lou Gehrig, first base/ Kiki Cuyler, right field
Jimmie Foxx, third base/ Wally Berger, center field
Al Simmons, center field/ Bill Terry, first base
Joe Cronin, shortstop/ Travis Jackson, shortstop
Bill Dickey, catcher/ Gabby Hartnett, catcher
Lefty Gomez, pitcher/ Carl Hubbell, pitcher

YOGI BERRA, ELSTON HOWARD
The only two players from the same major league club to catch in one All-Star Game. The New York Yankees' Berra entered the first All-Star Game of 1961 in the ninth inning as a pinch-hitter for starting American League catcher John Romano of the Cleveland Indians. After taking over behind the plate in the bottom of the ninth Berra was replaced by Yankee teammate Howard with two out in the inning. Howard finished the game, which the National League won, 5-4, in 10 innings.

BRAVES FIELD
Scheduled site of the 1953 All-Star Game, with the National League's Boston Braves due to serve as hosts. However, the Braves franchise shifted to Milwaukee in March 1953 and the Cincinnati Reds, next up among N.L. cities

in the All-Star rotation, took over as hosts. The N.L. won the '53 All-Star Game, 5-1, at Crosley Field.

Braves Field was the site of one All-Star Game, the 1936 classic, won by the National League, 4-3.

JIM BUNNING
The only major leaguer to pitch three perfect innings twice in All-Star Game history. Representing the Detroit Tigers, Bunning accomplished the feat as the American League's starting pitcher in 1957 and as the A.L. starter again in the second game of 1961. He pitched in eight All-Star Games overall.

Seven other pitchers have worked three perfect innings in an All-Star Game. The complete list follows:

1957/Jim Bunning, A.L./First through third
1958/Billy O'Dell, A.L./Seventh through ninth
*1959/Don Drysdale, N.L./First through third
*1961/Warren Spahn, N.L./First through third
**1961/Jim Bunning, A.L./First through third
1966/Denny McLain, A.L./First through third
1967/Gary Peters, A.L./Sixth through eighth
1980/Steve Stone, A.L./First through third
1986/Roger Clemens, A.L./First through third
*First All-Star Game of the season.
**Second All-Star Game of the season.

STEVE CARLTON
The only major leaguer to pitch in two All-Star Games indoors. Carlton, representing the St. Louis Cardinals, pitched one inning in the 1968 game at Houston's Astrodome and, as a member of the Philadelphia Phillies, worked one inning at Seattle's Kingdome in 1979.

Only eight other players have appeared in two indoor All-Star Games. Carl Yastrzemski (Boston Red Sox) also played in the 1968 and 1979 contests, while Gary Carter (Montreal Expos, New York Mets), Keith Hernandez (St. Louis Cardinals, Mets), Dave Parker (Pittsburgh Pirates, Cincinnati Reds), Jim Rice (Red Sox), Mike Schmidt (Philadelphia Phillies), Frank White (Kansas City Royals) and Dave Winfield (San Diego Padres, New York Yankees) played in the '79 game and in the '86 classic at the Astrodome.

BILL CAUDILL
Pitcher who has struck out every batter he has faced in All-Star Game competition—and the relief specialist has pitched against three batters. Working the seventh inning of the 1984 game, Caudill, representing the

354

Boston Braves center fielder Wally Berger (center), shown crossing bats with National League teammates Kiki Cuyler (left) and Joe Medwick before the 1934 All-Star Game in New York, was the only member of either the A.L. or N.L. starting lineup who failed to make baseball's Hall of Fame.

Oakland A's, fanned Tim Raines of the Montreal Expos, Ryne Sandberg of the Chicago Cubs and Keith Hernandez of the New York Mets.

Bobby Shantz also struck out all three batters that he faced in his All-Star Game career. The Philadelphia Athletics' Shantz fanned Whitey Lockman of the New York Giants, Jackie Robinson of the Brooklyn Dodgers and Stan Musial of the St. Louis Cardinals in the fifth inning of the 1952 classic.

Only two other pitchers have struck out "all" of their All-Star Game opponents—Cy Blanton of the Pittsburgh Pirates, 1937, and Jesse Orosco of the New York Mets, 1983. Blanton faced just one hitter in his All-Star Game career, Joe DiMaggio, and he fanned the New York Yankees' star in the fourth inning of the '37 game. And Orosco has pitched against only Ben Oglivie, fanning the Milwaukee Brewers' power hitter in the seventh inning of the '83 classic.

ROBERTO CLEMENTE
The only player to strike out four times in an All-Star Game. In the National League's 15-inning, 2-1 triumph over the American League in 1967, the Pittsburgh Pirates' star struck out in the third, sixth, ninth and 11th innings against Dean Chance, Gary Peters, Al Downing and Jim (Catfish) Hunter, respectively. Clemente collected an infield single in the first inning and grounded out in the 14th.

CLEVELAND INDIANS
The last team failing to have a player appear in an All-Star Game that the franchise hosted. No member of the Indians—pitcher Jim (Mudcat) Grant was the lone Cleveland player to make the American League squad— played in the 1963 All-Star Game, contested at Cleveland Stadium.

In 1962, Senators pitcher Dave Stenhouse, the lone Washington player named to the A.L. team, did not appear in that season's first All-Star Game played at District of Columbia Stadium; in 1950, pitcher Ray Scarborough, the only White Sox player selected for the A.L. squad, did not get into the classic at Chicago's Comiskey Park; in 1937, pitcher Wes Ferrell, catcher Rick Ferrell and second baseman Buddy Myer, Washington's three representatives, were not used in the game played at the Senators' Griffith Stadium; in 1936, outfielder Wally Berger, the lone Braves choice, did not play for the National League in the contest at Boston's Braves Field. (First baseman George McQuinn, the St. Louis Browns' lone selection for the 1940 game at St. Louis' Sportsman's Park, did not appear in the '40 contest. However, the Cardinals, not the Browns, were the host team for that game.)

CLEVELAND STADIUM
The most frequent All-Star Game site, having played host to four midsummer classics. All-Star Games were played at Cleveland's lakefront ball park in 1935, 1954, 1963 and 1981.

COMISKEY PARK, BRIGGS STADIUM
Home ball parks of the American League's Chicago White Sox and Detroit Tigers, they were sites of the 1950 and 1951 All-Star Games, marking the first time that one league had played host to the midsummer classic in consecutive years. The '51 game, scheduled to be hosted by the Philadelphia Phillies, was moved to Detroit to help celebrate the 250th anniversary of the Michigan city's

founding. Accordingly, the Phillies staged the 1952 game.

MORT COOPER, WALKER COOPER
The only brother combination to form a starting battery in All-Star Game history. Both members of the St. Louis Cardinals, the Coopers were National League starters in both 1942 and 1943. Pitcher Mort worked three innings in the '42 game and 2 1/3 innings in the '43 classic and was the losing pitcher in each contest. Catcher Walker went 1 for 2 at the plate in each game.

JOE CRONIN, BILL TERRY
The only two men to play for and manage an All-Star Game squad in one year—and both performed the feat in 1934. Cronin, representing the Washington Senators, managed the American League All-Stars and played the entire game at shortstop. He collected a single and a double in five at-bats. The New York Giants' Terry managed the National League club and played the entire game at first base. He went 1 for 3. Cronin's American Leaguers won, 9-7.

The Cooper boys, Mort (left) and Walker, are the only brothers to form a starting battery in All-Star Game history. Mort pitched to Walker in both the 1942 and 1943 classics.

TONY CUCCINELLO
Brooklyn Dodgers infielder who was the last batter in major league baseball's first All-Star Game. Cuccinello, pinch-hitting for New York Giants pitcher Carl Hubbell in the ninth inning of the 1933 game at Chicago's Comiskey Park, struck out against Lefty Grove of the Philadelphia A's. The American Leaguers downed the National Leaguers, 4-2.

DOMINIC DiMAGGIO, JOE DiMAGGIO
The only brothers to hit safely in the same All-Star Game—and they achieved the feat twice. In the 1941 game, Boston Red Sox outfielder Dom DiMaggio singled in his only at-bat and New York Yankees outfielder Joe DiMaggio collected a double in four at-bats. In the 1949 contest, Dom singled and doubled in five at-bats and Joe singled and doubled in four at-bats.

JOE DiMAGGIO
The first rookie to play in an All-Star Game. DiMaggio, who made his big-league debut on May 3, 1936, was the American League's starting right fielder a little more than two months later in the majors' fourth All-Star Game. The New York Yankees' newcomer batted third and played the entire game, going 0 for 5 at the plate and making an error.

JOE DiMAGGIO
New York Yankees star who played in every inning of every All-Star Game for seven straight seasons, 1936 through 1942.

The only other major leaguer to play as many as six consecutive complete All-Star Games was Detroit Tigers second baseman Charlie Gehringer, who played every inning of the first six contests in history, 1933 through 1938.

LEO DUROCHER
Brooklyn Dodgers shortstop who circled the bases on a bunt play in the 1938 All-Star Game. Batting in the seventh inning with the National League ahead, 2-0, and Cincinnati's Frank McCormick on first base, Durocher bunted against Boston Red Sox pitcher Lefty Grove. The Red Sox's Jimmie Foxx, playing third base, fielded the ball and threw it past first base and into right field. New York Yankees outfielder Joe DiMaggio retrieved the ball and threw toward the plate. McCormick scored on the play—and so did Durocher, as DiMaggio's throw sailed beyond the plate. Durocher was credited with a single and Foxx and DiMaggio were charged with errors. The "gift" runs helped the N.L. to a 4-1 triumph.

FENWAY PARK
The scheduled site for the 1945 All-Star Game, a contest that was canceled because of wartime travel restrictions. Seven midsummer interleague exhibition games replaced the All-Star clash, with the White Sox playing the Cubs

at Chicago's Comiskey Park, the Giants meeting the Yankees at New York's Polo Grounds, the Indians facing the Cincinnati Reds at Cleveland Stadium, the Braves opposing the Red Sox at Boston's Braves Field, the Browns squaring off against the Cardinals at St. Louis' Sportsman's Park, the A's battling the Phillies at Philadelphia's Shibe Park and the Senators going against the Brooklyn Dodgers at Washington's Griffith Stadium. The Detroit Tigers were denied permission to travel to Pittsburgh to play the Pirates. Proceeds from the seven exhibitions—American League teams won five of the games—went to the War Service Relief Fund.

Fenway Park played host to the 1946 All-Star Game.

BOB FRIEND, VERNON LAW
Pittsburgh teammates who started and won the first and second All-Star Games, respectively, of 1960. The Pirate righthanders pitched a total of 5 2/3 innings (Law also worked in relief in the first game), yielding no runs and only two hits.

Pittsburgh relief ace Roy Face pitched 1 2/3 innings of hitless and scoreless ball in the first All-Star Game of 1960, meaning that Pirate pitchers worked a total of 7 1/3 innings in the '60 All-Star contests and gave up no runs and only two hits.

FRANKIE FRISCH
The first of only five players to lead off the first inning of an All-Star Game with a home run. The St. Louis Cardinals' Frisch, the first man to bat for the National League in the bottom of the first of the 1934 classic, drilled a homer off Lefty Gomez of the New York Yankees.

Lou Boudreau of the Cleveland Indians (1942), Willie Mays of the San Francisco Giants (1965), Joe Morgan of the Cincinnati Reds (1977) and Bo Jackson of the Kansas City Royals (1989) also have struck first-inning, leadoff home runs in All-Star Game competition. Boudreau, Mays and Morgan connected in the top half of the inning; Jackson clubbed his homer in the bottom half.

STEVE GARVEY
Of players whose teams never lost an All-Star Game in which they appeared, the one with the best record—10-0. First baseman Garvey represented the National League's Los Angeles Dodgers in the All-Star Game from 1974 through 1981 and wore a San Diego Padres uniform in the 1984 and 1985 games. Garvey contributed greatly to the 10 victories, posting a lifetime .393 batting average in All-Star competition with two home runs (six extra-base hits overall) and seven runs batted in. He twice was named the All-Star Game's most valuable player.

LEFTY GOMEZ

A notoriously poor hitter (he finished his major league career with 133 hits in 904 at-bats for a .147 batting average), he nonetheless drove in the first run in All-Star Game history. With Jimmie Dykes of the Chicago White Sox on second base and Joe Cronin of the Washington Senators on first in the second inning of the inaugural All-Star Game in 1933, the New York Yankees' pitcher went to the plate against Bill Hallahan of the St. Louis Cardinals and singled home Dykes.

The only pitcher to win three All-Star Games, receiving credit for the American League's 4-2, 4-1 and 8-3 victories in 1933, 1935 and 1937. The New York Yankees' standout lefthander was the A.L.'s starting pitcher in five of the first six midsummer classics.

The first of six pitchers to win an All-Star Game and a World Series game in the same season. Gomez, of the New York Yankees, got the victory in the 1937 All-Star Game and then won two games against the New York Giants in the '37 World Series.

Also winning an All-Star Game and a World Series contest in the same year: Paul Derringer of the Cincinnati Reds, 1940; Frank (Spec) Shea, Yankees, 1947; Vernon Law, Pittsburgh Pirates, 1960; Sandy Koufax, Los Angeles Dodgers, 1965, and Don Sutton, Dodgers, 1977. Like Gomez, Derringer, Shea, Law and Koufax won two World Series games in the years they posted All-Star/Series "doubles." Sutton was 1-0 in the '77 Series.

RICH (GOOSE) GOSSAGE

The only player who has represented four teams in All-Star Game competition. Gossage pitched in the 1975 classic as a member of the Chicago White Sox, the 1977 game for the Pittsburgh Pirates, the 1978 and 1980 games while with the New York Yankees and the 1984 and 1985 games as a representative of the San Diego Padres.

HANK GREENBERG

Detroit first baseman who had exactly 100 runs batted in at the All-Star Game break of 1935 (at which time the Tigers had played 75 games)—but didn't make the American League's All-Star roster that year. Lou Gehrig of the New York Yankees played the entire July 8, 1935, All-Star Game at first base for the A.L. squad (whose other first baseman, Jimmie Foxx of the Philadelphia Athletics, was stationed at third base against the National Leaguers).

The only other player to have 100 or more RBIs at an All-Star Game break was Tommy Davis of the Los Angeles Dodgers. Davis had 106 RBIs entering the second All-Star Game of 1962, which was played on July 30. By then, the Dodgers had played 106 games.

Chicago White Sox star Jimmie Dykes crosses the plate with the first run in All-Star Game history, courtesy of a single by a notoriously poor hitter—Yankees pitcher Lefty Gomez.

Greenberg finished with 170 RBIs in '35; Davis totaled 153 in '62.

BILLY HERMAN

The only player to make two appearances in one All-Star Game. Herman, second baseman for the Chicago Cubs, first appeared in the 1934 All-Star Game in the third inning as a-pinch-hitter for New York Giants pitcher Carl Hubbell and popped out. Then, in the seventh inning, National League Manager Bill Terry of the New York Giants needed to replace his starting second baseman, Frankie Frisch of the St. Louis Cardinals, who was hobbled by charley-horse problems. Lacking a replacement, Terry asked permission of American League Manager Joe Cronin to insert Herman at second base, and Cronin agreed to Herman's re-entry into the game.

CHARLIE HOUGH

The only pitcher in All-Star Game history to strike out three batters in one inning without retiring the side. Representing the Texas Rangers in the 1986 classic, knuckleball specialist Hough yielded a leadoff double to San Francisco's Chris Brown in the eighth inning but proceeded to strike out the Giants' Chili Davis, Montreal's Hubie Brooks and the Expos' Tim Raines in order. End of inning with no scoring? Wrong. Davis had struck out on a wild pitch, Brown advancing to third on the play and Davis being retired on a throw to first base by Boston Red Sox catcher Rich Gedman, who was bedeviled by Hough's fluttering pitches. Brooks had fanned on a pitch that got away from Gedman, the passed ball enabling Brown to score and Brooks to reach first (as Gedman opted for a play on Brown at the plate instead of throwing to first base for a sure out on Brooks). Brooks moved to second on a balk before Raines struck out. Steve Sax of the Los Angeles Dodgers then singled home Brooks, and Dave Righetti of the New York Yankees replaced Hough for the American League. The National League failed to score again, and the A.L. held on for a 3-2 triumph.

Pitchers striking out three batters in one inning of an All-Star Game:

1934/1st/Hubbell, N.L.*/Ruth, Gehrig, Foxx
1934/2nd/Hubbell, N.L./Simmons, Cronin, Gomez
1938/7th/Grove, A.L.*/Brown, Hack, Herman
1943/5th/Vander Meer, N.L./Keltner, Wakefield, York
1943/7th/Javery, N.L./Case, Keltner, Stephens
1948/5th/Sain, N.L.**/Stephens, Doerr, Evers
1949/1st/Spahn, N.L./D. DiMaggio, Williams, Parnell
1952/5th/Shantz, A.L.**/Lockman, J. Robinson, Musial
1955/10th/Nuxhall, N.L.*/Vernon, Rosen, Sullivan
1955/12th/Conley, N.L.**/Kaline, Vernon, Rosen
1961a/10th/Miller, N.L./Wilhelm, Gentile, Maris
1961b/9th/Miller, N.L.*/Mantle, Howard, Sievers

1963/8th/Radatz, A.L./Mays, McCovey, Groat
1967/6th/Jenkins, N.L./Fregosi, Carew, Oliva
1968/7th/McDowell, A.L./Haller, Mays, McCovey
1968/8th/Seaver, N.L./Powell, Mantle, Monday
1972/9th/McGraw, N.L./Jackson, Cash, Grich
1977/1st/Palmer, A.L./Garvey, Cey, Bench
1980/6th/Reuss, N.L.**/Porter, Bell, John
1982/4th/Carlton, N.L./Cooper, Fisk, Thornton
1982/7th/Soto, N.L./White, Wilson, Bell
1983/1st/Stieb, A.L./Dawson, Murphy, Schmidt
1984/4th/Valenzuela, N.L.**/Winfield, Jackson, Brett
1984/5th/Gooden, N.L.**/Parrish, Lemon, Davis
1984/7th/Caudill, A.L.**/Raines, Sandberg, Hernandez
1986/4th/Valenzuela, N.L.**/Mattingly, Ripken, Barfield
1986/8th/Fernandez, N.L.*/Jacoby, Rice, Mattingly
1986/8th/Hough, A.L.*/C. Davis, Brooks, Raines
> aFirst game of season
> bSecond game of season
> *Consecutive
> **Only three batters of inning

REGGIE JACKSON
The major leaguer with the highest home run total at the time of the first or only All-Star Game of a season, having smashed 37 homers by the All-Star break of 1969. Jackson's Oakland A's had played 92 games when the '69 All-Star Game was played on July 23.

New York Yankee sluggers Roger Maris and Mickey Mantle established an All-Star-break high for homers in 1961, having clouted 40 by the second All-Star Game of that season (played July 31). At that juncture, the Yankees had played 101 games.

Jackson finished the 1969 season with 47 home runs; Maris slugged a major league-record 61 homers in 1961 and Mantle walloped 54 in '61.

HARMON KILLEBREW, HARVEY KUENN
When these two American Leaguers failed to play in the second All-Star Game of 1959, it marked the only time in All-Star Game history that a league did not have at least one of its "big three" offensive departmental leaders—the league pacesetter in batting average, home runs or runs batted in—play in the contest. The Washington Senators' Killebrew, whose 33 homers and 81 RBIs were leading the American League at the second All-Star break, was on the '59 A.L. squad but wasn't used in game two by Manager Casey Stengel of the New York Yankees. Kuenn, the A.L.'s top hitter with a .343 mark, was not a member of the second-game A.L. team; the Detroit Tigers' star was sidelined because of

a knee injury. Despite the absence of Killebrew and Kuenn from the lineup, the A.L. All-Stars won the second classic of '59 by a 5-3 score.

HARVEY KUENN, JOE DiMAGGIO
The only two batters in history to make the last out in three All-Star Games. Representing the Detroit Tigers, Kuenn grounded into a game-ending force-out against the New York Giants' Johnny Antonelli in 1956 and fouled out against the Chicago Cubs' Don Elston to end the first All-Star Game of 1959; in 1960, as a member of the Cleveland Indians, he flied out against the Pittsburgh Pirates' Vernon Law for the last out of that season's first All-Star Game. The New York Yankees' DiMaggio popped out against the Cubs' Lon Warneke to end the 1936 game, flied out against the Giants' Carl Hubbell to conclude the 1940 contest and grounded into a double play against the Cincinnati Reds' Ewell Blackwell to close the 1950 classic.

The only other player to bat last in three All-Star Games was Stan Musial of the St. Louis Cardinals. Musial grounded out against Joe Coleman of the Philadelphia Athletics to end the 1948 game, struck out against the Athletics' Bobby Shantz for the last out of the 1952 game (although the National League won the rain-shortened, five-inning game) and homered in the 12th inning off Frank Sullivan of the Boston Red Sox to cap the 1955 classic.

VERNON LAW, SANDY KOUFAX
The only pitchers to win an All-Star Game, a World Series game and the Cy Young Award in one season, with the Pittsburgh Pirates' Law achieving the "triple" in 1960 and the Los Angeles Dodgers' Koufax accomplishing the feat in 1965. Law posted a 20-9 record in '60, sharing the National League lead with 18 complete games; he started and won that season's second All-Star Game and then beat the New York Yankees twice in that fall's World Series. Koufax went 26-8 in '65 and topped the N.L. in numerous categories, including victories, strikeouts (382) and earned-run average (2.04); he won the All-Star Game in a relief role and notched two World Series triumphs against Minnesota.

AL LOPEZ
His 0-5 record ranks as the worst managerial mark in All-Star Game history. Lopez managed the American League All-Stars when they lost to the National Leaguers in 1955, 1960 (twice), 1964 and 1965.

LYNN'S ALL-STAR GAME 'FIRST'
The American League already had scored three runs in the third inning of the 1983 All-Star Game at Chicago's Comiskey Park, increasing its lead over the National League to 5-1. Now, Milwaukee Manager Harvey Kuenn's A.L. team had runners on second and third base in that inning and the Brewers' Robin Yount, the league's Most Valuable Player in 1982, was striding to the plate. A base hit at this juncture seemingly would ensure that the American Leaguers

would get over the hump. And what a hump it was: The A.L. had lost 11 consecutive All-Star Games (and 19 of the previous 20). Yount, though, was walked intentionally, loading the bases. That brought up lefthanded-hitting outfielder Fred Lynn of the California Angels. Lynn worked the count to 2 and 2, then drilled a pitch into the right-field stands. The American League rode the first grand slam in All-Star Game history to a 13-3 victory.

Supporting Cast:
• **Jim Rice.** Boston outfielder who, with the A.L. leading, 2-1, started the third-inning fireworks by homering to left field.
• **Dave Winfield.** After Kansas City's George Brett tripled and Milwaukee's Ted Simmons popped out in the third, the New York Yankees' slugger delivered a run-scoring single up the middle. A.L. 4, N.L. 1.
• **Rod Carew.** After Cleveland's Manny Trillo singled Winfield to second base and California's Doug DeCinces flied out, the Angels' Carew singled home Winfield for a 5-1 A.L. advantage. On the throw to the plate, Trillo took third base and Carew moved to second. Yount was then walked.
• **Atlee Hammaker.** Giants lefthander who had gone in to pitch for the N.L. at the beginning of the third inning. When relieved by Houston's Bill Dawley after giving up Lynn's bases-full homer, Hammaker had this log: 2/3 innings pitched, six hits and seven runs (all earned) allowed, one walk and no strikeouts. He had an N.L.-leading 1.70 earned-run average entering the game.
• **Dave Stieb.** Toronto pitcher who earned the victory, allowing no hits and one unearned run in the first three innings. He walked one and struck out four.
• **Mario Soto.** Having allowed the A.L. two runs (both unearned) in the first two innings, Cincinnati's Soto was saddled with the loss for St. Louis Manager Whitey Herzog's N.L. team.

CONNIE MACK
Selected to manage the 1939 American League All-Star team under special circumstances, he had to relinquish the duties and was replaced by the man who normally would have gotten the managerial assignment. While the All-Star Game managerial format normally involves using pennant-winning managers of the previous season, the scenario differed for the American League in 1939 because the junior league wanted to honor its senior manager, Mack, in baseball's centennial season. Accordingly, Mack, manager of the Philadelphia A's since the A.L.'s inception in 1901, was named to manage the A.L. club. Joe McCarthy, who guided the New York Yankees to the A.L. pennant and World Series title in 1938, wound up managing the squad, though, when illness forced Mack to miss the game.

BILL MADLOCK, JON MATLACK
The only players to share an Arch Ward Trophy, symbolic of the most valuable player in the All-Star Game and named in honor of the game's founder, a former sports editor of the Chicago Tribune. The dual honor for the National

California's Fred Lynn raises a triumphant fist as he circles the bases and then gets a warm reception at the plate after hitting the first bases-loaded home run in All-Star Game history, helping the American League to a 13-3 victory in the 1983 classic.

League players came in 1975 when Chicago Cubs third baseman Madlock broke a 3-3 tie in the ninth inning with a bases-loaded single and New York Mets pitcher Matlack pitched two scoreless innings of relief (during which he struck out four batters). The N.L. won, 6-3, with Matlack notching the victory.

JUAN MARICHAL
One of only five pitchers to receive the Arch Ward Trophy as the All-Star Game's most valuable player and the only Ward Trophy-winning pitcher not to be credited with a victory in his "MVP" performance. Marichal, of the San Francisco Giants, pitched one-hit, scoreless ball in the first three innings of the 1965 classic and left the game with a 5-0 lead. The American League eventually tied the score, though, before the N.L. nailed down a 6-5 triumph. Sandy Koufax of the Los Angeles Dodgers picked up the victory with one scoreless inning of relief.

Other Arch Ward Trophy-winning pitchers were the New York Mets' Jon Matlack, who shared honors with third baseman Bill Madlock of the Chicago Cubs, 1975; Don Sutton of the Los Angeles Dodgers, 1977; LaMarr Hoyt of the San Diego Padres, 1985, and Roger Clemens of the Boston Red Sox, 1986.

WILLIE MAYS
The only player to hit two home runs off the same pitcher in All-Star Game competition. Representing the New York Giants, Mays socked a homer off Whitey Ford of the New York Yankees in the 1956 contest. Then, as a member of the San Francisco Giants, he connected against Ford in the second All-Star Game of 1960.

The lone player to start all eight All-Star Games from 1959 through 1962, when a two-games-a-year format was in effect.

The only other player to appear in all eight All-Star Games from '59 through '62 was Stan Musial of the St. Louis Cardinals.

The first of three players to win the Arch Ward Trophy as the All-Star Game's most valuable player twice, taking the honor in 1963 and 1968. In '63, the San Francisco Giants' star collected a single, walked once, stole two bases, drove in two runs, scored twice and made an outstanding catch in the National League's 5-3 triumph. He singled and scored for the N.L. in '68 in the only 1-0 game in All-Star history.

The other two-time Arch Ward Trophy winners are Steve Garvey of the Los Angeles Dodgers (1974, 1978) and Gary Carter of the Montreal Expos (1981, 1984).

Center fielder for the New York and San Francisco Giants and the New York

Cardinals slugger Joe Medwick, shown crossing the plate after his three-run homer in the 1934 All-Star Game at New York's Polo Grounds, put his name in the record books later that season by also homering in the World Series.

Mets who played 11 All-Star Games in their entirety, a record, and appeared in 24 midsummer classics overall, a mark equaled by only Stan Musial of the St. Louis Cardinals and Hank Aaron of the Milwaukee and Atlanta Braves and the Milwaukee Brewers. Musial is next on the "complete game" list, having played 10 All-Star Games from start to finish, while Aaron ranks third with nine; Ted Williams of the Boston Red Sox and Brooks Robinson of the Baltimore Orioles are next on the total-games chart with 18 appearances each.

JOE MEDWICK

The first player in major league history to hit a home run in the All-Star Game and in the World Series in the same season. Playing for the St. Louis Cardinals, Medwick homered in the 1934 All-Star Game and in the first game of the '34 World Series. A list of all players hitting same-season homers in All-Star Game and World Series competition follows:

1934/Medwick, Cards/1 All-Star HR/1 Series HR
1936/Lou Gehrig, New York Yankees/1/2
1937/Lou Gehrig, New York Yankees/1/1
1939/Joe DiMaggio, New York Yankees/1/1
1952/Jackie Robinson, Brooklyn Dodgers/1/1

1955/Mickey Mantle, New York Yankees/1/1
1956/Mickey Mantle, New York Yankees/1/3
1964/Ken Boyer, St. Louis Cardinals/1/2
1965/Harmon Killebrew, Minnesota Twins/1/1
1971/Roberto Clemente, Pittsburgh Pirates/1/2
1971/Frank Robinson, Baltimore Orioles/1/2
1977/Steve Garvey, Los Angeles Dodgers/1/1

The only man to collect four hits in an All-Star Game and four hits in a World Series game. Medwick, of the St. Louis Cardinals, went 4 for 5 (a home run and three singles) in Game 1 of the 1934 World Series and was 4 for 5 (two singles, two doubles) in the 1937 All-Star Game.

Only two other players—Boston Red Sox sluggers Ted Williams and Carl Yastrzemski—have collected four hits in an All-Star Game. Williams belted two homers and two singles while going 4 for 4 in the 1946 contest; Yastrzemski hit three singles and a double in his 4-for-6 performance in the 1970 classic.

STU MILLER
San Francisco Giants pitcher who struck out three batters in one inning in both All-Star Games of 1961. In the 10th inning of the first game, he struck out Baltimore's Hoyt Wilhelm, the Orioles' Jim Gentile and Roger Maris of the New York Yankees—but the American League still managed to score a run on a two-out walk and a wild throw. In the ninth inning of the second game, Miller allowed a leadoff single to Al Kaline of the Detroit Tigers before striking out the Yankees' Mickey Mantle and Elston Howard and the Chicago White Sox's Roy Sievers.

Overall in the 1961 games, Miller worked 4 2/3 innings, allowed one hit, one unearned run and one walk, and struck out nine batters. He was the winning pitcher in the first game, thanks to the National League's two-run 10th-inning rally that produced a 5-4 victory. The '61 contests marked Miller's only All-Star Game appearances.

JOE MORGAN
The last of seven players to end an All-Star contest with a game-winning hit. Facing Dave McNally of the Baltimore Orioles with the score tied, 3-3, and one out in the bottom of the 10th inning of the 1972 All-Star Game, the Cincinnati Reds' second baseman singled home Nate Colbert of the San Diego Padres from second base. The National League's 4-3 triumph marked the start of an 11-game N.L. winning streak.

Also ending All-Star Games with victory-producing hits were: Ted Williams, Boston Red Sox slugger whose three-run ninth-inning home run off Claude

Passeau of the Chicago Cubs lifted the American League to a 7-5 triumph in 1941; the St. Louis Cardinals' Stan Musial, whose 12th-inning leadoff homer against the Red Sox's Frank Sullivan made the N.L. a 6-5 winner in 1955; Roberto Clemente, Pittsburgh Pirates standout who delivered a 10th-inning single off Hoyt Wilhelm of the Baltimore Orioles that enabled the N.L. to prevail, 5-4, in the first game of 1961; the Philadelphia Phillies' Johnny Callison, whose three-run homer off Dick Radatz of the Red Sox in the ninth inning of the 1964 game pulled the N.L. to a 7-4 victory; the Los Angeles Dodgers' Maury Wills, whose 10th-inning single off Pete Richert of the Washington Senators in 1966 slipped the N.L. past the A.L., 2-1; the Chicago Cubs' Jim Hickman, who came through with a 12th-inning single against Clyde Wright of the California Angels in the 1970 classic, the hit scoring the Cincinnati Reds' Pete Rose—who barreled into Cleveland Indians catcher Ray Fosse—and giving the N.L. a 5-4 triumph.

STAN MUSIAL

St. Louis Cardinals first baseman who was the only non-member of the Cincinnati Reds to be elected by fans to the National League's starting lineup for the 1957 All-Star Game. Because of ballot-stuffing by Cincinnati fans, Reds players topped the voting for seven of the N.L.'s eight positions (pitching selections were made by the manager). Reds voted to starting berths were: Johnny Temple, second base; Don Hoak, third base; Roy McMillan, shortstop; Frank Robinson, left field; Gus Bell, center field; Wally Post, right field, and Ed Bailey, catcher. With the final ballots yet to be counted but the Reds fans' voting onslaught evident, Commissioner Ford Frick, thinking that more-deserving players were being victimized by the ballot avalanche, ruled that three heavy vote-getters from Cincinnati—Post, Bell and first baseman George Crowe—would not start regardless of the final ballot figures. Crowe, it turned out, finished second to Musial, anyway. Frick allowed second-place finishers Hank Aaron (Milwaukee Braves) and Willie Mays (New York Giants) to start in place of Post and Bell, respectively. Bell, named a reserve by N.L. Manager Walter Alston of the Brooklyn Dodgers, contributed a two-run pinch double in the game, which the American League won, 6-5. Starters Temple, Hoak, McMillan, Robinson and Bailey went 2 for 9 overall at the plate and played flawlessly afield.

Getting out the vote was nothing new for Cincinnati fans. In 1956, five Reds—Temple, McMillan, Robinson, Bell and Bailey—were elected as N.L. starters. All started, as scheduled, and they collected four hits in 13 at-bats (while playing errorless ball) as the N.L. scored a 7-3 triumph. Additionally, Reds first baseman Ted Kluszewski drilled two doubles in two at-bats after entering the game in the sixth inning.

The only player in All-Star Game history to collect two pinch hits in one year. The St. Louis Cardinals' Musial singled off Frank Lary of the Detroit Tigers while batting for the Pittsburgh Pirates' Bill Mazeroski in the eighth inning of the first All-Star Game of 1960. In the second All-Star contest of '60, played two days later, Musial was sent up in the seventh inning to hit for Stan Williams of the Los Angeles Dodgers and belted a home run off Gerry Staley of the Chicago White Sox.

NATIONAL LEAGUE
While the National League's All-Star Game players have worn uniforms of their respective teams since 1934 (and American League players have done so since the game's inception in 1933), the N.L. All-Stars wore special uniforms for the inaugural game. N.L. President John Heydler instructed A.G. Spalding & Bros. to make up a set of gray uniforms for the '33 All-Star Game with the words "National League" sewn across the shirt fronts. The senior-league players also wore caps with "NL" affixed to them.

The winning team in all eight extra-inning contests played in All-Star Game history. The National Leaguers defeated the American Leaguers, 4-3, in 14 innings in 1950; 6-5 in 12 innings in 1955; 5-4 in 10 innings in the first game of 1961; 2-1 in 10 innings in 1966; 2-1 in 15 innings in 1967; 5-4 in 12 innings in 1970; 4-3 in 10 innings in 1972, and 2-0 in 13 innings in 1987.

NEW YORK YANKEES
The only team to have six players start in one All-Star Game. With managers responsible for choosing the starting lineups at the time, Yankees Manager Joe McCarthy selected the following American League batting order for the 1939 classic: Doc Cramer, Boston Red Sox, right field; Red Rolfe, Yankees, third base; Joe DiMaggio, Yankees, center field; Bill Dickey, Yankees, catcher; Hank Greenberg, Detroit Tigers, first base; Joe Cronin, Red Sox, shortstop; George Selkirk, Yankees, left field; Joe Gordon, Yankees, second base, and Red Ruffing, Yankees, pitcher. The A.L. won, 3-1, with Selkirk contributing a run-scoring single and DiMaggio clouting a bases-empty home run.

Apparently resenting accusations that he favored Yankee representatives in All-Star play, McCarthy didn't use any of the five New York players available to him for the 1943 game. He proved he could win without the Yankee contingent, though, as the A.L. scored a 5-3 victory in the '43 contest.

American League club that has played host to the All-Star Game three times— and gone on to win the A.L. pennant in each of those seasons. All-Star Games were played at Yankee Stadium in 1939, 1960 and 1977, years in which World Series also were contested at the Yankees' ball park.

1959-1962
The four-season span in which two All-Star Games were played each year, with the doubling-up aimed at providing additional revenue for the players'

pension fund, helping needy old-time players and boosting youth baseball. The two 1959 All-Star Games were played approximately four weeks apart, while the contests in 1961 and the games in 1962 were held 20 days apart. In 1960, though, the All-Star clashes were played within two days of each other.

1965
The year in which the National League first surpassed the American League in All-Star Game triumphs. After the first All-Star Game in 1933 through the 1963 contest—a span of 34 games—the A.L. held the lead in victories. In 1964, though, the N.L. won, 7-4, and tied the series at 17-17 with one ite. The National Leaguers' 6-5 triumph in '65 thrust the senior league in front. Through 1991, the N.L. had widened the gap to 37-24-1, thanks largely to 19 victories in the 20 games that were played from 1963 through 1982.

1981
The year in which the All-Star Game marked the return of major league baseball action after a 50-day strike had forced cancellation of 712 regular-season games. Players walked off their jobs following games of June 11, 1981, and the labor dispute wasn't settled until July 31, at which time it was agreed that the All-Star Game—originally scheduled for July 14 in Cleveland—would be played August 9 and that the regular season would resume August 10. Paced by Gary Carter's two home runs and Mike Schmidt's game-winning two-run homer in the eighth inning, the National League defeated the American League, 5-4.

1983
The only year in which at least one player from each of the current 26 big-league teams appeared in the All-Star Game. Overall, there have been eight All-Star Games in which every club in the majors has had a representative play in the contest; the seasons of those classics and the number of teams in the big leagues at the time: 1933, 16; 1944, 16; 1946, 16; 1949, 16; 1953, 16; 1961 (first game), 18; 1973, 24; 1983, 26. (The big leagues expanded from 16 to 18 clubs in 1961, from 18 to 20 in 1962, from 20 to 24 in 1969 and from 24 to 26 in 1977.)

GAYLORD PERRY, JIM PERRY
The only brothers to pitch in the same All-Star Game and one of seven brother combinations to appear in the same classic. Gaylord, of the San Francisco Giants, pitched the sixth and seventh innings of the 1970 game for the National League and Jim, of the Minnesota Twins, worked the seventh and eighth innings for the American League. Gaylord yielded four hits and two runs; Jim surrendered one hit and one run.

Other brothers appearing in the same All-Star Game: outfielders Dominic DiMaggio (Boston Red Sox) and Joe DiMaggio (New York Yankees), 1941, 1949 and 1950; pitcher Mort Cooper and catcher Walker Cooper (both of the St.

All-Star pitchers Carl Hubbell (left) of the New York Giants and Lefty Grove of the Philadelphia A's show the contrast in uniform style in baseball's first midsummer classic in 1933. National Leaguers wore a special gray uniform while American Leaguers wore the uniforms of their respective teams.

Louis Cardinals), 1942 and 1943; outfielders Dixie Walker (Brooklyn Dodgers) and Harry Walker (Cardinals, Philadelphia Phillies), 1943 and 1947; outfielders Felipe Alou (Atlanta Braves) and Matty Alou (Pittsburgh Pirates), 1968; outfielder Carlos May (Chicago White Sox) and first baseman Lee May (Cincinnati Reds), 1969, and catcher Sandy Alomar Jr. (Cleveland Indians) and second baseman Roberto Alomar (San Diego Padres, Toronto Blue Jays), 1990 and 1991.

PHILADELPHIA PHILLIES
The only team in the major leagues to go four straight All-Star Games without a representative appearing in one of the contests. No Phillies players competed in the 1968, 1969, 1970 and 1971 contests, although Philadelphia did have one representative on each National League squad—in order pitchers Woodie Fryman, Grant Jackson, Joe Hoerner and Rick Wise.

Only two other teams have gone as many as three consecutive All-Star Games without a player getting into the classic. No Boston Bees players appeared for the N.L. from 1936 through 1938, and no Cleveland Indians representatives played in the game for the American League from the second contest in 1962 through 1964.

PITTSBURGH PIRATES
The only team to have as many as eight players appear in one All-Star Game. In the first All-Star Game of 1960, the Pirates' Bob Skinner (left field), Bill Mazeroski (second base) and Bob Friend (pitcher) started for the National League and Pittsburgh's Roberto Clemente (right field), Dick Groat (shortstop), Smoky Burgess (catcher), Roy Face (pitcher) and Vernon Law (pitcher) also got into the contest.

POLO GROUNDS
The first two-time site of the All-Star Game, having played host to baseball's second "Dream Game" in 1934 and to the 10th classic in 1942.

National League left fielder Joe Medwick was the only player to start in both the '34 and '42 games, first representing the St. Louis Cardinals and then the Brooklyn Dodgers. Three other players—all National Leaguers— appeared in both Polo Grounds contests: Billy Herman (Chicago Cubs and Dodgers), Mel Ott (New York Giants) and Arky Vaughan (Pittsburgh Pirates and Dodgers).

PAUL RICHARDS, GENE MAUCH
The only All-Star Game managers who never managed teams in World Series competition. Normally, a league's All-Star pilot is the man who directed his team to the pennant in the previous year. However, Casey Stengel, who managed the New York Yankees to the American League championship in 1960, was not retained by the Yanks for 1961 and was inactive that season.

Accordingly, Richards, manager of the 1960 A.L. runner-up Baltimore Orioles, guided the '61 A.L. All-Stars. Johnny Keane, manager of the 1964 National League pennant-winning and World Series champion St. Louis Cardinals, resigned after the Series and became manager of the Yankees. Mauch, who had guided the Philadelphia Phillies to a second-place tie in '64, directed the N.L. squad in the 1965 All-Star Game.

BROOKS ROBINSON, CARL YASTRZEMSKI
The only players from losing All-Star teams to win most-valuable-player honors in the showcase game. Robinson, third baseman for the Baltimore Orioles, won the Arch Ward Trophy in 1966 when he singled twice and tripled for the American League in a 2-1, 10-inning loss to the National League. Boston Red Sox standout Yastrzemski hit three singles and a double in his Ward Trophy-winning performance of 1970—but the N.L. All-Stars won the '70 classic, 5-4, in 12 innings.

BROOKS ROBINSON
Longtime Baltimore Orioles third baseman who played in 15 American League defeats in All-Star Game competition, the most losses suffered by any All-Star participant. Overall, Robinson appeared in 18 All-Star Games from 1960 through 1974, with the A.L. winning twice (1971 and the second game of 1962) and tying once (game two of 1961).

FRANK ROBINSON
The only player to hit an All-Star Game home run and a World Series homer off the same pitcher in the same year. The Baltimore Orioles' Robinson walloped a homer off Pittsburgh's Dock Ellis in the third inning of the 1971 All-Star Game and then connected against the Pirates' righthander in the second inning of the first game of the '71 Series.

STEVE ROGERS
The last of seven pitchers who have started All-Star Games in their home ball parks. Rogers, representing Montreal, started and won the 1982 game at the Expos' Olympic Stadium.

Also starting All-Star Games in their home parks were: Carl Hubbell, New York Giants, Polo Grounds, 1934; Johnny Vander Meer, Cincinnati Reds, Crosley Field, 1938; Red Ruffing, New York Yankees, Yankee Stadium, 1939; Curt Simmons, Philadelphia Phillies, Shibe Park, 1952; Don Drysdale, Los Angeles Dodgers, Memorial Coliseum, 1959 (second game); Whitey Ford, Yankees, Yankee Stadium, 1960 (second game). Vander Meer was a winner in his home-park All-Star start, Drysdale and Ford were losers and Hubbell, Ruffing and Simmons did not get decisions.

COOKIE ROJAS

One of 14 players (seven from each league) to hit a pinch homer in All-Star Game competition—and the American League reserve did it while batting for the Minnesota Twins' Rod Carew, who was on the way to his second A.L. batting championship. Rojas, who finished his 16-season career in the majors with only 54 homers (and a .263 batting average), connected off Bill Stoneman of the Montreal Expos with a man on base in the eighth inning of the 1972 classic. The homer by the Kansas City Royals' second baseman boosted the A.L. into a 3-2 lead, but the National League rebounded for a 4-3 triumph in 10 innings.

Besides Rojas, A.L. players to slam pinch homers are: Larry Doby, Cleveland Indians, 1954, against Milwaukee Braves pitcher Gene Conley; Harmon Killebrew, Twins, first game of 1961 (Mike McCormick, San Francisco Giants); Pete Runnels, Boston Red Sox, second game of 1962 (Art Mahaffey, Philadelphia Phillies); Reggie Jackson, Oakland A's, 1971 (Dock Ellis, Pittsburgh Pirates); Carl Yastrzemski, Red Sox, 1975 (Tom Seaver, New York Mets); Frank White, Royals, 1986 (Mike Scott, Houston Astros).

N.L. players hitting pinch homers: Mickey Owen, Brooklyn Dodgers, 1942 (Al Benton, Detroit Tigers); Gus Bell, Cincinnati Reds, 1954 (Bob Keegan, Chicago White Sox); Willie Mays, New York Giants, 1956 (Whitey Ford, New York Yankees); Stan Musial, St. Louis Cardinals, second game of 1960 (Gerry Staley, White Sox); George Altman, Chicago Cubs, first game of 1961 (Mike Fornieles, Red Sox); Willie Davis, Los Angeles Dodgers, 1973 (Nolan Ryan, California Angels); Lee Mazzilli, Mets, 1979 (Jim Kern, Texas Rangers).

FRANKLIN D. ROOSEVELT

The first President of the United States to attend an All-Star Game. Roosevelt was present at the 1937 game, played at Griffith Stadium in Washington. There was a wild scramble for the President's ceremonial first pitch, and New York Giants outfielder Joe Moore came up with the ball.

AL ROSEN, RAY BOONE

The first players to hit consecutive home runs in an All-Star Game. Rosen, of the Cleveland Indians, smashed a three-run homer off Robin Roberts in the third inning of the 1954 classic and Boone, of the Detroit Tigers, followed with a homer against the Philadelphia Phillies' pitcher. The blasts staked the American League to a 4-0 lead in a game that the A.L. All-Stars won, 11-9.

The only other back-to-back home runs in All-Star history were struck by the A.L.'s Ted Williams (Boston Red Sox) and Mickey Mantle (New York Yankees) in the sixth inning of the 1956 game, the National League's Steve Garvey and Jim Wynn (both of the Los Angeles Dodgers) in the second inning of the 1975 game and the A.L.'s Bo Jackson (Kansas City Royals) and Wade Boggs (Boston

Franklin D. Roosevelt became the first U.S. President to attend an All-Star Game when he threw out the first ball for the 1937 classic at Washington's Griffith Stadium.

Red Sox) in the first inning of the 1989 classic.

BOB RUSH
The winning pitcher in the shortest game in All-Star history, working the final two innings of the National League's 3-2 victory over the American League in 1952 in a contest that was called after five innings because of rain. Rush, the ace of the Chicago Cubs' pitching staff, gave up four hits and both A.L. runs in his stint.

Bob Lemon of the Cleveland Indians, who yielded two hits and two runs in two innings, was the losing pitcher for the A.L.

ST. LOUIS CARDINALS
The team that accounted for the entire starting infield for the National League squad in the 1963 All-Star Game. Three Cardinals—first baseman Bill White, shortstop Dick Groat and third baseman Ken Boyer—were voted to starting berths, while St. Louis' Julian Javier was named to replace Bill Mazeroski, the leading vote-getter at second base, when the Pittsburgh Pirates' standout was unable to play because of a leg injury.

SEVEN

The fewest number of teams to be represented in the starting lineups of an All-Star Game, with only Oakland (five players), New York (three) and Minnesota (one) placing players in the American League's game-opening lineup in 1975 and just Cincinnati (four players), Los Angeles (three), St. Louis (one) and Pittsburgh (one) landing players on the National League's starting unit. The '75 lineups: N.L.—Pete Rose, Reds, right field; Lou Brock, Cardinals, left field; Joe Morgan, Reds, second base; Johnny Bench, Reds, catcher; Steve Garvey, Dodgers, first base; Jim Wynn, Dodgers, center field; Roy Cey, Dodgers, third base; Dave Concepcion, Reds, shortstop, and Jerry Reuss, Pirates, pitcher. A.L.—Bobby Bonds, Yankees, center field; Rod Carew, Twins, second base; Thurman Munson, Yankees, catcher; Reggie Jackson, A's, right field; Joe Rudi, A's, left field; Graig Nettles, Yankees, third base; Gene Tenace, A's, first base; Bert Campaneris, A's, shortstop, and Vida Blue, A's, pitcher.

There were 24 teams in the major leagues in 1975.

17

The number of times that Willie Mays and Hank Aaron played on the winning side in All-Star Game history—a record total. Each player appeared in 24 All-Star Games; Aaron had a record of 17-5-1 as a National Leaguer (representing the Milwaukee and Atlanta Braves) and 0-1 as an American Leaguer (Milwaukee Brewers), while Mays went 17-6-1 as an N.L. player (New York and San Francisco Giants and New York Mets).

FRANK (SPEC) SHEA

The first rookie pitcher to win an All-Star Game. After fashioning a 15-5 record and a 1.66 earned-run average for Oakland of the Pacific Coast League in 1946, Shea compiled an 11-2 record for the New York Yankees by the All-Star Game break of 1947 and was selected to appear in the midsummer classic in his first major league season. Working the fourth through the sixth innings for the American League, Shea allowed one run and three hits (including a home run by Johnny Mize of the New York Giants) in a game that the A.L. won, 2-1.

Shea finished with a 14-5 record for the Yankees in '47.

AL SIMMONS

Chicago White Sox outfielder who received the most votes from fans in the nationwide newspaper poll that was used to select the teams for the first All-Star Game in 1933. Simmons collected 346,291 votes, outdistancing runner-up Chuck Klein of the Philadelphia Phillies by 4,008 votes. Following Klein, who attracted 342,283 votes, were: Gabby Hartnett, Chicago Cubs, 338,653; Joe Cronin, Washington Senators, 337,766, and Lefty Grove, Philadelphia A's, 327,242. The New York Yankees' Babe Ruth, nearing the end of his career at age 38, was sixth in the balloting with 320,518 votes.

Basically, fans picked the players (including the pitchers) again in 1934, the rival managers chose the rosters from 1935 through 1937, the eight managers from each league named the squads from 1938 through 1946, fans selected the eight "position" starters from 1947 through 1957 (with managers naming the remainder of the squads) and managers, coaches and players picked the position starters from 1958 through 1969 (managers again completing the teams). Fans regained the honor of choosing the position starters in 1970 (with managers selecting the rest of the players), a process that remains in effect.

BILL TERRY
Not only the National League's manager in the 1934 All-Star Game, but the N.L.'s leading batter at the '34 All-Star break with a .367 average (108 hits in 294 at-bats). Terry, manager and first baseman of the New York Giants, collected a single in three at-bats in the All-Star contest, which the N.L. lost,

Terry finished the '34 season with a .354 batting mark, second to the .362 figure posted by N.L. batting champion Paul Waner of Pittsburgh.

TEXAS RANGERS
With the Toronto Blue Jays having played host to the All-Star Game for the first time in 1991, the Rangers are the only present-day major league club yet to stage the midsummer classic.

TICKET PRICES
Admission to the first All-Star Game in major league history, played July 6, 1933, at Comiskey Park in Chicago, cost $1.65 for a box seat, $1.10 for a grandstand location and 55 cents for a bleacher ticket.

TUESDAY
Traditionally, the day of the week on which the All-Star Game is played—but the classic has been contested on every day of the week except Friday and Saturday. Forty-nine of the 62 All-Star Games have been played on Tuesday, six on Monday, five on Wednesday, one on Thursday (the first game, in 1933) and one on Sunday (in the strike-shortened season of 1981).

FERNANDO VALENZUELA
Pitching in relief in the 57th All-Star Game, he matched a record established in the second All-Star contest when he struck out five straight batters. Valenzuela, of the Los Angeles Dodgers, fanned Don Mattingly (New York Yankees), Cal Ripken Jr. (Baltimore Orioles) and Jesse Barfield (Toronto Blue Jays) in the fourth inning of the 1986 game and then struck out Lou Whitaker (Detroit Tigers) and pitcher Ted Higuera (Milwaukee Brewers) in the fifth to tie the All-Star consecutive-strikeout mark set 52 years earlier by Carl Hubbell of the New York Giants. Hubbell, like Valenzuela a screwball pitcher, struck out Babe Ruth (Yankees), Lou Gehrig (Yankees), Jimmie Foxx (Philadelphia

A's), Al Simmons (Chicago White Sox) and Joe Cronin (Washington Senators) in the first two innings of the 1934 game.

ARCH WARD
Chicago Tribune sports editor who founded the All-Star Game in 1933 as the featured sports event of Chicago's Century of Progress Exposition.

Ward, also founder of the Chicago College All-Star Football Game (1934) and the All-America Football Conference (1946), died on July 9, 1955, at age 58 and was buried in Chicago on July 12, the day baseball's 22nd All-Star Game was played at Milwaukee's County Stadium. Game time was delayed one-half hour to allow baseball dignitaries time to travel from Ward's funeral to Milwaukee.

Arch Ward (right) posed with American League President Will Harridge in 1940, seven years after becoming the founding father of baseball's All-Star Game.

LON WARNEKE
The only pitcher to hit a triple in an All-Star Game (no pitcher has connected for a home run), achieving the feat in the sixth inning of the first All-Star classic in 1933. Warneke, of the Chicago Cubs, rapped his triple—the first All-Star extra-base hit by a pitcher—off Alvin Crowder of the Washington Senators.

Only three other pitchers have managed extra-base hits in All-Star Game history. Bucky Walters of the Cincinnati Reds (1941), Johnny Podres of the Los Angeles Dodgers (second game, 1962) and Steve Carlton of the St. Louis Cardinals (1969) all struck doubles, with Carlton's blow representing the last hit by a pitcher in an All-Star Game.

LON WARNEKE
The only man to play in an All-Star Game and umpire in the classic. Representing the Chicago Cubs, Warneke pitched in the 1933, 1934 and 1936 games. He later became a National League umpire and worked the right-field line during the 1952 All-Star contest.

DON WERT
A lifetime .242 big-league hitter who batted only .200 in 1968, he nonetheless played in the All-Star Game in '68 and collected a hit in his only career All-Star at-bat. Wert, who had a .220 average at the All-Star break as the Detroit Tigers' third baseman, entered the game in the sixth inning for the American League and doubled off Tom Seaver of the New York Mets in the eighth.

LOU WHITAKER
American League player who arrived in Minneapolis, site of the 1985 All-Star Game, without his uniform and was forced to purchase a replica jersey from a souvenir vendor. Whitaker, the A.L.'s starting second baseman, had left Detroit without his home Tigers uniform and a replacement was lost in shipment. While the souvenir jersey had the familiar old-English "D" on the front, it was numberless on the back. So, using a marking pen, Whitaker made a reasonable facsimile of his number 1 and was ready for action.

Whitaker played error-free ball at second base in the '85 All-Star Game but was hitless in two at-bats before leaving the contest in the sixth inning.

DICK WILLIAMS
Of the All-Star managers meeting the usual criterion of having managed a major league pennant-winner the previous season, the only one to represent a club other than the team he led to a league championship a year earlier. Williams, who managed the Oakland A's to the American League pennant and World Series title in 1973 and then resigned, was named California manager three weeks before the 1974 All-Star Game and was in an Angels uniform when he directed the A.L. All-Stars in the '74 classic.

When Detroit Tigers second baseman Lou Whitaker forgot to take his uniform to the 1985 All-Star Game in Minneapolis, he was forced to put together a makeshift outfit purchased from a souvenir vendor.

MAURY WILLS

The winner of the first Arch Ward Trophy, presented to the All-Star Game's Most Valuable Player. The award was initially given in 1962, a year in which Wills stood out in the first All-Star contest of the season. Wills, shortstop for the Los Angeles Dodgers, entered the game in the sixth inning as a pinch-runner for Stan Musial of the St. Louis Cardinals. After stealing second base, he scored the game's first run on a single by Dick Groat of the Pittsburgh Pirates. In the eighth, Wills led off with a single and raced to third on a single to left field by San Francisco's Jim Davenport. When the Giants' Felipe Alou followed with a foul fly to short right field, Wills tagged up after the catch and slid home with the National League's final run in a 3-1 triumph.

WILBUR WOOD

The pitcher with the highest victory total, 18, at the time of the first or only All-Star Game of a season—but he wasn't selected to his league's All-Star squad that year, 1973. Wood, a knuckleball specialist for the Chicago White Sox, boasted an 18-14 record when the '73 All-Star Game was played on July 24. His heavy loss total no doubt contributing to the lack of an All-Star invitation, Wood went on to compile a 24-20 mark for the White Sox in '73.

Chicago lefthander Wilbur Wood, shown comparing knuckleball grips with teammate Hoyt Wilhelm in 1967, was an All-Star snub in 1973 when he led the American League at the break with 18 victories.

Whitey Ford of the New York Yankees and Don Drysdale of the Los Angeles Dodgers share the All-Star-break record for victories, having attained 19 triumphs at the time of the second All-Star Game of 1961 and the second classic of 1962, respectively. Ford's Yankees had played 101 games by the second-game break and Drysdale's Dodgers had played 106; Wood's White Sox had played 98 games by the All-Star break of '73.

Ford finished with a 25-4 record in '61; Drysdale went 25-9 in '62.

YANKEE STADIUM
The first and last ball park to play host to an All-Star Game and a World Series in the same year, doing so in 1939 and in 1977. Yankee Stadium also was an All-Star site (second game of the season) and World Series host in 1960.

Six other ball parks have served as hosts for baseball's two prime attractions in the same year: Fenway Park, Boston, 1946; Ebbets Field, Brooklyn, 1949; Cleveland Stadium, Cleveland, 1954; Memorial Coliseum, Los Angeles, 1959 (second All-Star Game of the season); Metropolitan Stadium, Bloomington, Minn., 1965; Riverfront Stadium, Cincinnati, 1970.

While teams hosting the All-Star Game have reached the World Series nine times overall, only three All-Star hosts—the '39 New York Yankees, the '59 Los Angeles Dodgers and the '77 Yanks—have won the Series.

FOURTH INNING
Charting the masterpieces: perfect games and no-hitters

GROVER CLEVELAND ALEXANDER

The highest-ranking pitcher on the big leagues' career-victory list never to have thrown a nine-inning no-hitter in the majors. While Alexander, whose 373 victories place him in a third-place tie with Christy Mathewson among the majors' all-time winningest pitchers, never threw a no-hit game Charles (Bumpus) Jones (two lifetime victories) and Bobo Holloman (three) did toss no-hitters. Following are charts showing 300-game winners who failed to pitch no-hitters and pitchers with fewer than 20 career victories who did achieve no-hit fame:

Did Not Pitch No-Hitter		Pitched No-Hitter	
Grover C. Alexander	373-208	Charles (Bumpus) Jones	2-4
Charles (Kid) Nichols	361-208	Wilson Alvarez	3-3
Tim Keefe	342-224	Bobo Holloman	3-7
Steve Carlton	329-244	George Davis	7-11
Don Sutton	324-256	Mike Warren	9-13
Mickey Welch	307-209	Bill McCahan	16-14
Eddie Plank	305-181	Tommy Greene	17-12
Lefty Grove	300-141		
Early Wynn	300-244		

Jones pitched his no-hitter for Cincinnati in 1892, Holloman for the St. Louis Browns in 1953, Alvarez for the Chicago White Sox in 1991. Davis for the Boston Braves in 1914, Warren for the Oakland A's in 1983 and McCahan for the Philadelphia A's in 1947. Alexander narrowly missed a no-hitter for the Philadelphia Phillies on June 5, 1915, going 8 2/3 innings against St. Louis before allowing the Cardinals' only hit of the game.

LEON (RED) AMES

New York Giants pitcher who threw a five-inning no-hitter in his major league debut. Ames' first appearance in the big leagues came in the second game of a doubleheader at St. Louis on September 14, 1903, and the 21-year-old righthander struck out seven batters and walked two while holding the Cardinals hitless in a 5-0 triumph. The game was halted after five innings because of darkness.

AL ATKISSON

The only man to pitch no-hitters in each of his first two years in the big leagues. Atkisson hurled his no-hit games for Philadelphia of the American Association (a major league at the time), the gems coming in a 10-1 victory over Pittsburgh in 1884 and a 3-2 triumph against New York in 1886. He did not pitch in the majors in 1885.

The only other pitcher to record two no-hitters by the end of his first two years in the big leagues was Johnny Vander Meer of the Cincinnati Reds. Both of Vander Meer's no-hit performances came in 1938, his second season in the majors.

Steve Busby fired no-hitters for the Kansas City Royals in his first two full seasons in the majors, 1973 and 1974. He had pitched in five games for Kansas City in 1972, however.

JIMMY AUSTIN

Third baseman who played in eight major league no-hitters—three of them on August 30 (1910, 1912 and 1916). On August 30, 1910, Austin played third for the New York Highlanders in the second game of a doubleheader when teammate Tom Hughes held Cleveland hitless through nine innings. Hughes then yielded seven hits in the next two innings and wound up a 5-0 loser. Two years to the day later, Austin was playing third for the Browns when St. Louis' Earl Hamilton tossed a 5-1 no-hitter against the Detroit Tigers. And, exactly four years after Hamilton's masterpiece, Austin again was stationed at third base for the Browns in a no-hit game; this time, though, Austin and his teammates were the victims, falling to Hubert (Dutch) Leonard of the Boston Red Sox in a 4-0 contest.

No other major leaguer has appeared in three no-hitters that occurred on the same date.

JOHN BALAZ

One of five players (all members of the 1974 and 1975 California Angels) to appear in no-hit games exactly one year apart—and he played in only 59 games in his two-year major league career. Balaz played left field for the Angels in teammate Nolan Ryan's no-hitter against the Minnesota Twins on September 28, 1974, and he was in right field for California in Oakland's four-man (Vida Blue, Glenn Abbott, Paul Lindblad and Rollie Fingers) no-hitter against the Angels on September 28, 1975. Bruce Bochte, Dave Chalk, Morris Nettles and Lee Stanton also played for the Angels in both games, a 4-0 California victory and a 5-0 A's triumph.

GEORGE BRADLEY

The first pitcher in major league history to throw a no-hitter, accomplishing

St. Louis Browns pitcher Bob Holloman, who won only three major league games, celebrated one of those victories, a no-hitter against the Philadelphia Athletics,with his wife and son in 1953.

the feat for St. Louis' National League club in a 2-0 triumph over Hartford on July 15, 1876. The N.L., baseball's first "big league," had begun its first season of operation the previous April.

TED BREITENSTEIN
The first of five pitchers to notch no-hitters in two major leagues. Breitenstein pitched his first no-hitter for the St. Louis Browns of the American Association in 1891, then recorded his second for the National League's Cincinnati Reds in 1898.

Others pitching no-hitters in two major leagues: Cy Young, Cleveland, N.L., 1897, and Boston, A.L., 1904, 1908; Tom Hughes, New York, A.L., 1910, and Boston, N.L., 1916; Jim Bunning, Detroit, A.L., 1958, and Philadelphia, N.L., 1964; Nolan Ryan, California, A.L., 1973 (2), 1974, 1975; Texas, A.L., 1990, 1991, and Houston, N.L., 1981.

TED BREITENSTEIN, JIM HUGHES
The first pitchers in big-league history to throw nine-inning no-hitters in

different games on the same day. In National League contests played April 22, 1898, Cincinnati's Breitenstein pitched an 11-0 no-hit game against Pittsburgh and Baltimore's Hughes stopped Boston without a hit in an 8-0 triumph.

More than ninety years later, no-hitters were thrown on the same day in different leagues—a first in the majors. On June 29, 1990, Oakland's Dave Stewart tossed a no-hitter at Toronto in a 5-0 American League victory; later that night, the Los Angeles Dodgers' Fernando Valenzuela held St. Louis hitless in a 6-0 N.L. conquest.

On May 2, 1917, Cincinnati's Fred Toney and Chicago's Jim (Hippo) Vaughn threw nine-inning no-hitters against each other in an N.L. game that was scoreless entering the 10th inning. The Reds broke through for two hits and a run in the 10th against Vaughn and wound up 1-0 winners, with Toney holding the Cubs hitless throughout.

SMOKY BURGESS
He caught two no-hit games in his big-league career—and his club lost both contests. Playing for the Cincinnati Reds on May 26, 1956, in Milwaukee Burgess caught a combined nine-inning no-hitter by Johnny Klippstein, Hershell Freeman and Joe Black; the Braves got a 10th-inning hit, though, and two more in the next inning and scored a 2-1 victory in 11 innings. Three years later, in another May 26 game also played in Milwaukee, Burgess was behind the plate for Pittsburgh when the Pirates' Harvey Haddix pitched 12 perfect innings against the Braves. Milwaukee won that 1959 contest, 1-0 getting one hit in a 13-inning triumph.

JEFF BURROUGHS
The only player in major league history to slug a bases-loaded home run in a no-hit game of nine or more innings. Texas' left fielder hit a first-inning grand slam off Oakland's Vida Blue on July 30, 1973, in a game in which the Rangers' Jim Bibby pitched a 6-0 no-hitter against the A's.

Ed Cartwright of the St. Louis Browns hit a bases-full smash and a three-run shot—both homers coming in an 11-run third inning—in support of George Nicol's no-hit pitching on September 23, 1890, in a 21-2 mauling of Philadelphia. The Browns-Athletics American Association game was shortened to seven innings because of darkness.

BERT CAMPANERIS
The player who has appeared in the most no-hit games in the major leagues, 11. He was a member of the winning team five times. The no-hitters in which Campaneris played (with capitalization indicating participation with the victorious club):

Date	Club	No-Hit Pitcher
MAY 8, 1968	OAKLAND	JIM (CATFISH) HUNTER VS. MINNESOTA
Aug. 13, 1969	Oakland	Jim Palmer, Baltimore
July 3, 1970	Oakland	Clyde Wright, California
SEPT. 21, 1970	OAKLAND	VIDA BLUE VS. MINNESOTA
July 30, 1973	Oakland	Jim Bibby, Texas
July 19, 1974	Oakland	Dick Bosman, Cleveland
SEPT. 28, 1975	OAKLAND	BLUE-ABBOTT-LINDBLAD-FINGERS VS. CALIFORNIA
July 28, 1976	Oakland	Odom-Barrios, Chicago
SEPT. 22, 1977	TEXAS	BERT BLYLEVEN VS. CALIFORNIA
May 14, 1977	Texas	Jim Colborn, Kansas City
JULY 4, 1983	N.Y., A.L.	DAVE RIGHETTI VS. BOSTON

Campaneris played shortstop in the first 10 games and was at third base for the New York Yankees in Righetti's no-hitter.

DON CARDWELL
Two days after being traded from the Philadelphia Phillies to the Chicago Cubs in May 1960, he tossed a no-hitter for the Cubs in the second game of a doubleheader at Wrigley Field. Facing the St. Louis Cardinals, Cardwell allowed only one baserunner. After walking the Cards' Alex Grammas with one out in the first inning, he proceeded to retire the next 26 batters—the final out coming when Cubs left fielder Walt Moryn made a shoetop catch of Joe Cunningham's liner. Chicago won, 4-0, in the May 15 game.

JAMES (DOC) CASEY
The first of four major leaguers to appear in no-hit games in five consecutive years. Third baseman Casey played in no-hitters while with the Chicago Cubs in 1903, 1904 and 1905 and in no-hit performances while a member of the Brooklyn Dodgers in 1906 (three times) and 1907.

Others appearing in no-hit contests in five straight seasons: Deron Johnson, Philadelphia Phillies, 1969 through 1972, and Oakland A's, 1973; Bill North, Cubs, 1972, and A's, 1973 through 1976; Bert Campaneris, A's, 1973 through 1976, and Texas Rangers, 1977 (two games).

JOE CHRISTOPHER
The first player to make his major league debut in a perfect game. Christopher, playing for Pittsburgh, took over in right field for Roman Mejias in the 10th inning of Pirate lefthander Harvey Haddix's 12-inning perfect game against the Milwaukee Braves on May 26, 1959. Mejias had left the game for a pinch-hitter.

Only two other players have broken into the majors under perfect-game

Don Cardwell, traded by Philadelphia to Chicago two days earlier, was literally surrounded by Cubs fans after pitching a no-hitter against the St. Louis Cardinals in the second game of a 1960 doubleheader at Wrigley Field.

circumstances—and they did it in the same contest. Byron Browne and Don Young made their first big-league appearances on September 9, 1965—Browne played left field and Young was in center field for the Chicago Cubs—when Sandy Koufax of the Los Angeles Dodgers fired a 1-0 perfect game against Chicago.

Outfielder Joe Rudi made his Oakland A's debut on May 8, 1968, in the game in which A's pitcher Jim (Catfish) Hunter recorded a perfect game against the Minnesota Twins, 4-0. Rudi, though, had entered the majors in 1967 with the Kansas City A's and played 19 games for the Kansas City club.

LARRY CORCORAN
The first man to pitch two no-hitters in the majors—and the first to toss three as well. Corcoran, who pitched all three of his gems for the Chicago club of the National League, notched his first no-hitter on August 19, 1880, against Boston, his second on September 20, 1882, against Worcester and his third on June 27, 1884, against Providence. He won by 6-0, 5-0 and 6-0 scores.

HUGH DAILY
One-armed pitcher who on September 13, 1883, pitched a no-hitter for Cleveland in a 1-0 National League triumph over Philadelphia. Daily, who had

part of his left arm amputated as a youngster, spent six seasons in the major leagues. He struck out 19 batters in an 1884 Union Association game and established a big-league season record for righthanders in '84 by striking out 483 batters.

DETROIT TIGERS
Club that played an American League-record 39 consecutive seasons without getting a no-hit pitching performance. In the second game of a July 4, 1912, doubleheader, against St. Louis, the Tigers' George Mullin threw a 7-0 no-hitter against the Browns. However, from 1913 through 1951, no Detroit pitcher turned in a no-hitter. Virgil Trucks tried to make up for lost time in 1952, fashioning two no-hitters for the Tigers in a little more than three months. His gems were 1-0 victories over the Washington Senators and New York Yankees on May 15 and August 25, respectively.

BILL DINNEEN
The last umpire in a big-league no-hit game to have pitched a no-hitter himself in the majors. Dinneen, who umpired in Bill Dietrich's 8-0 no-hitter for the Chicago White Sox against the St. Louis Browns on June 1, 1937, pitched a 2-0 no-hit game for the Boston Red Sox against the White Sox in the first game of a September 27, 1905, doubleheader.

GEORGE ESTOCK
Boston Braves pitcher who in his only major league start (he made 36 relief appearances) and lone decision was victimized by a no-hitter. Matched against Pittsburgh's Cliff Chambers in the second game of a May 6, 1951, doubleheader in Boston, Estock yielded eight hits and three runs in eight innings. Chambers walked eight Braves batters in his complete-game performance, but held Boston hitless in a 3-0 victory.

The no-hitter was the last triumph in a Pirates uniform for Chambers, who had led Pittsburgh in victories in 1949 (13) and 1950 (12). The gem against Boston gave Chambers a 3-2 record three weeks into the 1951 season, but on June 15—having dropped to a 3-6 mark—he was traded to the St. Louis Cardinals.

FORBES FIELD
A major league ball park for 61 years (mid-1909 until mid-1970), but never the site of a no-hitter. Jeff Tesreau of the New York Giants was on the brink of no-hit fame at Pittsburgh's Forbes Field, though, while pitching against the Pirates on May 16, 1914. Tesreau held the Bucs hitless for 8 2/3 innings before yielding a single to Joe Kelly, Pittsburgh's center fielder and leadoff hitter. Tesreau retired the next batter, finishing with a one-hit, 2-0 triumph.

KEN FORSCH, JACK MORRIS
Pitchers who tossed the earliest calendar-date no-hitters in major league

history, recording their masterpieces in April 7 games. Forsch, pitching for the Astros, threw his no-hit game against the Atlanta Braves in 1979, posting a 6-0 victory at Houston; Morris, a member of the Detroit Tigers, stopped the White Sox without a hit in 1984, collecting a 4-0 triumph at Chicago. Forsch's no-hitter came in the Astros' second game of the '79 season, while Morris' gem came in the Tiger pitcher's second contest of '84 and Detroit's fourth game overall.

FOUR
The number of players who have ended their big-league careers in perfect games. John Anderson and Ossee Schreckengost of the Chicago White Sox saw their final major league action on October 2, 1908, in Cleveland—the day on which Addie Joss pitched a perfect game against the Sox. Schreckengost caught for Chicago that afternoon and Anderson pinch-hit for the Sox in Cleveland's 1-0 victory. And while Chicago played four more games that season, neither player got into another contest. Seventy-six years later, on the final day of the regular season, Texas' Marv Foley and Mickey Rivers bowed out of the majors in California pitcher Mike Witt's perfect game. Foley pinch-hit and Rivers saw duty as the designated hitter for the Rangers in the September 30, 1984, game in Arlington, Tex., in which Witt retired all 27 Texas batters in a 1-0 Angels triumph.

One other player has finished his big-league career on the day in which his club was involved in a perfect game. Pitcher Tom Sturdivant of the New York Mets worked in both games of a June 21, 1964, doubleheader against Philadelphia, the relief roles marking his final appearances in the majors. In the first game of the twin bill, the Phillies' Jim Bunning pitched a 6-0 perfect game against the Mets in New York.

JAMES (PUD) GALVIN
The last big-leaguer to throw a no-hitter from 45 feet, which was baseball's prescribed pitching distance from the National League's inception in 1876 through 1880. Galvin, a member of the N.L.'s Buffalo club, held Worcester hitless on August 20, 1880, and was a 1-0 winner.

The pitching distance was moved to 50 feet from the plate in 1881.

JAMES (PUD) GALVIN
Winner of the most lopsided nine-inning no-hit game in major league history. Clearly, August 4, 1884, was a long day for the Detroit club of the National League; not only did Buffalo's Galvin pitch a no-hit, no-run game against Detroit, he received offensive support galore. The final score: Buffalo 18, Detroit 0.

The modern record for the most one-sided outcome in a nine-inning no-hitter

Detroit's Jack Morris received a well-deserved hug from catcher Lance Parrish after his April 7, 1984, no-hit performance against the Chicago White Sox. Morris matched the record for the earliest calendar-date no-hitter in big-league history.

is 15-0, the score by which Frank Smith of the Chicago White Sox beat Detroit in the second game of a September 6, 1905, doubleheader.

BILL HAWKE

Baltimore pitcher who threw the first big-league no-hitter from 60 feet, 6 inches, which became the majors' required pitching distance in 1893 (and remains the measurement in use today). Pitching against Washington on August 16, 1893, Hawke hurled no-hit ball while posting a 5-0 victory. Hawke pitched his gem from a rubber slab; previously, pitchers threw from a boxed-in area—a "pitcher's box"—that was 50 feet from home plate.

KEN HOLTZMAN

The last major leaguer to notch a no-hitter without recording a strikeout, achieving that oddity on August 19, 1969, when he pitched the Chicago Cubs to a 3-0 triumph over Atlanta. Holtzman walked three Braves.

Holtzman fired a second no-hitter on June 3, 1971, leading the Cubs past Cincinnati, 1-0. He struck out six Reds and walked four.

WILLIAM (DUMMY) HOY

The only man to play in no-hitters in three major leagues. In the American Association, outfielder Hoy played for St. Louis in 1891 when the Browns' Ted Breitenstein pitched a no-hitter against Louisville. In the National League, Hoy and his Washington teammates were held hitless in 1893 by Baltimore's Bill Hawke and his Cincinnati club was victimized in 1897 by Cleveland's Cy Young; in 1899, he played behind Deacon Phillippe when the Louisville pitcher tossed a no-hitter against New York. And Hoy played for the American League's Chicago White Sox in 1901 when the Sox went nine innings without a hit against Cleveland's Earl Moore (before Chicago broke through for two hits and two runs in the 10th and beat Moore, 4-2).

TOM HUGHES

Of pitchers who wound up losing no-hit games, the one who suffered the worst defeat. Hughes, of the New York Highlanders, held Cleveland hitless for 9 1/3 innings in the second game of an August 30, 1910, American League doubleheader before yielding a single to Harry Niles. Cleveland collected six more hits off Hughes and won, 5-0, in 11 innings.

TIM HULETT

Infielder who had appeared in two no-hitters after his first eight major league games. Hulett, playing his fourth big-league contest, was at second base for the Chicago White Sox on September 29, 1983, when Mike Warren of the Oakland A's held the Sox hitless in a 3-0 triumph. On April 7, 1984, Hulett saw action at third base (but didn't start) for the Sox—it was his eighth game in the majors—as Jack Morris of the Tigers pitched a 4-0 no-hitter against Chicago.

CHARLES (BUMPUS) JONES

Pitcher who broke into the majors by hurling what proved to be the last big-league no-hitter from a distance of 50 feet—and this man won only one other game in the majors. Jones made his major league debut on the final day of the 1892 season, achieving a 7-1 no-hitter for Cincinnati against Pittsburgh. In 1893, a season in which Jones posted a 1-4 record before bowing out of the big leagues, the pitching distance was moved to its present length of 60 feet, 6 inches.

Jones' 1892 masterpiece, accomplished on October 15, ranks as the latest calendar-date no-hitter of nine innings or longer in major league history.

ADDIE JOSS

The only major leaguer to toss two nine-inning no-hitters against the same club. Joss, who spent all nine of his big-league seasons with Cleveland, pitched a perfect game against the Chicago White Sox on October 2, 1908, and came back with a second no-hitter against the White Sox on April 20, 1910. Cleveland was a 1-0 winner in each game.

SAM KIMBER

The only man to pitch a major league no-hitter that ended in a tie game. Kimber, a member of the Brooklyn club of the American Association, shut out Toledo for 10 innings on October 4, 1884, not allowing a hit. However, Toledo's Tony Mullane matched Kimber's scoreless pitching—he allowed four hits—in a game that was halted after 10 innings because of darkness.

Kimber's effort in the 0-0 game marked the majors' first no-hitter exceeding nine innings.

ED KONETCHY

Boston Braves first baseman who in consecutive games against the New York Giants in 1916 spoiled no-hit bids—and wound up with the Braves' only hit in each contest. In the second game of a September 28, 1916, doubleheader, the Giants' Ferdie Schupp had a no-hitter until Konetchy singled in the seventh inning. After Schupp nailed down a one-hit, 6-0 victory, rain postponed the next day's Braves-Giants game. In the opening game of the September 30 twin bill between the same clubs, New York's Rube Benton carried a no-hitter into the eighth inning before Konetchy delivered another single. Benton went on to win his one-hitter by a 4-0 score.

Benton's September 30 triumph was the Giants' 26th consecutive victory, a major league record. Boston won the second game of that day's doubleheader, though, ending New York's winning streak.

SANDY KOUFAX

The first pitcher to toss a no-hitter in a Cy Young Award-winning season—and he accomplished the no-hitter/Cy Young feat twice. The Los Angeles Dodgers' lefthander pitched an 8-0 no-hit game against San Francisco on May 11, 1963, and went on to win the National League's '63 Cy Young honor with a 25-5 record, 306 strikeouts and a 1.88 earned-run average. In 1965 he hurled a 1-0 perfect game against the Cubs on September 9 en route to a 26-8 mark, 382 strikeouts, a 2.04 ERA and another Cy Young Award.

Houston's Mike Scott is the only other pitcher to throw a no-hitter and win the Cy Young Award in the same year. Scott held San Francisco hitless and struck out 13 Giants batters while winning, 2-0, on September 25, 1986. The Astros' righthander later was named the N.L.'s Cy Young winner for '86 after compiling a season record of 18-10, an N.L.-leading 2.22 earned-run average and a league-high 306 strikeouts.

JOE LAFATA

New York Giants first baseman-outfielder who appeared in one big-league game in 1948—Rex Barney's 2-0 no-hitter for Brooklyn. Brought up from Minneapolis of the American Association, Lafata was called upon as a pinch-hitter in the ninth inning of the Giants' September 9 game against the Dodgers and struck out against Barney.

Lafata appeared in 127 big-league games overall, playing 62 games for the Giants in 1947 and 64 for the National League club in 1949.

CHARLIE LEA

The only pitcher born outside the United States to throw a major league no-hitter outside the U.S. Lea, born in Orleans, France, in 1956, pitched a 4-0 no-hit victory for the Montreal Expos over the San Francisco Giants in the second game of a May 10, 1981, National League doubleheader at Montreal's Olympic Stadium.

HUBERT (DUTCH) LEONARD

Boston Red Sox pitcher who fired a no-hitter against St. Louis the day after the Browns drove him from the mound in the first inning. On August 29, 1916, Leonard started the first game of a doubleheader but retired only one Browns batter. He allowed two hits, two runs and a walk, hit a batter and uncorked a wild pitch. The next day, Leonard allowed only two baserunners —both on walks—and held St. Louis hitless in a 4-0 triumph.

When Leonard was knocked out of the August 29 game, he was relieved by 21-year-old Babe Ruth (who was on the way to a 23-victory season for the Red Sox).

SAL MAGLIE

The losing pitcher in Don Larsen's perfect game in the 1956 World Series, but the last man to pitch a no-hitter in the majors prior to Larsen. Larsen pitched his 2-0 Series gem for the New York Yankees against the Brooklyn Dodgers on October 8, 1956. Thirteen days earlier, in the final week of the National League season, Maglie had fashioned a no-hit game against Philadelphia as the Dodgers downed the Phillies, 5-0.

Three other pitchers have tossed big-league no-hitters and then absorbed the loss in the majors' next nine-inning no-hit game. Jim Tobin of the Boston Braves held the Brooklyn Dodgers hitless on April 27, 1944; in the big leagues' next no-hitter, Tobin was the loser when the Cincinnati Reds' Clyde Shoun baffled the Braves in a May 15, 1944, game. Cleveland's Bob Feller threw a no-hit game against the Detroit Tigers on July 1, 1951; 11 days later, the New York Yankees' Allie Reynolds pitched a no-hitter against Feller and the Indians. Bo Belinsky of the Los Angeles Angels stopped the Baltimore Orioles without a hit on May 5, 1962; in the major leagues' next no-hit game, Belinsky and the Angels lost to Earl Wilson of the Boston Red Sox on June 26, 1962.

Dodgers ace Sandy Koufax posed with comedian Milton Berle on September 9, 1965, after pitching a perfect game against the Chicago Cubs en route to a 26-8 record and the National League Cy Young Award.

BILL McCAHAN
The losing pitcher when Don Black of the Cleveland Indians pitched a no-hitter against the Philadelphia A's on July 10, 1947, he proceeded to throw the major leagues' next no-hit game eight weeks later. Working against Washington on September 3, McCahan faced only 28 batters in his gem—the Senators' lone baserunner was the result of an error—and pitched the A's to a 3-0 American League victory.

Hugh (One Arm) Daily and Mal Eason are the only other major leaguers to be a losing pitcher in an opponent's no-hit game and then hurl the big leagues' next no-hitter. On September 13, 1883, Cleveland's Daily held Philadelphia hitless in a National League game after he had lost the majors' previous no-hit game (pitched by Hoss Radbourn of Providence seven weeks earlier). And on July 20, 1906, Brooklyn's Eason pitched an N.L. no-hitter against the St. Louis Cardinals 2 1/2 months after he had been the losing pitcher in the big leagues' last hitless game (turned in by John Lush of the Phillies).

MIKE McCORMICK
San Francisco pitcher who allowed a hit during his June 12, 1959, outing against Philadelphia, but was still credited with a no-hit game against the Phillies—a five-inning no-hitter. Entering the bottom of the sixth inning, the Phils not only trailed the Giants, 3-0, they had failed to collect a hit off McCormick. The Phillies loaded the bases in the sixth, though, with McCormick walking two batters and yielding a single to Richie Ashburn. However, rain prevented the inning from being finished and, under the rules, records reverted to the last completed inning, the fifth. And McCormick had an abbreviated no-hitter.

MILWAUKEE BRAVES
National League club that was involved in six no-hitters (all played in Milwaukee) during its 13-season history and won all six games—despite being no-hit victims in two of the contests. Three Milwaukee pitchers accounted for four of the no-hitters, with Jim Wilson (1954), Lew Burdette (1960) and Warren Spahn (1960, 1961) tossing hitless games. In 1956, Cincinnati's Johnny Klippstein, Hershell Freeman and Joe Black held the Braves without a hit for nine innings, but Milwaukee collected a hit in the 10th and went on to win in 11 innings. In 1959, Pittsburgh's Harvey Haddix pitched 12 perfect innings against Milwaukee, only to lose on one hit in 13 innings.

TONY MULLANE
Pitching for Louisville of the American Association in an 1882 game, he hurled the major leagues' first no-hitter from a 50-foot distance. The length from the pitcher's box to home plate had been increased from 45 to 50 feet effective with the beginning of the 1881 season, but it wasn't until late in the 1882 season—September 11—that a no-hit game was pitched from the new distance, with

Mullane achieving the feat in a 2-0 triumph over Cincinnati.

GEORGE MULLIN
The only man in major league history to toss a no-hitter on his birthday. Mullin, of the Detroit Tigers, turned 32 years old on July 4, 1912, the day he held the St. Louis Browns hitless in the second game of a doubleheader. Mullin's 7-0 gem was the first no-hit game thrown by a Tigers pitcher.

GRAIG NETTLES
The player who has appeared in the most major league games without participating in a no-hit game. From 1967 through 1988, Nettles played in a total of 2,700 games for the Minnesota Twins, Cleveland Indians, New York Yankees, San Diego Padres, Atlanta Braves and Montreal Expos but his name never appeared in a no-hit box score.

NEW YORK METS
The major league team that currently has gone the longest time without holding another club hitless in a game. The Mets, who entered the National League in 1962, have allowed at least one hit in every game in their 30-year history.

Only one other existing big-league club—the San Diego Padres, born in 1969—has never held another team hitless.

NEW YORK YANKEES
While every major league club has been held hitless in a game at some time during its history, the Yankees currently have gone the longest time without being victimized. The last time the Yanks were no-hit was on September 20, 1958, when Baltimore's Hoyt Wilhelm accomplished the feat.

MILT PAPPAS
Having retired the first 26 San Diego batters in a September 2, 1972, game, this Chicago Cubs pitcher had a one-ball, two-strike count on Padres pinchhitter Larry Stahl as he attempted to nail down a perfect game. But Pappas proceeded to throw three straight balls in the two-out, ninth-inning situation. After walking Stahl, Pappas induced another pinch-hitter, Garry Jestadt, to pop out. While denied a perfect game, Pappas had completed an 8-0 no-hitter.

GEORGE (KEWPIE) PENNINGTON
Pitcher who made his only big-league appearance in the April 14, 1917, game in which Eddie Cicotte of the Chicago White Sox pitched a no-hitter. Working in relief for St. Louis, Pennington hurled a scoreless ninth inning as the Browns suffered an 11-0 trouncing.

Shortly after his stint in Cicotte's no-hit game, the 20-year-old Pennington was released to Newark of the International League.

PHILADELPHIA PHILLIES
National League club that went 57 consecutive seasons (1907 through 1963) without getting a no-hit performance from a member of its staff—a record span of no-hit futility in the major leagues. Actually, the Phils' no-hit failure lasted for more than 58 years in terms of the calendar date—from John Lush's no-hitter against Brooklyn on May 1, 1906, until Jim Bunning's perfect game against the New York Mets on June 21, 1964.

LEE RICHMOND
Retiring all 27 Cleveland batters he faced in a June 12, 1880, National League game, Worcester's Richmond hurled the big leagues' first perfect game and accounted for the majors' first no-hitter by a lefthanded pitcher. Worcester defeated Cleveland, 1-0.

PETE ROSE
The most recent of four players to appear in a National League-leading eight no-hitters. Rose, who played in all eight no-hit games while a member of the Cincinnati Reds, appeared in no-hitters pitched by the Reds' Jim Maloney (1965, two; 1969), George Culver (1968) and Tom Seaver (1978), and in hitless games hurled against Cincinnati by Ken Johnson of the Houston Colts (1964), Don Wilson of the Houston Astros (1969) and Rick Wise of the Philadelphia Phillies (1971).

Pee Wee Reese, Johnny Callison and Hank Aaron also participated in eight N.L. no-hit games.

AMOS RUSIE
The youngest pitcher in major league history to throw a no-hitter of nine or more innings. Rusie was just two months past his 20th birthday when, pitching for the New York Giants in a July 31, 1891, National League game, he beat Brooklyn, 6-0, without allowing a hit.

The youngest no-hit pitcher in modern big-league history was the Philadelphia Phillies' John Lush, who was about seven months past his 20th birthday when he hurled his gem on May 1, 1906. He also defeated Brooklyn, 6-0, in an N.L. contest.

Only four other major leaguers pitched no-hitters before reaching age 21: John Montgomery Ward, Providence, N.L., 1880 (perfect game); Richard Burns, Cincinnati, Union Association, 1884; Matt Kilroy, Baltimore, American Association, 1886, and Nick Maddox, Pittsburgh, N.L., 1907.

NOLAN RYAN

Holds the strikeout record for a nine-inning no-hit game in the majors. Pitching for the California Angels on July 15, 1973, Ryan held Detroit hitless and struck out 17 Tiger batters en route to a 6-0 triumph.

After nine innings of a June 14, 1965, Reds-Mets game, Cincinnati's Jim Maloney had 15 strikeouts while holding New York hitless in a 0-0 deadlock. Maloney struck out two more Mets in the 10th inning before New York's Johnny Lewis dashed the righthander's no-hit hopes in the top of the 11th by blasting a leadoff, game-winning home run. Maloney then recorded his 18th and final strikeout of the game (prior to yielding his second and last hit of the contest). Mets reliever Larry Bearnarth kept Cincinnati in check in the bottom of the 11th as New York hung on for a 1-0 victory.

NOLAN RYAN

The oldest pitcher to toss a major league ho-hitter of nine innings or more. Ryan was three months past his 44th birthday when he hurled a 3-0 no-hit game for the Texas Rangers against the Toronto Blue Jays on May 1, 1991. A year earlier, Ryan had hurled a 5-0 no-hitter against the Oakland Athletics.

The only other 40-year-old pitchers to record no-hitters in the majors were the Boston Red Sox's Cy Young, who was three months past his 41st birthday when he held the New York Highlanders hitless in 1908, and the Milwaukee Braves' Warren Spahn, who had just turned 40 when he stopped the San Francisco Giants without a hit in a 1961 game.

ST. LOUIS BROWNS

The only major league team to hold an opposing club hitless on consecutive days. On May 5, 1917, Browns pitcher Ernie Koob hurled a 1-0 no-hitter against the Chicago White Sox. The next day, in the second game of a doubleheader, St. Louis' Bob Groom stopped the Sox without a hit in a 3-0 decision.

The no-hitters were the second and third involving the Browns and White Sox in a little more than three weeks. On April 14, Chicago's Eddie Cicotte had pitched an 11-0 no-hit game against the Browns at St. Louis' Sportsman's Park, also site of the no-hitters thrown by Koob and Groom.

ST. LOUIS CARDINALS

Club that was victimized by Cincinnati Reds pitcher Hod Eller's no-hitter on May 11, 1919—and then didn't suffer no-hit ignominy again for 40 consecutive seasons, 1920 through 1959, a record span. In fact, in calendar-date terms, it was 41 years and four days after Eller's gem that the Cardinals next went hitless, with Don Cardwell of the Chicago Cubs tossing a no-hitter against the Cards in the second game of a May 15, 1960, doubleheader.

When New York's Johnny Lewis (circling the bases) hit a leadoff home run in the 11th inning of a June 14, 1965, game against Cincinnati, he ruined the day for Reds righthander Jim Maloney, who had not allowed a hit up to that point in a 0-0 nail-biter.

RAY SCHALK
He caught the most no-hitters in big-league history, four. Schalk was on the receiving end of no-hit games pitched by Jim Scott and Joe Benz (both in 1914), Eddie Cicotte (1917) and Charley Robertson (1922, a perfect game), all of the Chicago White Sox.

MIKE SCOTT
The only pitcher in major league history to toss a title-clinching no-hitter. Entering the 1986 season, a no-hit game had not been pitched in a contest that decided a divisional race, league championship or World Series crown. But on September 25, 1986, Scott, pitching for Houston on a day when the Astros' "magic number" for clinching the National League West title was at "1," held San Francisco hitless and struck out 13 Giants. The drama-packed 2-0 triumph at Houston's Astrodome eliminated the (Cincinnati Reds—the Astros' last mathematical threat—from West Division title contention.

Allie Reynolds of the New York Yankees is the only other big-league pitcher to hurl a no-hitter on the day his team clinched a championship. Reynolds' 8-0 no-hit game at Yankee Stadium on September 28, 1951, did not sew up a title, though; instead, the gem against the Boston Red Sox in the first game of a doubleheader assured the Yankees of at least a tie for first place in the American League pennant race. In the nightcap, the Yanks clinched the A.L. flag with an 11-3 triumph.

SEPTEMBER 20
The date on which the most no-hit games of nine or more innings have occurred in the major leagues. Six no-hitters have been thrown on September 20, the first achieved by Larry Corcoran of Chicago's National League club in 1882 and the last accomplished by Bob Moose of the Pittsburgh Pirates in a 1969 N.L. game. Other pitchers hurling no-hit games on September 20: James Callahan, Chicago, American League, 1902; Nick Maddox, Pittsburgh, N.L., 1907; Frank Smith, Chicago, A.L., 1908, and Hoyt Wilhelm, Baltimore, A.L., 1958.

Five no-hitters have been pitched on April 30, May 15 and September 18. Some historians may contend that six no-hit games have been thrown in the big leagues on May 15—the sixth coming in the Federal League in 1915. However, The Sporting News does not recognize the Federal League, which operated in 1914 and 1915, as a major league.

BOB SKINNER
Outfielder who played in two no-hit games, one as a teammate of a no-hit pitcher and the other as a member of the victimized team—and, startlingly, Skinner's club lost when its pitcher hurled a no-hitter and his team won when it was the victim of no-hit pitching. Skinner was Pittsburgh's left fielder on

Houston Astros righthander Mike Scott had two reasons to celebrate in 1986 after becoming the first pitcher in major league history to pitch a title-clinching no-hitter.

May 26, 1959, when Pirates lefthander Harvey Haddix hurled a 12-inning perfect game against the Milwaukee Braves. The Pirates ended up 1-0 losers, though, when the Braves scored a run on one hit in the 13th inning. On April 23, 1964, Skinner was Cincinnati's left fielder when the Reds were held hitless by Houston Colts pitcher Ken Johnson. Despite Johnson's performance, Cincinnati prevailed, 1-0, thanks to two ninth-inning Colt errors (one of which was made by Johnson).

WARREN SPAHN

The first big-league pitcher to throw no-hitters in consecutive years. Spahn was 39 years old and in his 16th season with the Braves when he spun his first

New York righthander Allie Reynolds was the center of attention in 1951 when he pitched no-hitters against Cleveland and Boston, the latter assuring the Yankees of at least a tie in the American League pennant race.

no-hit game in the majors on September 16, 1960, against the Philadelphia Phillies. Then, five days past his 40th birthday, Milwaukee's Spahn hurled hitless ball against the San Francisco Giants on April 28, 1961.

Sandy Koufax of the Los Angeles Dodgers matched Spahn's feat by pitching no-hitters in 1962 and 1963, surpassed the accomplishment by fashioning another no-hitter in 1964 and then ran his consecutive-year streak of no-hitters to four in 1965 with a perfect game. Steve Busby threw no-hitters in 1973 and 1974 for the Kansas City Royals, while Nolan Ryan, the only other major leaguer to hurl no-hit games in consecutive seasons, pitched two no-hitters for

California in 1973 and unfurled no-hit games for the Angels in 1974 and 1975. Ryan also pitched no-hitters for the Texas Rangers in 1990 and 1991.

BILL STONEMAN
Pitcher who fired the majors' first complete-game no-hitter hurled outside the United States, a 7-0 triumph for the Montreal Expos over the New York Mets in the first game of an October 2, 1972, doubleheader at Montreal's Jarry Park. The no-hit game was the second in the big leagues for Stoneman, who had held the Philadelphia Phillies hitless in a 7-0 victory on April 17, 1969, at Philadelphia's Connie Mack Stadium.

Besides Stoneman's gem in 1972, three other major league no-hitters have been thrown outside the U.S. On May 10, 1981, in the second game of a doubleheader at Montreal's Olympic Stadium, the Expos' Charlie Lea no-hit the San Francisco Giants in a 4-0 triumph. On June 29, 1990, Oakland's Dave Stewart tossed a no-hitter at Toronto's SkyDome, beating the Blue Jays by a 5-0 score. On May 23, 1991, Philadelphia's Tommy Greene hurled a no-hitter at Olympic Stadium, beating the Expos, 2-0.

JOHNNY VANDER MEER
The first man to pitch two no-hitters in the big leagues in one season—and he accomplished the feat with a flair, hurling consecutive no-hit games. Vander Meer, of the Cincinnati Reds, held the Boston Bees hitless in a June 11, 1938, game and then notched a no-hitter on June 15 against the Brooklyn Dodgers. He finished the '38 season with a 15-10 record.

Also throwing two no-hitters in the majors in one season were Allie Reynolds, Virgil Trucks, Jim Maloney and Nolan Ryan. Reynolds turned the trick in 1951 for the New York Yankees (his second no-hitter coming in his final start of the regular season and giving him a 17-8 season mark), Trucks achieved the feat in 1952 for the Detroit Tigers (his second no-hit game proving his final victory of the year in a 5-19 season), Maloney did it in 1965 for the Cincinnati Reds (en route to a 20-9 mark) and Ryan accomplished his no-hit "double" in 1973 for the California Angels (on the way to a 21-16 record).

Maloney's 1965 no-hitters came in a 10-inning complete-game effort (which he won) and in an 11-inning contest (which he lost) wherein he hurled hitless ball through 10 innings before allowing two hits in the 11th.

MIKE WARREN
The last rookie to hurl a no-hitter in the major leagues. Working for Oakland in a September 29, 1983, game, the 22-year-old Warren pitched no-hit ball against the Chicago White Sox as the A's posted a 3-0 victory.

WASHINGTON SENATORS
Club that went an American League-record 29 consecutive seasons, 1918 through 1946, without being victimized by a no-hitter. Boston's Ernie Shore, replacing Red Sox starting pitcher Babe Ruth when Ruth was ejected after issuing a game-opening base on balls, pitched perfect ball the rest of the way in a June 23, 1917, contest against Washington. It wasn't until September 3, 1947, that the Senators were again held hitless, this time by Bill McCahan of the Philadelphia A's. Shore's victory, coming in the first game of a double-header, was by a 4-0 score; McCahan won, 3-0.

VIC WERTZ
Detroit outfielder whose two-out home run in the bottom of the ninth inning on May 15, 1952, enabled Tiger teammate Virgil Trucks to post a 1-0 no-hit victory over the Washington Senators. Wertz's dramatic smash came against Bob Porterfield.
Seven other players have slugged home runs in 1-0 no-hit games:

Date	No-Hit Pitcher, Club	Home Run Hitter	Inn.
May 15, 1944	Clyde Shoun, Cin.	Chuck Aleno	5
April 30, 1946	Bob Feller, Cleve.	Frankie Hayes	9
July 12, 1951	Allie Reynolds, N.Y., A.L.	Gene Woodling	7
Sept. 20, 1958	Hoyt Wilhelm, Balt.	Gus Triandos	7
June 14, 1965	Jim Maloney,Cin.	*Johnny Lewis	11
Aug. 19, 1965	Jim Maloney, Cin.	Leo Cardenas	10
Sept. 17, 1968	Gaylord Perry, S.F.	Ron Hunt	1

*Of the eight players whose homers have provided the only runs in 1-0 no-hit games, only Lewis connected for the team victimized by the no-hitter. Playing for the New York Mets, Lewis socked an 11th-inning homer off Cincinnati's Maloney after the Reds' pitcher had hurled hitless ball through 10 innings (thereby gaining credit for a no-hitter).

The late-inning homers by the Indians' Hayes, the Mets' Lewis and the Reds' Cardenas all came in the top half of the innings indicated.

Cincinnati's Aleno hit only one other homer in his major league career.

EARL WILSON
The last American League pitcher to hurl a no-hitter and hit a home run in the same game. Wilson, of the Boston Red Sox, stopped the Los Angeles Angels without a hit on June 26, 1962, and socked a bases-empty home run off Bo Belinsky in a 2-0 decision.

RICK WISE
The last major league pitcher to slug a home run during his no-hit perfor-

mance—and the only pitcher to hit two homers while recording a no-hitter. The Philadelphia Phillies' Wise held the Cincinnati Reds hitless in a 4-0 National League triumph on June 23, 1971, and drilled a two-run homer off Ross Grimsley and a bases-empty shot off Clay Carroll.

MIKE WITT
The only pitcher in major league history to hurl a perfect game of nine or more innings in his club's last game of the season. Witt, of the California Angels, did not allow a Texas Rangers batter to reach base on the final day of the 1984 regular season.

Harry Vickers of the Philadelphia A's pitched perfect ball against the Washington Senators in a five-inning game played on the last day of the 1907 season. However, many historians do not recognize no-hitters of fewer than nine innings.
A complete list of major league no-hit performances—including those of fewer than nine innings—that have occurred on the last day of a team's season:
*Oct. 4, 1891, Ted Breitenstein, St. Louis, vs. Louisville, A.A., 8-0
Oct. 15, 1892, Charles (Bumpus) Jones, Cincinnati, vs. Pittsburgh, N.L., 7-1
**Oct. 15, 1892, Jack Stivetts, Boston, vs. Washington, N.L., 6-0
**Oct. 5, 1907, H. Vickers, Phil., vs. Washington, A.L., 4-0 (perfect game)
Sept. 28, 1975, Vida Blue (5 inn.), Glenn Abbott (1 inn.), Paul Lindblad (1 inn.), Rollie Fingers (2 inn.), Oakland, vs. Calif., A.L., 5-0
Sept. 30, 1984, Mike Witt, California, vs. Texas, A.L., 1-0 (perfect game)
*First game of a doubleheader
**Five-inning second game of a doubleheader

ZERO
The number of times triple plays have been made in no-hit-game history.

California righthander Mike Witt saved his best for last in 1984, becoming the first pitcher in big-league history to throw a perfect game of nine or more innings on the final day of the regular season.

FIFTH INNING
Trivial facts
about storied moments
in postseason history

WILLIE AIKENS
The only player to hit two home runs in one game twice in the same World Series. Playing for the Kansas City Royals against the Philadelphia Phillies in the 1980 Series, first baseman Aikens rifled two homers off Bob Walk in Game 1 (the Royals lost, 7-6) and connected off Larry Christenson and Dickie Noles in Game 4 (Kansas City won, 5-3).

MIKE ANDREWS
Oakland player whose fielding lapses prompted his "firing" by A's Owner Charlie Finley during the 1973 World Series. Andrews, signed by the A's in August of '73 after his release by the Chicago White Sox, made two costly errors against the New York Mets in the 12th inning of Game 2 of the '73 fall classic, and Finley announced the next day that he was deactivating him.

Supporting Cast:
• **Willie Mays.** His 12th-inning single in Game 2 at Oakland broke a 6-6 tie and ignited a four-run Mets outburst. The hit was the last for Mays in his major league career.
• **John Milner.** With the bases loaded later in the Mets' 12th, Milner hit a ground ball to Andrews at second base. Andrews, who had entered the game in the eighth inning as a pinch-hitter, let the ball get through his legs and two runs scored. Mets 9, A's 6.
• **Jerry Grote.** Batting after Milner, he also grounded to Andrews. The A's infielder made a poor throw to first baseman Gene Tenace, pulling him off the bag, and another run scored. While the A's mounted a rally in the bottom of the 12th—they scored once and had the bases loaded with only one out—the Mets hung on for a 10-7 triumph.

Finley tried to place Andrews on the disabled list, citing a shoulder injury, and even got the veteran player to sign a statement saying he was hurting physically. The day after Finley instructed Andrews to pack his bags, Finley himself received a directive. Commissioner Bowie Kuhn ordered Finley to reinstate the 30-year-old Andrews, much to the delight of Andrews' teammates, who had reacted angrily to Finley's move. And, later, the commissioner fined the A's boss.

Oakland second baseman Mike Andrews made two costly 12th-inning errors in Game 2 of the 1973 World Series that resulted in embarrassment on the field and face-covering dejection in the A's dugout.

411

Andrews, who had batted .308 and fielded flawlessly in part-time duty for the Boston Red Sox in the 1967 World Series, was back in uniform for Game 4 of the '73 Series. Called upon as a pinch-hitter in that contest, he received a rousing greeting from New York fans before grounding out. The at-bat proved his last in the big leagues.

A's Manager Dick Williams, who was in the process of guiding the A's to their second straight Series championship, told his players before Game 3 that he would not be back in 1974. While Williams reportedly had tired of Finley's interference long before the Andrews affair and may have intended to resign anyway, the "firing" of Andrews seemingly ensured the manager's departure.

JIMMY ARCHER
The first man to play for both American League and National League teams in World Series competition. Archer caught one game for the Detroit Tigers in the 1907 Series against the Chicago Cubs; in 1910, he played three games for the Cubs (one at first base, two behind the plate) against the Philadelphia A's in the fall classic.

HANK BAUER, LOU PINIELLA, GEORGE STALLINGS
The only World Series managers with unbeaten records in the fall classic. Each managed in only one Series, with Stallings leading the Boston Braves to a four-game sweep of the Philadelphia Athletics in 1914, Bauer guiding the Baltimore Orioles to a four-games-to-none rout of the Los Angeles Dodgers in 1966 and Piniella directing the Cincinnati Reds past the Oakland Athletics in four games in 1990.

While Stallings' Braves were the first club to win a World Series in four games, the 1907 Chicago Cubs were the first team to go unbeaten in a Series. The '07 Cubs won four games and tied one against the Detroit Tigers.

JOHNNY BENCH
Victim of an Oakland A's ruse in the 1972 World Series. With Cincinnati ahead, 1-0, in the eighth inning of Game 3 and Reds runners on third and second base with one out, A's reliever Rollie Fingers had a 3-2 count on Reds cleanup hitter Bench. At this juncture, Oakland Manager Dick Williams went to the mound. With first base open, the forthcoming strategy was obvious—or so it seemed. Bench, who had led the National League in 1972 with 40 home runs and 125 runs batted in (and won N.L. Most Valuable Player honors), would not be given a hittable pitch in this situation. Instead, the A's would pitch to first baseman Tony Perez. After Williams gestured toward first base and headed toward the dugout, A's catcher Gene Tenace dutifully extended his mitt for an intentional fourth ball. One problem, though: As Fingers let go of what virtually everyone assumed was "ball four," Tenace stepped back behind the plate and the ball dipped into the strike zone. Bench was trans-

fixed—and an embarrassed strikeout victim.

Following the trickster antics against Bench that resulted in the called third strike, the A's did issue an intentional walk—to Perez. Denis Menke then fouled out, ending the inning, but the Reds held on for a 1-0 triumph at Oakland.

BOSTON, PHILADELPHIA
Cities represented in the 1914 and 1915 World Series—but the matchups for the two fall classics were entirely different. In 1914, the National League's Boston Braves downed the American League's Philadelphia A's in the Series. A year later, the Braves dropped to second place in the N.L. and the A's plummeted to last place in the A.L.—but the Philadelphia Phillies succeeded the Braves as N.L. champions and the Boston Red Sox supplanted the A's as A.L. titlists. In the continuation of the Boston-Philadelphia rivalry, the Red Sox prevailed over the Phils in the 1915 Series.

Oddly, in neither 1914 nor 1915 did the Boston club play its World Series home games in its own ball park. In the '14 Series, the Braves played their home contests at the Red Sox's Fenway Park, citing it as a more attractive facility than their South End Grounds. In '15, the Red Sox opted to play their Series home games at the Braves' new park (Braves Field) because its seating capacity was superior to Fenway's.

LOU BOUDREAU
The last player-manager to appear in—and win—a World Series. Boudreau played the entire 1948 Series at shortstop for Cleveland and guided the Indians to a four games-to-two triumph over the Boston Braves.

Managers who won World Series in which they made at least one playing appearance:

Year—Player, Manager, Club	Pos.	G	AB-H	B.A.
1903—Jimmy Collins, Boston, A.L.	3B	8	36-9	.250
1906—Fielder Jones, Chicago, A.L.	CF	6	21-2	.095
1907—Frank Chance, Chicago, N.L.	1B	4	14-3	.214
1908—Frank Chance, Chicago, N.L.	1B	5	19-8	.421
1909—Fred Clarke, Pittsburgh, N.L.	LF	7	19-4	.211
1912—Jake Stahl, Boston, A.L.	1B	8	32-9	.281
1915—Bill Carrigan, Boston, A.L.	C	1	2-0	.000
1916—Bill Carrigan, Boston, A.L.	C	1	3-2	.667
1920—Tris Speaker, Cleveland, A.L.	CF	7	25-8	.320
1924—Bucky Harris, Washington, A.L.	2B	7	33-11	.333
1926—Rogers Hornsby, St. Louis, N.L.	2B	7	28-7	.250
1933—Bill Terry, New York, N.L.	1B	5	22-6	.273

| 1934—Frank Frisch, St. Louis, N.L. | 2B | 7 | 31-6 | .194 |
| 1948—Lou Boudreau, Cleveland, A.L. | SS | 6 | 22-6 | .273 |

GEORGE BRETT
The only player in big-league history to slug three home runs in a postseason game that his club lost. Brett hit bases-empty homers for the Kansas City Royals against the Yankees' Jim (Catfish) Hunter in the first, third and fifth innings of Game 3 of the 1978 American League Championship Series. New York overcame Brett's performance, though, and notched a 6-5 victory.

Only three other major leaguers have hit three homers in a postseason game—the Yankees' Babe Ruth (who accomplished the feat in Game 4 of the 1926 World Series and again in Game 4 of the 1928 classic), the Yanks' Reggie Jackson (Game 6 of the 1977 World Series) and the Pittsburgh Pirates' Bob Robertson (Game 2 of the 1971 National League Championship Series).

MARK BROUHARD
Outfielder who played in only one postseason game in his major league career—an American League Championship Series game in which he went 3 for 4, drove in three runs and scored four times (the latter feat tying the Championship Series record). Playing left field for Milwaukee against California in Game 4 of the 1982 A.L. title series, Brouhard singled, doubled and homered as the Brewers won, 9-5, and tied the best-of-five playoff at two games apiece.

Brouhard, who had not seen action for the Brewers in almost a month, was penciled into the lineup only because of an injury to outfielder Ben Oglivie.

Milwaukee, which had lost the first two games of the series, beat the Angels, 4-3, in Game 5 and reigned as the A.L. champion.

BUSCH STADIUM TARPAULIN
An unlikely central figure in the 1985 National League Championship Series—and nearly a tragic interloper. As the St. Louis Cardinals worked out in their home ball park before Game 4 of the '85 N.L. pennant playoff, a light rain began to fall. The batting cage was removed and the Cardinals' Vince Coleman, coming off a season in which he established a big-league rookie record with 110 stolen bases, started walking toward the dugout when he paused and turned to flip his glove—just as the tarpaulin-spreading device was activated. A mechanized, 150-foot-long aluminum cylinder began rolling across the infield to position the tarpaulin, and the tube ran across Coleman's left foot and up his leg. The 24-year-old left fielder fell to the ground, crying out in pain. Once Coleman was extricated and examined, observers' worst fears were not realized: As potentially career-threatening as the accident appeared, Coleman had suffered no lasting injuries, only contusions and a bone chip on the knee.

But the suddenly hobbled Coleman, the catalyst in St. Louis' speed-oriented offense, was through for postseason play in '85.

Tito Landrum took over for Coleman in left field that night and, by game's end, was himself in the spotlight. Landrum went 4 for 5 and drove in three runs in Game 4 as the Cardinals pummeled the Dodgers, 12-2, and deadlocked the Championship Series. The Cards advanced to the '85 World Series, and Landrum continued to fill in admirably—he batted .360 in seven games against the Kansas City Royals.

DONIE BUSH, GABBY HARTNETT, EDDIE SAWYER
The only men to have lost all World Series games in which they managed. Each manager was at the helm in only one Series—and was victimized by a sweep. Bush's Pittsburgh Pirates fell to the New York Yankees in four games in 1927, Hartnett's Chicago Cubs dropped four straight to the Yankees in 1938 and Sawyer's Philadelphia Phillies were vanquished by the Yanks in four consecutive games in 1950.

CINCINNATI REDS
The last team whose World Series participants were all first-time performers in the fall classic. No Reds player who appeared in the 1961 World Series had seen Series action (for any club) previously, and the experience-shy Cincinnati team lost to the New York Yankees, four games to one, in the '61 Series.

Other teams whose World Series players were all first-time participants in the classic: Boston Red Sox and Pittsburgh Pirates, 1903 (first-time status was automatic since the Series was introduced that year); Philadelphia A's and New York Giants, 1905 (the year that the second Series was played); Chicago Cubs, 1906; Detroit Tigers, 1907; Red Sox, 1912, and St. Louis Browns, 1944.

CINCINNATI REDS
Club that compiled the best cumulative won-lost record in the major leagues in 1981—but didn't qualify for postseason play. A 50-day players strike interrupted the '81 season and resulted in the adoption of a split-season format, with first-half divisional winners (those teams leading their divisions at the time of the June 12 walkout) to face the champions of the second-half race (which began with the post-strike resumption of play on August 10) in a best-of-five divisional title series. The extra tier of playoffs proved disastrous for the Reds, who finished the first half with a 35-21 record, one-half game behind Los Angeles, and ended the second half with a 31-21 record, 1 1/2 games behind Houston. While the Dodgers (63-47 overall) and Astros (61-49) wound up battling for the West Division crown and a berth in the National League Championship Series, the Reds sat at home—despite compiling the majors' top overall mark in '81, 66-42.

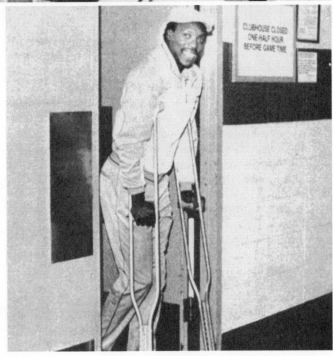

When St. Louis rookie sensation Vince Coleman was attacked by a Busch Stadium tarpaulin before Game 4 of the 1985 N.L. Championship Series, he had to be removed from the field on a stretcher and limped through the remainder of the postseason on crutches.

CLARK'S DRAMATIC SHOT

With his team ahead in the best-of-seven 1985 National League Championship Series, three games to two, but trailing Los Angeles by a 5-4 score in the ninth inning of Game 6, St. Louis' Jack Clark approached the plate. There were two out and Cardinals perched on second and third base. While first base was open, Dodgers Manager Tom Lasorda elected to take his chances with cleanup hitter Clark, who had hit 22 home runs and driven in 87 runs during the regular season. Clark jumped on the first pitch, belting the ball into the left-field bleachers. The three-run, pennant-deciding blow in the October 16 game sent shock waves through the Dodger Stadium crowd. Cardinals 7, Dodgers 5.

Supporting Cast:

•**Ken Dayley.** Relief pitcher who retired the Dodgers in order in the ninth inning, nailing down the N.L. pennant for St. Louis.

•**Mike Marshall.** Los Angeles outfielder whose eighth-inning homer off Cardinals reliever Todd Worrell had broken a 4-4 tie. Worrell turned out to be the winning pitcher.

•**Willie McGee.** St. Louis outfielder who, with the Dodgers ahead, 4-1, in the seventh inning, rifled a two-run single off Dodgers starter Orel Hershiser (and subsequently scored the tying run). In the ninth inning, he kept St. Louis' hopes alive with a one-out single and a steal of second base. Ozzie Smith's walk and Tommy Herr's groundout put runners on second and third with two men out and Clark coming up.

•**Tom Niedenfuer.** While he had struck out Clark when working out of a seventh-inning jam, Niedenfuer yielded Clark's momentous homer in the ninth. Charged with the defeat, Niedenfuer also was the Dodgers' loser in the previous game of the N.L. playoffs.

•**Ozzie Smith.** His seventh-inning triple off Niedenfuer, who had just come in to pitch, scored McGee and tied the game, 4-4. Two days earlier, the Cardinal shortstop's ninth-inning homer off Niedenfuer had given St. Louis a 3-2 victory in Game 5.

•**Andy Van Slyke.** When Lasorda decided to have righthanded reliever Niedenfuer pitch to righthanded batter Clark in the ninth inning, it was the lefthanded-hitting Van Slyke (13 homers, 55 RBIs in the regular season) who was on deck.

JACK COOMBS

The first man to pitch for both American League and National League teams in World Series play. Coombs hurled for the A.L.'s Philadelphia A's in the 1910 and 1911 Series and he pitched for the N.L.'s Brooklyn Dodgers in the 1916 classic.

STEVE CRAWFORD

Boston Red Sox relief pitcher who failed to win a game during the 1986 American League season, finishing with a 0-2 record while making 40

Jack Clark's dramatic ninth-inning home run in Game 6 of the 1985 National League Championship Series brought the Cardinals to their feet and sent the Los Angeles Dodgers packing for a long winter.

appearances, but was credited with the victory in Game 5 of the '86 A.L. Championship Series against the California Angels and then was the winning pitcher in Game 2 of the '86 World Series against the New York Mets.

MIKE CUELLAR, TOM SEAVER

Pitchers who started against each other in a World Series game in a year in which both won the Cy Young Award. Baltimore's Cuellar, who shared the 1969 American League pitching honor with Denny McLain of the Detroit Tigers, and '69 N.L. honoree Seaver of the New York Mets were the starting pitchers in Games 1 and 4 of the 1969 Series. Cuellar tossed a six-hitter in the opener and defeated Seaver and the Mets, 4-1; Seaver copped Game 4, a 2-1, 10-inning decision in which he allowed six hits and beat Dick Hall (one of three Orioles who worked in relief of Cuellar).

The only other World Series in which the season's Cy Young honorees started against each other was the 1968 classic, in which N.L. winner Bob Gibson of the St. Louis Cardinals and Detroit's McLain (an outright winner this time in the A.L.) dueled in Games 1 and 4. Gibson downed McLain and the Tigers in both contests, striking out a Series-record 17 batters in a 4-0 victory in Game 1 and coasting to a 10-1 triumph in Game 4.

Jim (Catfish) Hunter of the Oakland A's and Mike Marshall of the Los Angeles Dodgers are the only other men to pitch in the same World Series game in a year in which each was a Cy Young recipient. In Game 1 of the 1974 Series, both made ninth-inning relief appearances; in Game 3 of that classic, A.L. Cy Young winner Hunter started and worked 7 1/3 innings (and got credit for a 3-2 victory), while N.L. award winner Marshall pitched two innings of relief.

MIKE CUELLAR, ROSS GRIMSLEY
Baltimore pitchers who combined on a one-hitter in Game 4 of the 1974 American League Championship Series—a contest that the Orioles lost, 2-1, to the Oakland A's. Cuellar didn't allow a hit in 4 2/3 innings, but permitted nine bases on balls (including four straight, one of which was an intentional walk, in the fifth inning that boosted the A's into a 1-0 lead). Reggie Jackson collected Oakland's only hit, a seventh-inning double that scored Sal Bando and extended the A's edge to 2-0 in a game that nailed down the third consecutive A.L. pennant for Oakland, a three games-to-one victor in the playoff.

The only other time a team has been held to fewer than two hits in a Championship Series game occurred in the sixth game of the 1990 N.L. playoffs when Cincinnati's Danny Jackson (six innings), Norm Charlton (one inning) and Randy Myers (two innings) held Pittsburgh to one hit. First baseman Carmelo Martinez collected the Pirates' lone hit—a fifth-inning double—in the October 12, 1990, game, in which Cincinnati clinched the pennant with a 2-1 victory.

BILL DINNEEN
The first of six major leaguers to have played and umpired in World Series competition. Dinneen notched three pitching victories for the Boston Red Sox in the 1903 Series, then umpired in seven fall classics from 1911 through 1932.

Also playing and umpiring in World Series were George Moriarty, George Pipgras, Ed Rommel, Frank Secory and Lon Warneke.

Ken Burkhart and Bill Kunkel were World Series eligibles (Burkhart for the St. Louis Cardinals in 1946, Kunkel for the New York Yankees in 1963) who didn't see playing action in the classic, but later umpired in the Series.

TIM FLANNERY
San Diego pinch-hitter who hit the crucial ground ball that first baseman Leon Durham of the Chicago Cubs muffed in the seventh inning of the fifth and decisive game of the 1984 National League Championship Series. Trying to clinch their first pennant since 1945, the Cubs—13-0 and 4-2 winners in the first two games of the best-of-five playoff but 7-1 and 7-5 losers in Games 3 and 4—held a 3-0 lead midway through Game 5 in San Diego. Pitcher Rick Sutcliffe, 16-1 in the regular season for Chicago after his mid-June acquisition from the Cleveland Indians, then yielded sixth-inning sacrifice flies to Graig

Nettles and Terry Kennedy (following Alan Wiggins' bunt single, Tony Gwynn's single and a walk to Steve Garvey) . . . and that elusive N.L. flag was slipping away from the Cubs.

Supporting Cast:
•**Jody Davis.** After Durham had rapped a two-run home run in the first inning off the Padres' Eric Show, catcher Davis staked the Cubs to a 3-0 lead with a second-inning homer off Show. Sutcliffe maintained that three-run edge through five innings, allowing only two infield hits.
•**Carmelo Martinez.** With the Cubs ahead, 3-2, San Diego's left fielder drew a leadoff walk against Sutcliffe in the seventh inning.
•**Garry Templeton.** Padres shortstop who sacrificed Martinez to second, bringing Flannery to the plate to bat for reliever Craig Lefferts. Flannery, a utility infielder, grounded to Durham, and the ball squirted through his legs. Martinez dashed home on the miscue, tying the score at 3-3.
•**Ryne Sandberg.** After Wiggins followed Durham's error with a check swing single, Cubs second baseman Sandberg saw Gwynn's smash—a potential double-play ball—take a bad hop over his shoulder and rocket into right-center for a two-run double. Padres 5, Cubs 3. Gwynn, who took third on a throw to the plate, then scored on a single by Garvey, whose five-RBI performance (capped by a game-winning, two-run homer in the ninth inning) had jolted the Cubs in Game 4.

The Padres went on to win by the 6-3 score, copping the club's first N.L. pennant in the franchise's 16th year of operation.

BUD HARRELSON
The only man to be in uniform for the New York Mets in all 19 of the National League club's World Series games. Harrelson played shortstop for the N.L. champions in all five games of the 1969 fall classic against the Baltimore Orioles and in all seven games of the 1973 Series against the Oakland A's, and he also served as third-base coach for the Mets in the club's seven-game battle against the Boston Red Sox in 1986.

BUCKY HARRIS
He guided Washington to the 1924 World Series title in his first season as the Senators' manager (at age 27, he also was the club's second baseman) and directed the New York Yankees to the 1947 Series crown in his first year as the Yanks' pilot—a first-season championship "double" that is unequaled in Series managerial history. Harris' 1924 Senators and 1947 Yankees were four games-to-three Series victors over the New York Giants and Brooklyn Dodgers, respectively.

The only other manager to win pennants in his first year at the helm of two teams is Pat Moran, who led the Philadelphia Phillies to the National League title in 1915 and managed the Cincinnati Reds to the N.L. pennant in 1919. Moran's 1915 Phils lost the World Series in five games to the Boston Red Sox, while his 1919 Reds won the Series in eight games against the Chicago White Sox.

BILLY HATCHER
Houston center fielder who supplied perhaps the most dramatic moment in the drama-filled sixth game of the 1986 National League Championship Series, hitting a one-out home run in the bottom of the 14th inning that enabled the Astros—down three games to two in the playoff—to tie the New York Mets, 4-4. As it turned out, though, Hatcher's homer—a shot to left field that was barely fair—merely gave the Astros a stay of execution. Two innings later, the Mets wrapped up the best-of-seven title series.

Supporting Cast:
• **Bob Knepper.** Houston pitcher who took a two-hit shutout—and a 3-0 lead—into the ninth inning of Game 6. But the Mets broke through against Knepper in the ninth as pinch-hitter Lenny Dykstra tripled, Mookie Wilson singled and, following a groundout, Keith Hernandez doubled. With the score now 3-2, Dave Smith relieved Knepper and allowed two walks and Ray Knight's game-tying sacrifice fly.
• **Wally Backman.** After the clubs battled through the 13th inning in a 3-3 deadlock, the Mets seized the lead in the 14th when Backman stroked a run-scoring single following Gary Carter's single, Darryl Strawberry's walk and a forceout.
• **Jesse Orosco.** Reliever who, with New York ahead, 4-3, came on to pitch in the bottom of the 14th in hopes of wrapping up the N.L. pennant for the Mets. But, after Bill Doran, struck out, Hatcher belted his clutch home run. (Hatcher had hit only six homers during the 1986 season.)
• **Aurelio Lopez.** Having allowed New York's run in the 14th, the Astros' reliever was victimized again in the 16th as the Mets scored three times (Lopez was charged with two of the runs, Jeff Calhoun with one). Strawberry opened the inning with a double (Hatcher got a slow start on the fly ball) and Knight singled him home. Calhoun later wild-pitched a run home, while Dykstra contributed an RBI single in the inning as the Mets built a 74 advantage.
• **Kevin Bass.** After Hatcher and Glenn Davis delivered RBI singles in the Astros' half of the 16th, Bass strode to the plate with two on and two out and struck out against Orosco. The final score, in the majors' longest postseason game in history (in terms of time, 4 hours and 42 minutes, as well as innings): Mets 7, Astros 6. New York had won its first N.L. pennant in 13 years.

DAVE HENDERSON
Boston outfielder who, three innings after deflecting a California Angels smash over the wall for a crucial home run and with the Red Sox one strike away from postseason elimination, smashed a two-run homer in the top of the

Dave Henderson's valiant leap in Game 5 of the American League Championship Series against the California Angels turned Bobby Grich's long fly ball into a home run and almost spelled doom for the Boston Red Sox.

ninth that gave the Sox a 6-5 lead in Game 5 of the 1986 American League Championship Series. Boston squandered the edge in the bottom of the ninth, but came back to win, 7-6, in 11 innings at Anaheim Stadium on a sacrifice fly by . . . Henderson.

Supporting Cast:
•**Bob Boone.** Angels catcher who drilled a bases-empty homer in the third

Henderson turned his misery into ecstasy with a dramatic two-run, ninth-inning home run that kept the Red Sox alive and vaulted them toward the A.L. pennant.

inning, cutting Boston's lead to 2-1.

•**Rich Gedman.** Boston catcher who, with his team trailing three games to one in the best-of-seven series, smacked a two-run homer in the second inning.

•**Bobby Grich.** California first baseman who hit the sixth-inning drive that glanced off Henderson's glove and dropped over the center-field fence. Doug DeCinces' double had preceded the homer, a blast that thrust the Angels into a 3-2 lead.

•**Mike Witt.** Angels starting pitcher who took a 5-2 lead into the ninth—California had scored seventh-inning runs on Rob Wilfong's pinch double and Brian Downing's sacrifice fly—before faltering. Bill Buckner led off Boston's ninth with a single and, after Dave Stapleton ran for Buckner and Jim Rice struck out, Don Baylor homered. His lead now cut to 5-4, Witt got Dwight Evans to pop out, but then gave way to reliever Gary Lucas as Gedman (3 for 3 at the plate at that point) came up to bat.

•**Donnie Moore.** After Lucas hit Gedman with a pitch, Moore came on in relief and, after battling Henderson to a two-ball, two-strike count, yielded the go-ahead homer to Henderson, who had entered the game in the fifth inning as a replacement for injured Red Sox center fielder Tony Armas.

•**Ruppert Jones.** Pinch-running in the Angels' ninth for Boone (who led off the inning with a single), Jones advanced to second on Gary Pettis' sacrifice and scored on Wilfong's single off Joe Sambito, his slide around Gedman making the score 6-6.

•**Calvin Schiraldi.** The loser in relief the night before in a game that the Red Sox had led, 3-0, entering the bottom of the ninth but wound up losing, 4-3, in 11 innings, he was Boston's fifth and last pitcher of the day. Entering Game 5 after the Red Sox had seized a 7-6 lead in the top of the 11th on Henderson's sacrifice fly (which followed Moore's hitting of Baylor with a pitch, Evans' single and Gedman's bunt single), he retired the Angels in order and nailed down the victory for fellow reliever Steve Crawford. Boston's Crawford had wriggled out of a one-out, bases-loaded jam in the ninth when the score was tied.

Boston's victory in the dramatic game—which also featured Red Sox left fielder Rice's leaping catch against the wall of a Pettis drive in the 10th inning and Angels left fielder Downing's wall-banging catch of Ed Romero's smash in the 11th (after Boston had regained the lead)—sent the teams back to Boston for Game 6 and, if necessary, Game 7. The Red Sox, given new life, coasted to a 10-4 triumph and an A.L. pennant-winning 8-1 decision at Fenway Park.

TOMMY HERR
St. Louis Cardinals second baseman who drove in two runs with one sacrifice fly in the 1982 World Series. Batting against Milwaukee pitcher Moose Haas with Willie McGee on third base and Ozzie Smith on second in the second inning of Game 4, Herr belted a one-out drive to center field. The Brewers' Gorman Thomas tracked down the long smash and, after Thomas made the catch, McGee tagged up and headed for the plate. Herr's "conventional" sacrifice fly turned into a one-for-the-book occurrence, though, when Thomas subsequently slipped on the warning track. Smith not only sped on to third base, but raced home behind McGee. Despite Herr's two-RBI sacrifice fly, which sent the Cardinals ahead, 3-0, Milwaukee rebounded for a 7-5 triumph.

TOMMY JOHN
The last of three pitchers to start and win a World Series game for both a National League club and an American League team. John started and won a game for the N.L.'s Los Angeles Dodgers against the New York Yankees in the 1978 Series and was a starter and winner for the A.L.'s Yankees against the Dodgers in the 1981 fall classic.

Jack Coombs posted four Series victories as a starting pitcher for the A.L.'s Philadelphia A's (winning three times in 1910 and once in 1911) and won one game as a starter for the N.L.'s Brooklyn Dodgers in 1916. And Hank Borowy was a Series starter and winner for the N.L.'s Chicago Cubs in 1945 two years after a victorious starting assignment for the Yankees in the fall classic. (Borowy also won in relief for the Cubs in the '45 Series.)

KANSAS CITY ROYALS, NEW YORK METS

The only teams to lose the first two games of a World Series in their home ball park and then rebound to win the Series crown—and they accomplished the feat in successive years. Kansas City lost the first two games of the 1985 Series at Royals Stadium, falling to St. Louis by 3-1 and 4-2 scores, but then won two of three games at the Cardinals' Busch Stadium before copping the Series title with two victories in Kansas City. The Mets dropped the opening two games of the 1986 Series at Shea Stadium, losing 1-0 and 9-3 decisions to Boston, but then won two of three games at the Red Sox's Fenway Park before seizing the Series championship with two victories in New York.

JIM KONSTANTY

The relief ace (74 appearances, all out of the bullpen) of the 1950 National League champion Philadelphia Phillies—but, astonishingly, the Phils' starting pitcher in Game 1 of the 1950 World Series. Konstanty, who won N.L. Most Valuable Player honors in '50 with a 16-7 record and 2.66 earned-run average, was Phils Manager Eddie Sawyer's first-game pitching choice after staff leader Robin Roberts (20 victories) was forced to pitch three times in the last five days of the season. The late-season loss of pitcher Curt Simmons (17 triumphs) to the Army and nagging injuries to Bob Miller and Bubba Church also took their toll on the Phils' staff and contributed to Sawyer's surprise selection of Konstanty to open the Series. The 33-year-old Konstanty was up to the challenge, though, allowing only one run and four hits against the New York Yankees in eight innings. However, the Yanks won as Vic Raschi tossed a two-hit, 1-0 shutout.

Konstanty, who had pitched exclusively in relief (133 appearances overall) for the Phillies since joining the club in 1948 (he had made a total of 13 starts for the Cincinnati Reds and Boston Braves earlier in his career), returned to bullpen duty in Games 3 and 4 of the 1950 Series, which the Yankees won in a sweep.

TITO LANDRUM

Acquired by the Baltimore Orioles from the St. Louis Cardinals' organization on August 31, 1983, the cutoff date for postseason eligibility, Landrum entered the '83 American League Championship Series with only three home runs in 227 regular-season major league games—but he broke a 0-0 tie against the Chicago White Sox in Game 4 of the playoffs by lining a one-out, 10th-inning home run off Britt Burns. The Orioles scored two more runs after the blast by Landrum (who spent most of the season in the minor leagues), and the 3-0 triumph at Comiskey Park clinched the best-of-five playoff for Baltimore, three games to one.

JON MATLACK

The last of four pitchers to start the opening game of a World Series despite compiling a losing record in the regular season. Matlack started Game 1 of the 1973 Series for the New York Mets after compiling a season mark of 14-16. Despite yielding only two runs and three hits in six innings, he was a 2-1 loser to the Oakland A's.

Alvin Crowder, 9-11 overall in 1934 (4-10 for Washington, 5-1 for Detroit), started and lost for the Tigers, 8-3, in Game 1 of the 1934 World Series against the St. Louis Cardinals. After turning in a 9-10 season record in 1944, Denny Galehouse of the St. Louis Browns pitched a complete-game 2-1 victory over the St. Louis Cardinals in the first game of the '44 Series. And Don Drysdale put together a 13-16 season for the Los Angeles Dodgers in 1966 before starting—and suffering a 5-2 loss—in the opening game of the '66 Series against the Baltimore Orioles.

STUFFY McINNIS
The first man to play for World Series championship teams from both major leagues. First baseman McInnis saw action for Series-winning clubs from the American League in 1911 (Philadelphia A's), 1913 (A's) and 1918 (Boston Red Sox) and from the National League in 1925 (Pittsburgh Pirates).

McInnis also played on one World Series loser, the 1914 A's.

BOB MOOSE
With defending World Series champion Pittsburgh and Cincinnati tied, 3-3, with two out in the bottom of the ninth inning of the fifth and deciding game of the 1972 National League Championship Series, Pirates reliever Moose fired a wild pitch that gave the Reds the N.L. pennant.

Supporting Cast:
•**Johnny Bench.** With his team trailing, 3-2, entering the bottom of the ninth, the majors' leader in home runs (40 in '72) sent the Cincinnati crowd into a frenzy with a game-tying shot over the right-field fence off Pittsburgh's Dave Giusti, who had just entered the game.
•**George Foster.** A future two-time N.L. home run champion, this 23-year-old reserve outfielder went in to run for Tony Perez after Perez followed Bench's homer with a single.
•**Denis Menke.** His single advanced Foster to second base.
•**Cesar Geronimo, Darrel Chaney.** The Reds' seventh- and eighth-place hitters, they were up next. When the count reached 2-0 on Geronimo, Moose replace Giusti. Geronimo and Chaney were retired on a fly ball and a popup, respectively, but Geronimo's drive advanced Foster to third base.
•**Hal McRae.** Sent up as a pinch-hitter for Reds relief pitcher Clay Carroll, he was at the plate in the ninth when Moose let fly with a wild pitch that skipped past catcher Manny Sanguillen and scored Foster, giving Cincinnati a 4-3 triumph and a berth in the World Series.

• **Roberto Clemente.** Pirates' Hall of Fame-bound right fielder who went 1 for 3 in the game and received an eighth-inning intentional walk from Cincinnati's Tom Hall in what proved his last career plate appearance. Clemente was killed in a plane crash about 2 1/2 months later.

NINE GAMES
While 84 of the 88 World Series played through 1991 were contested under a best-of-seven format, four Series—including the first one in 1903—were best-of-nine confrontations. While none of the best-of-nine Series was played to the limit, three of those fall classics did require eight games. The best-of-nine World Series:

Year—Winner, Games Won	Loser, Games Won
1903—Boston Red Sox, A.L., 5	Pittsburgh Pirates, N.L., 3
1919—Cincinnati Reds, N.L., 5	Chicago White Sox, A.L., 3
1920—Cleveland Indians, A.L., 5	Brooklyn Dodgers, N.L., 2
1921—New York Giants, N.L., 5	New York Yankees, A.L., 3

1954
The last year in which the season's major league batting champions met in the World Series. Willie Mays of the National League pennant-winning New York Giants won the '54 N.L. hitting title with a .345 average, while Bobby Avila of the American League champion Cleveland Indians captured the A.L. batting crown with a .341 mark. In the '54 World Series, which the Giants won in four straight games, Mays batted .286 and Avila hit .133.

The only other World Series matchups of batting-title winners occurred in 1909 and 1931. In 1909, Detroit's Ty Cobb won the A.L. batting title with a .377 mark as the Tigers advanced to the Series against Pittsburgh, led by the N.L.'s top hitter, Honus Wagner, who fashioned a .339 mark. The Pirates won the Series in seven games, with Wagner hitting .333 and Cobb finishing at .231. The St. Louis Cardinals won the '31 Series against the Philadelphia A's, but got little help from N.L. batting champion Chick Hafey in another seven-game battle. Hafey, a .349 hitter during the season, managed only a .167 mark in the Series. Philadelphia's Al Simmons, the A.L. batting titlist with a .390 figure, hit .333 against the Cardinals.

1976
The last year in which no pitcher started more than one game for either side in the World Series. In the '76 Series, which National League titlist Cincinnati won in four games, the Reds called upon Don Gullett, Fred Norman, Pat Zachry and Gary Nolan as starters; the American League champion New York Yankees used Doyle Alexander, Jim (Catfish) Hunter, Dock Ellis and Ed Figueroa.

The Yankees' four-game Series sweeps of 1927 (over the Pittsburgh Pirates)

Cincinnati Manager Sparky Anderson couldn't contain his enthusiasm after George Foster had scored the winning run on a wild pitch by Pittsburgh's Bob Moose to give the Reds the 1972 National League pennant.

and 1950 (against the Philadelphia Phillies) also featured different starting pitchers throughout for both clubs.

JORGE ORTA
Pinch-hitting for Kansas City with the Royals trailing the St. Louis Cardinals, 1-0, in the ninth inning of Game 6 of the 1985 World Series, he hit a ground ball on which first-base umpire Don Denkinger made a hotly disputed call—a call that helped the American League champions, down three games to two in the Series, to a game-winning, two-run rally.

Supporting Cast:

• **Brian Harper.** Pinch-hitting for Cardinals starting pitcher Danny Cox, who had shut out the Royals over seven innings, he delivered a run-scoring bloop single in the eighth inning that gave St. Louis a 1-0 lead at Royals Stadium.

• **Pat Sheridan.** Kansas City's lefthanded-hitting right fielder and the first man scheduled to bat in the bottom of the ninth. With Cardinals lefthander Ken Dayley ready to begin his second inning of relief, righthanded hitter Darryl Motley was announced as a pinch-hitter for Sheridan. St. Louis Manager Whitey Herzog then summoned hard-throwing righthander Todd Worrell, and Royals Manager Dick Howser countered with Orta, a lefthanded batter, to hit for Motley.

• **Jack Clark.** St. Louis first baseman who fielded Orta's ensuing grounder and threw to Worrell, who was covering first. Television replays indicated Orta was out on the play, but Denkinger called him safe. Herzog argued vehemently, but to no avail. Kansas City's Steve Balboni then lifted a catchable popup near the first-base dugout, but Clark inexplicably failed to make the play and the ball fell untouched. Balboni then singled, with Orta stopping at second base.

• **Jim Sundberg.** After Onix Concepcion ran for Balboni, Sundberg bunted into a forceout at third base.

• **Hal McRae.** Pinch-hitting for Buddy Biancalana, he was at the plate when Cardinals catcher Darrell Porter committed a passed ball. With runners now at second and third, McRae was walked intentionally (and replaced by pinch-runner John Wathan).

• **Dane Iorg.** Batting for Royals reliever Dan Quisenberry, he poked a single to right field that scored Concepcion and Sundberg and gave Kansas City a Series-squaring 2-1 triumph over St. Louis.

The Royals won their first World Series crown the next night. The Cardinals, two outs away from nailing down the Series title in Game 6 and clearly showing the effects of the game that got away (because of an umpire's apparent mistake and their own faulty play), unraveled in Game 7 and dropped the Series finale, 11-0.

ROGER PECKINPAUGH

Washington shortstop who made errors in six of the seven games of the 1925 World Series—including two misplays in both Game 2 and Game 7. His eight errors established a Series record for one player (regardless of position) that still stands and helped the Pittsburgh Pirates to a four games-to-three triumph.

The Senators' Peckinpaugh had been voted the A.L.'s "most valuable player to a club" (the terminology in those days) in '25.

DEACON PHILLIPPE

The only pitcher to win three games in a World Series for the losing club. Pitching for the Pittsburgh Pirates in the 1903 Series against the Boston Red

Kansas City catcher Jim Sundberg was understandably ecstatic after scoring the winning run in the ninth inning of Game 6 of the 1985 World Series against the St. Louis Cardinals.

Sox, Phillippe was a winner in Games 1, 3 and 4 (and a loser in Games 7 and 8) as the Pirates fell to the Red Sox, five games to three.

Phillippe pitched five complete games and 44 innings (both records) in the Series, which ran for 13 days.

ALLIE REYNOLDS
The only pitcher to win at least one World Series game in five consecutive years. Reynolds, of the New York Yankees, beat the Brooklyn Dodgers in Game 1 of the 1949 Series (on a two-hit shutout), defeated the Philadelphia Phillies in Game 2 of the 1950 classic (allowing one run in 10 innings), stopped the New York Giants in Game 4 of the 1951 Series (yielding two runs), downed the Dodgers twice in 1952 (via a shutout in Game 4 and a relief stint in Game 7) and won over Brooklyn in Game 6 of the 1953 Series (while working two innings of relief).

Reynolds was a two-time World Series loser in the 1949-1953 streak and fashioned a 7-2 Series record overall (having posted a victory against Brooklyn in 1947).

Only four other pitchers have even appeared in five consecutive Series—the Yankees' Eddie Lopat, Vic Raschi, Whitey Ford and Ralph Terry. Lopat and Raschi, like Reynolds were Series pitchers from '49 through '53; Ford and Terry appeared in the Series from 1960 through 1964.

JIM RICE
Boston Red Sox left fielder who collected only five hits and batted just .161 in the seven-game 1986 American League Championship Series against the California Angels—but set a Championship Series record by scoring eight runs. Rice, who had two singles, a double and two home runs, scored in every inning in which he collected a hit or a base on balls (he drew one walk). He also scored after reaching base on a fielder's choice and after getting aboard on an error.

In 1989 Championship Series play, Oakland's Rickey Henderson and San Francisco's Will Clark tied Rice's mark of eight runs scored.

BOBBY RICHARDSON
After driving in only seven runs (in 194 at-bats) for the New York Yankees in the final 75 games of the 1960 season and finishing the year with 26 runs batted in, he established a World Series record with 12 RBIs (in 30 at-bats) in the Yanks' seven-game classic against the Pittsburgh Pirates in '60. Richardson set a one-game Series mark with six RBIs in Game 3, a contest in which he slugged a bases-full home run off Pirates reliever Clem Labine in the first inning. He drilled two triples and knocked in three runs in Game 6.

The New York Yankees lost the 1960 World Series to the Pittsburgh Pirates, but they weren't lacking for offense. The biggest producer was little second baseman Bobby Richardson, who received a warm welcome after hitting his third-game grand slam.

Richardson, who became a front-line Yankee player in 1957 and retired after the 1966 season, never had more than 59 RBIs in one major league season.

PETE ROSE, BUD HARRELSON

Combatants in a 1973 National League Championship Series fight that led to a stoppage of play when New York Mets fans rained debris on Cincinnati left fielder Rose. With the playoff deadlocked at a game apiece and the Mets ahead, 9-2, in the fifth inning of Game 3 at New York's Shea Stadium, Rose collected a one-out single off Jerry Koosman. Joe Morgan then grounded into a first base-to-shortstop-to-first double play—John Milner was the Mets' first baseman and Harrelson the shortstop—but not before Rose made a hard slide into Harrelson in an attempt to break up the play. Harrelson and Rose began pushing and shoving and soon fell to the ground, flailing away at each other. Players from both benches and bullpens raced onto the field. After order was restored, Rose took his position in left field—and was soon the target of garbage-throwing fans. Cincinnati Manager Sparky Anderson pulled his club off the field and the Reds didn't return until a Mets contingent—headed by Manager Yogi Berra and outfielder Willie Mays— made a trip to left field and pleaded with the fans to settle down. The unruliness ended, and New York went on to win by the 9-2 score.

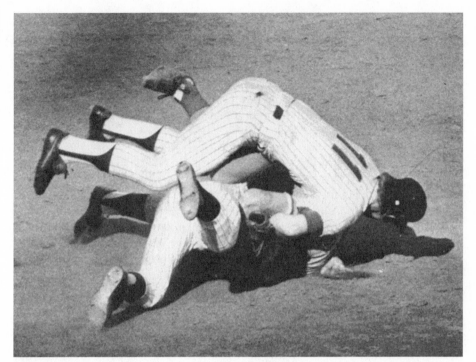

Push came to shove in the 1973 N.L. Championship Series when Mets shortstop Bud Harrelson and Cincinnati's Pete Rose exchanged unpleasantries. Mets third baseman Wayne Garrett (11) arrived on the scene in short order.

Rose got "revenge" the next day at Shea when he belted a game-winning, 12th-inning home run off Harry Parker—he circled the bases with a fist raised high—as the Reds edged the Mets, 2-1, and squared the Championship Series at two games each. New York won the best-of-five title playoff, though, with a subsequent 7-2 triumph.

CLARENCE (PANTS) ROWLAND
The first of eight World Series managers with no playing experience in the major leagues. Rowland, in his only Series managerial role, piloted the Chicago White Sox to a four games-to-two triumph over the New York Giants in 1917.

Other World Series managers who never played in the big leagues: Ed Barrow, who guided the Boston Red Sox into the Series in 1918; Joe McCarthy, Chicago Cubs, 1929, and New York Yankees, 1932, 1936 through 1939 and 1941 through 1943; Eddie Sawyer, Philadelphia Phillies, 1950; Johnny Keane, St. Louis Cardinals, 1964; Earl Weaver, Baltimore Orioles, 1969 through 1971, 1979; Jim Frey, Kansas City Royals, 1980, and Paul Owens, Phillies, 1983. Barrow was a Series winner in 1918, McCarthy won seven times (missing only in 1929 and 1942), Keane was triumphant in 1964 and Weaver prevailed in

1970. Teams managed by Sawyer, Frey, and Owens failed to win the Series.

VERN RUHLE
Houston Astros pitcher who was at the center of a major controversy that flared in Game 4 of the 1980 National League Championship Series. Houston, leading the best-of-five playoff, two games to one, was locked in a 0-0 battle with Philadelphia when the Phillies came to bat in the top of the fourth inning.

Supporting Cast:
•**Bake McBride, Manny Trillo.** The Phils' first two batters in the fourth, they collected singles off Ruhle.
•**Garry Maddox.** He followed Trillo to the plate and hit a low, soft liner to Ruhle, who wheeled and threw to Houston first baseman Art Howe in an apparent attempt to double up the baserunner, who was off the bag. The Phillies mounted a strenuous protest, insisting that Ruhle had trapped the ball. (Television replays were inconclusive.) And as the Phils voiced their grievance, Howe ambled down to second base, touched the bag and thereby put in a claim for a triple play.
•**Doug Harvey.** Home-plate umpire who first indicated the play was a "trap," then asked for help after acknowledging that he didn't have a clear view of the action because Maddox had stepped into his line of vision. Harvey conferred with his fellow umpires and with N.L. President Chub Feeney (seated nearby) and, accepting their collective judgment, ruled the play a catch—and a double play. Since time had been called after Ruhle's throw to Howe, the subsequent triple-play attempt by Howe was not allowed (and McBride returned to second base). The next batter, Larry Bowa, ended the inning by grounding out.

The Phillies went on to win Game 4, prevailing by a 5-3 score in 10 innings, and then won a 10-inning, 8-7 stem-winder that gave them their first N.L. pennant in 30 years.

77
The number of postseason games—divisional-playoff, Championship Series and World Series contests—in which Reggie Jackson has appeared, a major league record. Jackson has played in five divisional-playoff games (the extra tier of playoff competition that was part of the 1981 split season), 45 Championship Series games and 27 World Series games. Jackson, whose divisional-playoff action came with the New York Yankees, has played in 20 Championship Series games with Oakland, 14 as a member of the Yankees and 11 while a California Angels player. And he participated in 12 World Series games for the A's and 15 with the Yanks. (Jackson also played for the Yankees against the Red Sox in the one-game playoff that broke a 1978 A.L. East title tie. However, a championship-season tie-breaking game isn't considered part of postseason play because the contest applies directly to the regular season and all records from the game are included in regular-season statistics.)

Umpire Doug Harvey was forced to the sideline during Game 4 of the 1980 Championship Series for a chat with N.L. President Chub Feeney. Both the Houston Astros and Philadelphia Phillies were vehemently protesting a call that, after considerable confusion and deliberation, became a double play.

The all-time leader in World Series games played is Yogi Berra, who appeared in 75 contests for the Yankees from 1947 through 1963, while the No. 1 man in Championship Series games played is Jackson, whose 45 appearances have come from 1971 through 1986. (Berra played in 74 percent of all World Series games contested from '47 through '63; Jackson participated in 64 percent of all A.L. Championship Series games played from '71 through '86.)

LONNIE SMITH
The first man to bat in big-league postseason play in Canada in both the National League and the American League. Smith was Philadelphia's center fielder and leadoff batter on October 7, 1981, at Montreal's Olympic Stadium when the Phillies and Expos met in Canada's first postseason game—the opening game of the N.L. East divisional playoffs. (The divisional playoff competition, which would determine Championship Series entrants, was an extra round in the majors' postseason structure and part of the split-season format adopted during the strike-torn season of '81.) Four years later, on October 8, 1985, at Toronto's Exhibition Stadium, Smith became the first

player to bat in an A.L. postseason game when, as Kansas City's left fielder, he led off for the Royals in Game 1 of the Championship Series against the Blue Jays.

LONNIE SMITH
The last of four players to see World Series duty in at least one game for three different Series-winning franchises, having played for the Philadelphia Phillies in 1980, the St. Louis Cardinals in 1982 and the Kansas City Royals in 1985. Smith, an outfielder/designated hitter, played in all 20 games of the '80, '82 and '85 Series. In addition, Smith played for Atlanta in the 1991 World Series, but the Braves lost to Minnesota.

Bullet Joe Bush and Wally Schang were teammates on the 1913 Philadelphia A's, 1918 Boston Red Sox and 1923 New York Yankees, all of whom won World Series crowns. And Stuffy McInnis played for the Series-winning A's of 1911 and 1913, Red Sox of 1918 and Pittsburgh Pirates of 1925.

OZZIE SMITH
Switch-hitting shortstop who, when he went to the plate as a lefthanded batter for St. Louis against Los Angeles in the ninth inning of Game 5 of the 1985 National League Championship Series, had not slugged a home run as a lefthanded hitter in his eight-year major league career (a span that included 2,967 regular-season at-bats as a lefthanded batter). However, with the score tied, 2-2, and one out, Smith picked on a 1-2 pitch from Dodgers reliever Tom Niedenfuer and slammed the ball off the cement facing above the right-field wall at Busch Stadium. The homer not only gave the Cardinals a 3-2 victory, it enabled St. Louis to take a three-games-to-two lead in the playoffs. The Cards won the N.L. pennant-deciding series in six games.

BILL TERRY
The last player-manager to hit a home run in a World Series. Terry, first baseman and manager of the New York Giants, slugged a bases-empty homer off Washington's Monte Weaver in the fourth inning of Game 4 of the 1933 Series. The Giants won that contest, 2-1, in 11 innings and wrapped up the Series title over the Senators in five games.

The only other player-managers to rap Series home runs were Fred Clarke of the Pittsburgh Pirates and Bucky Harris of the Senators. Clarke, an outfielder, hit two homers against the Detroit Tigers in the 1909 classic, and second baseman Harris slammed two homers against the Giants in 1924.

JIM THORPE
Famed Olympic Games athlete and college and pro football star who "appeared" in one World Series game—but, in fact, never got onto the playing field in that contest. Listed as the New York Giants' starting right fielder for Game 5 of the

Ozzie Smith's first major league home run as a lefthanded hitter resulted in a jubilant trot around the bases and a Game 5 victory for St. Louis over Los Angeles in the 1985 N.L. Championship Series.

1917 Series in Chicago, the righthanded-hitting Thorpe was sixth in the batting order as the Giants faced White Sox lefthander Reb Russell. After yielding a walk and two hits to New York's first three batters of the game, Russell gave way to righthander Eddie Cicotte. By the time Thorpe was due to hit in the first inning, the Giants already had scored one run and had two men on base. At this juncture, Giants Manager John McGraw sent up lefthanded-hitting Dave Robertson, New York's starting right fielder in the first four games, to bat for Thorpe. Robertson delivered a run-scoring single, then took over in right field in a game that the Giants wound up losing, 8-5.

Robertson, who went 3 for 5 in Game 5, hit safely in all six Series games—the White Sox prevailed, four games to two—and was the top hitter in the classic with a .500 average (11 hits in 22 at-bats).

MOOKIE WILSON
New York Mets outfielder who was at bat with two out in the 10th inning of Game 6 of the 1986 World Series when the game-tying run was wild-pitched home. Wilson then proceeded to hit a grounder to Boston first baseman Bill Buckner, who misplayed the ball into a game-deciding error. The two runs that scored during Wilson's at-bat capped a three-run rally and enabled the Mets—on the brink of elimination—to beat the Red Sox, 6-5, in New York and deadlock the Series at three games apiece.

Supporting Cast:
•**Dave Henderson.** Boston outfielder who snapped a 3-3 tie in the top of the 10th with a leadoff homer against Rick Aguilera. The Red Sox expanded their lead to 5-3 later in the inning when Wade Boggs doubled and Marty Barrett singled him home.
•**Wally Backman, Keith Hernandez.** The Mets' first two batters in the bottom of the 10th, they flied out against Red Sox reliever Calvin Schiraldi.
•**Gary Carter.** He kept the Mets' faint hopes alive by lining a single on a 2-1 pitch.
•**Kevin Mitchell.** Batting for Aguilera, he rifled a one-strike pitch for a base hit.
•**Ray Knight.** With Carter on second base and Mitchell on first, the Mets were down to their last strike when Knight swung at a no-ball, two-strike offering and looped a single to center field. Carter scored on the play, cutting New York's deficit to 5-4, and Mitchell advanced to third.
•**Bob Stanley.** Boston reliever who entered the game at this juncture and battled Wilson to a 2-2 count, bringing the Red Sox within one strike of the Series championship for the second time. Wilson fouled off the next two pitches before Stanley uncorked a wild pitch that scored Mitchell, tied the game at 5-5 and sent Knight to second base. Wilson hit two more foul balls and then slapped another 3-2 offering to Buckner, who let the grounder get through his legs. Knight raced home on the error, and the Mets had a storybook 6-5 victory.

The Mets went on to win the '86 World Series, scoring an 8-5 comeback triumph over the Red Sox in Game 7 (a contest that was delayed one night because of rain).

GEORGE WRIGHT

A pennant winner in his only season as a big-league manager—a distinction unequaled in major league history. Wright, a middle infielder on brother Harry Wright's Boston clubs in the National League's first three seasons of existence (1876 through 1878), took the managerial reins of Providence's N.L. club in 1879 and guided the team to a first-place finish. Harry Wright, whose teams had won N.L. flags in 1877 and 1878, saw his Boston club finish second to Providence in '79.

George Wright played briefly for Boston again in 1880 and 1881 before rounding out his big-league playing career with Providence in 1882.

SIXTH INNING
Dealing with trades—
the twists and turns
of the swap mart

FELIPE ALOU, MATTY ALOU
Brothers who were sold by the same major league team on the same day. On September 6, 1973, the New York Yankees sent first baseman-outfielder Felipe Alou to the Montreal Expos and dispatched outfielder Matty Alou to the St. Louis Cardinals. Felipe had joined the Yankees in the first week of the 1971 season, while Matty had been a member of the Yanks since November 1972.

JAY BELL, BERT BLYLEVEN
Involved in a 1985 trade between the Minnesota Twins and the Cleveland Indians, they had a noteworthy introduction to each other in the major leagues in 1986. Bell, who as a Twins' minor-league infielder had been part of a three-for-one deal with the Indians that sent veteran pitcher Blyleven to Minnesota on August 1, 1985, appeared in his first big-league game on September 29, 1986, and homered for Cleveland on the first pitch he saw in the majors—a pitch thrown by Minnesota's Blyleven. Not only did Bell enter the record books with a homer on his first at-bat, he took Blyleven with him. The home run was the 47th allowed by Blyleven in '86, establishing a big-league record for the most homers yielded by one pitcher in one year. (By season's end, Blyleven had given up 50 homers, which remains the major league record.

VIDA BLUE, JOE RUDI, ROLLIE FINGERS
Three standout Oakland players whom A's Owner Charlie Finley attempted to sell in June 1976. Faced with the prospect of losing some of his top, unsigned players to free agency at the end of the '76 season, Finley readied plans to sell pitcher Blue to the New York Yankees for a reported $1.5 million and outfielder Rudi and reliever Fingers to the Boston Red Sox for $1 million apiece. "I'm disappointed with the necessity of having to make these sales," Finley said after announcing completion of the transactions on June 15. "But I just refused to let these players drive me into bankruptcy with their astronomical salary demands." On the night of the sales, the Red Sox were in Oakland to play the A's and Rudi and Fingers changed clubhouses and uniforms. However, Boston Manager Darrell Johnson did not use either player that evening. The next day, Commissioner Bowie Kuhn ordered the Red Sox and Yankees to refrain from using their new players until he finished an

investigation into the deals. On June 18, Kuhn voided the sales, saying they were not in "the best interests of the game."

Rudi and Fingers played out their options with the A's in 1976 and, achieving free-agent status, signed with the California Angels and San Diego Padres, respectively. Blue, who agreed to contract terms with Finley just before the June 15 sale (the Yankees did not want to acquire an unsigned player m fear of losing him to free agency), pitched for the A's again in 1977 before being traded.

BOSTON RED SOX, CHICAGO CUBS
Teams that made the first deal in major league baseball's initial interleague trading period, which came after the 1959 season. Previously, transactions between teams of the American League and clubs in the National League could be made only after a player had cleared waivers in his league. Starting on November 21, 1959, and continuing for 3 1/2 weeks, clubs could make waiver-free interleague trades—and the Red Sox and Cubs went right to work. On November 21, Boston dealt first baseman Dick Gernert to the Cubs for pitcher Dave Hillman and first baseman-outfielder Jim Marshall.

By the first interleague trading deadline of December 15, 1959, 30 players had changed leagues.

DAN BROUTHERS
Hall of Fame-bound first baseman who, in an era of disbanding franchises and short-lived leagues, played for Boston of the National League in 1889, Boston of the Players League in 1890 and Boston of the American Association (a major league at the time) in 1891.

BILL CAMPBELL
Of the players available in major league baseball's initial free-agent reentry draft (held November 4, 1976), the first to sign a contract. Campbell, The Sporting News' Fireman of the Year in the American League in '76 when he fashioned a 17-5 record for the Minnesota Twins, signed a long-term contract with the Boston Red Sox two days after the draft.

OWNIE CARROLL
The only player in major league history to be traded three times in deals for future Hall of Fame members. A righthanded pitcher who compiled a 65-89 record for four clubs in a big-league career that began in 1925 and ended in 1934, Carroll was first traded in May 1930 when he, George Wuestling and Harry Rice were sent from the Detroit Tigers to the New York Yankees for Mark Koenig and future Hall of Famer Waite Hoyt. Sold to Cincinnati later in 1930, Carroll and Reds teammate Estel Crabtree were dealt to the St. Louis Cardinals in December 1932 for Cooperstown-bound Jim Bottomley. And in February

Though it does not appear in the playing records of either Rollie Fingers or Joe Rudi (with Manager Darrell Johnson), both were brief members of the Boston Red Sox in 1976. After being sold to Boston by Oakland Owner Charlie Finley on June 15, both donned their new uniforms for one game (neither played) before the deal was voided.

1933, the Cards dispatched Carroll and Jake Flowers to the Brooklyn Dodgers for Gordon Slade and future Hall of Fame inductee Dazzy Vance.

Only one other player, Curt Davis, was involved in three trades involving future Hall of Famers. Davis was swapped in separate deals for Chuck Klein and Dizzy Dean and in a trade with Joe Medwick.

CEPEDA, SADECKI, TORRE
Players who went round-robin for each other in a series of major league trades. First baseman Orlando Cepeda was dealt from the San Francisco Giants to the St. Louis Cardinals for pitcher Ray Sadecki on May 8, 1966. Cepeda then was swapped from St. Louis to the Atlanta Braves for catcher-first baseman Joe Torre on March 17, 1969. And on October 13, 1974, Sadecki and pitcher Tommy Moore were traded from the Mets to the Cardinals for Torre.

LU CLINTON
American Leaguer who played one game for Kansas City in 1965—a game that he apparently wasn't supposed to play. When the California Angels placed Clinton on waivers in early September of '65—marking the third time that waivers had been asked that year on the 27-year-old outfielder—the A.L. office failed to designate the waivers as irrevocable (as befits a three-time waiver situation). Believing that Clinton could still be recalled from the waiver wire, all A.L. clubs except one—Cleveland—passed on him. When A.L. officials discovered that the waivers should have been listed as irrevocable, they informed all teams of the oversight and gave clubs with a lower standing than the fourth-place Indians a chance to enter a claim. And the last-place A's did just that. With California playing in Kansas City on the night of the waiver wildness (September 8), Clinton donned an A's uniform and went hitless in one at-bat against his former team. The following day, the A.L. office notified the A's that the Clinton case was being reopened and that Kansas City should not use Clinton pending a ruling. After Commissioner Ford Frick's entry into the matter and following a disclosure that Cleveland had claimed Clinton earlier in year, too, it was decided on September 10 that—procedurally amiss or not—the first-come Indians would be first-served. Clinton was awarded to the Tribe.

Clinton's one appearance with Kansas City happened to come in one of the most memorable games in the Athletics' 13 seasons in the Missouri city. It was the contest in which Bert Campaneris of the A's became the first player in major league history to play all nine positions in one game.

COFFMAN-FISCHER, DAVIS-NORDHAGEN
These major league players were traded even up for each other—twice. On June 9, 1932, the St. Louis Browns dealt righthanded pitcher Dick Coffman to the Senators for lefthander Carl Fischer. The following December, the Senators

Jim (Catfish) Hunter, the American League's reigning Cy Young Award winner, was the center of considerable attention on December 31, 1974, when he ended a bidding war by agreeing to a contract with the New York Yankees after being declared a free agent because of Oakland's breach of contract.

swapped Coffman back to the Browns for Fischer. Fifty years later, in a June 15, 1982, transaction, the Philadelphia Phillies sent outfielder Dick Davis to the Toronto Blue Jays for outfielder Wayne Nordhagen. The same day, the Phils traded Nordhagen to Pittsburgh for outfielder Bill Robinson. Then, just a week later, the Pirates and Blue Jays hooked up in a one-for-one deal—Nordhagen going back to Toronto in exchange for Davis.

Other players have been swapped twice for each other, but in most cases the transactions involved additional players and/or cash. Among players traded for each other twice in multi-player deals were: Larry Benton and Hugh McQuillan, Spud Davis and Jimmie Wilson, Kiddo Davis and Chick Fullis, Ron Northey and Harry Walker, Fred Sanford and Dick Starr, Smoky Burgess and Andy Seminick, Hoot Evers and Bill Wight, Ray Katt and Dick Littlefield, Larry Doby and Tito Francona, Tim Cullen and Ron Hansen and Jim Essian and Dick Allen.

NATE COLBERT
Of the 24 players available in the majors' first free-agent re-entry draft (conducted in November 1976), the only one who didn't hook on with a big-league club. While 22 of the pool's players were drafted (13 were picked the maximum 13 times), Colbert and Willie McCovey, both of whom finished the '76 season with brief stints for the Oakland A's, went unclaimed. McCovey eventually signed with the San Francisco Giants (the team for whom he had played from 1959 through 1973), but former San Diego star Colbert did not

444

catch on with another major league team.

DECEMBER 31, 1974
The date on which pitcher Jim (Catfish) Hunter, declared a free agent a little more than two weeks earlier because the deferred-compensation portion of his contract had been breached by the Oakland A's, ended the frenzied auction for his services by agreeing to a five-year contract with the New York Yankees. The deal reportedly was worth more than $3 million. Major league club officials, caught up in baseball's first free-agent bidding war, had flocked to Hunter's home state of North Carolina to make pitches for the 28-year-old righthander, who had just won the American League's Cy Young Award after a 25-victory season for the A's (which marked his fourth straight year of winning 20 games).

BRUCE ELLINGSEN
The player Cleveland received from Los Angeles in the April 4, 1974, one-for-one deal that sent Pedro Guerrero to the Dodgers' organization. Ellingsen, nearing his 25th birthday, was a lefthanded pitcher who in 1973 had posted a 5-10 record (with a 6.71 earned-run average) for Class AAA Albuquerque. Third baseman Guerrero, just 17 years old, had played only 44 games of professional ball at that juncture, all in a rookie league. Ellingsen went on to appear in 16 major league games, all for the 1974 Indians, and compiled a 1-1 record with a 3.21 ERA. On the other hand, Guerrero, who saw his first extensive duty for Los Angeles in 1981, developed into one of the majors' top hitters—both for average and power. Through 1991, Guerrero boasted a .302 career batting average in a total of 1,493 games with Los Angeles and St. Louis.

The Ferrell brothers, Rick (left) and Wes (right), greet Washington Manager Bucky Harris after their June 1937 trade from the Red Sox to the Senators.

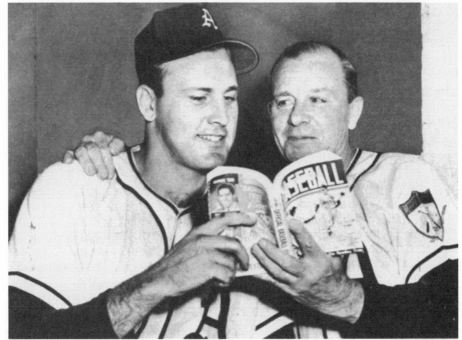

Outfielder Gus Zernial (left), one of 57 players to perform with the Philadelphia A's and not play under Manager Connie Mack, looks over an Official Baseball Guide with Jimmie Dykes, the A's manager from 1951 through 1953. Zernial played 528 games in the four years that the A's remained in Philadelphia after Mack's retirement.

He had knocked in 100 or more runs three times and topped the 30-homer mark on three occasions.

RICK FERRELL, WES FERRELL
A major league brother battery, the Ferrells were traded together by the Boston Red Sox to the Washington Senators on June 10, 1937. Rick, a catcher, had batted .301 for Boston in 1935 and .312 in 1936, while pitcher Wes had won 25 games for the Red Sox in '35 and 20 in '36. Accompanying the Ferrells to Washington was outfielder Mel Almada. In return, the Red Sox received outfielder Ben Chapman and pitcher Bobo Newsom from the Senators.

57
In the 54-year history of the Philadelphia A's, the number of players to perform for that team who did not play for Connie Mack. Of the 57, outfielder Gus Zernial appeared in the most games (528) for the Philadelphia club without ever playing under Mack and he was the only non-pitcher to play for the Philadelphia A's all four years (1951 through 1954) that Mack didn't manage the team.

Of the Philadelphia A's pitchers who never played for Mack (there were 25, compared with 32 non-pitchers), Morrie Martin appeared in the most games for the Philadelphia club (111) and was the only hurler to pitch for the team in all four of the non-Mack years.

VERN GEISHERT, FRANK DUFFY
The players the San Francisco Giants received when they sent George Foster to the Cincinnati Reds in a May 29, 1971, swap. Geishert, a pitcher, never saw action for the Giants and appeared in only 11 big-league games in his entire career, all for the 1969 California Angels. In fact, Geishert, after being shifted from Cincinnati's Class AAA farm club to San Francisco's top affiliate in the wake of the deal, left baseball. Duffy, an infielder, batted .179 for the Giants in 21 games, then was traded in November 1971 to the Cleveland Indians. While not an immediate sensation with the Reds, Foster eventually made his mark. In a six-season period, 1976 through 1981, he drove in 671 runs for Cincinnati and drilled 198 home runs. Foster led the National League in RBIs in 1976, 1977 and 1978 with totals of 121, 149 and 120 and paced the N.L. in homers in '77 and '78 with 52 and 40.

Nobody could blame catcher Ron Hassey for being a little confused after being involved in three trades between the New York Yankees and Chicago White Sox in a 7 1/2-month span. When all was said and done, Hassey ended up splitting the 1986 season between the Yanks and the White Sox.

447

RON HASSEY

A catcher who in a 7 1/2-month period was involved in three trades between the New York Yankees and the Chicago White Sox and in a 20-month span was part of four trades between major league clubs in New York and Chicago. On December 12, 1985, the Yankees swapped Hassey and pitcher Joe, Cowley to the White Sox for pitcher Britt Burns, shortstop Mike Soper and outfielder Glen Braxton. Before donning a White Sox uniform, Hassey was sent back to the Yanks in a seven-player deal that was made on February 13, 1986, and featured the move of pitcher Neil Allen from the Yanks to the Sox and the speedy return of Braxton to the Chicago organization. Then, on July 30, 1986, the Yankees and White Sox completed a six-player trade, with Hassey again becoming property of the White Sox and outfielder Ron Kittle heading the contingent moving to the Yanks. Hassey's Chicago-New York shuttle had begun on December 4, 1984, when the Cubs included him in a four-man package that was dispatched to the Yankees for pitcher Ray Fontenot and outfielder Brian Dayett.

REGGIE JACKSON

The first player selected when big-league baseball's free-agent re-entry draft made its debut in the fall of 1976. Jackson, who played for the Baltimore Orioles in '76, was picked by the Montreal Expos, who chose first because their record was the worst in the majors that year. Jackson eventually signed with the New York Yankees.

FRANK LANE

Major league baseball's noted wheeler-dealer of the 1950s, he outdid himself in 1956 while serving the first of two years as general manager of the St. Louis Cardinals. "Trader Frank" made 10 trades involving 45 players in '56, swinging seven-, nine- and 10-player deals. With his business-first, sentiment-later approach obvious from the start (as evidenced by the disappearance of the traditional birds-on-bat insignia from the front of Cardinal uniforms), Lane shook up the St. Louis populace on June 14 when he shipped longtime Cardinal favorite Red Schoendienst to the New York Giants. Accompanying the second baseman to New York were heralded rookie outfielder Jackie Brandt, catcher Bill Sarni, pitcher Dick Littlefield and minor league infielder Bobby Stephenson (who was assigned to Minneapolis). In return, the Cards received shortstop Alvin Dark, first baseman-outfielder Whitey Lockman, catcher Ray Katt and pitcher Don Liddle.

Lane's 45-man trade count in 1956 did not include single players bought or sold in cash transactions.

It was Lane, as Cleveland's general manager, who helped engineer an August 3, 1960, "trade" of managers. The exchange sent Jimmie Dykes from the Tigers to the Indians and Joe Gordon from Cleveland to Detroit.

TOM LAWLESS
The player the Montreal Expos obtained from Cincinnati for Pete Rose in the August 16, 1984, trade that resulted in the immediate appointment of Rose as the Reds' player-manager. Rose, who had starred for Cincinnati from 1963 through 1978, replaced Vern Rapp as the Reds' pilot. Under Rapp, Cincinnati had compiled a 51-69 record in '84. Lawless, a 27-year-old infielder who had been playing for Cincinnati's Class AAA affiliate at Wichita, was assigned to Montreal's top farm club at Indianapolis.

Other instances in which players were traded or released to pave the way for their managerial appointments, or situations in which managers moved to other clubs in return for compensation or "considerations":

DECEMBER 1913—BUCK HERZOG. Infielder Herzog became playing manager of the Cincinnati Reds after he and catcher Grover Hartley were traded from the New York Giants to Cincinnati for outfielder Bob Bescher.
JULY 1916—CHRISTY MATHEWSON. Pitcher Mathewson became manager of the Reds (he pitched in one game for Cincinnati in '16) after he, infielder Bill McKechnie and outfielder Edd Roush were traded from the Giants to Cincinnati for infielder Buck Herzog and outfielder Red Killefer.
NOVEMBER 1923—DAVE BANCROFT. Infielder Bancroft became playing manager of the Boston Braves after he and outfielders Casey Stengel and Bill Cunningham were traded from the Giants to Boston for outfielder Billy Southworth and pitcher Joe Oeschger.
OCTOBER 1928—BUCKY HARRIS. Harris, playing manager of the Washington Senators, became manager of the Detroit Tigers (he appeared in seven games for Detroit in 1929) after a trade in which the Tigers sent infielder Jack Warner to Washington.
NOVEMBER 1933—JIMMIE WILSON. Catcher Wilson became playing manager of the Philadelphia Phillies after he was traded from the St. Louis Cardinals to Philadelphia for catcher Spud Davis and infielder Eddie Delker.
JANUARY 1934—BOB O'FARRELL. Catcher O'Farrell became playing manager of the Reds after he and pitcher Syl Johnson were traded from the Cardinals to Cincinnati for pitcher Glenn Spencer and cash.
DECEMBER 1951—EDDIE STANKY. Infielder Stanky became playing manager of the Cardinals after he was traded from the Giants to St. Louis for pitcher Max Lanier and outfielder Chuck Diering.
SEPTEMBER 1958—SOLLY HEMUS. Infielder Hemus became playing manager of the Cardinals after he was traded from the Phillies to St. Louis for third baseman Gene Freese.
MAY 1963—GIL HODGES. First baseman Hodges became manager of the Senators after being released as a player by the New York Mets. The day after Hodges was given his freedom to take the managerial position, the Washington club sold outfielder Jim Piersall to the Mets as an apparent "consideration."
OCTOBER 1967—GIL HODGES. Hodges, manager of the Senators, became

manager of the Mets in a transaction that involved his release as Washington's pilot, a cash payment from New York to Washington and the November dispatch of pitcher Bill Denehy from the Mets to the Senators.

NOVEMBER 1976—CHUCK TANNER. Tanner, manager of the Oakland A's, became manager of the Pittsburgh Pirates after the Pirates sent catcher Manny Sanguillen and cash to Oakland in exchange for Tanner's services.

MATHEWSON, McKECHNIE, ROUSH

Principals in the only major league trade involving three future Hall-of-Famers. Amazingly, the swap did not involve a mix of the three; instead, the Cincinnati Reds acquired all three of the Cooperstown-bound figures—Christy Mathewson, Bill McKechnie and Edd Roush—in the five-man swap with the New York Giants that was made on July 20, 1916. While a deal netting one team three eventual Hall-of-Famers would appear decidedly one-sided (if not a case of highway robbery), all was not as it now seems.

The 35-year-old Mathewson, after all, was going to Cincinnati to manage, not pitch (the Giants' 372-game winner would pitch only once—it was a winning effort—for the Reds). And McKechnie was an infielder of marginal ability, a .234 lifetime hitter who won his way to the Hall of Fame via his managerial skill (which he exhibited by directing three National League franchises to pennants and managing four N.L. championship teams overall). The acquisition of Roush, though, clearly was a coup for Cincinnati in terms of bolstering its playing talent. Only 23 years old at the time of the deal, outfielder Roush went on to win two batting crowns while a member of the Reds and attained a .325 career average in the majors.

In return for Mathewson, McKechnie and Roush, New York received infielder Buck Herzog (who had played for the Giants in the 1911, 1912 and 1913 World Series) and outfielder Red Killefer from Cincinnati. Herzog didn't distinguish himself in his third stint with the New York club and, after appearing in the 1917 Series with the Giants and then being traded two more times, bowed out of the big leagues in 1920 with a .259 career batting mark. Killefer appeared in only two games for the Giants, then left the majors for good as a .248 hitter.

KEVIN McREYNOLDS

Outfielder who on December 11, 1986, was traded from San Diego to the New York Mets in an eight-man deal that netted the Padres five players—including outfielder-infielder Kevin Mitchell and pitchers Kevin Brown and Kevin Armstrong. While tripling their pleasure in the "Kevin" department, the Padres also acquired promising outfielders Shawn Abner and Stanley Jefferson in the swap and sent pitcher Gene Walter and infielder Adam Ging to the Mets.

Curt Flood, the man who instigated the fight against baseball's reserve system, sat out the 1970 season before becoming a member of the 1971 Washington Senators in a comeback that lasted only 13 games.

OAKLAND A'S
American League team for whom Felipe Alou played in 1971, Matty Alou played in 1972 and Jesus Alou played in 1973. Felipe, an A's regular in 1970, played only two games for Oakland in '71 before being traded to the New York Yankees. Matty appeared in 32 games for the A's in '72 following his late-August acquisition from the St. Louis Cardinals. And Jesus played 36 games for Oakland in '73 after being obtained in a July 31 transaction with the Houston Astros. (Matty moved on to the Yankees in November 1972, while Jesus played for Oakland again in 1974 before drawing his release from the A's organization in March 1975.)

OCTOBER 7, 1969
Date of the seven-man St. Louis Cardinals-Philadelphia Phillies trade that involved Curt Flood and precipitated Flood's court fight against baseball's

reserve system. The swap sent outfielder Flood (a Cardinal since 1958 and a lifetime .293 hitter in the majors), catcher Tim McCarver, outfielder Byron Browne and pitcher Joe Hoerner from St. Louis to Philadelphia for first baseman Dick Allen, second baseman Cookie Rojas and pitcher Jerry Johnson. Contending that he should be able to make a deal for himself and not be shipped around without his approval (he also had been swapped in 1957 from Cincinnati to St. Louis), Flood sat out the 1970 season and began a long assault on the reserve clause, which reserved a player's services to one team from one year to the next until the player was traded, sold or released or until he retired. As compensation for Flood's failure to report, the Cards sent first baseman-outfielder Willie Montanez (in April 1970) and pitcher Bob Browning (in August 1970) to the Phillies.

Flood, assured that a return to action would not affect his court case, was induced back to the playing field in 1971 by Washington Senators Owner Bob Short. The Phillies, to whom Flood technically belonged, agreed to let Flood join the Senators in a November 3, 1970, deal that sent first baseman-catcher Greg Goossen, first baseman-outfielder Gene Martin and pitcher Jeff Terpko to the National League team. The 33-year-old Flood played only 13 games for Washington in '71—he batted .200—before leaving the club and major league baseball for good.

The U.S. Supreme Court upheld baseball's reserve system in 1972.

DAVE REVERING
Power-hitting prospect whom the Oakland A's were to receive—along with an estimated $1.75 million—as the result of a December 9.1977, trade sending Vida Blue, a three-time 20-game winner for the A's, to the Cincinnati Reds. A's Owner Charlie Finley, defying Commissioner Bowie Kuhn's directive that the commissioner's office should be consulted before any transaction involving $400,000 or more was made, was foiled on January 30, 1978, when Kuhn voided the deal.

First baseman Revering, who had slugged 29 home runs and driven in 110 runs at Class AAA Indianapolis in 1977, wound up with the A's after all, going to Oakland along with an undisclosed amount of cash in a February 25, 1978, trade in which the Reds received relief pitcher Doug Bair. And Blue, the American League's Cy Young Award winner in 1971, wound up in the National League after all—but with the San Francisco Giants, not the Reds. In a March 15, 1978, deal, the A's sent the lefthanded pitcher to the Giants for seven players and an estimated $390,000.

JIMMY RING
A 118-149 pitcher in 12 National League seasons, he was the third man in two memorable trades—first, a swap involving a future Pro Football Hall of Fame

inductee and a future member of baseball's Hall of Fame and, second, a stunning deal featuring the exchange of two of the major leagues' best and most colorful players (both of whom also won places at Cooperstown). In February 1921, the Cincinnati Reds traded outfielder Earle (Greasy) Neale, a veteran of five N.L. seasons at that juncture, and pitcher Ring to the Philadelphia Phillies for pitcher Eppa Rixey. After only 22 games with the Phillies, Neale was sold back to the Reds, for whom he wound up his big-league career in 1924. Neale, a lifetime .259 hitter in 768 games in the majors, later became coach of the National Football League's Philadelphia Eagles (he had coached Washington and Jefferson to an appearance in the 1922 Rose Bowl) and directed the Eagles to NFL championships in 1948 and 1949. In 1969, Neale was elected to the Pro Football Hall of Fame. Rixey, an eight-year major leaguer at the time of the 1921 Phils-Reds trade, went on to pitch 13 years for Cincinnati and finished his big-league career with a 266-251 record. In 1963, Rixey was named to baseball's Hall of Fame. Ring, who was traded to the New York Giants in December 1925, accompanied Giants second baseman Frankie Frisch (a homegrown New Yorker and crowd favorite) to St. Louis in the momentous December 1926 swap that sent second baseman Rogers Hornsby, playing manager of the Cardinals' '26 World Series champions, to New York's N.L. club.

BROOKS ROBINSON, CARL YASTRZEMSKI
Of players who spent their entire major league careers with one club, the ones who performed for the most years—23. Robinson broke into the big leagues with Baltimore in 1955 and played for the Orioles through 1977, while Yastrzemski made his debut in the majors with Boston in 1961 and was a member of the Red Sox through 1983. Players who spent 20 or more seasons in the majors, all with one team:

Years	Player, Club, League	Career Span
23	Brooks Robinson, Baltimore, A.L.	1955-1977
23	Carl Yastrzemski, Boston, A.L.	1961-1983
22	Cap Anson, Chicago, N.L.	1876-1897
22	Al Kaline, Detroit, A.L.	1953-1974
22	Stan Musial, St. Louis, N.L.	1941-1963
22	Mel Ott, New York, N.L.	1926-1947
21	Walter Johnson, Washington, A.L.	1907-1927
21	Ted Lyons, Chicago, A.L.	1923-1946
21	Willie Stargell, Pittsburgh, N.L.	1962-1982
20	Luke Appling, Chicago, A.L.	1930-1950
20	Red Faber, Chicago, A.L.	1914-1933
20	Mel Harder, Cleveland, A.L.	1928-1947

BRAGGO ROTH, RED SHANNON
Major leaguers who twice were traded as a package, first for two players and then for three. On June 27, 1919, the Philadelphia A's swapped outfielder Roth

and infielder Shannon to the Boston Red Sox for outfielder Amos Strunk and infielder Jack Barry (whose subsequent retirement did not nullify the deal). The following January, the Red Sox dealt Roth and Shannon to the Washington Senators for outfielder Mike Menosky, infielder Eddie Foster and pitcher Harry Harper.

While other big-league pairs have been traded together twice, additional players usually accompanied the two to their new teams. Among other players swapped together twice were Johnny Hodapp and Bob Seeds, Red Kress and Bobo Newsom, Billy Cox and Preacher Roe, Clint Courtney and Bob Chakales, Ryne Duren and Jim Pisoni, Tom Morgan and Mickey McDermott, Ken Brett and Jim Lonborg, Joe Ferguson and Bobby Detherage and Ed Farmer and Gary Holle. (After Cox and Roe were traded together for a second time—the circumstances being a December 1954 relocation from the Brooklyn Dodgers to the Baltimore Orioles—Roe retired. The deal then was completed in March 1955 with an additional exchange of players and cash.)

RON SANTO
The first major league player to exercise his right to refuse a trade under the Basic Agreement's "10 and five" rule. In February 1973, big-league owners and players agreed on a new contract containing a stipulation that a player who had 10 or more years of major league service and had spent the last five years with the same club had the right to veto a trade. On December 5, 1973, Santo, a Chicago Cub since entering the majors in 1960, vetoed a deal that would have sent him to California (reportedly for Angels pitching prospects Andy Hassler and Bruce Heinbechner). The power-hitting third baseman, wanting to stay in Chicago, consented a week later to a swap shipping him to the crosstown White Sox. In return, the Sox received catcher Steve Swisher and pitchers Steve Stone, Ken Frailing and Jim Kremmel.

The "10 and five" rule had received its first test in March 1973 when Minnesota made plans to deal pitcher Jim Perry, a big-leaguer since 1959 and a Twins pitcher since 1963, to Detroit. Perry agreed to go to the Tigers, thus becoming the majors' first player with "10 and five" veto privileges to consent to a trade. In return for Perry, the Twins received pitching prospect Danny Fife and cash from the Tigers in the March 27 swap.

ED SAUER, HANK SAUER
Brothers who were involved in separate National League deals on the same day in 1949—and Ed Sauer was peddled twice before the day was out. On June 15, the St. Louis Cardinals sent Ed, an outfielder, to the Pittsburgh Pirates for cash, and the Pirates turned around and shipped Ed to the Boston Braves for catcher Phil Masi. Also that day, the Cincinnati Reds traded outfielders Hank Sauer and Frankie Baumholtz to the Chicago Cubs for outfielders Harry Walker and Peanuts Lowrey.

SEVEN

The number of games that Ernie Broglio won for the Chicago Cubs in the remainder of his big-league career after the Cubs gave up outfielder Lou Brock to obtain Broglio from the St. Louis Cardinals in a June 15, 1964, trade. While the swap was, in fact, a six-player deal—pitcher Bobby Shantz and outfielder Doug Clemens accompanied Broglio to Chicago and pitchers Paul Toth and Jack Spring moved to St. Louis with Brock—the principals clearly were Broglio, a 21-game winner for St. Louis in 1960 and an 18-game winner for the Cards in 1963, and Brock, a fleet outfielder whose enormous potential had gone largely untapped since his arrival in the majors at the end of the 1961 season. Broglio, who had a 3-5 record for the Cards in '64, was 4-7 for the Cubs the rest of the year and, beset by arm problems, finished 1-6 and 2-6 for Chicago in 1965 and 1966, respectively. He never pitched again in the majors, his big-league career having ended before he turned 31. Brock, batting .251 for the Cubs at the time of the trade, hit .348 for St. Louis in 103 games and helped the '64 Cardinals to the National League pennant and World Series crown. Brock went on to collect 3,023 career hits in the majors, steal a record 938 bases (including 118 in 1974, still an N.L. mark) and win election to the Hall of Fame in 1985.

17, 64

The number of transactions made between the New York Yankees and the Kansas City Athletics from March 1955 through June 1961 and the number of players involved in those deals. The powerful Yankees seemed to trade quantity for quality when dealing with the also-ran A's, often obtaining future stars, solid players or stretch-run help for packages of steady-but-unspectacular performers. In the view of many, the Yankees had developed a "parent club-farm team" relationship with Kansas City, tapping the Midwest pipeline for just the right player when the situation demanded it. The irony was that until '55—when the Philadelphia A's moved to Kansas City—K.C., in fact, had been a New York farm club, serving as a longtime Class AAA affiliate of the Yankees. The heavy trading between the two clubs came to a halt when Charlie Finley took ownership of the A's in December 1960.

Nine players made "round-trips" between New York and Kansas City during the six-year trading binge. Traded from the Yankees to the A's and then back to the Yanks were Enos Slaughter, Ralph Terry, Bob Cerv, Bob Martyn, Jack Urban and Milt Graff (the last three of whom, though, never appeared in a regular-season game with the Yankees); going from the Athletics to the Yanks and then back to the A's were Harry (Suitcase) Simpson, Murry Dickson and Art Ditmar.

Typical of the Yankees' good fortune in their dealings with Kansas City was the pinstripe success enjoyed by Roger Maris, Ralph Terry and Enos Slaughter. Outfielder Maris, infielder Joe DeMaestri and first baseman Kent Hadley were obtained from the A's in a December 11, 1959, swap in which New York traded pitcher Don Larsen, outfielders Hank Bauer and Norm Siebern and first baseman Marv Throneberry to Kansas City. Maris won the American League's Most Valuable Player honor the next two seasons while smashing a total of 100 home runs for the Yankees (including a record 61 in 1961). Terry began his big-league career with the Yankees in 1956 before moving to Kansas City in a June 15, 1957, deal. After what critics of Yankees-A's bartering called a little "seasoning," pitcher Terry was reacquired by New York in a May 26, 1959, deal and posted a 16-3 record for the Yankees in 1961, won 23 games in 1962 and notched 17 victories in 1963. Slaughter, a Yankee reserve in 1954, was traded to Kansas City on May 11, 1955, but was reacquired by New York via an August 25, 1956, purchase. The 40-year-old outfielder hit .289 for the Yanks in the last month of the season, then starred in the '56 World Series (hitting a game-winning homer and batting .350).

Kansas City profited from the swap mart, too, most notably as a result of its October 15, 1956, purchase of outfielder Cerv from the Yankees. In 1958, Cerv blossomed into one of the top power hitters in the majors, walloping 38 homers, driving in 104 runs and batting .305 for the A's.

ROYLE STILLMAN
Having driven in one run and batted .091 in 20 games for the 1976 Baltimore Orioles, this outfielder-first baseman was one of the 24 players available in major league baseball's first free-agent re-entry draft, held November 4, 1976. Stillman, like the other 23 big-leaguers on the open market, was eligible for the draft after failing to sign a contract in '76 and playing out his option that year (part of which he spent in the minor leagues). Obviously, Stillman, who wound up signing with the Chicago White Sox on December 5, was not one of the plums of the draft. Others in the pool were: Reggie Jackson, Don Gullett, Sal Bando, Rollie Fingers, Joe Rudi, Don Baylor, Bobby Grich, Doyle Alexander, Bert Campaneris, Bill Campbell, Dave Cash, Gene Tenace, Eric Soderholm, Nate Colbert, Paul Dade, Tito Fuentes, Wayne Garland, Willie McCovey, Richie Hebner, Gary Matthews, Steve Stone, Tim Nordbrook and Billy Smith.

The re-entry draft was formulated in an agreement between management and the MLPA as an outgrowth of arbitrator Peter Seitz's decision in December 1975 to grant free-agent status to pitchers Andy Messersmith and Dave McNally, both of whom had played without contracts in '75 (Messersmith with the Los Angeles Dodgers and McNally with the Montreal Expos until his retirement in June). Seitz's decision, upheld in subsequent court challenges, struck at the centerpiece of baseball's reserve system, the renewal clause, by which a team could renew the contract of a player into perpetuity. Seitz's ruling, in effect, no longer bound a player to one club until that player was released, traded or sold. (Messersmith moved to Atlanta, signing a free-agent contract in April 1976. McNally remained in retirement.)

Royle Stillman, who had seen only limited service for the Orioles, was probably the least known player among the 24 who made up baseball's first free-agent re-entry list in 1976. Stillman was signed by the White Sox.

PETE SUDER

One of eight men to play for all three managers in Philadelphia A's history. Infielder Suder played 1,014 games for Connie Mack (who guided the club from its inception in 1901 through 1950), 312 games for Jimmie Dykes (the American League team's pilot from 1951 through 1953) and 69 games for Eddie Joost (who directed the last Philadelphia A's entry, the 1954 club).

Also playing for all three Philadelphia A's pilots (with figures in parentheses indicating the number of games played under, in order, Mack, Dykes and

St. Louis Cardinals fans well remember Ernie Broglio and Bob Sykes, the pitchers who were traded in deals for outfielders Lou Brock (1964) and Willie McGee (1981), respectively. Broglio went on to win seven games for the Cubs and Sykes never appeared in a game for the Yankees.

Joost): Joe Astroth (108, 250, 77), Ed Burtschy (9, 7, 46), Joost (561, 337, 19), Alex Kellner (87, 92, 27), Carl Scheib (196, 127, 1) Bobby Shantz (69, 81, 7) and Elmer Valo (843, 302, 95).

ZERO

The number of games in which pitcher Bob Sykes appeared in the majors after the October 21, 1981, trade in which the New York Yankees dealt minor league outfielder Willie McGee to the St. Louis Cardinals in exchange for Sykes. Sykes, 26 years old, had a 23-26 career record in the majors at the time of the deal; McGee, two weeks from his 23rd birthday, had played five years in the minor leagues and was coming off a .322 season in Class AA ball. Sykes, a lefthander who had incurred various arm and shoulder ailments earlier in his career, was troubled again by injuries in 1982. After compiling a 1-2 record for Class AAA Columbus and a 2-1 mark for Class AA Nashville in '82, Sykes disappeared from baseball. McGee, meanwhile, helped the Cardinals to the 1982 World Series title and won the National League's Most Valuable Player honor in 1985 when he hit a league-leading .353 in the Cards' pennant-winning year.

A December 14, 1982, deal in which the Cardinals sent promising prospects Bobby Meacham (shortstop) and Stan Javier (outfielder) to the Yankees for three not-so-prime minor leaguers was viewed in many baseball circles as an apparent "pot sweetener" for the McGee deal.

SEVENTH INNING
Major accomplishments
in the minor leagues

BUZZ ARLETT
He slugged four home runs in one game twice in a five-week span of the 1932 International League season. Playing for Baltimore in a June 1 game against Reading, outfielder Arlett belted four homers and drove in seven runs as the Orioles defeated the Keys, 14-13. Then, in the first game of a July 4 Baltimore-Reading doubleheader, he repeated the four-homer salvo and knocked in nine runs as the Orioles romped to a 21-10 victory. (For good measure, Arlett homered once in the nightcap of the Independence Day twin bill.)

The switch-hitting Arlett, who finished the '32 season with 54 home runs, hit 30 or more homers eight times in the minor leagues. His only big-league experience came in 1931 when, after 13 years with Oakland of the Pacific Coast League, he played a full season with the Philadelphia Phillies. After performing capably for the Phils (.313 batting average, 18 homers and 72 RBIs), Arlett was back in the minors the next season and excelling for Baltimore.

ORIE ARNTZEN
The Sporting News' Minor League Player of the Year in 1949—at age 39. Pitching for Albany of the Eastern League, Arntzen compiled a 25-2 record. He walked only 41 batters in 216 innings and fashioned a 2.79 earned-run

Arntzen, who broke into professional ball in 1931, spent one season in the major leagues. As a member of the 1943 Philadelphia Athletics, he won four of 17 decisions.

JOE BAUMAN
The all-time single-season homer champion in Organized Baseball (the umbrella under which both the major leagues and the National Association's minor leagues fall). Bauman slammed 72 home runs for Roswell of the Longhorn League in 1954, achieving his record total in 138 games and also driving in 224 runs and batting an even .400.

From 1952 through 1955, Bauman averaged 55 homers per season in the Longhorn League (compiling yearly totals of 50, 53, 72 and 46).

TED BEARD
Hollywood outfielder who in a 3 1/2-week span of the 1953 Pacific Coast

League season accomplished the feats of slugging four home runs in one game and reeling off 12 consecutive hits over four contests.

Beard, a 5-foot-8, 165-pounder, had attracted attention in 1950 when, in a stint with the Pittsburgh Pirates, he became the first player since Babe Ruth (in 1935) to homer over the right-field stands at Forbes Field.

Beard, who spent parts of five seasons with the Pirates and saw limited service with the Chicago White Sox in two other years, batted .198 with six homers in 474 career at-bats in the majors.

STEVE BILKO

One of the most feared hitters in the history of the high minors, as reflected by his successive 50-plus homer seasons for Los Angeles of the Pacific Coast League. Playing 162 games for the PCL's Angels in 1956, Bilko smashed 55 home runs, knocked in 164 runs and batted .360 (all league-leading figures). In 1957, Bilko slammed 56 homers for the Angels and drove in 140 runs—both league highs—while hitting .300 in 158 games.

Bilko also topped the PCL in homers in 1955, hitting 37 for Los Angeles in 168 games. He batted .328 that year and had 124 RBIs.

WADE BOGGS, CAL RIPKEN JR.

The opposing third basemen in the longest game in Organized Baseball history, a 33-inning International League contest between Pawtucket and Rochester that was played in 1981. Boggs collected four hits in 12 at-bats for Pawtucket, while Ripken was 2 for 13 for Rochester. Both played errorless ball in the field.

Two years later, Ripken won Most Valuable Player honors in the American League while playing shortstop for the Baltimore Orioles and Boggs, having settled into the third-base job for the Boston Red Sox, captured his first A.L. batting championship.

FRAN BONIAR

Dodger farmhand who enjoyed two of the best seasons in minor league history, batting .435 for Hornell of the Pony League in 1955 and .436 for Reno of the California League in 1957.

Outfielder Boniar, who embellished those seasons with home run/runs-batted-in totals of 18 and 100 and then 11 and 138, never made the major leagues and played as high as the Class AAA level only briefly.

IKE BOONE

The minors' Ty Cobb, having posted the best lifetime average, .370, in

Steve Bilko, one of the most prodigious power hitters in minor league history for the Pacific Coast League's Los Angeles Angels, is pictured (right) with another Bilko, Phil Silvers, who played Sergeant Ernie Bilko in the late 1950s on television's hit comedy series 'The Phil Silvers Show.'

baseball's "bush leagues." Boone, a .319 career hitter in the majors in 356 games (he batted .333 and .330 for the Boston Red Sox in 1924 and 1925), played 1,857 games in the minor leagues and posted such full-season averages as .407, .402, .389 and .380. And, in an 83-game stint (310 at-bats) for the Pacific Coast League's Missions club in 1930, he batted .448.

Danny Boone, Ike's brother, also was a robust minor league hitter. A onetime pitcher (he went 8-13 for the Philadelphia A's, Detroit Tigers and Cleveland Indians in a big-league career that ended in 1923), Danny became an outfielder and batted .356 in 1,336 minor league games.

The Boones combined for 101 minor league home runs in 1929, Ike slugging 55 for the PCL Missions and Danny walloping 46 for High Point of the Piedmont League.

RAY BOYER
Pawtucket player who figured in the battle for the 1980 International League batting championship—despite the fact he hit .238 in '80. When Pawtucket came to bat in the bottom of the ninth inning of its season finale against Toledo, the Mud Hens' Dave Engle had a batting average of .30674 and Pawtucket's Wade Boggs had a league-leading mark of .30695. With little threat of extra innings (Toledo led, 6-1), Engle surely had made his last trip to the plate of the season. Boggs, though, would bat fourth in the Pawtucket ninth—if the Red Sox's top farm club got that far into the order. Toledo players, wanting Engle to win the batting title by whatever means, made certain Pawtucket got that far. After Pawtucket's first two batters were retired in the ninth, the light-hitting Boyer was walked intentionally. Boyer, thinking turnabout was fair play in this help-a-teammate-in-need scenario, set out for second base in hopes of being thrown out to end the game. No luck. He didn't even draw a throw. Boyer then trotted toward third base and, again, the Toledo catcher (Ray Smith) ignored him. What next? With Boggs at the plate ("We were losing and I wanted to hit," Wade said later), Boyer lit out for home plate—and pitcher Wally Sarmiento sailed a pitch to the screen. Toledo had achieved its objective: Boggs would have to bat. And, with the batting title on the line, the Pawtucket star grounded out. Toledo had won (6-2)—and so had Engle (.30674 to Boggs' .30622).

GEORGE BRUNET
A pitcher in Organized Baseball for 33 consecutive seasons, 1953 through 1985, and the minor leagues' all-time leader in strikeouts with 3,175. He also holds the Mexican League record for career shutouts, 55, despite the fact he didn't enter the league until 1973, a year in which he turned 38 years old. And Brunet was an effective Mexican League hurler even at age 48, fashioning a 1.93 earned-run average in 186 innings of work in 1983.

Brunet posted a 69-93 record in 15 big-league seasons. The lefthander was a 13-

game winner twice for the California Angels, and he tossed 15 shutouts overall in the majors.

JOHN CANTLEY
Opelika pitcher who hit three bases-loaded home runs in a June 5, 1914, Georgia-Alabama League game against Talladega, a contest he won, 19-1.

WALTER CARLISLE
He pulled off an unassisted triple play in a 1911 Pacific Coast League game — while playing center field. With Los Angeles runners on first and second base and no one out in the sixth inning of a July 19 contest, Roy Akin drove a pitch toward center field. Vernon's Carlisle, breaking in on the ball, made a sensational shoe-top catch. Carlisle, seeing that the runners had been in flight, proceeded to second base and stepped on the bag and then continued on to first to complete the triple killing.

MOOSE CLABAUGH
Outfielder whose 62-homer output in the low minors in 1926 earned him a late-season shot in the major leagues. After his remarkable season for Tyler of the East Texas League, Clabaugh was obtained by Brooklyn and appeared in 11 National League games in '26. Used mainly as a pinch-hitter, the 24-year-old Clabaugh had one hit (a double) in 14 at-bats—and never again played in the majors.

Clabaugh did more than hit the long ball in the minors. He wound up winning five minor league batting championships and had a lifetime hitting mark of .339 in baseball's "bushes."

NIG CLARKE
Corsicana catcher who stroked eight—count 'em eight—home runs against Texarkana in a June 15, 1902, Texas League game. Taking advantage of a short fence—the game was played at a non-league park in Ennis because Sunday games were not permitted in Corsicana—Corsicana hit 21 home runs and won a 51-3 laugher. Seven Corsicana players had five or more hits in the contest, and Clarke was one of three hitters who went 8 for 8.

While some historians claim Clarke hit only three homers in the game (the typographical similarity of an "8" and a "3" being cited in various ways for an alleged mixup), the latest studies support the credibility of the eight-homer feat.

Clarke played in the majors from 1905 through 1911 and again in 1919 and 1920. He hit a total of six homers in 506 big-league games (with the Cleveland Indians, Detroit Tigers, St. Louis Browns, Philadelphia Phillies and Pittsburgh Pirates).

Corsicana catcher Nig Clarke took advantage of a short fence during a 1902 Texas League game and hit eight home runs against Texarkana. Bob Crues put together an incredible season for Amarillo of the West Texas-New Mexico League in 1948, hitting 69 home runs, driving in 254 runs and batting .404.

TONY CLONINGER

A hard-throwing pitcher who in a 10-game stint with Cedar Rapids of the Three-I League in 1959 compiled a 0-9 record and a 9.59 earned-run average (with 58 walks in 46 innings contributing to his troubles).

Two years after his Three-I League disaster, Cloninger was with the Milwaukee Braves. A 7-2 pitcher for the National League club in 1961, Cloninger parlayed his improved control into 19- and 24-victory seasons for Milwaukee in 1964 and 1965 and a total of 113 major league victories.

BOB COLEMAN

A manager in the minors for 35 seasons, he first guided a team in 1919 (Mobile) and last piloted a minor league club in 1957 (Evansville). Coleman, second on the minors' managerial victory list with 2,496 games won, had four managerial stints—totaling 20 years—with Evansville's Three-I League franchise. He guided the Indiana team from 1928 through 1931, 1938 through 1942, 1946 through 1949 and 1951 through '57.

Coleman, a former reserve catcher in the majors, managed the Boston Braves in 1944 and for more than half of the 1945 season.

CORDELE
The Georgia-Florida League team that in 1952 didn't exactly rely on the long ball. The Cordele Athletics, fifth-place finishers in the league with a 66-73 record, hit one home run in the entire season. Third baseman Ralph Betcher connected for Cordele in the club's 73rd game of the year.

BOB CRUES
In 1948, while playing for Amarillo of the West Texas-New Mexico League, he put together what surely ranks—in terms of sheer numbers, regardless of the competition or playing conditions—as the greatest all-around single-season performance in professional baseball history. Competing in a Class C league little-known as a breeding ground for future major leaguers but well-known for its small ball parks, Crues hammered 69 home runs and drove in 254 runs (a record for Organized Baseball)—and he posted those figures in a 140-game schedule. Sure, but could he hit for average? Would you believe .404? That's the batting mark Crues fashioned, based on his 228 hits in 565 at-bats.

MATTHEW MARIO (MATT) CUOMO
An outfielder who appeared in 81 games for the Pittsburgh Pirates' Brunswick farm club of the Georgia-Florida League in 1952 and batted .244 with one home run and 26 runs batted in.

While Cuomo never realized most players' ambition of reaching the big leagues, Brunswick teammate Fred Green did. Lefthanded pitcher Green, a 20-game winner for Brunswick, made the majors in 1959 and was a member of the 1960 World Series-champion Pittsburgh Pirates. On the other hand, Mario Cuomo made the "big time" in another field—he was elected governor of New York in 1982 and re-elected to that post in 1986 and 1990.

STEVE DALKOWSKI
Pitcher who could throw a ball through a brick wall—that, or 10 feet *over* it. Regarded as one of the prime prospects in baseball history, Dalkowski had blazing—perhaps even unprecedented—speed. But the lefthander also had monumental—perhaps even unprecedented—control problems. Signed by the Baltimore Orioles in 1957, Dalkowski averaged 17 walks and 15 strikeouts per nine innings in his first five seasons of pro ball (1,022 walks and 907 strikeouts in 537 innings) while compiling a 19-52 won-lost record. Dalkowski abruptly harnessed his skills in 1962, averaging nearly 11 strikeouts and not quite 6 1/2 walks per nine innings for Elmira of the Eastern League. And he had a shot at making the Orioles' roster in the spring of 1963 until beset by arm problems. Never again the overpowering pitcher he once was (but, by the same token, never again the wild man of his earlier days), Dalkowski began to drift.

Lefthander Steve Dalkowski, shown warming up in 1963 under the watchful eye of Orioles pitching coach Harry Brecheen, might have been the fastest, and wildest, pitcher ever to play Organized Baseball.

Baltimore released him during the 1965 season and he caught on with a California Angels farm club. But Dalkowski never pitched again professionally after '65, winding up with a 46-80 career record in the minors. Through at age 26 without having thrown a pitch in the majors, Dalkowski stood out as a classic case of what-might-have-been.

JOE DiMAGGIO
Owner of the longest hitting streak (56 consecutive games) in major league history, he has the second longest batting streak in minor league history. Playing his first full season of professional ball in 1933, the 18-year-old DiMaggio hit safely in 61 straight games for San Francisco of the Pacific Coast League.

DOUGLAS
The Arizona-Mexico League team that in an August 19, 1958, game against Chihuahua hit nine home runs—one by each player in the lineup. Connecting for the Copper Kings were left fielder Ron Wilkins, center fielder Andy Prevedello, right fielder Fred Filipelli, first baseman Frank (Dutch) Van Burkleo, second baseman Luis Torres, third baseman Darrell McCall, shortstop Don Pulford, catcher Rich Binford and pitcher Bob Clear (also the club's

GUILTY!

SET NEW ALL TIME ORGANIZED BASEBALL RECORD

NEVER ACCOMPLISHED BEFORE — LIKELY NEVER AGAIN

DOUGLAS, ARIZONA, POPULATION 12,000. SMALLEST SPORTS MINDED CITY IN CLASS C BASEBALL. WINNERS OF 1958 ARIZONA-MEXICO LEAGUE PENNANT. ON AUGUST 19th AT CHIHUAHUA, MEXICO EACH OF THE ABOVE NINE DOUGLAS PLAYERS HIT AN "OUT OF THE PARK" HOME RUN. THE DISTANCES GREATER THAN SEVERAL MAJOR LEAGUE PARKS.

Douglas, Ariz., was rightfully proud of its nine players who went on a record-setting home run binge in a 1958 Arizona-Mexico League game.

manager). Wilkins went 6 for 6 as the Copper Kings won, 22-8, in a contest stopped after eight innings because of darkness.

DICK DRAGO, DARRELL CLARK
Rocky Mount teammates who in a May 15, 1966, Carolina League double-header both pitched seven-inning no-hitters against Greensboro. Drago was a 5-0 victor in the opener and Clark was a 2-0 winner in the nightcap.

Drago went on to win 108 games in a 13-year big-league career that began in 1969 with the Kansas City Royals. While Clark never made the majors, his batterymate on May 15, 1966, was Jim Leyland, who 20 years later was managing the Pittsburgh Pirates.

HARRY DUNLOP
Bristol catcher whose error with two out in the ninth inning of a May 13, 1952, Appalachian League contest against Welch gave teammate Ron Necciai the opportunity to shoot for a game-total 27 strikeouts. Necciai had 25 strikeouts and was one out away from completing a no-hitter when he faced Welch center fielder Bobby Hammond. Having allowed three baserunners to that point (a hit batsman, a walk and an error), the 19-year-old Necciai proceeded to strike out Hammond—but the low pitch eluded Dunlop and Hammond reached first base. With his strikeout total at 26, Necciai then fanned left fielder Bob Kendrick to nail down a 7-0 no-hit triumph that featured, incredibly, 27 strikeouts.

Dunlop was Bill Bell's catcher when Bell hurled consecutive no-hitters for Bristol on May 22 and May 26—meaning that the Bristol receiver had caught three no-hitters in 14 days.

While Dunlop never made it to the big leagues as a player, he has served as a coach for the Kansas City Royals, Chicago Cubs, Cincinnati Reds and San Diego Padres.

VALLIE EAVES, JERRY EAVES
A father-son combination that pitched for the Hobbs club of the Southwestern League—in the same season. Jerry Eaves, 20, worked in 15 games and compiled a 2-4 record for Hobbs in 1957 and father Vallie, a 45-year-old former major leaguer who served the Hobbs club mainly in an advisory role, posted a 1-0 record in four appearances that year.

Vallie Eaves, who broke into the big leagues in 1935 with the Philadelphia A's and also pitched for the Chicago White Sox and Chicago Cubs, managed a 4-8 record in the majors.

EL PASO, BEAUMONT
Texas League teams that scored a total of 89 runs in successive games in the 1983 season. On April 30, host El Paso scored in each of its at-bats—the Diablos had four six-run innings and one five-run outburst—and outslugged Beaumont,

Rocky Mount pitchers Dick Drago (left) and Darrell Clark (right) posed with Manager Al Federoff after their no-hitters in both ends of a 1966 doubleheader. Eleanor Engle looked out of place in the Harrisburg Senators' dugout in her brief 1952 stay with the Inter-State League team.

35-21, in a wind-swept game that featured 56 hits (nine of which were home runs) and nine errors. El Paso's Mike Felder and Stan Levi each rapped two home runs, with Felder driving in nine runs and Levi knocking in seven (Levi also scored seven times). Any notion that the Texas League rivals had ended their scoring binge with the completion of the April 30 contest was disproved in their very next meeting when Beaumont struck for 11 runs in the top of the first inning on the way to a 13-0 lead. El Paso battled back, eventually coming within 15-13, but Beaumont wound up a 20-13 winner in a May 1 game that had "only" 36 hits (including five homers) and four errors.

ELEANOR ENGLE
A 24-year-old stenographer who in June 1952 signed to play with the Harrisburg Senators of the Inter-State League. After watching her work out at shortstop, one veteran scout cracked, "She threw like a girl." Whatever that meant, there were other opinions. One reporter said she "scooped up hard grounders and threw to first base like a pro," and a club director suggested that "she can hit the ball a lot better than some of the fellows on the club." Harrisburg Manager Buck Etchison vehemently opposed the presence of Mrs. Engle on his roster, and National Association President George Trautman, backed by Commissioner Ford Frick, quickly voided the signing and made it known that any future such attempts in Organized Baseball to sign female players would be subject to severe penalties.

Mrs. Engle, while having appeared in uniform for Harrisburg, never played for the Senators.

FRANK ETCHBERGER, JIM MITCHELL
Minor league pitchers who tossed no-hitters—in the same game. The hard-to-fathom double no-hitter unfolded on August 20, 1952, in Batavia, N.Y., as Bradford slipped past Batavia, 1-0, in a Pony League game. Bradford's Etchberger walked five batters and struck out six while holding Batavia hitless; Mitchell issued one base on balls, hit a batter and fanned seven Bradford hitters in his no-hit loss. The game's only run was scored in the eighth inning on a walk, a sacrifice, a wild pitch and an error by Batavia's player-manager, shortstop George Genovese.

59
The number of minor leagues in operation in 1949, a record one-season total.

LEW FLICK
Little Rock outfielder who banged out nine consecutive hits in a 19-inning Southern Association game played on July 21, 1946. Playing against the Memphis Chicks in the first game of a doubleheader, Flick hit safely in his first nine at-bats before grounding out. He followed up his 9-for-10 plate performance by going 3 for 3 in the nightcap.

Flick teammate Kerby Farrell, who went on to manage the Cleveland Indians in 1957, had eight hits for Little Rock in the opener of the twin bill. Despite the heroics by Flick and Farrell and the fact Little Rock pulled off a triple play in the long contest, the Travelers wound up 8-6 losers.

.477
Willie Mays' batting average for the Minneapolis Millers when he left the American Association club to make his major league debut with the New York Giants in May 1951. Mays' 35-game statistics for the Millers included eight home runs and 30 runs batted in.

LOU FRIERSON, CECIL DUNN
Players who gave the minor leagues two five-homers-in-one-game performers in less than two calendar years. On May 30, 1934, Frierson smacked five home runs for Paris in a West Dixie League game (a contest that Paris lost), and on April 29, 1936, Dunn belted five homers for Alexandria in an Evangeline League game.

PETE GRAY
One-armed outfielder who had a scintillating minor league season before winning a spot on the St. Louis Browns' roster in 1945. Appearing in 129 games for Memphis of the Southern Association in 1944, Gray batted .333, stole a league-leading 68 bases and topped the league's outfielders in fielding percentage with a .983 figure. Additionally, he struck out only 12 times and, despite an obvious inability to hit for power, managed to rap five home runs for the Chicks.

BRUCE HAROLDSON
Lewiston relief pitcher who entered an August 6, 1961, Northwest League game against Tri-Cities in the sixth inning with the bases loaded and no one out and retired the side—with one pitch. Tri Cities' Ray Youngdahl slapped Haroldson's first offering to third baseman Dick Green, who stepped on the bag for one out and threw on to Ossie Chavarria. After getting the forceout at second base, Chavarria rifled the ball to first baseman Ed Olsen to nail Youngdahl and complete a triple play.

Five years later, Green and Chavarria were teammates with the Kansas City A's.

JOE HAUSER
The only player in Organized Baseball history to have two 60-homer seasons. First baseman Hauser slugged 63 home runs for Baltimore of the International League in 1930 and belted 69 for Minneapolis of the American Association in 1933.

Hauser played six seasons in the big leagues—all of them before his 60-homer productions in the minors. His best year in the majors was 1924, when he hit 27 homers and drove in 115 runs for the Philadelphia A's. In 1929, as a member of the Cleveland Indians, Hauser wound up his big-league career at age 30.

LEE HEFFNER
Welch third baseman who started triple plays in consecutive innings for his Appalachian League team in a July 26, 1954, game against Johnson City. In the seventh inning, Heffner fielded a ground ball, stepped on third base for one out and threw on to second for out No. 2. The relay to first base completed the triple killing. In the eighth inning, Heffner snared a line drive and rifled a throw to second base to double up the runner. The relay to first caught another runner off base.

Lodi of the California League pulled off two triple plays in one game in 1978. In a July 25 contest, Lodi turned a first-inning line drive off the bat of Fresno's Jim Rothford into a triple play and then converted a fifth-inning grounder by Bill Young into an around-the-horn triple killing. (Bob Brenly, three years away from making his major league debut with the San Francisco Giants, was a Fresno baserunner when each triple play occurred.)

HOLLYWOOD
The Pacific Coast League club whose players trotted out for an April 1, 1950, game against Portland attired in T-shirt-style uniform tops and pin-striped shorts. "This isn't a gag (April Fools' Day or not), nor are we 'going Hollywood,' " Stars Manager Fred Haney said of the shorts. "It stands to reason that players should be faster wearing them—and that half step down to first wins or loses many games." And, of course, the outfits seemed a natural for yet-to-come steamy summer days. Fans greeted the scantily clad Hollywood players with catcalls and hoots, and Portland Manager Bill Sweeney joined in the kidding by wearing an apron and a purple hat (over a long, curly wig) when he appeared at home plate for the lineup exchange, at which he presented Haney with a bouquet of pansies.

While the shorts style subsequently was tried out elsewhere in the minors in 1950, the Hollywood club wound up wearing the "briefs" infrequently.

WALTER JUSTIS
Three years after seeing his only big-league service (two appearances with the Detroit Tigers), he pitched four no-hitters for Lancaster during the 1908 Ohio State League season.

BILL KENNEDY
Rocky Mount pitcher who in 1946 posted a 28-3 Coastal Plain League record, embellished by a 1.03 earned-run average and 456 strikeouts in 280 innings.

Hollywood Stars Manager Fred Haney models the uniform that caught everybody by surprise on April 1, 1950. Hub Kittle, at age 63, became the oldest player in Organized Baseball history when he started and pitched one inning for Springfield, the Cardinals' Triple-A affiliate, in 1980.

Kennedy reached the majors in 1948 and wound up pitching for five clubs (Cleveland Indians, St. Louis Browns, Chicago White Sox, Boston Red Sox and Cincinnati Reds) in a big-league career that ended in 1957.

HUB KITTLE

At age 63, the oldest man to play in an Organized Baseball game. While serving as a minor league pitching instructor for the St. Louis Cardinals, Kittle, six months past his 63rd birthday, started for Springfield against Iowa in an August 27, 1980, American Association game. He retired the side in order in the first inning—two fly balls and a groundout doing the trick—and, as planned, threw one pitch in the second inning before leaving the contest.

Kittle, a longtime minor league pitcher and manager, never played in the major

Pawtucket first baseman Dave Koza gets a warm reception after delivering a 33rd-inning single that beat Rochester and ended the longest game in baseball history.

leagues but did serve as a coach with the Houston Astros and the St. Louis Cardinals. He was, in fact, pitching coach for the 1982 World Series-champion Cards.

DAVE KOZA

Pawtucket first baseman whose bases-loaded single ended the longest game in Organized Baseball history, a 33-inning International League contest between Pawtucket and Rochester that began on the night of April 18, 1981, in Pawtucket and ended on June 23 in the Rhode Island city. Thirty-two innings of the game were played April 18-19—the contest was suspended at 4:07 a.m. with the clubs were deadlocked, 2-2 (Rochester having seized a 1-0 lead in the seventh inning, Pawtucket tying the game in the ninth and each club scoring a run in the 21st). When play resumed more than nine weeks later on Rochester's next visit to Pawtucket, the home club broke through in its first at-bat. Marty Barrett was hit by a pitch, Chico Walker singled Barrett to third and, with no one out, Russ Laribee was walked intentionally. Rochester pitcher Cliff Speck then was summoned to replace reliever Steve Grilli, who had entered the game at the outset of the inning. Speck and Koza battled to a 2-2 count before Koza singled to left field. Pawtucket 3, Rochester 2.

After battling 8 hours and 7 minutes in the April portion of the marathon, the two clubs needed just 18 minutes in the June continuation to decide the issue. The total time of 8:25 also established a professional record.

DICK LANE

After hitting five home runs in 125 minor league games (123 in the Cotton States League and two in the Southern Association) in 1947, he slammed five homers in one Central League game in 1948. Playing for Muskegon against Fort Wayne on July 3, Lane homered in the first, fourth (connecting twice), seventh and eighth innings and knocked in 10 runs. Three of Lane's homers were off Walter (Boom-Boom) Beck, Fort Wayne's player-manager and a former big-league pitcher.

Lane, who finished the '48 season with 12 home runs for Muskegon, saw his only major league service in 1949. Playing for the Chicago White Sox, outfielder Lane got into 12 games but managed only five hits (all singles) in 42 at-bats.

TONY LAZZERI

While Babe Ruth made major league history by cracking 60 home runs in 1927, it was Lazzeri—a teammate of Babe's on the '27 New York Yankees— who was the first man to smash 60 homers in an Organized Baseball season. Playing 197 games for Salt Lake City in 1925, Lazzeri drilled exactly 60 homers and knocked in 222 runs for the Pacific Coast League team.

JIM LEMON

He accomplished the feat of slugging four home runs in an all-star game— the 1955 Southern Association classic. Playing for the league's All-Stars against first-place Birmingham, Chattanooga's Lemon socked homers in the first, third, seventh and ninth innings and drove in seven runs in the July 19 game, which the All-Star squad won, 10-5.

Lemon had big seasons for the Washington Senators in 1959 and 1960, hitting 33 home runs in '59 and 38 in '60 and notching exactly 100 RBIs each year.

BOB LENNON

While the New York Giants marched toward a National League pennant and World Series championship in 1954, Giants farmhand Lennon buoyed the New Yorkers' hopes of future success by clouting 64 home runs for Nashville of the Southern Association in '54. Lennon never made the grade with the Giants, though; in fact, he appeared in only 29 games for New York (three in '54, 26 in 1956) and failed to hit a homer for the N.L. club.

While his banner season at Nashville (a noted home run haven because of its cozy Sulphur Dell home grounds) shot Lennon into the spotlight as a potential big-league slugger, the Brooklyn native finished his career with one home run in the majors (in 79 at-bats). Playing for the Chicago Cubs in an April 30, 1957, game at Brooklyn's Ebbets Field, Lennon hammered a three-run shot off the Dodgers' Sal Maglie.

D.C. MILLER
Wichita Falls outfielder who finished the 1947 Big State League season with 57 home runs and 196 runs batted in—and did not lead the league in either category. Sherman-Denison's Buck Frierson, who had played briefly with the Cleveland Indians in 1941, was the Big State's homer and RBI champion in '47, boasting totals of 58 and 197.

BRENT MUSBURGER
A noted television sports journalist of today and a former newspaper reporter in Chicago, he served as a Midwest League umpire in 1959 before pursuing other interests.

KENNY MYERS
Las Vegas slugger who bashed two bases-loaded home runs in the third inning of a 1947 Sunset League game—teammate Ned Klingensmith, a pitcher, also smacked a grand slam in the believe-it-or-not inning—as the Wranglers annihilated Ontario, 30-5. In addition to his exploits in Las Vegas' 16-run inning, Myers hit two other homers in the contest.

Myers later became a noted scout for the Brooklyn and Los Angeles Dodgers and the California Angels.

Armando Flores, playing for Laredo, hit two bases-full homers in the eighth inning of a June 25, 1952, Gulf Coast League game, and Redwood's Lance Junker walloped two grand slams in the ninth inning of a June 30, 1983, California League contest.

RON NECCIAI, BILL BELL
The pitching wunderkinds of the Pittsburgh Pirates' Bristol farm club of the Appalachian League in 1952. Necciai, a month from his 20th birthday, struck out 27 batters in a nine-inning no-hitter against Welch on May 13 and then fanned 24 Kingsport batters on May 21 before being promoted within the Pirates' organization. Bell, 18, pitched consecutive no-hit games against Kingsport (May 22) and Bluefield (May 26) and fired a third no-hitter, a seven-inning affair, against Bluefield (August 25).

One of Necciai's 27 strikeout victims on May 13 reached base when the catcher couldn't handle the third strike, meaning that one Welch batter (right fielder Bob Ganung, who grounded out) was not retired on strikes.

Necciai posted a 4-0 record for Bristol in 1952, notching 109 strikeouts and

John Neves didn't hit much for Fargo-Moorhead of the Northern League in 1951, but he did raise some eyebrows with his backward '7' uniform number.

allowing only 10 hits in 43 innings. After going 7-9 with 172 strikeouts in 126 innings for Burlington of the Carolina League, Necciai finished the '52 season with the Pirates, for whom he was 14 with 31 strikeouts in 55 innings. Bell, who had started the 1952 season with Burlington as he fought control problems, went 11-3 for Bristol and also earned a call-up from Pittsburgh. In four appearances with the '52 Pirates, Bell was 0-1.

After 1952, the careers of Necciai and Bell plummeted. Wildness continued to haunt Bell (he had walked 11 batters in his first no-hitter of 1952), and arm problems and other physical ailments contributed to both pitchers' rapid decline. Only Bell, with one relief appearance for Pittsburgh in 1955, appeared in the majors after '52.

JOHN NEVES
A .240-hitting second baseman for Fargo-Moorhead of the Northern League in 1951, he wore a backward "7" on his uniform—reflecting the fact that spelling out S-E-V-E-N in reverse fashion would produce his last name.

1956
The year in which three minor league players walloped 60 or more home runs. Leading the way was Dick Stuart, who poled 66 homers for Lincoln of the Western League. Ken Guettler hit 62 homers for Shreveport of the Texas League that season, while Forrest (Frosty) Kennedy rapped exactly 60 for the Southwestern League's Plainview club.

BOB OJEDA
The winning pitcher in the longest game in the history of professional baseball. Ojeda worked only one inning and threw just 13 pitches, but he was credited with the victory in Pawtucket's 3-2, 33-inning triumph over Rochester in a 1981 International League game. Ojeda replaced Bruce Hurst, who had allowed no runs and two hits over five innings, in the top of the 33rd of a 2-2 game. After Ojeda held Rochester at bay, Pawtucket scored a game-winning run in the bottom of the inning.

Ojeda was Pawtucket's eighth pitcher of the game. The loser was Steve Grilli, the fifth of Rochester's six hurlers. Grilli succeeded Jim Umbarger, who had pitched 10 innings of shutout relief (allowing only four hits, striking out nine and walking none).

ROGER OSENBAUGH
Sacramento hurler who, according to Manager Tommy Heath, needed a "stiff workout" against Los Angeles on June 22, 1957, to combat the effects of a recent illness and an accompanying lack of pitching time. "Stiff" hardly describes the kind of workout Osenbaugh got against the Angels. Los Angeles raked Osenbaugh for 22 runs and 18 hits—nine of them home runs— before Heath

decided his pitcher had endured enough, a decision that came after 6 2/3 innings. Hitting stars for the Angels included Bert Hamric, who rapped three home runs, and George (Sparky) Anderson, who walloped a bases-full homer (his first professional home run since 1953).

Despite the merciless pounding, Osenbaugh was effective enough overall for Sacramento in 1957 (9-14 record, 4.36 earned-run average for a team that finished 63-105) to be drafted by the Pittsburgh Pirates at the '57 winter meetings. Osenbaugh failed to make the Pirates' roster in 1958, though, and never appeared in the major leagues.

PAUL OWENS
Best known as manager of the 1983 National League champion Philadelphia Phillies (as the club's general manager, he fired Manager Pat Corrales at midseason and took over the managerial reins himself), he was a two-time .400 hitter in the low minors. In 1951, Owens broke into pro ball by batting a Pony League-leading .407 for Olean. Six years later, as Olean's player-manager, Owens again topped the league (renamed the New York-Pennsylvania League) in hitting and did so with a familiar figure—.407.

SATCHEL PAIGE
At age 50, he made 37 pitching appearances for Miami of the International League in 1956—and compiled an earned-run average of 1.86. He won 11 games, lost four and walked only 28 batters while striking out 79 in 111 innings.

RANCE PLESS
Denver player who socked four bases-loaded home runs for the American Association club in a 34-day period of the 1957 season. Pless' spree began July 3 when, in his debut with the Bears after his acquisition from Omaha, he hit two home runs, one of them a grand slam. Pless hit another bases-full shot three nights later, connected again with the bases loaded on July 30 and cracked another grand slam on August 5.

PONCA CITY, GREENVILLE
Sooner State League clubs that executed triple plays in successive half innings of the first game of a June 28, 1957, doubleheader. Ponca City's Carl Reynolds lined into a triple play in the bottom of the first inning of the opener, and Greenville's Carlos Mobley followed with a triple-play liner in the top of the second.

CHARLEY PRIDE
He had a 0-1 pitching record for Fond du Lac of the Wisconsin State League in 1953 and made three appearances without a decision (but collected two hits in five at-bats) for Missoula of the Pioneer League in 1960 before eventually

Former Negro League great Satchel Paige made 37 appearances for Miami of the International League in 1956 at age 50, finishing 11-4 with a 1.86 ERA.

making it big in another line of work—country-and-western singing.

FRANK RAMSAY
The night after Bristol's Bill Bell had baffled Bluefield for his third no-hitter of the 1952 Appalachian League season, teammate Ramsay went to the mound against the Bluefield club and pitched a 1-0 no-hit game.

Ramsay's no-hitter, which came on August 26, was the Bristol staff's third of the year against Bluefield and its fifth and last of the season overall.

Jackie Robinson gets a handshake from Montreal Royals teammate George Shuba after hitting a home run in his first game in Organized Baseball at Jersey City's Roosevelt Stadium on April 18, 1946.

GARY REDUS, WILLIE AIKENS

Organized Baseball performers who not only cracked the stratospheric .400 batting level in a minor league season, but topped the .450 mark in the process. Redus, playing in the short-season (68 games) Pioneer League in 1978, batted .462 for Billings. In 1986, Aikens hit .454 for Puebla of the Mexican League.

JOE RELFORD

With Statesboro fans taunting the visiting Fitzgerald club with jeers of "Put in the batboy" after the hometown club built a 13-0 lead in a July 19, 1952, Georgia State League game, Fitzgerald Manager Charlie Ridgeway did just that—and the 12-year-old Relford was the youngster he summoned. Getting approval from umpire Ed Kubick, Ridgeway sent up Relford as a pinch-hitter in the eighth inning and the batboy (a black who broke the league's color barrier) grounded sharply to third base. Relford stayed in the game, taking over in center field, and sparkled defensively by making a sensational catch against the fence.

The next day, the Georgia State League fired Kubick for his role in the batboy-playing affair and slapped Ridgeway with a fine and suspension.

BOB RIESENER
New York Yankee farmhand who compiled a 20-0 record for Alexandria of the Evangeline League in 1957. Riesener led the league in victories, winning percentage (obviously), shutouts (four) and earned-run average (2.16).

Riesener was promoted to New Orleans of the Southern Association late in the '57 season. While the switch was easy geographically (a simple move downstate), it was tough competitively. The righthander started twice for the Pelicans and suffered 12-6 and 8-2 setbacks.

Tony Napoles fashioned an 18-0 record for Peekskill of the North Atlantic League in 1946, then went 4-0 in the playoffs for the league's championship team.

JACKIE ROBINSON
The first black in modern major league baseball, he broke into Organized Baseball on April 18, 1946, at Jersey City's Roosevelt Stadium by collecting four hits—including a home run—in Montreal's 14-1 International League trouncing of the Jersey City club.

Robinson went on to lead the International League in batting, hitting .349.

GENE RYE
Playing for Waco in an August 6, 1930, Texas League game against Beaumont, he walloped three home runs—in one inning. Rye's cannonading came in the eighth inning, a frame in which Waco scored 18 runs.

Outfielder Rye had a cup of coffee in the major leagues in 1931, appearing in 17 games for the Boston Red Sox. He collected seven hits (all singles) in 39 at-bats.

WARREN SANDEL
The first pitcher Jackie Robinson faced in Organized Baseball. Lefthander Sandel started for Jersey City in the Giants' 1946 International League opener against the Montreal Royals and induced Robinson to ground out in the Montreal player's first at-bat in the pro ranks. But on his second trip to the plate, Robinson rifled a three-run homer off Sandel.

Gene Rye enjoyed his moment in the sun in 1939 when he walloped three home runs in one inning for Waco in a Texas League game against Beaumont. Newark outfielder Bob Seeds was devastating in a 1938 game against Buffalo, homering in four consecutive innings.

ROY SANNER
A combination outfielder-pitcher, Houma's Sanner won the Evangeline League's "triple crown" in 1948 by slugging 34 home runs, knocking in 126 runs and batting .386—and, for good measure, he hung up a 21-2 pitching record that season with 251 strikeouts in 199 innings.

PETE SCHNEIDER
A pitcher for the Cincinnati Reds from 1914 through 1918 and with the New York Yankees in 1919, he became a minor league outfielder and slugged five home runs—two of them with the bases loaded—and a double in a May 11, 1923, game for the Vernon club of the Pacific Coast League. Schneider drove in 14 runs in his one-for-the-book performance, which came in a 35-11 Vernon romp against Salt Lake City.

BOB SEEDS
Newark outfielder who on May 6, 1938, against Buffalo homered in four consecutive innings, went 6 for 6 overall and drove in 12 runs as the Bears

dismantled the Bisons by a 22-9 score. Seeds hit a bases-empty home run in the fourth inning, a two-run shot in the fifth, a bases-full homer in the sixth and two-run drive in the seventh.

Seeds continued his rampage the next day, hitting three homers as Newark thrashed Buffalo, 14-8. The former American Leaguer belted 28 homers in 59 games for Newark in '38, then was sold to the New York Giants. (In a total of 615 big-league games, coming before and after his sizzling stretch for Newark in '38, Seeds hit only 28 home runs.)

BILL SISLER
The hard-to-track minor league pitcher who broke into Organized Ball in 1923 and pitched professionally as late as 1948 (at age 44)—despite run-of-the-mill skills. Sisler, obviously able to sell his abilities regardless of his prior production, apparently signed contracts with as many as 50 professional clubs (most of them in the low minors), but often had two or fewer decisions with a team before moving on.

Sisler achieved a career-high eight victories for the Staunton club of the Virginia League in 1942.

KEVIN STOCK, BOB LOSCALZO
Modesto players who both hit for the cycle in their club's 23-4 California League pasting of Visalia on May 20, 1985. Second baseman Stock, who knocked in seven runs, lashed his single, double, triple and home run (a bases-loaded shot) in five at-bats, while left fielder Loscalzo went 4 for 7 with four RBIs.

BILL THOMAS
The winningest pitcher in minor league history, notching 383 victories in a pro playing career that began in 1926 and ended in 1952. He enjoyed his best season in 1946 when, at age 41, he won 35 games for Houma of the Evangeline League.

Thomas, who won 15 or more games in 15 minor league seasons, never pitched in the majors.

325
The most hits achieved by one player in one season in Organized Baseball history. Outfielder Paul Strand established the record in 1923, a year in which he played 194 games for Salt Lake City of the Pacific Coast League (extended seasons were common in the PCL) and won the league batting championship with a .394 mark.

Strand, who in 1922 had collected 289 hits for Salt Lake City while appearing in 178 games, won a return trip to the big leagues because of his lusty hitting in the PCL (he had pitched for Boston's Miracle Braves of 1914 and had seen brief outfield duty in the majors). But in 47 games for the Philadelphia A's in 1924, Strand batted only .228 (38 hits in 167 at-bats) and was back in the minor leagues to stay by midseason.

MARV THRONEBERRY
While coming to symbolize the ineptitude of the early-day New York Mets with his not-so-marvelous play for the National League club, Throneberry was, in fact, a slugging marvel as a New York Yankee farmhand. Playing for Denver, he led the American Association in home runs and runs batted in for three consecutive seasons. Throneberry hit 36 homers and drove in 117 runs for the Bears in 1955, walloped 42 homers and knocked in 145 runs in 1956 and had 40 homers and 124 RBIs in 1957.

FRED TONEY
Pitching for Winchester against Lexington in a May 10, 1909, Blue Grass League game, he threw a 17-inning, 1-0 no-hitter.

Eight years later, as a member of the Cincinnati Reds, Toney hurled a 10-inning, 1-0 no-hit game against the Chicago Cubs in a contest that also featured hitless pitching by Cubs starter Jim Vaughn through 9 1/3 innings.

JOHNNY VANDER MEER
Fourteen years after pitching consecutive no-hit games for the Cincinnati Reds, he pitched another no-hitter—in the Texas League. In his first full season out of the big leagues (except for military service) since he first appeared in the majors in 1937, the 37-year-old Vander Meer pitched for Tulsa in 1952 and, on July 15, held Beaumont hitless in a 12-0 victory.

ED WALSH
Son of big-league pitching great Big Ed Walsh, he stopped Joe DiMaggio's Pacific Coast League batting streak at 61 games in 1933. Pitching for Oakland against San Francisco on July 26, he held DiMaggio hitless in five at-bats.

Eight years later, another son of a major league pitching star victimized DiMaggio. Jim Bagby Jr., pitching in relief for the Cleveland Indians on July 17, 1941, got the New York Yankees' DiMaggio to ground into a double play in his last at-bat of the game, ending the Yankee Clipper's major league-record batting streak at 56 games.

STAN WASIAK
A minor league manager for a record 37 consecutive years, 1950 through 1986 (although illness limited him to a one-game stint in 1982). Guiding Vero Beach of the Florida State League in '86, he became the first manager to reach (and

Marv Throneberry, who later won the hearts of New York Mets fans with his inept play, was a devastating slugger during his minor league days at Denver. Stan Wasiak, who managed 37 straight years in the Dodgers' organization, surpassed the 2,500-victory plateau in 1986.

then surpass) 2,500 career victories in the minors.

While Wasiak piloted the Los Angeles Dodgers' Class AAA affiliate in Albuquerque from 1973 through 1976, most of his managerial career was spent in the low minors.

JOE WILHOIT
Wichita outfielder who hit safely in 69 consecutive games in 1919, a record for Organized Baseball. Wilhoit batted .505 during his streak, collecting 151 hits in 299 at-bats, and finished the season with a Western League-leading .422 batting average.

Wilhoit, who played in the National League in 1916, 1917 and 1918, won another look in the majors after his success at Wichita. Appearing in six games for the Boston Red Sox late in the 1919 season, he went 6 for 18 at the plate. But in 1920, Wilhoit was back in the minors to stay.

EIGHTH INNING
Fathers and sons—
and more—
from baseball's family tree

HANK AARON, TOMMIE AARON
The top career homer-hitting brother combination in major league history, having slugged a total of 768 home runs. Hank, of course, is the big leagues' all-time leader; he drilled 755 homers in 23 seasons with the Milwaukee Braves, Atlanta Braves and Milwaukee Brewers. Tommy, five years younger than Hank and a major leaguer for seven years with the Braves (when they were based in both Milwaukee and Atlanta), hit 13 homers—eight of them in 1962, when he appeared in 141 games for the Milwaukee Braves.

HANK AARON, TOMMIE AARON
The only brother teammates to appear in a Championship Series, with Hank playing in all three games of the 1969 National League playoffs for Atlanta (going 5 for 14 at the plate with three home runs and seven runs batted in) and Tommie making an unsuccessful pinch-hitting appearance for the Braves against the New York Mets.

ART ALLISON, DOUG ALLISON
The first brother combination to play major league baseball. Doug Allison already was established as the starting catcher for Hartford of the newly formed National League (baseball's first "major league") when, on June 3, 1876, outfielder-first baseman Art Allison made his big-league debut as a member of the N.L.'s Louisville club. Louisville downed New York, 8-1.

Two other brother combinations played in the National League during its initial season of 1876. George, Sam and Harry Wright performed for Boston, and Fred and Pete Treacey saw duty for New York.

FELIPE ALOU, JESUS ALOU, MATTY ALOU
The brother combination amassing the most hits in one major league season, getting an aggregate of 505 in 1968. Felipe, playing for the Atlanta Braves, tied Cincinnati's Pete Rose for the National League lead with 210 hits, while Matty collected 185 hits for the Pittsburgh Pirates and Jesus contributed 110 for the San Francisco Giants.

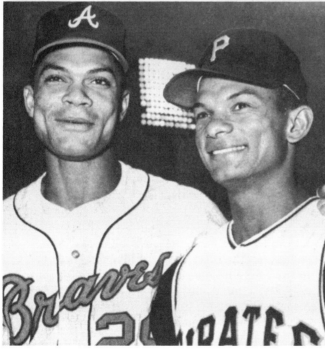

Brothers Hank (left) and Tommie Aaron combined for 768 major league home runs, Hank accounting for 755. Felipe (left) and Matty Alou are the only brother combination ever to finish 1-2 in a batting race.

FELIPE ALOU, JESUS ALOU, MATTY ALOU

They logged the most games played of any brother combination in big-league history, totaling 5,129. Felipe appeared in 2,082 games during his career, Matty played in 1,667 and Jesus was a participant in 1,380.

The record for most career games played by two brothers is 4,542, a figure reached by Hall of Fame outfielders Paul (2,549 games) and Lloyd (1,993) Waner.

MATTY ALOU, FELIPE ALOU

The only brothers to finish 1-2 in a major league batting race. Matty won the 1966 National League batting championship, hitting .342 for the Pittsburgh Pirates. Felipe, playing for the Atlanta Braves, was the N.L. runner-up with a .327 mark.

KEN ASPROMONTE, BOB ASPROMONTE

The only brothers to play in the first games of expansion teams. Ken played second base for the Los Angeles (now California) Angels when that American League expansion club made its debut on April 11, 1961. Bob was at third base for the Houston Colt .45s (now Astros) when that new National League team played its first game on April 10, 1962.

JIM BAGBY SR., JIM BAGBY JR.

The only father-son combination to pitch in World Series competition. Jim Sr. was the losing pitcher for the Cleveland Indians in Game 2 of the 1920 Series and the winning pitcher in Game 5; Jim Jr. worked three innings of relief for the Boston Red Sox in Game 4 of the 1946 fall classic.

The Bagbys figured prominently in two of baseball's most memorable games— one of which was the World Series contest that the elder Bagby won. In that October 10, 1920, game, Indians second baseman Bill Wambsganss turned the only unassisted triple play in Series history, Cleveland's Elmer Smith socked the first bases-loaded homer in Series play and Bagby himself entered the record books by becoming the first pitcher to smash a Series homer. Then, on July 17, 1941, the younger Bagby, then with Cleveland and working in relief of starter Al Smith, induced New York's Joe DiMaggio to ground into an eighth-inning double play; the at-bat was DiMaggio's last on a hitless night that ended the Yankee star's 56-game hitting streak.

JIM BAILEY, ED BAILEY

The last brother battery to start a big-league game, with Jim pitching and Ed catching for the Cincinnati Reds in the second game of a September 10, 1959, doubleheader in Chicago against the Cubs. Jim, who was making his major league debut, worked 7⅔ innings and was charged with a 6-3 loss; Ed caught the entire game and went 0 for 4 at the plate.

Brothers Ken and Clete Boyer, who played in the majors chiefly with the Cardinals and Yankees, respectively, both reached the 150-homer mark. Bert Campaneris of the A's and Jose Cardenal of the Angels (and later the Indians) were second cousins who twice finished 1-2 in A.L. stolen bases.

Jim Bailey pitched in only two other major league games, both in relief, and brother Ed was his catcher both times. Ed, on the other hand, had an extensive career in the majors, playing in 1,212 games.

GUS BELL, BUDDY BELL
With Gus Bell having played for the National League in the 1953, 1954, 1956 and 1957 All-Star Games, an All-Star "first" occurred in 1973 when son Buddy played for the American League—never before had a father-son combination appeared in the midsummer classic. Gus represented the Cincinnati Reds in his four All-Star appearances, while Buddy was a member of the Cleveland Indians in '73 and an All-Star participant for the A.L. in 1980, 1981, 1982 and 1984 as a Texas Rangers player.

DENNIS BENNETT, DAVE BENNETT
The last lefthanded-righthanded brother combination to pitch for the same big-league team in the same game. Lefthander Dennis Bennett, who had a seven-season major league career, started for the Philadelphia Phillies against

the New York Mets on June 12, 1964, and lasted 2 1/3 innings in an 11-3 loss. Righthander Dave, in his only appearance in the majors, worked the ninth inning for the Phils and allowed two hits and one run.

KEN BOYER, CLETE BOYER
Brothers who each reached the 150-homer mark in the majors, a feat unmatched by any other brothers. In fact, Ken Boyer socked 282 home runs and Clete walloped 162.

Members of only one other brother twosome can claim as many as 125 homers each—Joe and Vince DiMaggio, with Joe blasting 361 and Vince hitting exactly 125. And, besides the Boyers and the DiMaggios, only one other pair of brothers can boast of individual homer totals of 100 or more—Bob (156) and Emil Meusel (106).

BERT CAMPANERIS, JOSE CARDENAL
Second cousins who twice finished 1-2 in American League stolen-base competition. In 1965, Campaneris topped the A.L. with 51 steals while playing for the Kansas City A's and, Cardenal, a member of the California Angels, was second with 37. Three years later, Campaneris had an A.L.-high 62 thefts for the Oakland A's and Cardenal was the league runner-up with 40 for the Cleveland Indians.

BILLY CONIGLIARO, TONY CONIGLIARO
The last brothers to slug home runs in the same big-league game as teammates. Playing for the Boston Red Sox against the Washington Senators on September 19, 1970, Billy Conigliaro smacked a three-run homer off Jim Hannan in the fourth inning and Tony hit a bases-empty shot against Joe Grzenda in the seventh. The Red Sox won, 11-3.

BILLY CONIGLIARO, TONY CONIGLIARO
The brother combination with the most home runs in one major league season as teammates. Billy Conigliaro, playing his first full season in the majors, hit 18 homers for the Boston Red Sox in 1970 and Tony walloped 36 for the American League club.

Hank and Tommy Aaron rank one behind the Conigliaros' total of 54. They established their National League-leading mark in 1962 when Hank rapped 45 homers for Milwaukee and Tommy hit eight for the Braves.

MORT COOPER, WALKER COOPER
The only brother battery in World Series history. Mort was a six-time starting pitcher for the St. Louis Cardinals in Series play, getting the call twice in each fall classic from 1942 through 1944, and brother Walker was in the Cards' lineup in all six contests.

492

Brothers Billy (left) and Tony Conigliaro combined for 54 home runs while playing for the Boston Red Sox in 1970.

JOSE CRUZ, HECTOR (HEITY) CRUZ
The last brothers to hit home runs in the same major league game. In the Astros-Cubs game of May 4, 1981, Houston's Jose Cruz smashed a three-run-home run against Mike Krukow in the first inning and Chicago's Hector Cruz rapped a bases-empty homer off Joaquin Andujar in the sixth. The Astros beat the Cubs, 5-4.

HERM DOSCHER, JACK DOSCHER
The first father-son combination to play in the major leagues Herm Doscher, a third baseman, started his big-league career with Troy of the National League in 1879 and finished with the N.L.'s Cleveland club in 1882. Son Jack, a lefthanded pitcher, made his debut in the majors on July 2, 1903 as a starter for the Chicago Cubs. He subsequently moved on to Brooklyn and wound up his big-league career with Cincinnati in 1908.

8
The number of Hall-of-Famers whose sons played in the major leagues.

Hall of Famer	Son	Son's Career Span	Years	Games	Avg. or Won-Lost
Earl Averill	Earl	1956-63	7	449	.242
Yogi Berra	Dale	1977-87	11	853	.236
Eddie Collins	Eddie	1939-42	3	132	.241
Fred Lindstrom	Charlie	1958	1	1	1.000
Connie Mack	Earle	1910-1914	3	5	.125
Jim O'Rourke	Jim	1908	1	34	.231
George Sisler	Dave	1956-62	7	247	38-44
	Dick	1946-1953	8	799	.276
Ed Walsh	Ed	1928-32	4	79	11-24

8, 25

The number of major league games in which brothers Felipe, Matty and Jesus Alou appeared together as teammates and the number of big-league games overall in which the three Alous appeared together. Felipe Alou, a San Francisco Giants outfield regular and a member of the National League club since June 1958, was the team's right fielder and leadoff batter in a September 10, 1963, game in New York—a major league contest in which, for the first time, he was joined by both Matty and Jesus (also property of the Giants). Never before had more than two brothers appeared in the same big-league game. Called up from San Francisco's Tacoma farm club and facing the Mets' Carlton Willey, Jesus made his major league debut by grounding out in the eighth inning while pinch-hitting for shortstop Jose Pagan. Matty also just up from Tacoma but a full-season member of the Giants in 1961 and 1962, followed Jesus to the plate and struck out as a pinch-hitter for pitcher Bob Garibaldi. Felipe then grounded out against Willey, ending the historic inning. The three Alous then appeared in the same game seven more times for the '63 Giants.

After the trading of Felipe Alou to the Milwaukee Braves in December 1963, the three Alous appeared in the same Giants-Braves game six times in 1964 and nine times in 1965. And when Felipe and Matty played for the New York Yankees in 1973 and Jesus saw action for the Oakland A's that year, the three Alous appeared in the same Yanks-A's game twice.

The Alous remain the only family to have had three brothers play m the same major league game. The only other brother threesomes to have played for the same big-league team in one season were Harry, George and Sam Wright of Boston's 1876 N.L. club and Jose, Hector (Heity) and Cirilo (Tommy) Cruz of the N.L.'s St. Louis Cardinals in 1973.

WES FERRELL
Cleveland Indians pitcher who on April 29, 1931, tossed a no-hitter in which

the game's only questionable call came on a ball hit by his brother, catcher Rick Ferrell of the St. Louis Browns. Rick hit an eighth-inning smash that appeared headed to left field, but Indians shortstop Bill Hunnefield raced into the hole, snared the ground ball and whistled a throw to first base—a throw that pulled Lew Fonseca off the bag. Most observers were amazed that Hunnefield got to the ball, and thus a "hit" ruling seemed possible; by the same token, a good throw clearly would have gotten the baserunner. The decision: Error— Hunnefield. The miscue was one of three that the Cleveland infielder made that day, an afternoon on which Wes Ferrell completed a 9-0 no-hit game.

59
The most major league home runs hit in one season by a brother combination— and the figure was attained twice, both times by the DiMaggios. In 1937, Joe DiMaggio clubbed an American League-leading 46 homers for the New York Yankees and brother Vince, a rookie with the Boston Bees of the National League, socked 13. Four years later, a third DiMaggio brother, Dominic, got into the act. Joe hit 30 homers for the Yankees in 1941, Vince drilled 21 for the Pittsburgh Pirates and second-year major leaguer Dom hit eight for the Boston Red Sox.

Yankees Manager Yogi Berra, shown giving instructions to son Dale Berra in 1985, is one of eight Hall of Famers whose sons made it to the major leagues.

BOB FORSCH, KEN FORSCH

Besides Gaylord and Jim Perry and Phil and Joe Niekro, the only other brother twosome in major league history to be made up of two 100-victory pitchers. While the Perry and Niekro combinations each boast a 300-game winner (Gaylord, Phil) and a 200-game winner, the Forsch brothers accounted for 164 (Bob) and 114 victories (Ken) during their careers.

MIKE GARBARK, BOB GARBARK

Of the 259 players who saw action in the American League in 1944, exactly two finished the season with .261 batting averages—and they were brothers. Mike Garbark, a catcher for the New York Yankees, achieved his .261 mark by collecting 78 hits in 299 at-bats; older brother Bob, also a catcher, reached that figure by going 6 for 23 as a member of the Philadelphia A's.

HEGANS, KENNEDYS

The only father-son combinations to hit safely in World Series play. Jim Hegan collected six hits in 32 at-bats for the Cleveland Indians in the 1948 and 1954 World Series; son Mike went 1 for 5 for the Oakland A's in the 1972 Series after going 0 for 1 for the New York Yankees in the 1964 fall classic. Bob Kennedy went 1 for 2 for the Indians in the '48 Series; son Terry was 4 for 19 for San Diego in the 1984 Series and 2 for 12 for San Francisco in the 1989 fall classic.

DANE IORG, GARTH IORG

The only brothers to see action for opposing teams in a Championship Series. Dane made four pinch-hitting appearances for the Kansas City Royals against Toronto in the 1985 American League Championship Series, while Garth was used in six games by the Blue Jays as a third baseman and pinch-hitter.

FERGUSON JENKINS

The only pitcher in big-league history to surrender home runs to all three Alou brothers. Pitching in each instance for the Chicago Cubs, Jenkins yielded two homers to Jesus Alou (the first in the opening game of a July 23, 1967 doubleheader, the second on May 31, 1973) and one each to Felipe Alou (April 25, 1968) and Matty Alou (September 5, 1971). Jesus played for the San Francisco Giants when he struck his first homer off Jenkins and was a member of the Houston Astros when he walloped No. 2. Felipe connected as an Atlanta Braves player, while Matty was with the St. Louis Cardinals when he homered against Jenkins.

No pitcher gave up home runs to all three DiMaggio brothers.

JIMMY JOHNSTON, DOC JOHNSTON

The first brother combination to appear in World Series competition and the first brothers to play in the same Series. After Jimmy Johnston pinch-hit and played right field for Brooklyn against the Boston Red Sox in the 1916 fall classic, Doc Johnston was a participant for Cleveland in the 1920 World Series—a postseason battle in which the Indians were matched against Brooklyn and Jimmy Johnston. In the '20 Series, Doc started four games at first base for Cleveland and brother Jimmy started four times at third base for Brooklyn. The Indians' Johnston pinch-hit in another game (and stayed in that contest, taking over at first base).

Since the Johnstons went head to head in the 1920 World Series, only two other sets of brothers have been Series opponents—the Meusels in 1921, 1922 and 1923 (Bob playing for the New York Yankees and Emil for the New York Giants) and the Boyers in 1964 (Kenny playing for the St. Louis Cardinals and Clete for the Yankees).

JIM LEFEBVRE
The only individual in big-league history to manage a father and son in the same season. In 1990 and 1991, Lefebvre was manager of Seattle Mariners teams that included outfielders Ken Griffey and Ken Griffey Jr.

The only other men to manage a father-son combination—not in the same year, however—were Connie Mack and Paul Richards. While directing the Philadelphia Athletics from 1901 through 1950, Mack manager Eddie Collins (1906-1914, 1927-1930) and Eddie Collins Jr. (1939, 1941-1942) and Earle Brucker (1937-1940, 1943) and Earle Brucker Jr. (1948). Richards, manager of the Chicago White sox from 1951 through 1954 and again in 1976, had Sam Hairston on his '51 Sox squad and Jerry Hairston on his '76 club.

Technically, Mack managed a third father-son combination—himself and his own son. As player-manager for Pittsburgh from late in the 1894 season through 1896, pilot Mack made decisions that affected catcher-first baseman Mack; then, in 1910, 1911 and 1914, Mack was in command of the A's (and long retired as a player) when son Earle played a total of five games for Philadelphia.

CONNIE MACK
The first man in big-league history to manage his son in the majors. Earle Mack, a "mascot" for his father's early Philadelphia A's teams and a .135-hitting catcher in 26 minor league games in 1910 (his pro debut), was a favorite of A's players and was called upon to catch for his father's team on October 5, 1910. Earle responded by hitting a single and a triple on a day in which he caught Eddie Plank and Jack Coombs in a 7-4 loss to the New York Highlanders. In 1911, Earle saw action at third base in two late-season games for Philadelphia and in 1914 he played first base in two end-of-the-year A's contests. (Earle Mack later served his father as an A's coach for more than 25 years.)

The only other two men to manage their sons in the major leagues were Yogi Berra and Cal Ripken. In 1985, infielder Dale Berra played 12 games for the

Yankees under his father (who subsequently was fired). Baltimore's Ripken managed sons Cal Jr. and Billy in 1987 but was dismissed six games into the 1988 season.

MICKEY MAHLER, RICK MAHLER
The last brothers to pitch for the same team in the same major league game. On September 25, 1979, the Mahlers worked a total of three relief innings for the Atlanta Braves against the Houston Astros, with Mickey pitching the sixth and seventh innings and Rick hurling in the eighth. Tommy Boggs was Atlanta's starting and losing pitcher as the Braves fell to the Astros, 8-0.

DENNY McLAIN
Pitcher who won the American League's Most Valuable Player Award in 1968—20 years after his father-in-law had captured the same honor. McLain compiled a 31-6 record and a 1.96 earned-run average while helping the Detroit Tigers to the A.L. pennant in '68. Cheering on Denny was wife Sharon, daughter of Cleveland Indians great Lou Boudreau. In 1948, Boudreau, Cleveland's player-manager, was named the A.L.'s MVP after batting .355, hitting 18 home runs and driving in 106 runs for the pennant-winning Indians (who, like McLain's Tigers, also won the World Series).

JOHNNY O'BRIEN, EDDIE O'BRIEN
Twin brothers who, as rookie major league infielders in 1953, each appeared in 89 games for the Pittsburgh Pirates. By the time their big-league careers had ended (Johnny finished up in 1959, Eddie in 1958), the twins had seen pitching duty. Johnny pitched 61 innings in the majors, allowed 61 hits and won one game; Eddie pitched 16 innings, allowed 16 hits and won one game. Eddie's lone victory—and only big-league decision—came in a 3-1 complete-game triumph for Pittsburgh over the Chicago Cubs in the first game of a September 14, 1957, doubleheader. In the nightcap of that twin bill, the Pirates lost, 7-3, with the defeat being charged to brother Johnny, who worked one inning of relief. The loss was Johnny's last decision in the majors, leaving him with a cumulative 1-3 record (he posted his only victory in 1956).

The O'Briens, already well-known athletically for their basketball exploits at Seattle University (Johnny was a consensus All-America selection in 1953), played in the same major league game for the first time on May 10, 1953, when Johnny entered the second game of a doubleheader (against the New York Giants) as a defensive replacement at second base and Eddie pinch-ran in the contest.

Eddie O'Brien spent his entire big-league career with the Pirates, appearing in 231 games (primarily as a shortstop-outfielder, having pitched in only five games). Johnny O'Brien saw service with the Pirates, St. Louis Cardinals and Milwaukee Braves in 339 games (mostly as a second baseman, with his

Tigers pitcher Denny McLain (right) and Manager Mayo Smith get a good-luck greeting from former Cleveland star Lou Boudreau before the final game of the 1968 World Series. McLain, a 31-game winner, was the A.L. MVP in '68, 20 years after Boudreau, his father-in-law, had won the same honor.

pitching duty limited to 25 games).

TOM PACIOREK
He appeared in the last regular-season major league game played by Julian Javier and in the first big-league contest played by Julian's son, Stan Javier Julian Javier took part in his last regular-season game on October 1, 1972 playing second base for the Cincinnati Reds against Paciorek and the Los Angeles Dodgers. Paciorek played first base and right field for the Dodgers in that game. And when Stan Javier made his big-league debut on April 15 1984, for the New York Yankees—he saw action in right field—Paciorek was at first base for the opposing Chicago White Sox.

GAYLORD PERRY, JIM PERRY
The first brothers to attain 20 pitching victories each in the same big-league season. In 1970, Gaylord Perry posted a 23-13 record for the San Francisco Giants and Jim compiled a 24-12 mark for the Minnesota Twins.

The only other brothers to achieve 20 victories apiece in the majors in the same year were Joe and Phil Niekro. Joe went 21-11 for the Houston Astros in 1979, while Phil was 21-20 for the Atlanta Braves that year.

The O'Brien twins, Johnny (left) and Eddie, were interchangeable rookie infielders for the Pittsburgh Pirates in 1953.

Jim (left) and Gaylord Perry, teammates with the Cleveland Indians in 1974 and part of 1975, combined for a record 529 big-league victories.

GAYLORD PERRY, JIM PERRY

The brother pitching combination with the most lifetime big-league victories, 529. Gaylord won 314 games while pitching from 1962 through 1983 for the San Francisco Giants, Cleveland Indians, Texas Rangers, San Diego Padres, New York Yankees, Atlanta Braves, Seattle Mariners and Kansas City Royals; Jim was a winner 215 times from 1959 through 1975 while a member of the Indians, Minnesota Twins, Detroit Tigers and Oakland A's. Phil (318) and Joe Niekro (221) rank second on the major league brothers' victory list with 539 triumphs.

The Perry brothers performed in the same major league—the American—at the same time for only four seasons, 1972 through 1975 (they were Cleveland teammates in 1974 and part of '75), and faced each other only once in a regular-season game. In the July 3, 1973, Detroit-Cleveland game, Jim started for the Tigers and Gaylord got the call for the Indians; Jim lasted 5 2/3 innings but wasn't involved in the decision, while Gaylord went 6 2/3 innings and was charged with the loss in a 5-4 Detroit victory.

HERMAN PILLETTE, DUANE PILLETTE

A father-son combination victimized by the Chicago White Sox in historic major league games. Herman Pillette was Detroit's losing pitcher—he tossed a complete-game seven-hitter—when Chicago's Charley Robertson threw a 2-0 perfect game against the Tigers on April 30, 1922. Son Duane went the distance for the St. Louis Browns in a 2-1, 11-inning loss in the last game in the Browns' 52-year history, a September 27, 1953, contest against the White Sox. (The Browns franchise moved to Baltimore after the '53 season and the club was renamed the Orioles.)

PETE ROSE
He appeared in the last major league game played by Ozzie Virgil Sr. and in the first big-league contest played by Ozzie Virgil Jr. In the second game of a June 27, 1969, doubleheader, Rose played right field for Cincinnati when Ozzie Sr., a member of the San Francisco Giants, bowed out of the majors as an unsuccessful pinch-hitter against the Reds. On October 5, 1980, Rose played first base for Philadelphia against the Montreal Expos when Ozzie Jr. made his big-league debut with a 1-for-5 batting performance as the Phillies' catcher.

Rose batted in the leadoff spot for his club in each game and collected two singles in each contest.

RAY SCHALK
The only player in major league history to catch a father-son combination—and he barely qualified for the distinction. Having caught the White Sox's Big Ed Walsh (a future Hall of Famer) in his early years as a big-league catcher, Schalk was midway through his second season as the Chicago club's manager when the chance developed to catch young Ed Walsh in the first game of a July 4, 1928, doubleheader. However, the opportunity to form the Sox battery with the 23-year-old Walsh came under trying circumstances: Schalk, under pressure to quit as manager, resigned on the morning of July 4, with the resignation to take effect at day's end. In his final major act as pilot of the White Sox, Schalk wrote his own name into the lineup for the opener of the doubleheader—it was his only catching appearance of the season and his 1,755th and last game as a Sox player—as Chicago faced the St. Louis Browns. Young Walsh, making his debut in the big leagues, yielded five runs in a four-inning stint and the Sox fell, 11-8.

Schalk, who removed himself from the game upon young Ed's departure, wound up his playing career in 1929 by appearing in five games for the New York Giants. Like the elder Walsh, Schalk won election to the Hall of Fame.

DICK SCHOFIELD, DICK SCHOFIELD
The only father-son combination to play in perfect games in the major leagues. The elder Schofield played shortstop for Pittsburgh on May 26, 1959, when the Pirates' Harvey Haddix fashioned a 12-inning perfect game against the Milwaukee Braves (only to lose in the 13th inning). And the younger Schofield

was at shortstop for California on September 30, 1984, when the Texas Rangers failed to get a baserunner against the Angels' Mike Witt.

NORM SHERRY, LARRY SHERRY

The last brother battery in major league history, teaming up for the Los Angeles Dodgers in a June 28, 1962, game against the New York Mets. Norm Sherry caught for the Dodgers in that contest and went hitless in four at-bats, while younger brother Larry entered the game in the eighth inning and worked two-thirds of an inning before being removed. Los Angeles won the game, 5-4, in 13 innings.

The Sherrys, big-league teammates in four seasons (all with the Dodgers), never formed a starting battery in the majors.

BILLY SULLIVAN SR., BILLY SULLIVAN JR.

The first of six father-son combinations to play in the World Series. Billy Sullivan Sr. caught for the Chicago White Sox in the 1906 Series, and Billy Jr. caught and pinch-hit for the Detroit Tigers in the 1940 fall classic. Other fathers and sons who competed in the Series:

Bagby—Jim Sr., Cleveland Indians, 1920
Bagby—Jim Jr., Boston Red Sox, 1946

Boone—Ray, Cleveland Indians, 1948
Boone—Bob, Philadelphia Phillies, 1980

Hegan—Jim, Cleveland Indians, 1948 and 1954
Hegan—Mike, New York Yankees, 1964; Oakland A's, 1972

Javier—Julian, St. Louis Cardinals, 1964, 1967 and 1968; Cincinnati Reds, 1972
Javier—Stan, Oakland Athletics, 1988 and 1989

Johnson—Ernie, New York Yankees, 1923
Johnson—Don, Chicago Cubs, 1945

Kennedy—Bob, Cleveland Indians, 1948
Kennedy—Terry, San Diego Padres, 1984; San Francisco Giants, 1989

26

The number of Hall-of-Famers whose brothers played in the big leagues. The figure includes Paul and Lloyd Waner, both of whom are in the Hall of Fame, and George and Harry Wright, another pair of brothers enshrined at Cooperstown, N.Y.

Hall of Famer	Brother	Brother's Career Span	Avg. or Years	Games	Won-Lost
Hank Aaron	Tommie	1962-71	7	437	.229
Fred Clarke	Josh	1898-11	5	223	.239
John Clarkson	Arthur	1891-96	6	96	39-39
	Walter	1904-08	5	78	18-16
Roger Connor	Joe	1900-05	3	90	.205
Stan Coveleski	Harry	1907-18	9	198	81-55
Dizzy Dean	Paul	1934-43	9	159	50-34
Ed Delahanty	Frank	1905-08	4	116	.228
	Jim	1901-12	11	1095	.283
	Joe	1907-09	3	269	.238
	Tom	1894-97	3	19	.239
Bill Dickey	George	1935-47	6	226	.204
Joe DiMaggio	Dom	1940-53	11	1399	.298
	Vince	1937-46	10	1110	.249
Johnny Evers	Joe	1913	1	1	.000
Buck Ewing	John	1883-91	6	129	53-63
Rick Ferrell	Wes	1927-41	15	374	193-128
Pud Galvin	Lou	1884	1	3	0-2
George Kell	Skeeter	1952	1	75	.221
George Kelly	Ren	1923	1	1	0-0
Heinie Manush	Frank	1908	1	23	.156
Christy Mathewson	Henry	1906-07	2	3	0-1
Jim O'Rourke	John	1879-83	3	230	.295
Gaylord Perry	Jim	1959-75	17	630	215-174
Wilbert Robinson	Fred	1884	1	3	.231
Joe Sewell	Luke	1921-42	20	1630	.259
	Tommy	1927	1	1	.000
Honus Wagner	Albert	1898	1	74	.226
Paul Waner	Lloyd	(Lloyd also is in Hall of Fame)			
Zack Wheat	Mack	1915-21	7	231	.204
George Wright	Harry	(Harry also is in Hall of Fame)			
	Sam	1876-81	3	12	.109

PAT UNDERWOOD

Detroit Tigers pitcher who broke into the major leagues by outdueling his brother Tom of the Toronto Blue Jays in a May 31, 1979, game. Pay was a 1-0 winner in his debut, yielding only three hits in 8 1/3 innings before getting relief help. Tom went the distance for Toronto and allowed only six hits—but one of them was an eighth-inning home run by Detroit right fielder Jerry Morales.

Dom and Joe were the American League representatives of the famed DiMaggio famly, with brother Vince spending his entire career in the N.L.

WALSH-SULLIVAN, WALSH-SULLIVAN

The battery for the Chicago White Sox in an early-October game in 1912, and again in a contest played late in the 1932 season—with the second pitcher-catcher combination being sons of the first. Big Ed Walsh and Billy Sullivan Sr. first served as a White Sox battery in 1904, gained particular attention in 1908 when Walsh won 40 games and last worked as a unit on October 4, 1912, when Walsh pitched the White Sox past the Detroit Tigers, 7-2. Then, on September 11, 1932, Walsh's son, Ed, a fourth-year major leaguer, started on the mound for the Sox and second-year man Billy Sullivan Jr. was behind the plate for the Chicago club in the second game of a doubleheader against the Washington Senators. In the only game in which young Walsh and young Sullivan teamed up as the White Sox's battery, Chicago absorbed a 9-4 defeat (loser Walsh departed after five innings, and so did Sullivan).

PAUL WANER, LLOYD WANER

The only brothers to collect 200 or more hits apiece in the same major league season—and they accomplished the feat in three consecutive years, 1927 through 1929. The Waners' highest combined hit total in one year was 460 (a record for a brother twosome), achieved in '27 when Paul amassed a major league-leading 237 hits for Pittsburgh and rookie Lloyd had 223 hits (second best in the N.L.) for the Pirates.

The brother combination compiling the most career hits in big-league history. Paul totaled 3,152 lifetime hits in the majors and Lloyd accounted for 2,459, an aggregate of 5,611.

Hall of Fame brothers and Pittsburgh teammates Lloyd (left) and Paul Waner combined for 5,611 major league hits.

Catcher Billy Sullivan Jr. (left) and Ed Walsh talk things over prior to a September 11, 1932, game in which both, literally, followed in their fathers' footsteps. Billy Sullivan Sr. and Big Ed Walsh had formed a battery 20 seasons earlier with the same team. The senior Walsh (left) is shown with his son in 1929.

The first of four brother combinations to play for the same team in the same World Series. Paul was stationed in right field and Lloyd manned center field for the Pittsburgh Pirates in the 1927 Series.

Subsequent Series-playing brother teammates were: Dizzy and Paul Dean, St. Louis Cardinals, 1934; Mort and Walker Cooper, Cardinals, 1942, 1943 and 1944; Felipe and Matty Alou, San Francisco Giants, 1962. (Virgil and Jesse Barnes of the 1922 New York Giants and Ken and George Brett of the 1980 Kansas City Royals also were brother teammates on Series teams, but Virgil Barnes didn't get into the '22 fall classic and Ken Brett wasn't used in the '80 Series.)

Of the four sets of brothers to have seen action for the same team in the same World Series, only the Deans didn't appear in at least one Series game together. Dizzy pitched for St. Louis in Games 1, 5 and 7 of the 1934 Series and pinch-ran in Game 4, while Paul pitched for the Cardinals in Games 3 and 6.

GEORGE WRIGHT, HARRY WRIGHT
The first brothers to play in the same major league game. A month and a half into the initial season of the National League (considered baseball's first "big league"), Boston's N.L. team employed George Wright at shortstop and Manager Harry Wright in right field in a contest against Louisville. Boston lost by a 3-0 score in the June 6, 1876, game, which proved Manager Wright's only playing appearance of the year.

ZERO
The number of Hall of Fame members whose fathers played in the major leagues.

NINTH INNING
Baseball's golden moments as depicted on the silver screen

'ALIBI IKE'
Based on the Ring Lardner character, this 1935 film comedy starred Joe E. Brown in the title role and focused on a Cub rookie's tendency to find an excuse for virtually everything—be it an on-field foulup or an off-the-field transgression. Also featured in the movie was 19-year-old Olivia de Havilland, a newcomer to Hollywood.

JUNE ALLYSON
Actress who was cast as Ethel Stratton in "The Stratton Story," the motion picture about big-league pitcher Monty Stratton's comeback bid after undergoing a leg amputation. Through dogged determination and aided by the support of his wife Ethel, Stratton enjoyed pitching success once more—albeit in the minor leagues.

'THE BABE RUTH STORY'
The eagerly awaited motion picture that had its official premiere in New York on July 26, 1948—and Ruth, leaving his hospital bed, was in attendance for part of the festivities. Three weeks later, baseball's legendary Bambino was dead. The film, which starred William Bendix in the title role, received generally unfavorable reviews. Otis L. Guernsey Jr. of the New York Herald Tribune put it this way: "It would be hard to find a more colorful American figure than the Babe for motion-picture documentation, and it would be difficult to do a worse job with him than has been done here."

Bendix, reflecting on the movie 13 years later, said: "Worst picture I ever made. It could have been great, I think. But it didn't work out that way. I remember going to the previews in Los Angeles. In the early part of the picture, when I'm discovered in the orphanage, the scene was full of 16- and 17-year-old kids. Do I have a kid playing me? No, I have to do it with makeup. And I'm 38 years old (42, actually) at the time. The audience laughed. I would have laughed, too, but I felt too bad."

BAY CITY BLUEBIRDS
The fictitious minor league baseball team around which the short-lived 1983 television series "The Bay City Blues" was built. The series, which lasted for less than a month in the fall of '83, focused on both the on-field exploits and -off-field escapades of players striving to make the major leagues.

Ethel Stratton, played by June Allyson, comforts husband Monty (James Stewart) after a hunting accident that resulted in the amputation of his leg in 'The Stratton Story.'

WILLIAM BENDIX

Television's bumbling Chester A. Riley cast as the heroic George Herman (Babe) Ruth? Say it ain't so. Well, it wasn't so—at least not chronologically. Bendix, you see, played the lead in "The Babe Ruth Story" (1948) five years before his visage as the well-meaning buffoon on "The Life of Riley" first appeared on TV (although he did create the Riley role on radio in 1943). And while hindsight has contributed to charges of miscasting, not everyone was upset with Bendix's portrayal of the Babe. Reviewing the "Ruth Story" in the New York Star in July 1948, Heywood Hale Broun wrote: "What saves the picture from being a solid bust is a good performance by Bendix. He looks pretty silly swinging a bat, but he has caught very well the boyish, expansive personality of the Babe, and when he is talking to kids, bargaining with Owner Jake Ruppert, or irritating Miller Huggins, well played by Fred Lightner, he makes us believe for a few moments that this is Babe Ruth himself."

In 1950, Bendix starred in another baseball movie, "Kill the Umpire," a comedy that depicted the ups and downs in the career of an umpire. Three years later, he assumed the Riley role on television.

William Bendix (left, as a teen-ager) was joined in his 1948 portrayal of Babe Ruth by William Frawley (center) and Charles Bickford (right). The Babe himself, just out of the hospital, enjoyed a moment at the picture's premiere with Claire Trevor, who portrayed Mrs. Babe Ruth.

JOHN BERARDINO

A major league infielder for 11 seasons, he has played Dr. Steve Hardy in the daytime television soap opera "General Hospital" since the highly popular show's inception in 1963. Berardino, an actor at age 6 in "Our Gang" background scenes and a bit player in films during his baseball days, played two hitches each with the St. Louis Browns, Cleveland Indians (he was a member of the 1948 World Series-champion Tribe) and Pittsburgh Pirates.

Soon after becoming entrenched as an actor in the 1960s, former ball player Berardino became actor Beradino (the "cleaner" spelling was convenient for

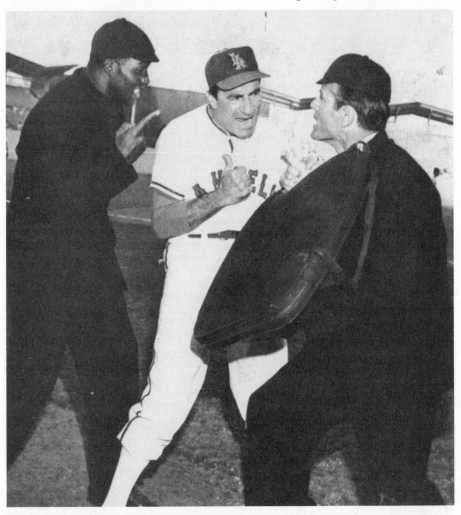

John Berardino, who already had given up baseball for an acting career and dropped the second 'r' from his last name, returned to the field in 1964 for a star-studded Hollywood-style game and was double-teamed by major leaguers-turned-umpires Vic Power (left) and Jim Piersall.

everyone and the second "r" was silent, anyway). Before the advent of "General Hospital," he was a regular in the television series "The New Breed" and appeared in TV's "I Led Three Lives."

CHARLES BICKFORD
The actor who played Brother Matthias, George Herman Ruth's "mentor" and father figure at Baltimore's St. Mary's Industrial School, in "The Babe Ruth Story."

RAMON BIERI
The actor who portrayed Dodgers Owner Walter O'Malley in the television drama "It's Good to Be Alive" and later played Babe Ruth in TV's "A Love Affair: The Eleanor and Lou Gehrig Story."

HARRIET BIRD
The seductress (Barbara Hershey) in "The Natural" who flirted with Roy Hobbs aboard a Chicago-bound train, invited Hobbs to her hotel room—and shot him.

JOE BOYD
The fanatical, middle-aged Washington Senators fan in the 1958 musical film "Damn Yankees," he said he'd sell his soul if it meant his lowly Senators would win the American League pennant. There was a buyer, all right—the devil himself. Suddenly, Joe Boyd (played by Robert Shafer) was transformed into young Joe Hardy (Tab Hunter), a power hitter of staggering dimensions, and the Senators were on their way.

"Damn Yankees" was a Broadway hit in 1955, with Shafer cast as Joe Boyd and Stephen Douglass starring in the Joe Hardy role.

BROOKLYN LOONS
The name of the baseball team that was willed to a cat in the 1951 film comedy "Rhubarb." The cat not only became owner of the Loons, but served as the club's good-luck charm as well. Good luck was nothing new to Rhubarb; in addition to being bequeathed the Loons, the feline also inherited a cool $30 million.

LeVAR BURTON
More than a year and a half after portraying young Kunta Kinte in the 1977 television production "Roots," he played Ron LeFlore in TV's "One in a Million," the story of LeFlore's rise from a prison inmate to a big-name outfielder for the Detroit Tigers.

MORRIS BUTTERMAKER
The swimming-pool cleaner and former minor leaguer ball player in a 1976 film who took over as coach of a Southern California kids-league team, the

Actor Tab Hunter donned a baseball uniform in the 1958 musical 'Damn Yankees' and powered the lowly Washington Senators to dizzying heights in the baseball world in his role as power-hitting Joe Hardy, whose feats would not be accomplished without a price.

Bears, that was really bad news—until, that is, the squad recruited a topnotch female pitcher, Amanda (Tatum O'Neal). Amanda, aided and abetted by her wisecracking teammates and directed by the beer-guzzling Buttermaker (Walter Matthau), helped turn "The Bad News Bears" into a surprisingly formidable unit (and a hit movie as well).

Sequels to "The Bad News Bears"—"The Bad News Bears in Breaking Training" (1977) and "The Bad News Bears Go to Japan" (1978)—were made without Matthau and O'Neal and generally were considered inferior to the original movie. "Breaking Training" told of the Bears' efforts to get to Houston's Astrodome in an attempt to win a berth against Japanese competition, and "Go to Japan" focused on the team's trip to the Orient and its adventures with promoter/con artist Marvin Lazar (Tony Curtis).

'CASEY AT THE BAT'
This 1927 film starred Wallace Beery, whose Casey character took a bottle of beer to the plate and slugged his prodigious home runs with one hand (when he wasn't striking out).

JOE CHARBONEAU
The American League's Rookie of the Year in 1980 as an outfielder with the Cleveland Indians (but a major leaguer for parts of only two other seasons), he was a member of the New York Knights in "The Natural."

'COLLEGE'
Buster Keaton starred in this 1927 movie about an athletically disinclined student who, while seeking approval from his favorite coed, tried out for the baseball team with absurd results.

GARY COOPER
Actor whose portrayal of Lou Gehrig in the 1942 film "The Pride of the Yankees" was widely hailed. The Gehrig film biography, which opened in New York about 13 months after the Iron Horse's death at age 37, also featured a sterling performance by Teresa Wright in the role of Gehrig's wife Eleanor.

RICHARD CRENNA
Still a few months away from initiating his memorable role as scatterbrained student Walter Denton in the "Our Miss Brooks" television show, he played the part of St. Louis Cardinals pitcher Paul Dean in "The Pride of St. Louis," a springtime-1952 motion picture about Paul's brother, Dizzy Dean.

DAN DAILEY
As colorful pitcher Dizzy Dean in "The Pride of St. Louis," he demonstrated how ol' Diz could master opposing batters—but not the English language. The latter shortcoming, magnified when former St. Louis Cardinals great Dean embarked on a broadcasting career, got plenty of attention in this film.

BLYTHE DANNER, EDWARD HERRMANN
They played the title roles in the 1977 television dramatization "A Love Affair: The Eleanor and Lou Gehrig Story."

DORIS DAY
Actress who portrayed Aimee Alexander, wife of pitching star Grover Cleveland Alexander, in the film "The Winning Team."

'DEATH ON THE DIAMOND'
Baseball is not a contact sport? The game is not violent? Let's see. In this 1934 motion picture, a star pitcher for the St. Louis Cardinals was shot as he rounded third base with the winning run; another Cardinal pitcher was strangled in the

When actor Gary Cooper accepted the role of Lou Gehrig in 'The Pride of the Yankees,'
former major leaguers Babe Herman (center) and Lefty O'Doul (right) were summoned to
work with the natural righthander.

In a scene from the 1952 film 'The Pride of St. Louis,' a concerned Dizzy Dean (actor Dan Dailey, kneeling, right) comforts brother Paul (Richard Crenna), who has just been struck by a line drive.

clubhouse; the Cards' catcher died of poisoning after consuming a hot dog, and two attempts were made on the life of a third St. Louis pitcher, one via gunfire aimed at a taxi cab in which the hurler (played by Robert Young of "Father Knows Best" and "Marcus Welby, M.D." fame) was riding, the other by a bombing device placed in the player's clothing. Obviously, this was a murder mystery, replete with the gambling crowd (a recurring element in early sports-oriented films). Despite the mayhem, there were plenty of laughs in this production.

MIKE DONLIN

A .356 hitter for the 1905 World Series-champion New York Giants and a lifetime .333 batter in the major leagues, he once left the game to tour with actress-wife Mabel Hite in vaudeville and on stage and eventually became a full-fledged stage and motion-picture actor—although he was seldom more than a "bit player."

JOANNE DRU
She appeared as Patricia Nash Dean, Dizzy's wife, in "The Pride of St. Louis."

'ELMER THE GREAT'
While Ring Lardner had created Elmer as a pitching sensation, this 1933 film made him into a slugger—in the person of Joe E. Brown. Elmer, possessing a strong swing but a weak mind, found trouble virtually everywhere he turned. But, when the big game came around, it was the Cubs' Elmer who proved troublesome (to the Yankees).

'FEAR STRIKES OUT'
The critically acclaimed 1957 film about Boston Red Sox player Jim Piersall (Anthony Perkins) and the mental illness that he suffered at the outset of his major league career. Piersall, heavily pressured to succeed by his father John (Karl Malden), was unable to cope with mounting stress—particularly the Red Sox's attempt to convert him from an outfielder into a shortstop.

The overall strain produced erratic behavior in Piersall, whose arguments, fights and clowning episodes alienated opponents and teammates alike and led to the ball player's hospitalization.

Norma Moore was cast as Jim Piersall's wife (Mary).

'FIREMAN, SAVE MY CHILD'
When Joe Grant (Joe E. Brown) wasn't experimenting with fire extinguishers or setting office buildings ablaze in this 1932 film, he was plying his trade as a big-league pitcher.

POP FISHER
The manager of the New York Knights in "The Natural." Pop was played by Wilford Brimley.

Assisting Pop was Knights Coach Red Blow (Richard Farnsworth).

HUCKLEBERRY FOX
Cast in "A Winner Never Quits," the television story of Pete Gray, he played the one-armed little California boy who made an inspirational trip to Memphis in 1944 to see Gray play for the minor league Chicks. The boy, devastated after his right arm had been amputated following a home accident, needed a boost and got it when he saw what amputee Gray could do on a ball field.

Anthony Perkins donned a Boston Red Sox uniform to portray Jim Piersall in the critically acclaimed 1957 movie about a young player's struggle against mental illness.

The real-life youngster depicted in the film, Nelson Gary Jr., became a standout outfielder and pitcher in kids-league and high school baseball in Southern California. While at one point hoping for a fling in professional baseball, Gary never advanced into the pro ranks.

WILLIAM FRAWLEY

Known to 1950s and 1960s television audiences for his portrayals of Fred Mertz on the "I Love Lucy" show and housekeeper Bub O'Casey on "My Three Sons," he had a featured role in the film "The Babe Ruth Story." Frawley played the part of Jack Dunn, owner-manager of the minor league Baltimore Orioles and the man who signed Ruth to his first professional baseball contract.

Frawley also appeared in the baseball movies "Alibi Ike," "Kill the Umpire," "Rhubarb" and "Safe at Home."

LOUIS GOSSETT JR.
He played Leroy (Satchel) Paige, famed Negro leagues pitcher who at age 42 finally got a chance in baseball's major leagues, in the 1981 made-for-television film "Don't Look Back."

'THE GREAT AMERICAN PASTIME'
A 1956 movie in which Tom Ewell managed a Little League baseball team — and managed to lose a lot of friends in the process.

'HEADIN' HOME'
A 1920 film in which Babe Ruth played a country bumpkin who apparently had no baseball skills. Apparently. Upon being angered, though, the Babe took

William Frawley (center), best known for his role as Fred Mertz in the 'I Love Lucy' show, acted in five baseball-related movies. His appearance with Yankee slugger Roger Maris (left) and Mickey Mantle (right) was in the 1962 film 'Safe at Home.'

a bat in hand and rocketed the ball for a five-block ride. His heretofore hidden talent now exposed, he soon became a big-leaguer and returned home a hero.

In 1927, Ruth appeared in a motion picture called "The Babe Comes Home," which seemingly was ignored by critics and moviegoers alike.

'THE HOT CORNER'
A 1956 Broadway comedy about the various crises that confronted a baseball manager (played by Sam Levene). Obviously not a knee-slapper, the play closed after five performances.

Eight years earlier, Levene had portrayed a newspaperman in the film "The Babe Ruth Story."

TAB HUNTER
The male lead in the movie version of "Damn Yankees," he also was cast as Jim Piersall in the 1955 television adaptation of the book "Fear Strikes Out." The television production of the Piersall story, presented on the program "Climax," was seen by U.S. audiences approximately 19 months before the motion picture about the Boston Red Sox player made its debut. Also starring in TV's "Fear Strikes Out" were Mona Freeman (as Jim's wife) and Robert Armstrong (as Jim's father).

IRIS, MEMO
Portrayed respectively by Glenn Close and Kim Basinger, they were two key women in ball player Roy Hobbs' life in "The Natural." Iris was Hobbs' in-the-stands inspiration, while Memo was the alluring niece of the team's manager.

'THE JACKIE ROBINSON STORY'
The 1950 film biography of modern major league baseball's first black player. Cast in the title role was a 31-year-old movie newcomer who exhibited composure, timing and grace on the screen: Jack Roosevelt Robinson, the Brooklyn Dodgers' star himself.

'THE KID FROM LEFT FIELD'
A 1953 movie about a 9-year-old batboy named Christy who received insightful ball-playing tips from his father—a former player roaming the stands as a peanut vendor—and relayed the helpful hints to his struggling team. The local nine proceeded to go on a winning binge and little Christy (Billy Chapin) was managerial timber.

Christy's father, Larry (Pop) Cooper, was played by Dan Dailey, who just a year earlier had portrayed Dizzy Dean in "The Pride of St. Louis." Anne Bancroft and Lloyd Bridges also were featured in "The Kid From Left Field."

Anthony Perkins might have received even more publicity for his portrayal of Jim Piersall in the movie 'Fear Strikes Out,' but Tab Hunter beat him to the punch, playing Piersall in a 1955 TV adaptation of the book.

Jackie Robinson appeared on the big screen in 1950 when he portrayed himself in 'The Jackie Robinson Story,' which also featured Minor Watson (center) as Branch Rickey and Richard Lane (right) as Clay Hopper, manager of the Montreal Royals.

A remake of "The Kid From Left Field" came to the screen—the small screen—in 1979. The made-for-television movie featured Gary Coleman and Robert Guillaume in the Chapin and Dailey roles.

'KILL THE UMPIRE'
The 1950 film comedy in which William Bendix played an umpire-hating baseball fan (and former player) who was so obsessed with the game that he couldn't hold a job once spring training began. To confront this vocational turmoil and at the same time satisfy his yearning to be close to baseball, Bendix character Bill Johnson decided to go to school. Umpire school. Before long, Johnson was calling 'em the way he saw 'em—and finding out that his new calling in life could be hazardous to his health (thanks to angry fans, players and gamblers).

Helpful baseball strategy tips from peanut vendor Larry (Pop) Cooper (Dan Dailey, left) to son Christy (center), a 9-year-old batboy . . .

PETE LaCOCK

A first baseman-outfielder for the Chicago Cubs (1972-1976) and Kansas City Royals (1977-1980), he is the son of longtime "Hollywood Squares" television host Peter Marshall and nephew of veteran actress Joanne Dru.

'LADIES' DAY'

A 1943 motion picture, starring Eddie Albert and Lupe Velez, that told of a young man who pitched woo and baseballs—and found it difficult to succeed with the latter when he was so wrapped up with the former.

MONK LANIGAN

The dimwitted catcher in "It Happens Every Spring" (1949). While opposing batters flailed away at the dancing pitches of Lanigan's new batterymate, Monk (Paul Douglas) had trouble catching on to the fact that his pitcher was using a special wood-resistant compound on the ball.

BINGO LONG, LEON CARTER

The star pitcher and catcher (portrayed by Billy Dee Williams and James Earl Jones, respectively) for the barnstorming black baseball team in "The Bingo

. . . helped turn the struggling local baseball team into an instant winner in the 1953 movie 'The Kid From Left Field.'

Long Traveling All-Stars and Motor Kings," a 1976 film release. Primarily a comedy, the movie also was a study of survival and of American race relations of 50 years ago.

FRANK LOVEJOY
Actor who played Rogers Hornsby, a playing rival of Grover Cleveland Alexander's and then Alexander's manager, in the Alexander film biography entitled "The Winning Team."

PEANUTS LOWREY
One of the many real-life ball players used as extras in baseball movies. Lowrey, an infielder-outfielder for 13 seasons with the Chicago Cubs, Cincinnati Reds, St. Louis Cardinals and Philadelphia Phillies, appeared in "The Pride of the Yankees," "The Stratton Story" and "The Winning Team" (in which, as outlined by the script, he conked Ronald Reagan, playing Grover Cleveland Alexander, with a thrown ball).

Additional examples of major leaguers appearing in baseball films include the use of Gene Bearden, Bill Dickey, Jimmie Dykes and Merv Shea in "The

One constant in the history of baseball-related movies is the use of major league extras, such as pitcher Gene Bearden, who is pictured above with actress June Allyson in a scene from 'The Stratton Story.'

Stratton Story" and the casting of Bob Lemon, Hank Sauer, Al Zarilla, John Berardino and George Metkovich in "The Winning Team."

SAM MALONE
Presented by scriptwriters as a former pitcher for the Red Sox, Malone (Ted Danson) owns and operates a Boston bar in the hit television series "Cheers," which made its debut in September 1982.

PHIL MANKOWSKI
The former part-time infielder for the Detroit Tigers and New York Mets who

Child actor Bryan Russell received a big assist from Yankee sluggers Roger Maris (left) and Mickey Mantle in the 1962 movie 'Safe at Home.'

produced guffaws in theaters nationwide when, as the third baseman for the New York Knights in "The Natural," he was struck in the groin by a batted ball while eyeballing a woman in the stands.

ROGER MARIS, MICKEY MANTLE
After Maris socked a major league-record 61 home runs in 1961 and Mantle walloped 54, the New York Yankee sluggers were the main attractions in a low-budget 1962 film called "Safe at Home." In the picture, a 10-year-old Florida boy named Hutch Lawton, played by Bryan Russell, bragged to friends—er, lied to friends—that he was an acquaintance of Maris and Mantle. What a tangled web we weave when first we practice to deceive.

527

BILL MAZEROSKI

Pittsburgh player who, merely following the script, hit into a game-ending triple play against the New York Mets as part of "The Odd Couple" motion picture. With the Mets leading the Pirates, 1-0, in the ninth inning of the made-for-Hollywood sequence, Mazeroski came to bat with the bases loaded and no one out and Jack Fisher pitching for New York. As sportswriter Oscar Madison (Walter Matthau) spoke on the telephone with his back to the field, Mazeroski grounded to Ken Boyer, who stepped on third base to start an around-the-horn triple play (with Jerry Buchek making the play at second base and Ed Kranepool handling the throw at first).

Roberto Clemente originally was scheduled to ground into the triple play, which was filmed at Shea Stadium in June 1967, but an impasse over film-appearance fees sent Mazeroski to the plate instead.

LUCAS McCAIN

The Old West character made familiar to television audiences by former big-league first baseman Chuck Connors in the late 1950s and early 1960s. McCain was a rifle-toting, law-preserving, marshal-helping homesteader in "The Rifleman" series.

Connors played in one game for the Brooklyn Dodgers in 1949 and appeared in 66 contests for the Chicago Cubs in 1951 (batting .239 for the Cubs with two home runs).

GUFFY McGOVERN

The blaspheming manager (Paul Douglas) of the lowly Pittsburgh Pirates in the 1951 movie "Angels in the Outfield." Guffy, a loudmouth who hated umpires and virtually every other segment of mankind, was directing his club toward a sorry finish in the National League when a messenger from above delivered some enticing news: Clean up your act, sir, and a few victories might come your way. The skipper turned over a new leaf and, sure enough, the Pirates made a turnaround in the standings. All wasn't divine, though, when an orphan girl (played by Donna Corcoran) noticed angels behind each Pittsburgh player and a newspaper reporter (Janet Leigh) tried to get to the bottom of this help from on high.

MAX MERCY

The name of the relentless and egocentric sportswriter in "The Natural." Portrayed by Robert Duvall, Mercy first met Roy Hobbs aboard a train in 1924 when a youthful Hobbs was an aspiring pitcher and then renewed acquaintances 15 years later when Hobbs, as an aging rookie outfielder, joined the New York Knights.

Pittsburgh's Bill Mazeroski shows actor Jack Lemmon the bat he used to ground into a triple play during the 1967 filming of 'The Odd Couple.'

Pirates Manager Guffy McGovern (right), played by actor Paul Douglas,
chats with real-life Pittsburgh slugger Ralph Kiner during filmning of the 1951 movie
'Angels in the Outfield.'

RAY MILLAND

Cast as the somewhat-nutty professor in "It Happens Every Spring," Milland took on a second baseball-related role in "Rhubarb," the film adaptation of H. Allen Smith's novel about a cat who owned a big-league ball club. Milland played a guardian for the cat, Rhubarb, and endured considerable travail when Rhubarb was targeted by bookies, gangsters and kidnapers.

MICHAEL MORIARTY

In the 1973 film "Bang the Drum Slowly," he portrayed pitcher Henry Wiggen, who was confronted with the to-be-kept-secret news that his roommate-batterymate was dying. The talented and intellectual Wiggen, the antithesis of his doomed friend, helped his teammate fulfill his wish of playing one more season of baseball.

GREG MULLEAVY
The son of a former big-league infielder, minor league manager and Brooklyn and Los Angeles Dodgers coach of the same name, he played the baseball cap-wearing husband (Tom) of Mary Hartman in the television show "Mary Hartman, Mary Hartman." The series, a satire of TV's soap operas, made its debut in January 1976.

'THE NATURAL'
The mystical 1952 novel by Bernard Malamud that was transformed to the screen in 1984, with Robert Redford starring as Roy Hobbs, a young man destined for major league stardom—but, because of a shooting, denied his date with baseball destiny for 15 years.

NEW YORK MAMMOTHS
The name of the baseball team managed by Dutch Schnell (Vincent Gardenia) in "Bang the Drum Slowly."

LLOYD NOLAN
Actor who played a feuding, Leo Durocher-like managerial character in "It Happened in Flatbush," a midsummer-1942 movie that attempted to depict the colorful playing style exemplified by the Brooklyn Dodgers.

MICHAEL NOURI
Perhaps best-known as the male lead opposite Jennifer Beals in the popular "Flashdance" film of 1983, he portrayed Bay City Bluebirds Manager Joe Rohner in the not-so-popular TV series "The Bay City Blues" of the same year. (The show ran from October 25 through November 15, then was canceled.)

BRUCE PEARSON
Name of the New York Mammoths' catcher (played by Robert De Niro) who was dying of Hodgkin's disease in "Bang the Drum Slowly," a highly praised film based on Mark Harris' mid-1950s novel.

'RAWHIDE'
A 1938 musical Western co-starring, believe it or not, Lou Gehrig. Yes, the Yankees' Iron Horse brandished a six-shooter instead of a Louisville Slugger. However, he preferred slinging to singing—he took aim at the bad guys with billiard balls in a memorable poolroom scene—and left the vocalizing to Smith Ballew, who portrayed a cowboy-lawyer.

RONALD REAGAN
In the presidential-election year of 1952, the 41-year-old Reagan was in the

New York Yankee slugger-turned-actor Lou Gehrig (white hat) takes his lumps from the bad guys during a saloon scene in the 1938 musical Western 'Rawhide.'

spotlight—because of his motion-picture portrayal of major league pitching star Grover Cleveland Alexander in "The Winning Team."

EDWARD G. ROBINSON
During a "down" period in his screen career, this noted movie tough guy played the part of a tryout-camp supervisor for the New York Giants in the 1953 movie "Big Leaguer."

BABE RUTH
He played himself in "The Pride of the Yankees," the film biography of Lou Gehrig, and was joined in the cast by noted Yankees Bill Dickey, Bob Meusel and Mark Koenig and sportscaster Bill Stern (all of whom played themselves).

VERNON SIMPSON
Name of the "It Happens Every Spring" character (portrayed by Ray Milland)

Edward G. Robinson (center) and Jeff Richards (left) receive technical advice from Hall of Fame pitcher Carl Hubbell during filming for the 1953 movie 'Big Leaguer.'

who stumbled upon a chemical compound that, applied to a baseball, made the ball repulsive to wood. More effective than even a split-fingered fastball, the chemical-compound pitch transformed Vernon from a chemistry instructor at a Midwest university into a big-league pitching star.

SIBBY SISTI
A longtime infielder-outfielder for the Boston Braves who wound up his major league career with the Milwaukee Braves in 1954, he was the man managing the Pittsburgh club in "The Natural."

'THE SLUGGER'S WIFE'
A 1985 Neil Simon movie about a dual-career relationship—he (Darryl Palmer, played by Michael O'Keefe) was a ball player, she (spouse Debby, played by Rebecca de Mornay) was a singer.

ROSCOE SNOOKER

A pill-popping arbiter with a twitching eye in the William Bendix vehicle "Kill the Umpire." Snooker was played by Tom D'Andrea, familiar to Bendix fans as Chester A. Riley's sarcastic friend, Jim Gillis, in "The Life of Riley" television series.

'SOMEWHERE IN GEORGIA'

The 1916 movie in which Ty Cobb played a bank clerk/ball player who was in love with the daughter of a small-town bank president. The film, completed in about two weeks and the product of Grantland Rice's writing, featured the Cobb character's ascent to the big leagues, his return to Georgia because of homesickness, a kidnaping and the seemingly obligatory just-in-time-arrival to win the big game.

'SPEEDY'

The 1928 film comedy starring Harold Lloyd and featuring a hilarious segment in which taxi driver Lloyd took a noted passenger, one Babe Ruth, on a breakneck-speed ride to the ball park. Also eliciting laughter from theater audiences was a scene in which Lloyd, working at a soda fountain, improvised a baseball scoreboard by fashioning numbers out of pretzels and doughnuts.

JAMES STEWART

He portrayed White Sox pitching ace Monty Stratton, whose big-league career was ended at age 26 because of a hunting accident, in the 1949 motion picture "The Stratton Story." After winning 15 games for Chicago in 1937 and again in 1938, rising star Stratton was the victim of a November 1938 hunting mishap that forced the amputation of his right leg. While he never pitched again in the majors, Stratton still staged an amazing comeback highlighted by his 18-victory season for Sherman of the Class C East Texas League in 1946.

JAMES STEWART, JUNE ALLYSON

Six years after playing Mr. and Mrs. Monty Stratton in "The Stratton Story," Stewart and Allyson were back in a baseball-related movie. This time around it was "Strategic Air Command," a 1955 film in which Stewart played Robert (Dutch) Holland, a big-league ball player who was called back into the Air Force at a crucial time in his baseball career, and Allyson portrayed his wife.

RUSTY TAMBLYN

The wayward youth in "The Kid From Cleveland," the late-summer movie of 1949 about a sports announcer's attempt to head off a budding case of juvenile delinquency. The announcer (George Brent) received a little help from his friends—the Cleveland Indians—along the way. The film obviously tried to capitalize on the popularity of the Indians, reigning World Series champions at the time, and featured newsreel footage of the Tribe in action.

Monty Stratton (James Stewart) shows mom (Agnes Moorehead) that baseball does indeed pay in a scene from the 1949 film 'The Stratton Story.'

James Stewart put on another baseball uniform in 1955 when he again teamed with actress June Allyson for the movie 'Strategic Air Command.'

Actor Cary Grant and actress Doris Day joined baseball stars Roger Maris, Mickey Mantle and Yogi Berra in the Yankee dugout during filming of the 1962 comedy-romance 'That Touch of Mink.'

Tamblyn, who in 1952 played Grover Cleveland Alexander's young brother Willie in "The Winning Team," became known as Russ Tamblyn when he stepped into more mature movie roles later in the '50s.

'THAT TOUCH OF MINK'
A 1962 comedy-romance set in New York that starred Cary Grant and Doris Day and featured brief appearances by Yankee stars Mickey Mantle, Roger Maris and Yogi Berra.

CLAIRE TREVOR
Actress who portrayed Mrs. Babe Ruth (Claire) in the film "The Babe Ruth Story."

BOB UECKER
A .200-hitting catcher for six big-league seasons (1962-1967), his flair for comedy—evidenced in beer commercials and as a talk-show guest—landed him a major role in the television series "Mr. Belvedere," which made its debut in March 1985. Uecker was cast as George Owens, whose family benefited from the wisdom of a cultured English servant but also had to endure the servant's barbed wit.

Actress Gwen Verdon played Lola, the alluring handmaiden of the devil, in the 1958 musical 'Damn Yankees.'

GWEN VERDON

Playing the handmaiden of the devil in the 1958 film musical "Damn Yankees," the theme of which was delivering a pennant to the Washington Senators at the expense of a diehard fan's soul, she had the assignment of keeping Senators rookie Joe Hardy in line (or out of line, depending upon your point of view).

RAY WALSTON
As Applegate (the devil) in the movie "Damn Yankees," he hatched the plot for the doormat Senators to beat out the New York Yankees. His right-hand woman in this sizable project was Lola (as in "Whatever Lola Wants, Lola Gets"), portrayed by Gwen Verdon. Walston and Verdon recreated the roles in which they earlier starred on Broadway.

JACK WARDEN
He was cast as Coach Morris Buttermaker in the television-series version of "The Bad News Bears," which aired in 1979 and 1980.

WAR MEMORIAL STADIUM
Former home park of Buffalo's minor league baseball team and longtime home field of football's Buffalo Bills, it served as the home of the New York Knights in "The Natural" and was the principal location for most of the baseball action in the 1984 film.

MINOR WATSON
Actor who was lauded for his portrayal of Brooklyn Dodgers President Branch Rickey in "The Jackie Robinson Story."

THE WHAMMER
The Ruthian-like major league slugger (Joe Don Baker) in "The Natural" whom farmboy Roy Hobbs struck out at a carnival. The Whammer-vs.-Hobbs matchup unfolded when a train transporting Hobbs to Chicago for a big-league tryout (the Whammer also was a passenger) made a whistle stop in a small town.

PAUL WINFIELD
He was cast as former Brooklyn catcher Roy Campanella in the 1974 television drama "It's Good to Be Alive," which focused on Campanella's fight to regain at least partial use of his limbs after a life-threatening and career-ending automobile accident in January 1958.

'A WINNER NEVER QUITS'
The 1986 made-for-television movie in which Keith Carradine played Pete Gray, the one-armed outfielder who overcame monumental odds and advanced to the major leagues despite his handicap. Gray appeared in 77 games for the 1945 St. Louis Browns and batted .218.

WOLVES
Name of the baseball team for which vaudeville comedians Dennis Ryan (Frank Sinatra) and Eddie O'Brien (Gene Kelly) played in the 1949 musical "Take Me Out to the Ball Game." Running the Wolves was K.C. Higgins— Esther Williams.

Frank Sinatra (left), Gene Kelly (center) and Jules Munshin sang and danced their way through the 1949 musical 'Take Me Out to the Ball Game.'

WONDERBOY
The name of Roy Hobbs' homemade bat in "The Natural."

WRIGLEY FIELD, LOS ANGELES
Longtime home of the Los Angeles Angels of the Pacific Coast League and home park of the American League's Los Angeles Angels expansion team in 1961. Its proximity to Hollywood made it a favorite setting for baseball movies of the 1940s and 1950s.

TENTH INNING
Touching other bases

CRAIG ANDERSON
New York Mets pitcher who, in relief, won both games of a May 12, 1962 doubleheader against the Milwaukee Braves—but never won another game in the major leagues, dropping his last 19 decisions. Anderson lost his final 16 decisions of '62 (and finished the year with a 3-17 record), had a 0-2 ledger in 1963 for the Mets and was 0-1 with the National League club in 1964.

Anderson, who pitched for the St. Louis Cardinals in 1961, compiled a 7-23 career record in the majors.

SPARKY ANDERSON, WHITEY HERZOG
The only managers in big-league history to have 100-victory seasons in both the American League and the National League. Anderson's Cincinnati Reds won 102 N.L. games in 1970, 108 in 1975 and 102 in 1976 and his Detroit Tigers totaled 104 A.L. victories in 1984. Herzog's Kansas City Royals won 102 A.L. games in 1977 and his St. Louis Cardinals won 101 times in the 1985 N.L. season.

ORVILLE ARMBRUST
Washington Senators pitcher whose only major league victory came against the New York Yankees on September 30, 1934—the day Babe Ruth played his last game for the Bronx Bombers. The 24-year-old Armbrust was a 5-3 winner in the season finale played at Washington, working seven-plus innings and allowing seven hits and all three Yankee runs. He walked one and struck out two. Ruth was 0 for 3 at the plate while appearing in his 2,084th and final game with the Yankees.

Ruth went on to play 28 more big-league games, all with the 1935 Boston Braves. Armbrust, whose start against the Yankees marked only his third appearance in the majors, never pitched again in the big leagues.

ERNIE BANKS
The first player to win a Most Valuable Player award in a season in which his team won fewer than half of its games—and he accomplished the feat two years in a row. In 1958, when the Chicago Cubs finished 72-82, the Cubs' Banks won National League MVP honors with a 47-homer, 129-RBI season that included a .313 batting average. A year later, the Cubs went 74-80 and Banks was an MVP repeater based on his 45 home runs, 143 runs batted in and .304 batting mark.

Another Cub, Andre Dawson, is the only other National Leaguer to be voted an MVP award when his club posted a losing record. The 1987 Cubs finished 76-85, but Dawson was a bright spot with an MVP season of 49 homers and 137 RBIs.

The only American League MVP to play on a sub-.500 team was Cal Ripken, who in 1991 won the award as a member of the 67-95 Baltimore Orioles. Ripken batted .323 with 34 home runs and 114 RBIs.

Hank Sauer is the only other player to win MVP selection while playing on a big-league team that failed to post a winning record. Sauer drilled 37 homers and knocked in 121 runs for the Cubs in his MVP season of 1952, a year in which Chicago compiled a 77-77 record.

DON BAYLOR
Normally the Boston Red Sox's designated hitter in 1986, he was stationed at first base on the night of April 29—and made an error that helped teammate Roger Clemens establish a big-league record of 20 strikeouts in a nine-inning game. Taking over for regular first baseman Bill Buckner (who was troubled by an elbow injury and assumed the "DH" role), Baylor camped under a fourth-inning pop foul off the bat off Seattle's Gorman Thomas—and dropped the ball. With eight strikeouts at that point, Clemens got another chance to dispose of Thomas via the strikeout route—and did just that. The Red Sox pitcher, appearing in only his 40th major league game, struck out the side in the fifth inning and fanned two batters in each of the final four innings to shatter the previous big-league mark of 19 strikeouts in a nine-inning contest.

Baylor appeared at first base only 13 times for Boston in 1986 and saw outfield duty in just three games.

BOSTON RED SOX
American League team that hit for the cycle against Chicago White Sox pitcher Orval Grove in a June 6, 1942, game—but could do nothing else against the righthander. Grove was tagged for a leadoff, first-inning home run by Boston's Dom DiMaggio and later in the game allowed a triple to Bill Conroy, a double to Jim Tabor and a single to Johnny Pesky. Grove's four-hit pitching lifted the White Sox to a 3-1 victory.

STEVE BRYE
Minnesota Twins left fielder whose misplay of a ninth-inning fly ball on the final day of the 1976 season enabled Kansas City's George Brett to win the American League batting championship—and infuriated the Royals' Hal McRae, whose own sights had been on the hitting crown. McRae wasn't upset with his Royals teammate; he was, however, enraged over the scenario that decided the title. Entering the last of the ninth inning of the game played in

Kansas City, Brett trailed A.L. leader McRae by the barest of margins, .3326 to .3322. Brett proceeded to hit a high fly ball to left, on which it appeared Brye would make a routine play (thus "assuring" McRae of the batting title). However, after running toward the ball, Brye stopped abruptly and the ball fell 10 to 15 feet in front of him. The ball took a high bounce on the artificial turf and went over Brye's head—and Brett circled the bases for an inside-the-park home run. The "gift" hit boosted Brett's average to .333 and meant that McRae, who followed Brett in the batting order, would have to hit safely to win the batting crown. Facing the Twins' Jim Hughes, McRae grounded out—after which the Royals player made two gestures toward the Minnesota dugout. McRae, a black player, later implied that he thought Minnesota Manager Gene Mauch had instructed his players to help Brett, who is white, win the title. Mauch was stunned by McRae's insinuation, saying he "would never, never do anything to harm the integrity of baseball." And Brye steadfastly maintained he simply made a "mistake by playing too deep."

The game actually began as a three-way battle for the hitting crown, with McRae entering the contest at .33078, Brett at .33073 and Minnesota's Rod Carew at .32945. Brett had a 3-for-4 afternoon, while McRae and Carew each went 2 for 4. The final, rounded-off averages: Brett, .333; McRae, .332, and Carew .331.

Brye never played again for the Twins, winding up his career with the Milwaukee Brewers (1977) and Pittsburgh Pirates (1978); pitcher Hughes, a 5-3 complete-game victor in the controversial contest and winner of 16 games in 1975 and nine in '76, found himself back in the minor leagues in 1977 and never won another game in the majors; Brett captured a second batting crown in 1980 and a third in 1990, thus becoming the only player in big-league history to win hitting titles in three decades; and McRae continued as one of the league's toughest hitters—but never again contended for a batting championship.

GENE CONLEY, DAVE DeBUSSCHERE
Pitchers who, when they appeared in the same 1963 major league game, were past and future members, respectively, of National Basketball Association championship teams. Conley, who played for the Boston Celtics' 1959, 1960 and 1961 NBA titlists, was the Red Sox's starting pitcher against the White Sox in an April 27, 1963, contest at Boston's Fenway Park. Ray Herbert started for Chicago, going 3 1/3 innings before being relieved by DeBusschere, who went on to play for the New York Knicks' NBA champions of 1970 and 1973. The two athletes were in the '63 American League game at the same time, at least briefly, as Conley pitched four-plus innings for Boston and DeBusschere, in a two-thirds-inning stint, worked in the fourth inning for Chicago.

CHUCK COTTIER, DICK WILLIAMS

Seattle's manager on April 29, 1986, when the Mariners were victimized by Roger Clemens' record 20-strikeout performance in a nine-inning major league game, Cottier had seen duty at second base for Washington on September 12, 1962, when the Senators' Tom Cheney established the big-league record for most strikeouts in one game, regardless of length, by fanning 21 Baltimore batters in a 16-inning contest. Fired from his Seattle managerial post about a week after Clemens' masterpiece, Cottier was succeeded on a permanent basis as Mariners pilot by Williams. And, curiously, it was Williams—as a pinch-hitter for Baltimore—who had been Cheney's 21st strikeout victim in that '62 Senators-Orioles game.

TED COX

Seattle Mariners third baseman who was credited with the first official game-winning RBI in American League history. After falling behind the Toronto Blue Jays, 2-0, in the first inning of their 1980 season opener, the Mariners tied the score in the bottom half of the inning and then went ahead in the same frame when Cox slammed a two-run double off Blue Jays pitcher Dave Lemanczyk. Seattle never relinquished the lead in the April 9 night game, posting an 8-6 triumph.

SAM CRAWFORD

In his first day as a major leaguer, this Cincinnati outfielder (and future Detroit Tigers star) played against Cleveland. And Louisville. Competing in. an era when schedules were more likely to develop occasional quirks, Cincinnati first played host to National League rival Cleveland on September 10, 1899, and then met the N.L.'s Louisville club on the Reds' home grounds later in the day. Crawford broke into the majors in the first game, rapping two singles in four at-bats against Cleveland as Cincinnati cruised to a 10-2 triumph. In the second contest, Crawford collected three hits—including the first of his major league-record 312 triples—and the Reds edged Louisville, 8-7.

BILL DAHLEN

Chicago shortstop whose 42-game batting streak was stopped in an August 7, 1894, National League contest in which teammates immediately ahead of and behind him in the batting order went 5 for 6. Second-place hitter Dahlen was hitless in six at-bats against Cincinnati, while leadoff man Jimmy Ryan and third-place hitter Walt Wilmot each cracked out five hits in a 17-hit Chicago attack that helped produce a 13-11 victory.

The next day, Dahlen started on a 28-game hitting streak.

MIKE FERRARO

The only former Seattle Pilots player to advance to the major league managerial ranks, performing for the Pilots in 1969 before managing the Cleveland Indians

In 1951, Gene Conley, pictured above with a Hartford teammate, was en route to the major leagues and even bigger and better things in the world of professional basketball.

in 1983 (100 games) and guiding the Kansas City Royals in 1986 (74 games). Ferraro appeared in five games as a pinch-hitter for the Pilots (who spent only one season in Seattle before moving to Milwaukee and becoming the Brewers), going 0 for 4 at the plate with one base on balls.

5

The uniform number that Hank Aaron first wore in the major leagues. Aaron wore number 5 while playing for the Milwaukee Braves in 1954, but asked for—and received—a double-digit number in 1955. Given '44,' Aaron wore the number for the rest of his big-league career.

GEORGE FOSTER
Cincinnati left fielder who was credited with big-league baseball's first official game-winning RBI, a statistic that was adopted in 1980 and rescinded following the 1988 season. Foster sent the Reds into the lead in the first inning of their April 9 season opener, drilling a two-run double off Atlanta's Phil Niekro. The Reds, behind the three-hit pitching of Frank Pastore, went on to a 9-0 triumph over the Braves in the afternoon contest.

BOB FRIEND
The last of only three pitchers in major league history to lose 200 or more games while failing to win at least 200. Friend had a lifetime 197-230 record for the Pittsburgh Pirates, New York Yankees and New York Mets in a big-league career that began in 1951 and ended in 1966.

Also losing 200 or more games in the majors without winning 200 were Chick Fraser (176-212) and Jim Whitney (193-207).

GENE GREEN
Cleveland outfielder who dropped two fly balls in the fifth inning of a 1962 game against Chicago, helping the White Sox collect a major league-record three sacrifice flies in one inning. In the second game of a July 1 doubleheader, the Sox had a runner on third base when Chicago pitcher Juan Pizarro hit a fifth-inning drive toward Green. The Indians' right fielder dropped the ball, but Pizarro was awarded a sacrifice fly because the official scorer ruled that the ball had traveled far enough to drive in the run had the catch been made. Later in the inning, Chicago's Nellie Fox hit another ball that Green dropped, with the scorer again crediting the batter with a sacrifice fly. The White Sox's Al Smith accounted for the lone "normal" sacrifice fly of the inning, with Green catching his drive (for the first out of the inning). Green's misplays contributed to a six-run White Sox inning, which Chicago rode to a 7-6 triumph.

AL GRUNWALD
Pittsburgh Pirates player who broke into the major leagues with a "cycle" performance—but, to Grunwald's dismay, he was pitching, not batting. Making his big-league debut in a fourth-inning relief role against the New York Giants in an April 18, 1955, game, Grunwald worked one-third of an inning and allowed four hits—a single by Don Mueller, a double by Monte Irvin, a triple by Willie Mays (the first man he faced) and a home run by Whitey Lockman. Grunwald was charged with four runs as the Giants, on the way to a 12-3

triumph, enjoyed an eight-run inning. Grunwald made nine pitching appearances overall in the majors, three with the '55 Pirates and six with the 1959 Kansas City A's. His career record was 0-1.

JACK HARPER
He played for big-league baseball's losingest and winningest clubs. A two-time 20-game winner in the majors, he pitched his rookie season for the 1899 Cleveland Spiders, compiling a 1-4 record for the National League club that lost a record 134 games while winning only 20. In 1906, Harper appeared in one game for the N.L.'s Chicago Cubs, a team that won a record 116 contests. Starting for the Cubs on June 6 against the New York Giants, he was struck on the hand by a line drive and left the game after the first inning— never to perform again in the majors.

SOLLY HEMUS
The only man in modern National League history to manage at least a full season in the league and never manage against a New York team. Hemus guided the St. Louis Cardinals during his entire 384-game major league managerial career, which stretched from 1959 until July 1961 and involved years in which there was no N.L. team in New York.

The four-year period from 1958 through 1961 marked the only time in modern big-league history that New York was not represented in the N.L.

ROGERS HORNSBY
The only player in major league history to attain a .400 batting average over a five-year period. Playing for the St. Louis Cardinals, Hornsby hit a composite .402 from 1921 through 1925 by fashioning National League-leading season averages of .397, .401, .384, .424 and .403. Hornsby collected 1,078 hits in 2,679 at-bats in that period.

LaMARR HOYT
The pitcher with the highest earned-run average in a Cy Young Award-winning year. Hoyt won the American League's Cy Young honor in 1983, putting together a 24-10 season for the Chicago White Sox despite a 3.66 ERA. The earned-run figure ranked 17th in the A.L. among pitchers working enough innings to qualify for the ERA title.

Only two other Cy Young Award winners who qualified for the ERA crown failed to finish in the top 10 of their league ERA races. Both instances occurred in 1967, when Jim Lonborg of the Boston Red Sox captured the A.L. Cy Young Award with a 3.16 ERA, the 18th-best mark in the league, and Mike McCormick of the San Francisco Giants took the N.L. Cy Young trophy with a 2.85 ERA, the 16th-best figure in the league.

San Diego Padres Owner Ray Kroc was not so happy when he grabbed the public-address-system microphone and chastised his team during its 1974 home opener.

KEN HUNT

Cincinnati Reds hurler whose major league career consisted of one season—a year in which he was named the National League's Rookie Pitcher of the Year by The Sporting News. After logging a 16-6 record for Columbia of the South Atlantic League in 1960, Hunt went to spring training with the parent Reds as a non-roster player in 1961—and made the club. Easing into Cincinnati's starting rotation early in the season, the 22-year-old Hunt got off to a 9-4 start with the Reds before slumping to a final 9-10 record and winding up in the bullpen for the N.L. champions. Nevertheless, he captured The Sporting News' N.L. rookie pitching honor. In 1962, Hunt encountered control problems in the spring and was sent back to the minor leagues—never to return.

Hunt's last appearance in the majors was as a ninth-inning reliever in the fifth and last game of the 1961 World Series against the New York Yankees.

JERRY KOOSMAN
The only pitcher to shut out the Milwaukee Brewers in 1979—and he performed the feat on the final day of the season, thus thwarting the Brewers' bid to equal the New York Yankees' major league record, established in 1932 and never matched, of playing an entire season without being blanked. Pitching for the Minnesota Twins on September 30, Koosman shut out Milwaukee, 5-0, despite allowing nine hits.

The 1979 Brewers went 95-66 and finished second in the American League East, while the 1932 Yankees captured the A.L. pennant with a 107-47 mark (the Yanks tied one game) and then won the World Series.

SANDY KOUFAX
The only pitcher to win the Cy Young Award in his last season in the major leagues. Koufax won his third Cy Young trophy in 1966 after compiling a 27-9 record for the Los Angeles Dodgers with 317 strikeouts and a 1.73 earned-run average. Following the '66 season, Koufax, six weeks from his 31st birthday, announced his retirement from baseball because of arthritic-elbow problems.

RAY KROC
San Diego Padres owner who, in the middle of the eighth inning of his fourth regular-season game as owner of a big-league club, grabbed the public-address-system microphone and, in a curt analysis of his team's performance, announced "that this is the most stupid baseball playing I've ever seen." Kroc's critique came in the Padres' 1974 home opener, an April 9 contest against the Houston Astros. That Kroc was frustrated proved no surprise; the Padres, after all, had opened the season in horrendous fashion, losing 8-0, 8-0 and 9-2 games in Los Angeles (and they were trailing 9-2 in this one against Houston). That he would share his thoughts with everyone in the stadium was a shocker; players on both clubs were angry over the public dressing-down, which they considered in extremely poor taste.

A day later, Kroc voiced his regret over the incident and said that a male streaker influenced his denunciation of the team. "The streaker just added gas to the fire," said Kroc, who had begun his previous night's remarks by saying "Ladies and gentlemen, I suffer with you" before being interrupted by the on-field streaker. After urging authorities to throw the streaker in jail, Kroc went on to offer a good-news, bad-news report to the stadium crowd—the good news being that San Diego had outdrawn Los Angeles in its home opener, the bad news being that the Padres were playing "stupid" baseball.

San Diego fell by a 9-5 score in its '74 home opener, then lost successive 9-1 games to Houston (meaning that the Padres had been outscored 52-9 while opening the season with six straight defeats). The club, managed by John McNamara, finished the season with a 60-102 record and finished last in the National League West.

JOHNNIE LeMASTER
Shortstop who in 1985 played for three major league clubs—all of whom finished in last place and lost at least 100 games. Perhaps fittingly, LeMaster's batting statistics reflected the company he was keeping (although, it should be pointed out, the infielder spent 2 1/2 months on the disabled list in '85 and had only 94 at-bats overall). LeMaster began the season with San Francisco and was hitless in 16 at-bats for the Giants, who wound up 62-100 and in the basement of the National League West. Traded to Cleveland in early May, he batted .150 for the Indians. Cleveland, on the way to a 60-102 record and a cellar finish in the American League East, dealt LeMaster to Pittsburgh before the month was out. Spending the balance of the season with the Pirates, LeMaster hit .155 for a team that went 57-104 and brought up the rear in the N.L. East.

LOS ANGELES ANGELS
Of the 10 modern big-league expansion franchises, the team that posted the best record in its first season of play. The Angels entered the American League in 1961 and compiled a 70-91 mark (.435 winning percentage) that year.

After playing surprisingly well in their first season, the Angels were just short of amazing in their second year. Eighth-place finishers in the A.L. in '61, the Angels leaped to third place in 1962 with an 86-76 record (.531) and finished only 10 games out of first place.

HEINIE MANUSH
From the inception of The Sporting News' end-of-season major league All-Star Team (1925) through the publication's 29th year of choosing the combined American League-National League "dream club" (1953, the St. Louis Browns' last season),he was the lone Browns player to win a spot on the select unit. Manush made it as an outfielder—along with Babe Ruth of the New York Yankees and Paul Waner of the Pittsburgh Pirates—on the 1928 team.

MAY 2, 1939
A notable day in Detroit baseball history, with Lou Gehrig, Fred Hutchinson and little William James Brown figuring in the goings-on. This was the afternoon on which New York's Gehrig ended his record consecutive-game playing streak, asking that he be scratched from the lineup for the Yankees-Tigers clash at Briggs Stadium after appearing in 2,130 straight major league contests. As Gehrig watched the proceedings (he would never play again in the majors), the Yanks crushed Detroit, 22-2. Among the victimized Tiger pitchers

was Hutchinson, a 19-year-old righthander who was making his big-league debut. Hutchinson, a standout Detroit pitcher after World War II and eventually the Tigers' manager, yielded four hits, five walks and eight runs in two-thirds of an inning. And, on this day, young Mr. Brown also made his debut. Born on May 2, 1939, in Crestline, O., William James (Gates) Brown became a 13-year Tiger player (1963-1975), a pinch-hitter deluxe and one of the most popular players in Detroit history.

MILWAUKEE BREWERS

The only team to play in both the West Division and East Division of a major league. When the American League West's Seattle Pilots abruptly moved to Milwaukee and became the Brewers prior to the 1970 season, the A.L. kept the franchise in the West Division for '70 and 1971. But when the second Washington Senators franchise, an A.L. East club, relocated in Texas after the '71 season and became the Rangers, the Brewers were switched to the East in 1972 and the Rangers were placed in the West.

JOHN MOHARDT

A college football teammate of George Gipp at Notre Dame from 1918 through 1920, a major league teammate of Ty Cobb with the Detroit Tigers in 1922 and a National Football League teammate of Red Grange with the Chicago Bears in 1925. Mohardt, a halfback with the Fighting Irish and the Bears, was an outfielder with the Tigers but played in only five big-league games. In his lone official at-bat in the majors, which came on April 21, 1922, Mohardt singled off Cleveland's Charlie Jamieson (an outfielder who was called upon to pitch in a lopsided game).

RICK MONDAY

Chicago Cubs center fielder who in the fourth inning of an April 25, 1976, game at Dodger Stadium snatched an American flag from two persons who were about to set the banner on fire. Los Angeles' Ted Sizemore was at the plate when a man and a youth ran onto the field and stopped in front of Cubs left fielder Jose Cardenal. Noticing that the flag-carrying intruders were fumbling with lighter fluid, Monday raced over, scooped up the flag and delivered it safely to a security guard. When Monday went to bat in the next inning, the crowd gave him a standing ovation.

"If you're going to burn the flag, don't do it in front of me," Monday said. "I've been to too many veterans hospitals and seen too many broken bodies of guys who tried to protect it...."

TERRY MULHOLLAND

San Francisco pitcher who had an undistinguished rookie season (1-7 record) in the major leagues in 1986—but didn't go unnoticed. Case in point: September 3, third inning, Giants vs. the New York Mets. Mulholland fielded a hard

Chicago Cubs center fielder Rick Monday reaches down to snatch an American flag that two persons were trying to set afire during a 1976 game at Dodger Stadium.

smash off the bat of Keith Hernandez and wheeled to throw to first base. However, the ball stuck in the webbing of Mulholland's glove and the 23-year-old lefthander couldn't pry it loose. What to do? Improvise, that's what. Mulholland kept his cool, ran toward first base and, when about seven feet from the bag, pitched his glove (with ball firmly embedded) to Giants first baseman Bob Brenly. Hernandez was out . . . and Mulholland was headed for the week's television highlight films.

NEW YORK METS

The last of only 10 big-league teams to post 100 or more victories in a season without having a pitcher win 20 games. The Mets, paced by Bob Ojeda's 18 victories, won 108 regular-season games in their World Series-championship season of 1986. Dwight Gooden won 17 games, Sid Fernandez collected 16 victories and Ron Darling was a 15-game winner for New York.

Year	Club	Won	Lost	Leading Winner on Staff
1915	Boston Red Sox	101	50	Rube Foster, Ernie Shore, 19
1931	St. Louis Cardinals	101	53	Bill Hallahan, 19
1941	New York Yankees	101	53	Lefty Gomez, Red Ruffing, 15
1942	Brooklyn Dodgers	104	50	Whitlow Wyatt, 19
1967	St. Louis Cardinals	101	60	Dick Hughes, 16
1975	Cincinnati Reds	108	54	Billingham, Gullett, Nolan, 15

1976	Cincinnati Reds	102	60	Gary Nolan, 15
1977	New York Yankees	100	62	Ed Figueroa, Ron Guidry, 16
1984	Detroit Tigers	104	58	Jack Morris, 19
1986	New York Mets	108	54	Bob Ojeda, 18

Of the 10 teams to win 100 games without benefit of a 20-game winner, only the 1942 Brooklyn Dodgers did not win the World Series. And those Dodgers didn't even win the pennant, finishing second to the National League-champion Cardinals (who won 106 games).

PHIL NIEKRO
The last pitcher in the majors to win and lose 20 or more games in the same season. Niekro went 21-20 for the Atlanta Braves in 1979, sharing the National League lead in victories with brother Joe of the Houston Astros and leading the major leagues in defeats.

1942
The last year in which there were no managerial changes in either the National League or the American League. Both circuits had eight clubs at the time.

The last year in which one league went an entire season without a managerial casualty was 1963, when each of the 10 N.L. pilots completed a 162-game schedule. (The A.L.'s last turnover-free season was 1962, a year in which the junior league also had 10 teams.)

96
The most hits gathered by any New York Met in 1972, marking the only time in modern big-league history that a team playing 150 or more games in a season failed to have a player reach the 100-hit plateau. The Mets' hits leader in '72 was Tommie Agee, who batted .227, two points higher than the club's National League-low .225 mark.

Injury problems contributed heavily to the Mets' low individual hit totals in 1972, with only two New York players managing 400 or more official at-bats (Agee was tops with the modest total of 422). Despite the batting woes, the '72 Mets finished third in the N.L. East race with an 83-73 record (six beginning-of-the-season games were canceled because of a players strike).

SPIKE OWEN
A former teammate of Boston's Roger Clemens at the University of Texas and a soon-to-be Red Sox teammate of the standout pitcher (Owen was traded to Boston during the stretch run of the 1986 season), he was at shortstop for the Seattle Mariners in the April 29, 1986, contest in which Clemens struck out a major league-record 20 batters in a nine-inning game. Owen, in fact, was Clemens' record-tying 19th strikeout victim as Seattle's leadoff batter in the

ninth inning. (After Owen's final-inning strikeout, the Mariners' Phil Bradley fanned for the fourth time in the game as Clemens rang up No. 20. Ken Phelps then grounded out to end the game, which the Red Sox won by a 3-1 score.)

Dave Henderson, part of the August 1986 trade that sent Owen to Boston and a postseason hitting star for the Red Sox in '86, played center field for the Mariners in the April 29 game at Fenway Park and struck out three times against Clemens.

MILT PAPPAS

The winning pitcher in the last game played by the original Washington Senators American League club, the losing pitcher in the first game played in the Los Angeles Angels' A.L. history and the loser in the last major league game played at Pittsburgh's Forbes Field. Pitching for the Baltimore Orioles on October 2, 1960, Pappas defeated Washington, 2-1, in the final game preceding the Senator franchise's move to Minnesota. On April 11, 1961, he was a loser against Los Angeles when the Angels made their A.L. debut with a 7-2 triumph over the Orioles, and on June 28, 1970, Pappas, then with the Chicago Cubs, fell to the Pirates, 4-1, in the Forbes Field finale.

REGGIE PATTERSON

Chicago Cubs pitcher who, during Pete Rose's quest to attain a major league-record 4,192 career hits, allowed Rose's 4,189th, 4,190th and 4,191st hits. Working in relief for Chicago in a September 6, 1985, game, righthander Patterson yielded a sixth-inning single to Cincinnati's Rose, who earlier in the day had homered off Cubs starter Derek Botelho for hit No. 4,188. Then, on September 8, Patterson, serving as a short-notice starter after scheduled pitcher Steve Trout had been injured in a bicycle mishap, was nicked for No. 4,190, a first-inning single by Rose. In the fifth inning, Rose, the Reds' manager-first baseman, tied Ty Cobb's lifetime mark of 4,191 hits by singling to right off Patterson.

Rose, with the baseball world watching his every move, was not expected to start in the September 8 contest because he had been sitting out against lefthanders all season and lefthander Trout was the anticipated starter for Chicago. Accordingly, fans nationwide were stunned to hear or see that Rose was indeed in the lineup on that Sunday afternoon at Wrigley Field (because of the Cubs' switch from a lefthanded to a righthanded starter). Also adding to the drama was the fact that Rose had thrust himself into a position of perhaps tying or even breaking Cobb's record away from his hometown fans—and doing so one day before the Reds would return to Cincinnati to open a home stand. (While Rose did tie Cobb on September 8, he then was retired on his final two at-bats of the day.)

GAYLORD PERRY, DON SUTTON

Of big-league baseball's 10 pitchers with 3,000 career strikeouts, the only two who never posted a league-leading season strikeout total in the majors. Perry, fourth in lifetime strikeouts with 3,534, achieved his strikeout high of 238 in 1973 for the Cleveland Indians; however, Perry's '73 total was only fourth best in the American League. In 1975, Perry had his highest seasonal ranking, tying for second place in the A.L. with 233 strikeouts while pitching for the Indians and the Texas Rangers. Sutton, sixth in career strikeouts with 3,431, had a high of 217 for the Los Angeles Dodgers in 1969, the seventh-best figure in the National League that year. Sutton's best ranking in one season was fourth, which he attained in 1972 and 1973 when he fanned 207 and 200 batters for the Dodgers.

MARINO PIERETTI

Of Washington's five principal starting pitchers in 1945 (each made 25 or more starts), the only non-knuckleballer. Pieretti, a rookie, compiled a 14-13 record for the '45 Senators. The knuckleball brigade was led by Roger Wolff (20-10), followed by Emil (Dutch) Leonard (17-7), Mickey Haefner (16-14) and Johnny Niggeling (7-12).

JUAN PIZARRO

He earned the first save in American League history. The pitching statistic for protecting a lead was introduced in the major leagues in 1969, and Boston's Pizarro netted the initial A.L. save in support of winning pitcher Bill Landis (who also had worked in relief) by hurling the final inning of a season-opening 5-4 Red Sox triumph over the Baltimore Orioles in a 12-inning game played on the afternoon of April 8.

CY RIGLER

Umpire who was wired for sound for an August 25, 1929, game at the Polo Grounds so his behind-the-plate calls could be heard in the stands. Wires from a microphone inserted into Rigler's mask were strung down the inside of his uniform and connected to metal plates on a shoe. Rigler stood on a metal sheet behind the catcher and once the umpire made contact with the sheet, his voice could be heard via stadium amplifiers. While the innovation clearly was in the spotlight that day at the New York Giants' home park, the Giants themselves attracted some attention by pounding the Pittsburgh Pirates, 10-5.

ROBIN ROBERTS

The only pitcher in major league history to defeat the Boston Braves, Milwaukee Braves and Atlanta Braves. Roberts was 12-6 against the Braves when the franchise was based in Boston, 21-24 against the club when it operated in Milwaukee and 1-0 against the team after it moved to Atlanta.

Al Travers, who allowed 26 hits and 24 runs during his one-game fling as a major league pitcher, later became a Catholic priest.

Only four big-league pitchers suffered losses to all three "versions" of the Braves: Ron Kline, Vernon Law, Joe Nuxhall and Curt Simmons.

SAN FRANCISCO GIANTS
National League club whose 1981 pitching staff became the first in major league history to notch more shutouts than complete games in a season. The Giants, getting six shutouts that involved more than one pitcher, blanked opponents nine times overall in '81 but had only eight complete games.

ERIC SHOW
San Diego pitcher off whom Cincinnati's Pete Rose collected his record-breaking 4,192nd major league hit in the first inning of a September 11, 1985, game. Rose, who had matched Ty Cobb's total of 4,191 hits on September 8 in Chicago, had not played against the Padres on September 9 in the opening game of a Reds home stand and had gone 0 for 4 in a September 10 contest against San Diego.

Supporting Cast:
•**Bruce Bochy.** Show's batterymate in the game played at Riverfront Stadium.
•**Tom Browning.** Cincinnati's starting and winning pitcher, yielding no runs

and five hits over 8 1/3 innings. John Franco and Ted Power each pitched one-third inning of relief to nail down a 2-0 victory.

• **Nick Esasky.** Cincinnati left fielder who drove in both of the game's runs, scoring Rose with a fielder's-choice grounder in the third inning and driving home the Reds' player-manager (who had tripled) with a sacrifice fly in the seventh inning.

• **Eddie Milner.** Cincinnati's leadoff batter, he fouled out in the first inning. Rose followed Milner to the plate, worked the count to 2-1 against Show and then lined what he called "the big knock"—lifetime hit No. 4,192 in the majors—into left-center field, and the crowd of 47,237 cheered wildly. Padres left fielder Carmelo Martinez fielded the ball, threw it in and one of baseball's great chases—if not the game's greatest chase—was over.

Show allowed seven Reds hits and two runs before leaving the game in the eighth inning for a pinch-hitter.

BILL SINGER
Los Angeles Dodgers pitcher who was credited with the major leagues' first save, which became an official relief-pitching statistic in 1969. Singer earned the save on April 7, 1969, in a season-opening National League game at Cincinnati, working three scoreless innings after taking over for Los Angeles starter and winner Don Drysdale. Singer did not allow a hit, walked one batter and struck out one as the Dodgers beat the Reds, 3-2.

JOHN SIPIN
San Diego Padres second baseman who belted triples in his first two big-league at-bats—but never collected another three-base hit in the majors. Breaking into the big leagues on May 24, 1969, Sipin rapped first- and fourth-inning triples off Ken Holtzman of the Chicago Cubs. Sipin had 227 more at-bats in the majors, all for the '69 Padres, and connected for 14 additional extra-base hits (12 doubles and two homers) while winding up with a .223 batting average.

The only other players to hit two triples in their first major league games were Ed Irwin of the Detroit Tigers in 1912, Roy Weatherly of the Cleveland Indians in 1936 and Willie McCovey of the San Francisco Giants in 1959. (Irwin, in fact, played in only one major league game. He was one of the amateur players whom the Tigers recruited to fill their ranks for a 1912 game against the Philadelphia A's when teammates of Detroit great Ty Cobb staged a walkout in the wake of Cobb's suspension for going into the stands in New York to confront a heckler. Irwin, who played third base and caught against the A's, was the only sandlotter to hit safely in the contest.)

WARREN SPAHN
The only big-league pitcher to win earned-run-average titles in three decades. Spahn captured National League ERA crowns with the Boston Braves in 1947

(2.33) and with the Milwaukee Braves in 1953 (2.10) and 1961(3.01.).

GIL TORRES
Washington Senators player who in less than a year's time hit into two triple plays at Griffith Stadium, with Detroit second baseman Eddie Mayo making the initial putout each time. In the seventh inning of the second game of a July 20, 1945, doubleheader, Torres smashed a line drive that a leaping Mayo snared and turned into a triple killing. Then, on May 8, 1946, Torres hit a third-inning liner that deflected off the bare hand of Tigers pitcher Hal Newhouser. Mayo caught the ball before it hit the ground and again was the triggerman on a triple play.

AL TRAVERS
A righthanded pitcher who surrendered 24 runs in his only major league appearance. A 20-year-old college student at St. Joseph's in Philadelphia, Travers was thrust into the big-league spotlight on May 18, 1912, despite the fact he wasn't good enough to make his college varsity baseball team. The scenario: Detroit superstar Ty Cobb had been suspended for going into the stands on May 15 in New York in pursuit of a heckler. Cobb's teammates decided to protest the suspension, which had been imposed by American League President Ban Johnson, by going on strike May 18 in Philadelphia (where the Tigers were to play the A's). To avoid a fine, forfeiture and possible loss of the Detroit franchise, Tigers Manager Hugh Jennings rounded up a quorum of Philadelphia-area sandlot players to play for his club. Nine locals, including Travers, performed in the game—although not all were starters. The 42-year-old Jennings and Tiger coaches James (Deacon) McGuire (46) and Joe Sugden (41) also appeared in the game, with Jennings failing in a pinch-hitting role, McGuire beginning the game as Travers' batterymate and Sugden playing first base. McGuire and Sugden each singled and scored a run. As for Travers, he pitched the entire game and allowed 26 hits in a 24-2 setback to the A's.

After his fling in the big leagues, Travers returned to his studies and later became a priest.

The Tigers ended their walkout after one game, and Cobb was back in action a short time later after completing his suspension.

ELMER VALO
Outfielder whose big-league playing career was affected by three franchise relocations. Valo spent his first 13 seasons in the majors with the Philadelphia A's, then accompanied the team to Kansas City when the American League club changed home bases after the 1954 season. A member of the Brooklyn Dodgers in 1957, he moved with the National League team to Los Angeles after the season when major league baseball made its historic double switch to the West Coast (with the New York Giants defecting to San Francisco). And after

A Toronto ball boy drops a towel over a sea gull that was accidentally killed when struck by a between-innings throw from New York Yankees outfielder Dave Winfield in a 1983 game.

playing for the Washington Senators in 1960, Valo found himself in Minnesota the following year when the Senators franchise moved to the Minneapolis-St. Paul area and was named the Twins.

DAVE WINFIELD

New York Yankees outfielder who accidentally killed a sea gull with a between-innings throw toward the bullpen during an August 4, 1983, game in Toronto and subsequently was charged with cruelty to animals. As Toronto prepared to bat in the fifth inning, Winfield, having just finished outfield warmups, winged a ball in the direction of a ball boy—but it struck a sea gull that had been lolling around on the outfield grass. After the deceased bird had been removed—Winfield stood with cap held over his heart—the game continued and the Yankees, paced by Winfield's two runs batted in, won, 3-1. Canadian fans, particularly respectful of wildlife, let fly with verbal blasts at Winfield, who was met after the game by several plainclothes officers and taken to a Toronto stationhouse. Charged with the crime and advised of his rights, Winfield posted a $500 bond.

A day later, Canadian officials, assured there was no criminal intent involved in the incident, announced that the case would be dropped.

WILBUR WOOD
The last pitcher in American League history to win and lose 20 or more games in the same season. Wood posted an A.L.-leading 24 victories for the Chicago White Sox in 1973 and dropped 20 decisions that year.

BILLY WYNNE
Chicago pitcher who won his first major league game at Milwaukee's County Stadium—but he didn't beat either the Braves or the Brewers while ringing up victory No. 1. Pitching for the White Sox in a June 16, 1969, game in Milwaukee—the Sox played a total of 20 "home games" in the Wisconsin city in 1968 and 1969—Wynne defeated the Seattle Pilots, 8-3.

Although Wynne didn't beat a Milwaukee team while winning his first big-league game al County Stadium, his victory did come against a club that became a County Stadium tenant the next year. The Pilots franchise, after one year in Seattle, was transferred to Milwaukee in '70.

TOM ZACHARY
Having suffered a "low" in 1927 when, as a Washington Senators pitcher, he allowed Babe Ruth's 60th home run, Zachary enjoyed a "high" just two years later when, as Ruth's teammate with the New York Yankees, he compiled a 12-0 record that ranks as the best single-season mark by an undefeated pitcher in big-league history.

AL ZARILLA, GUS ZERNIAL
The only players whose last names started with "Z" to play together in the same outfield. Zarilla and Zernial teamed up in April 1951, playing right and left field, respectively, as part of a Chicago White Sox outfield unit in four games. At the end of the month, Zernial was traded to the Philadelphia A's.

FRANK ZUPO, GEORGE ZUVERINK
The only "Z" battery in major league history. Zupo and Zuverink twice formed a one-inning battery for the Baltimore Orioles in 1957, the first time coming on July 1, 1957, when Zupo made his big-league debut with a 10th-inning catching appearance against the New York Yankees.